PROBLEM
SOLVING
AND STRUCTURED
PROGRAMMING
IN
BASIC

ADDISON-WESLEY PUBLISHING COMPANY

Reading, Massachusetts · Menlo Park, California

London · Amsterdam · Don Mills, Ontario · Sydney

PROBLEM SOLVING AND STRUCTURED PROGRAMMING IN BASIC

ELLIOT B. KOFFMAN
FRANK L. FRIEDMAN

Temple University

This book is in the

Addison-Wesley Series in

Computer Science and Information Processing

Consulting editor

Michael A. Harrison

Also by the authors:

Problem Solving and Structured Programming in FORTRAN

ISBN 0-201-03888-9
EFGHIJKLMN-AL-8987654321

To our wives: Caryn and Martha
The Koffman kids: Deborah, Richard and Robin
The Friedman flock: Dara and Shelley

Preface

Background

In this textbook, we have taken a new approach to teaching an introductory programming course in BASIC. BASIC has evolved over the years from a language intended mainly for student use to a relatively sophisticated language that is often used for large-scale software development projects. The widespread availability of BASIC compilers for personal computers should further stimulate the growth of BASIC as an important language for developing applications software in a variety of areas.

In addition, the low cost of microcomputers has made it economically feasible for many secondary schools to purchase their own computers and offer programming courses. Students will no longer learn just BASIC, but will move on to study other languages such as FORTRAN, COBOL and PASCAL in high school or college.

For these reasons, we feel it is important to teach BASIC in the same way that other high-level programming languages are taught. If BASIC is to be used as a serious tool for software development, then the principles of structured programming must be applied in order to design effective, reliable software that is readily maintained. If BASIC is to be a stepping stone to further study in computer science, then a firm foundation in the fundamentals of problem solving and programming is essential. It is unreasonable to expect students to discard unstructured programming techniques and practices that worked in BASIC just because a ''richer'' programming environment is available in a second programming language.

Consequently, we have stressed the development of good problem solving and programming habits throughout the textbook. We feel that these concepts should be introduced at the initial stage of development of a student's programming skills and that they are best instilled by examples, by frequent practice, and through instructor-student interaction. Therefore, we have concentrated on demonstrating problem solving and programming techniques through the presentation of numerous solved problems and example programs taken from a variety of applications areas. A minimal mathematical background is assumed.

Discipline and planning in both problem solving and programming are illustrated in the text from the beginning. We have attempted to integrate a number of relatively new pedagogic ideas into a unique, well-structured format that is uniformly repeated for each problem discussed. Three basic phases of problem solving are emphasized: the analysis of the problem; the stepwise specification of the algorithm (using flow diagrams); and, finally, the language implementation of the program.

Our goal is to bridge the gap between textbooks that stress problem solving approaches divorced from implementation considerations and programming manuals that provide the opposite emphasis. Language-independent problem analysis and algorithms are described in the same text as the language features required to implement the problem solution on the computer. For each new problem introduced in the text, the problem analysis and algorithm description are presented, along with the complete syntactic and semantic definitions of the new language features convenient for the implementation of the algorithm.

The top down or stepwise approach to problem solving is illustrated in the solution of each of the problems studied in the text. The use of subroutines is emphasized in the completed programs. Three pedagogic tools—a data definition table, a flow diagram and a program system chart—are used to provide a framework through which students may practice the definition and documentation of program variables in parallel with the stepwise development of algorithms.

The data definition tables provide a description of the attributes (initial values, sizes, etc.) and the use of each variable appearing in the problem solution. The flow diagram patterns that are used to represent decision and looping structures are similar to the D-chart of Dijkstra. Each algorithm is represented as a short sequence of individual flow diagram patterns corresponding to the algorithm subtasks; refinements of the subtasks are diagrammed separately. The program system chart illustrates the system structure and the data flow between system modules.

BASIC Syntax

Because there is no single widely-available form of structured BASIC, we emphasize three versions of BASIC in the text: the new Dartmouth BASIC, BASIC-PLUS and the American National Standard (ANS) for Minimal

BASIC. The only structured version of BASIC currently available is Dartmouth SBASIC. The control structures in SBASIC are being incorporated in Dartmouth BASIC, Edition 7, under development at Dartmouth College. In addition, a number of extended BASIC systems (such as Digital Equipment's BASIC-PLUS and Sperry Univac's UBASIC) support the one line IF-THEN-ELSE statement and the WHILE loop.

Each new control structure is introduced by first showing its flow diagram pattern and Dartmouth BASIC form; afterwards, its implementation in BASIC-PLUS and standard Minimal BASIC is described. All complete program solutions show the three versions of each structure. This is done by writing each program using the BASIC-PLUS form of the structures. Through the use of shading, the purpose of each structure is emphasized and separated from its implementation details. It is no coincidence that the shaded portion of the structure corresponds closely, if not exactly, to the Dartmouth BASIC form. The changes required for Minimal BASIC are enclosed in brackets at the right. Therefore, the text can be used with any version of BASIC. In fact, the standard Minimal BASIC is sufficient for solving all problems discussed in the first seven chapters.

Since this text presents a serious treatment of the BASIC language, we felt it essential that advanced features of string processing, array manipulation and file usage be thoroughly covered. These features are implemented differently on most BASIC systems; however, there is still a high degree of commonality.

The array manipulation features discussed are available on most extended BASIC systems and correspond to the proposed Level 1 extension to Minimal BASIC. The string processing chapter describes the syntactic forms for both Dartmouth BASIC, Edition 7, and BASIC-PLUS. The Dartmouth BASIC form is identical to the proposed Level 1 extension; the BASIC-PLUS form corresponds quite closely to a number of existing BASIC systems. The file usage chapter also describes the Dartmouth BASIC and BASIC-PLUS forms, which are similar to most other versions. There are tables at the end of these chapters showing comparable operations in a number of versions developed for Burroughs, Sperry Univac, Digital Equipment, Honeywell, Control Data, Hewlett Packard, Radio Shack and Commodore computers.

Textbook Organization

There is more than enough material for a one semester course. The first eight chapters represent the core of the textbook and should be studied by all students. The last three chapters contain advanced material on string processing, matrices and files. Each of these chapters can be studied independently of the others; consequently, the instructor should choose one or more of these chapters depending on student interest and time available.

Each chapter contains a description of common programming errors that may occur as well as hints for debugging. An extensive set of homework programming problems is provided at the end of each chapter, and exercises are inserted in the body of each chapter. Solutions to selected exercises are provided at the end of the text.

All chapters end with a summary and a table describing the BASIC statements introduced in the chapter. A glossary of all BASIC statements is also provided.

The text is organized so that students may begin working with the computer as soon as possible. Chapter 1 contains a short discussion of computer components and programming languages. This is followed by a description of some fundamental computer operations that are common to most computers, and their BASIC language forms. These operations include simple input and output, assignment, and the END statement. A simple payroll problem illustrates the application of these operations.

A section on using a time-sharing system followed by a complete discussion of interactive input and output is also included. Students should be able to write simple linear programs (no branching), and use strings to annotate their program output, and produce programs that draw pictures.

The stepwise approach to programming is introduced in Chapter 2. The data definition table and flow diagram are described, and problems involving decisions and loops are examined and solved. The algorithms are represented using flow diagram patterns for the IF-THEN-ELSE and the counter-controlled loop. The counter-controlled loop is introduced as a restricted form of the FOR loop. Students should use this structure to implement homework programs involving counting loops.

In Chapter 3, the syntactic forms of the decision structures are presented along with the general FOR loop. A number of problems illustrating the application of these new control structures are solved. The careful development of the algorithm and the progression from flow diagram to program implementation is stressed.

Chapter 4 describes the general form of expressions and the use of library functions. String variables are introduced and several applications are presented.

In Chapter 5, we introduce two additional control structures that are useful in the stepwise or top-down development of algorithms: the WHILE loop and the subroutine. The Minimal BASIC form of the subroutine is presented and some earlier problems are redone using this feature. The different syntactic forms of the WHILE loop are discussed and several applications of this conditional looping structure are presented.

The one-dimensional array or list is described in Chapter 6. The notion of a subscript is explained and several sample problems using arrays are solved, including an array search.

Chapter 7 provides a discussion of advanced control structures. The AND and OR logical operators are introduced along with the multiple-alternative decision structure. Several implementation forms of this structure are described including the Dartmouth SELECT structure and the Minimal BASIC ON-GOTO statement. Nested structures are discussed along with rules for structure entry and exit. A sorting algorithm is also presented.

User-defined functions and independent subprograms are described in Chapter 8. The program system chart is introduced as an important tool for documenting a large program system. We show how it is used to specify the flow of information and control between program modules.

String manipulation is covered in Chapter 9. The concepts of string length, substring, concatenation and string search are illustrated in a number of solved problems. The ASCII code is described along with the BASIC functions for converting strings to their code representations and vice versa.

Chapter 10 describes the use of two-dimensional arrays or matrices. The BASIC matrix operators are all introduced and applied in sample problems.

Files and techniques for formatting output with the PRINT USING and image features are described in Chapter 11. Most of the chapter is concerned with sequential file usage. An introduction to random access files and chaining is also provided.

It is our intention to provide sufficient material to accommodate the needs of a wide variety of students in an introductory programming course. The depth of understanding of the basic problem solving and programming techniques, as well as the proficiency demonstrated in the application of these techniques, will vary according to the skill of the student and the expectations of the instructor.

It is extremely important to teach students a careful, disciplined approach to computer problem solving in the first course as bad programming habits die slowly, if at all. If the proper foundation is provided in this course, it will be much easier for students to use BASIC effectively in later courses or to adapt what they have learned to the study of other programming languages.

We believe that structured versions of BASIC will become more prevalent in the future. In the meantime, students should be able to effectively use the programming concepts and control structure implementations described in this text regardless of the BASIC version available on their computer.

Acknowledgments

There are many people whose talents and influence are reflected in this text. We are especially indebted to Stephen Garland of Dartmouth College who carefully read all phases of the manuscript and gave numerous suggestions, insight, and advice. We would also like to acknowledge the contributions of Robert Cook (Central Michigan University), Thomas Dwyer (University of Pittsburgh) and William Linder (University of South Carolina) who read the first draft of the manuscript and provided valuable comments and criticisms. We would also like to thank two students at Temple University, James

Cardell and Nancy Klein, who tested the programs in the manuscript and provided solutions to exercises.

Lastly, we would like to thank all those involved in the actual production of the manuscript. In particular, we are extremely grateful to Fran Palmer Fulton, who served as production manager for the manuscript; Robert Lambiase, who provided the artwork; and Jacalyn Harriz and Mary McCutcheon for their excellent job of typing manuscript drafts.

Philadelphia
January 1979

E.B.K.
F.L.F.

CONTENTS

8
LARGER PROBLEMS:
USER-DEFINED FUNCTIONS,
SUBROUTINES AND SUBPROGRAMS
249

9
CHARACTER STRING MANIPULATION
287

10
TWO-DIMENSIONAL
ARRAYS AND MATRICES
331

11
FORMATTED OUTPUT AND FILES
363

INTRODUCTION

1

1.1   COMPUTER ORGANIZATION

A computer is a tool for representing and manipulating information. There are many different kinds of computers, ranging in size from hand-held calculators to large and complex computing systems filling several rooms or entire buildings. In the recent past, computers were so expensive that they could be used only for business or scientific computations; now there are personal computers available for use in the home (see Fig. 1.1).

Fig. 1.1   Radio Shack TRS-80 microcomputer. (Photo courtesy of Tandy Corp.)

The size and cost of a computer is generally dependent upon the amount of work it can turn out in a given time unit. Larger, expensive computers have the capability of carrying out many operations simultaneously, thus increasing their work capacity. They also have more devices attached to them for performing special functions, all of which increase their capability and cost.

Despite the large variety in the cost, size, and capabilities of modern

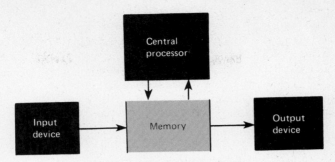

Fig. 1.2 Diagram of the basic components of a computer.

computers, they are remarkably similar in a number of ways. Basically, a *computer* consists of four components as shown in Fig. 1.2. (The lines connecting the various units represent possible paths of information flow. The arrows show the direction of information flow.)

All information that is to be processed by the computer must first be entered into the computer memory via an input device. The information in memory is manipulated by the central processor, and the results of this manipulation are also stored in the memory of the computer. Information in memory can be displayed through the use of appropriate output devices. These components and their interaction are described in more detail in the following sections.

1.1.1 The Computer Memory

The memory of a computer may be pictured as an ordered sequence of storage locations called *memory cells*. Each cell has associated with it a distinct *address*, which indicates its relative position in the sequence. Figure 1.3 depicts a computer memory consisting of 1000 cells numbered consecutively from 0 to 999. Some large-scale computers have memories consisting of millions of cells.

The memory cells of a computer are used to *represent* information. All types of information—numbers, names, lists, and even pictures—may be represented in the memory of a computer. The information that is contained in a memory cell is called the *contents* of the memory cell. Every memory cell contains some information—no cell is ever empty. Furthermore, no cell can ever contain more than one data item. Whenever a data item is placed into a memory cell, any information already there is destroyed, and cannot be retrieved. In Figure 1.3, the contents of memory cell 3 is the number −26, and the contents of memory cell 4 is the number 12.5.

Exercise 1.1: What are the contents of memory cells 0, 2, and 997 shown in Fig. 1.3?

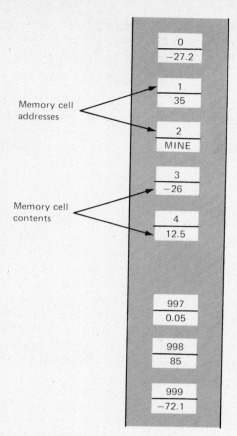

Fig. 1.3 A computer memory with 1000 memory cells.

1.1.2 The Central Processor Unit

The information representation capability of the computer would be of little use to us by itself. Indeed, it is the *manipulative* capability of the computer that enables us to study problems that would otherwise be impossible because of their computational requirements. With appropriate directions, modern computers can generate large quantities of new information from old, solving many otherwise impossible problems, and providing useful insights into others; and they can do so in exceptionally short periods of time.

The heart of the manipulation capability of the computer is the *central processor unit* (CPU). The CPU can retrieve information from the memory unit. (This information may be either data or instructions for manipulating data.) It can also store the results of manipulations back into the memory unit for later reference.

The CPU coordinates all activities of the various components of the computer. It determines which operations should be carried out and in what order. The transmission of coordinating control signals and commands is the function of the *control unit* within the central processor.

Also found within the central processor is the *arithmetic-logic unit*. The *arithmetic* portion consists of electronic circuitry wired to perform a variety of arithmetic operations, including addition, subtraction, multiplication, and division. The speed with which it can perform these operations is on the order of a millionth of a second. The *logic* unit consists of electronic circuitry to compare information and to make decisions based upon the results of the comparison. It is this feature, together with its powerful storage facility (the memory), that distinguishes the computer from the simple, hand-held calculators that many of us have used. Most of these calculators can be used only to perform arithmetic operations on numbers; they cannot compare these numbers, make decisions, or store large quantities of numbers.

1.1.3 Input and Output Devices

The manipulative skills of the computer would be of little use to us if we were unable to communicate with the computer. Specifically, we must be able to enter information into the computer memory, and display information (usually the results of a manipulation) stored in the computer memory. The input devices are used to *enter* data into the computer memory; the output devices are used to *display* results in a readable form.

Most of you will be using a computer terminal as both an input and output device. Terminals usually consist of a typewriter-like keyboard on which information required by the computer is typed (see Fig. 1.4, top). The results of a computation may be printed on a roll of paper fed through the terminal carriage or displayed on a video screen as *alphanumeric characters* (letters and numbers). Some terminals are equipped with *graphics capability* (see Fig. 1.4, bottom) which enables the output to be displayed as a two-dimensional graph or picture, and not just as rows of letters and numbers. With some graphics devices, the user can communicate with the computer by pointing at information displayed on the screen with an electronic pointer called a light pen, as shown in Fig. 1.4.

Computer terminals are widely used at ticket reservation counters for confirming reservations and printing tickets. They are also used at checkout counters in department stores to assist in keeping track of customer purchases and for inventory control.

In many computer systems, another type of input/output device is used to provide additional capability for information storage and retrieval (*secondary storage*). These devices can transfer huge quantities of information between the computer memory and a magnetic storage medium such as *magnetic tape, disk, or drum* (see Fig. 1.5). During a computer session, information

Fig. 1.4   Computer terminals: a standard "hard copy" terminal (top, photo courtesy Digital Equipment Corp.); a graphics terminal (bottom, photo courtesy IBM Corp.).

Fig. 1.5   Digital Equipment's VAX-11/780 computer system. (Photo courtesy Digital Equipment Corp.)

saved previously may be retrieved from a secondary storage device, and new information may be saved for future retrieval and use.

1.2   PROGRAMS AND PROGRAMMING LANGUAGES

1.2.1   Introduction

The computer is quite a powerful tool. Information *(input data)* may be stored in its memory and manipulated at exceptionally high speed to produce a result *(program output)*. We can describe a data manipulation task to the computer by presenting it with a list of instructions (called a *program*) that are to be carried out. Once this list has been provided to the computer, it can then assume responsibility and carry out *(execute)* these instructions.

The act of making up a list of instructions (writing a program) is called *programming*. Writing a computer program is very similar to describing the rules of a game to people who have never played the game. In both cases, a language of description understood by all parties involved in the communication is required. For example, the rules of the game must be described in some language, and then read and carried out. Both the inventor of the game and those who wish to play must be familiar with the language of description used.

Languages used for communication between man and the computer are called *programming languages*. All instructions presented to a computer must be represented and combined (to form a program) according to the *syntactic*

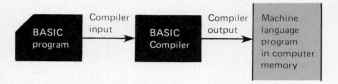

Fig. 1.6 Preparing a BASIC program for execution.

rules (grammar) of the programming language. There is, however, one significant difference between a programming language and a language such as French, English or Russian. The rules of a programming language are very precise and have no "exceptions" or "ambiguities." The reason for this is that a computer cannot think! It can only follow instructions exactly as given. It cannot interpret these instructions to figure out, for example, what the program writer *(programmer)* meant it to do. An error in writing an instruction will change the meaning of a program, and cause the computer to perform the wrong action.

In this book we shall concentrate on the BASIC (*B*eginner's *A*ll-purpose *S*ymbolic *I*nstruction *C*ode) programming language that was developed at Dartmouth College. BASIC was designed for use by students and others who require a relatively simple language with which to begin programming. Many of the programming and problem solving concepts you learn will be applicable to other programming languages as well as BASIC.

Most computers cannot execute BASIC programs directly. They must first be translated into the language understood by the computer (*machine language*). The translation is performed by a large program called a *compiler*. If the translation is successful, the machine language version of the program is stored in memory ready to be carried out or *executed*. This process is illustrated in Fig. 1.6.

There are two major advantages to programming in a *high-level language* like BASIC. First, BASIC is much closer to our own language than is machine language; hence, it is much easier to write BASIC programs. Second, BASIC programs are highly *portable*; a BASIC program written for one computer can often be executed on a variety of computers. On the other hand, a machine language program written for one computer will not normally execute on a different type of computer.

We will discuss a few of the fundamental features of the BASIC language in the next section. Others will be introduced throughout the rest of the text.

1.2.2 Executing a Program

In order to execute a program, the computer control unit examines each program instruction in memory, starting with the first, and sends out the command signals appropriate for carrying out the instruction. Normally, the in-

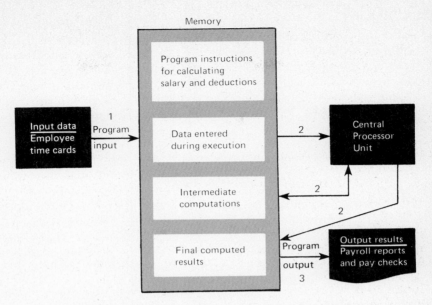

Fig. 1.7 The flow of information through the computer.

structions are executed in sequence; however, as we shall see later, it is possible to have the control unit skip over some instructions or execute some
instructions more than once.

   During execution, data may be entered into the memory of the computer,
and the results of the manipulations performed on this data may be displayed.
Of course, these things will happen only if the program contains instructions
telling the computer to enter or display the appropriate information.

   Figure 1.7 shows the relationship between a program for computing a
payroll and its input and output, and indicates the *flow of information* through
the computer during execution of the program. The data to be manipulated by
the program (employee time cards) must first be entered into the computer
memory (Step 1 in Fig. 1.7). As directed by the program instructions, the
central processor unit manipulates the data in memory, and places the results
of these computations back into memory (Step 2). When the computation process is complete, the results can be output from the memory of the computer
(Step 3) in the desired forms (as employee checks and payroll reports).

1.3 INTRODUCTION TO BASIC

1.3.1 Use of Symbolic Names in BASIC

   One of the most important features of BASIC is that it permits us to
reference data that are stored in memory through the use of symbolic names

(called *variable names* or, simply, *variables*), rather than numeric memory-cell addresses. The compiler *allocates* (assigns) one memory cell for each variable name used in our program. We need not be concerned with this address. We simply tell the compiler the name of each variable we want to use and let the compiler determine the address of the cell associated with that variable.

Variable names in BASIC consist of a single letter (A-Z) or a single letter followed by a digit (0-9). Examples of valid variable names would be:

A, C, C5, D9

Invalid variable names would be:

5C, A+, B36, TAX, 25

It is a good idea to choose the first letter in the description of the variable as its name. For a payroll program, we might use the variables H (for hours worked), R (for hourly rate), T (for tax amount), G (for gross salary), and N (for net pay). These are pictured in Fig. 1.8. The question mark in each box indicates that we have no idea of the current values of these variables although variables always have values.

Fig. 1.8 Using variable names to designate memory cells.

Exercise 1.2: Which of the following can be used as legal variable names in BASIC? Indicate the errors in the illegal names.

i) A	ii) M	iii) ZIP12	iv) 12Z
v) ITCH	vi) P3$	vii) G2	viii) 3X
ix) N1			

1.3.2 Some Computer Operations and Their BASIC Descriptions

There are a large number of computers available today and each has a unique set of operations that it can perform. These operations generally fall into three categories:

Input and output operations
Data manipulation and comparison
Control operations

Despite the large variety of operations in these categories, there are a few operations in each that are common to most computers. These operations are summarized in Fig. 1.9.

Input/Output Operations

Read
Print

Data Manipulation and Comparison

Add   Subtract   Multiply   Divide
Negate   Copy   Compare

Control Operations

Transfer
Conditional execution
Stop

Fig. 1.9 Common computer operations.

In the remainder of this chapter, we will describe some of these operations by showing how they are written in BASIC. We will do this by way of illustration, using a payroll processing problem.

Problem 1.1: Compute the gross salary and net pay for an employee of a company, given the employee's hourly rate, the number of hours worked, and the tax deduction amount.

1.3.3 Simple Data Manipulation—Assignment Statements

We will choose variables named H and R to represent the number of hours worked and the hourly wage rate, respectively. The variables G and N will be used to represent the computed gross and net salary, respectively. The variable T will represent the amount of tax to be withheld from the paycheck. For simplicity, we will assume the withholding tax amount to be $25 regardless of an employee's gross salary. (A more realistic tax schedule would calculate the amount of tax withheld by using a table of varying percentages based on the employee's gross salary.)

Our problem is to perform these two computations:

Compute gross salary as the product of hours worked and hourly wage rate;
Find net pay by deducting the tax amount from the gross salary.

We need to learn how to write BASIC instructions to tell the computer to perform these computations. This can be done using the BASIC *assignment statements*

```
LET G = H * R
LET N = G - T
```

These data manipulation statements are called assignment statements because they specify an assignment of value to a given variable. For example,
the statement

```
LET G = H * R
```

specifies that the variable G will be assigned the result of the multiplication
(indicated by *) of the values of the variables H and R. Figure 1.10 illustrates
the effect of the two assignment statements used for calculating gross and net
salary.

The effect of the first statement is to cause the value of the variable G to
be replaced by the *product* of the values of the variables H and R or 135. The
second statement causes the value of the variable N to be replaced by the
difference between the values of the variables G and T. We are assuming, of
course, that meaningful data items are already present in the variables H, R,
and T. Only the values of G and N are changed by this sequence of arithmetic
operations; the variables H, R, and T retain their original values.

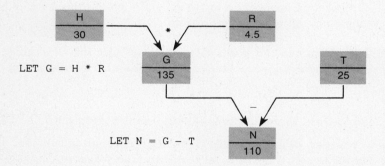

Fig. 1.10   Effect of assignment statements.

The general form of the assignment statement is shown in the display
below.

Assignment Statement

BASIC form:

```
LET result = operand₁ arithmetic—operator operand₂
```

Interpretation: Operand$_1$ and operand$_2$ represent the quantities being manipulated; arithmetic-operator indicates the manipulation to be performed. The
operands may be either variable names or numbers. The arithmetic-operator
is any of the symbols given in Table 1.1. The name of the variable that will be
assigned a new value is specified by result. The previous value of result is
destroyed when the new value is stored; however, the values of the operands
are unchanged.

Arithmetic-operator	Meaning
+	Addition
−	Subtraction
*	Multiplication
/	Division

Table 1.1   BASIC arithmetic operators

Example 1.1:   In BASIC, it is perfectly permissible to write assignment statements of the form

LET S = S + X

where the variable S is used on both sides of the equal sign. This is obviously not a mathematical equation, but it illustrates something that is often done in BASIC. This statement instructs the computer to add the value of the variable S to the value of the variable X and assign the result as the new value of the variable S. The previous value of S is destroyed in the process.

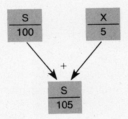

The statement above is used in Chapter 2, where it enables us to compute the sum of a large number of data items using only two variables (S and X) for data storage. The repeated execution of this statement accumulates the arithmetic sum of all the data items in the variable S.

Example 1.2:   Assignment statements can also be written with a single operand. The statement

LET A = B

instructs the computer to *copy* the value of the variable B into A. The statement

LET A = − B

instructs the computer to *negate* the value of the variable B and store the result in A. Neither of these statements affects the contents of the variable B. Negating a number is equivalent to multiplying it by −1. Thus, if the variable B contains −3.5, then the above statement will cause 3.5 to be stored in the variable A.

In Chapter 4, we will discuss more complex examples of assignment statements involving the use of multiple operators and more than two operands.

1.3.4   Storing Data in Memory—Program Constants and Variables

Information cannot be manipulated by the computer unless it is first stored in memory. There are two ways of initially placing data to be manipulated into computer memory: (1) by use of a "copy" assignment statement, or (2) by *reading* the data into memory during the execution of the program. Normally, the first approach is taken for a data item that is a *program constant* and does not change from one use of the program to the next. The second approach is taken for data that are likely to vary. In the payroll problem, the withholding-tax amount is always $25 regardless of which employee's net pay is to be computed. This value, therefore, may be copied into the variable T through the use of the assignment statement

LET T = 25

This statement defines the value of T as the constant 25 (the value 25 is stored in T); the statement must precede any other program statements that reference T.

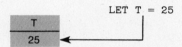

In the following section, we describe how data that are likely to vary with each execution of a program may be entered into computer memory.

1.3.5   The READ and DATA Statements

Since each employee of a company may work a different number of hours per week at a different hourly rate, the variables H and R do not represent program constants. Consequently, their values should be read into memory during program execution. This operation must be done prior to performing the calculations described earlier (Section 1.3.3).

The statement below instructs the computer to read data into variables H and R.

READ H, R

The effect of the READ statement is to cause the computer to enter a data item into each of the variables listed (H and R in this case). The prior values of these variables are lost.

All of the data items (values) to be entered by the READ statement must be listed in a corresponding DATA statement. The effect of the READ and DATA statements

READ H, R
DATA 30, 4.5

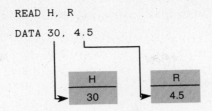

Fig. 1.11 Effect of READ and DATA statements.

is indicated in Fig. 1.11. The previous values of the variables H and R are destroyed by the data input process.

The displays below describe the READ and DATA statements.

READ Statement

BASIC form:

            READ list of variables

Interpretation: Data are entered into each variable specified in the list of variables. Commas are used to separate the variable names in the list. The data items are provided in DATA statements.

DATA Statement

BASIC form:

            DATA list of data items

Interpretation: Each number in the list of data items is entered into memory through the execution of a READ statement. Commas are used to separate the data items in the list.

The DATA statement may actually be placed anywhere in the program; however, we recommend placing it just after the READ statement which causes the last data item in the list to be entered into memory. The order of the data items in the DATA statement must correspond to the order of the variable names in the associated READ statement. If the order of the data items were somehow interchanged during preparation of the program, the values read into H and R would not be the ones desired.

To minimize the chance of this or other similar input errors going undetected, it is advisable to display or *echo print* the value of each variable used for storage of input data. Such a printout also provides a record of the data manipulated by the program. This record is often quite helpful to the programmer and to those who must read and interpret the program output. The statement used to display or print out the value of a variable is described in the next section.

1.3.6 The PRINT Statement

Thus far, we have discussed the BASIC instructions required for the entry of employee hours and wage rate, and the computation of gross salary and net pay. The computational results have been stored in the variables G and N, respectively. Yet all of this work done by the computer is of little use to us since we cannot physically look into a memory cell to see what is there. We must, therefore, have a way to instruct the computer to display or print out the value of a variable.

The BASIC instruction

```
PRINT G, N
```

would cause the values of the variables G and N to be printed on a line of program output (Fig. 1.12). The values of G and N are not altered by this operation.

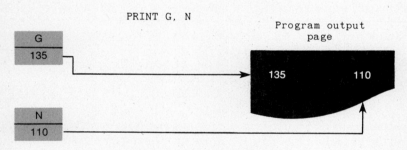

Fig. 1.12   Effect of PRINT statement.

The PRINT statement is described in the next display.

PRINT statement

BASIC form:

```
PRINT output list
```

Interpretation: The value of each variable in the output list is printed in sequence across an output line. Commas are used to separate items in the output list.

1.3.7   Stopping Computer Execution

Once all desired calculations have been performed and the results displayed, the computer must be instructed to stop execution of the program. The instruction that does this (END) is described in the next display.

END statement

BASIC form:

END

Interpretation: The END statement is always the last line of a BASIC program. It terminates program execution and indicates that there are no more BASIC statements in the program.

1.3.8   The Payroll Program

We can now collect all of the instructions that have been discussed, and order them to produce a complete BASIC program for Problem 1.1 (Fig. 1.13).

```
110 LET T = 25
120 READ H, R
130 DATA 30, 4.50
140 PRINT H, R
150 LET G = H * R
160 LET N = G - T
170 PRINT G, N
180 END
```

Fig. 1.13   Program for the payroll problem.

Each BASIC statement in Fig. 1.13 is preceded by a line number. The line numbers in a BASIC program must be in ascending numerical order. It is a good idea initially to count by tens as shown in Fig. 1.13 so that there is ample room to insert additional program statements that may be needed.

Blanks in BASIC statements are ignored by the compiler; you may, therefore, use blanks as you please in order to improve the readability of your program. However, you should try to be consistent. We will leave a blank after a comma and put a blank before and after operators such as * and −, and BASIC *keywords* such as LET, READ, DATA, and PRINT.

In the program of Fig. 1.13, the statements on lines 110 to 140 define the value of the program constant T and cause the values of the variables H and R to be entered and displayed. The statements on lines 150 to 170 are used to compute and display the values of G and N.

The END statement must be the very last statement in a program (largest line number). In addition to terminating program execution, it serves as a signal to the compiler that there are no more statements to be translated in the current program.

This program would generate two lines of output:

```
30          4.5
135         110
```

The data read into H and R are printed on the first line; the values computed for G and N are printed on the second line.

If we wished to rerun the program for a different employee who worked 35 hours and was paid $3.80 per hour, we could simply modify the DATA statement as shown below.

```
130 DATA 35, 3.80
```

Exercise 1.3: Can the order of any of the statements in the program in Fig. 1.13 be changed in any way without altering the results of the program? Which statements can be moved? Which cannot be moved? Why?

Exercise 1.4: What values will be printed by the Payroll Program for the alternate data statement

```
130 DATA 35, 3.80
```

Exercise 1.5: Let H, R, and T be the symbolic names of memory cells containing the information shown below:

H	R	T
40.0	16.25	0.18

What values will be printed following the execution of the following sequence of instructions?

```
10 LET G = H * R
20 LET T = G * T
30 LET N = G - T
40 PRINT H, R, G, T, N
50 END
```

1.4 USING THE COMPUTER

1.4.1 Introduction to Timesharing Computer Systems

Many of you will be interacting with a *timesharing* computer through a terminal. Timesharing enables the computer to serve many users concurrently. Because the operating speed of the computer is so fast, each user is often unaware that the computer is being shared with others.

All timesharing systems are somewhat different. However, in general, the procedure below must be followed in using BASIC on a timesharing system.

(1) The terminal should be turned on.
(2) If the terminal is not "hard-wired" to the computer, the computer must be dialed up and the telephone connected to the terminal.
(3) Obtain access to the computer by identifying yourself as a legitimate user.
(4) Indicate the type of system or compiler you desire to use (BASIC).
(5) Create a new program or retrieve an old one from secondary storage.
(6) Run or execute your program.
(7) After examining your program results, make any corrections or changes that may be necessary and rerun your program until it executes to your satisfaction.
(8) Save the final program on secondary storage if it will be needed later.
(9) When finished, logout or disconnect yourself from the timesharing system.

Your instructor will provide you with precise details of how all these functions are handled on your computer system. We provide an illustration of the above procedure in the next section.

1.4.2   Using a Timesharing System

In Fig. 1.14, we show a hypothetical terminal session in which our payroll program is entered and executed. All information typed by the computer system is underlined. The letters at left are for reference in the discussion that follows; they would not be printed at the terminal.

A. <u>FRIENDLY TIMESHARING SERVICE, TIME IS 3:47 P.M.</u>
This message was typed in response to our dialing-up the computer. It indicates that the computer is functioning and is available for our use.

B. <u>ACCOUNT –</u> SMITH
The computer requests our account name—we respond by typing our last name. After typing each line, the RETURN key on the terminal must be depressed.

C. <u>ID NUMBER –</u> 683425
The computer asks for our ID number—we respond (683425) and press RETURN.

D. <u>SYSTEM –</u> BASIC
The computer asks which system or compiler we desire—we type in BASIC and press RETURN.

E. <u>NEW OR OLD –</u> NEW
The computer asks whether we wish to create a new program (NEW) or use one that is in secondary storage (OLD)—we type in NEW and press RETURN.

```
A. FRIENDLY TIMESHARING SERVICE, TIME IS 3:47 P.M.
B. ACCOUNT - SMITH
C. ID NUMBER - 683425
D. SYSTEM - BASIC
E. NEW OR OLD - NEW
F. NEW FILE NAME - PAYROLL
G. READY

   110 LET T = 25
   120 READ H, R
   130 DATE 30, 4.50
   140 PRINT H, R
H. 150 LET G = H * R
   160 LET N = G - T
   170 PRINT * G, N
   180 END
   130 DATA 30, 4.50

I. LIST

   110 LET T = 25
   120 READ H, R
   130 DATA 30, 4.50
   140 PRINT H, R
   150 LET G = H * R
   160 LET N = G - T
   170 PRINT * G, N
   180 END

J. RUN

K. ILLEGAL STATEMENT AT LINE 170

L. 170  PRINT G, N

M. RUN

N. 30              4.5
   135             110

O. SAVE

P. READY

Q. LOGOUT
```

Fig. 1.14 Sample terminal session.

F. NEW FILE NAME - PAYROLL

We provide the name, PAYROLL, for our program. (If this program is later saved in secondary storage, it will be saved as the *file* named PAYROLL.)

G. <u>READY</u>
    The system is ready for our program.

H. The payroll program is typed in. Although the statements can be entered in any order, they are normally entered in sequence by line number. Line 130 is typed twice as the initial attempt contained an error (DATE instead of DATA). If you make a mistake in typing a line, simply retype it—line number and all; the computer only retains the last version of any line. On many systems, a special *rubout* key "erases" an erroneous character (or characters) as the line is being entered.

I. LIST
    We have asked the system to LIST our program so that we can verify that it has been entered correctly. The program lines are printed in numerical order. Note that only the corrected version of line 130 is printed.

J. RUN
    The command RUN causes the program to be translated and executed if there are no syntax errors in our BASIC statements.

K. <u>ILLEGAL STATEMENT AT LINE 170</u>
    The BASIC compiler found a syntax error at line 170; hence, it was not able to execute the program.

L. 170 PRINT G, N
    We reenter line 170.

M. RUN
    We instruct the computer to run our program again.

N. The program executes and the resulting output is printed.

O. SAVE
    We instruct the computer to save our program in seconday storage (file PAYROLL) as we may wish to use it during a later session.

P. <u>READY</u>
    The system indicates that it has finished saving our program.

Q. LOGOUT
    Typing LOGOUT disconnects us from the computer and terminates the session.

    The system commands LIST, RUN, and SAVE are used by us to tell the computer what to do with our program. In a single session, we can request as many listings (LIST) or executions (RUN) of a program as we desire. If we wish to use our program in a later session, we must save it during the current session (SAVE). In the next session, we enter the word OLD in response to the question NEW or OLD (step E), and specify the name of the file containing our program (step F). If we no longer need this program, we can erase it from secondary storage by later using the system command UNSAVE.

1.5 ADDITIONAL INPUT AND OUTPUT FEATURES

1.5.1 Annotated Output

The printout for our payroll program consists of four numbers only, with no indication of what these numbers mean. In this section, we shall learn how output values may be annotated using *quoted strings* (or strings) to make it easier for us to identify the variable values they represent. We will learn more about the use of strings in Chapter 4, but for the present it would be useful to know how to use them to clarify program output.

A *string* is a sequence of symbols enclosed in quotes. We can insert strings directly into BASIC print statements in order to provide descriptive messages in the program output. The string will be displayed exactly as it is typed (with the quotes removed).

For example, the statements

```
140 PRINT "HOURS = ", H, "RATE = ", R
170 PRINT "GROSS = ", G, "NET = ", N
```

contain four strings and would generate the two output lines:

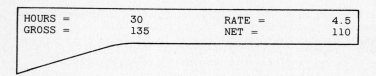

```
HOURS =          30        RATE =          4.5
GROSS =          135       NET =           110
```

An additional example of the use of strings to annotate output is provided in Fig. 1.15, which computes the average trip time and cost using the formulas below:

(1) time = distance / speed
(2) gallons used = distance / miles per gallon
(3) cost of trip = gallons used × cost per gallon

There are four data items for this program; trip distance (D), average speed (S), number of miles travelled on a gallon of gas (M), and cost of a gallon (C). The program computes the estimated time of the trip (T) and the total cost of gasoline (E).

The computations performed in this program are quite simple. Line 140 computes the time of a trip using formula (1) above; line 210 computes the number of gallons of gasoline using formula (2); line 220 computes the cost of the trip using formula (3).

The remaining statements are used for data entry and display. For each

```
100 PRINT "COMPUTE TRIP TIME AND COST"
105 READ D, S
110 DATA 320, 50
120 PRINT "DISTANCE = "; D; " MILES,"
130 PRINT "AVERAGE SPEED = "; S; " MPH"
140 LET T = D / S
150 PRINT "TIME OF TRIP = "; T; " HOURS"
160 PRINT
170 READ M, C
180 DATA 19.5, .60
190 PRINT "MILEAGE RATE = "; M; " MILES PER GALLON"
200 PRINT "COST PER GALLON = "; C; " DOLLARS"
210 LET G = D / M
220 LET E = G * C
230 PRINT "ESTIMATED TRIP EXPENSE = "; E; " DOLLARS"
240 END

RUN
```

COMPUTE TRIP TIME AND COST	*(line 100)*
DISTANCE = 320 MILES AVERAGE SPEED = 50 MPH	*(lines 120, 130)*
TIME OF TRIP = 6.4 HOURS	*(line 150)*
	(line 160)
MILEAGE RATE = 19.5 MILES PER GALLON	*(line 190)*
COST PER GALLON = .60 DOLLARS	*(line 200)*
ESTIMATED TRIP EXPENSE = 9.84615 DOLLARS	*(line 230)*

Fig. 1.15   Trip time and cost program and sample output.

line of output, the program statement that generated the output line is indicated in parentheses on the right.

A close examination of the program output for Fig. 1.15 reveals several important points concerning the print statements:

1. Each print statement initiates output on a new line, unless the previously executed print statement ended with a comma or a semicolon. (The output from the print statements at lines 120 and 130 appeared on the same line because the first print—at line 120—was terminated with a comma.)
2. The word PRINT by itself (line 160) generates a blank line.
3. All strings to be used as messages must appear in a print statement enclosed in quotes. A PRINT statement may be used to print a message only (line 100) or messages interspersed with variable values (lines 120, 130, 150, 190, 200, 230).
4. Either a comma or a semicolon may be used to separate items in an output list (following word PRINT). When a comma is used, the output items are printed in fixed columns across a page with spaces between them; when a semicolon is used, the output items are printed next to each other.
   a) The comma sets up *fields* or *zones* across a page. The number of characters in a field varies from computer to computer, but widths

of 15 are common. Each number is printed in a single field, regardless of the size of the number; however, a long string may use several fields. Both strings and numbers are printed starting in the left-most position of a field. However, for positive numbers, the left-most position will be blank.

b) When a semicolon is used as a separator in a print statement, variable size fields are used. For strings, the field size is equal to the length of the string. For numbers, the field size is equal to the length of the number plus one (for the sign). Again, if the number is positive, the sign position is left blank.

Example 1.3:   Let the variables D and B contain the values 257.5 and −195.75, respectively. Then

a) the statement

```
PRINT "DEPOSIT = "; D, "BALANCE = "; B
```

would produce the annotated output

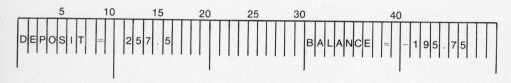

b) the statement

```
PRINT "THE CURRENT BALANCE IS ", B
```

would produce the output

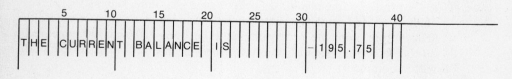

c) the statements

```
PRINT "DEPOSIT = "; D
PRINT "BALANCE = ", B
```

would produce the annotated output

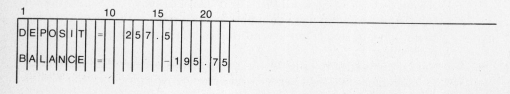

d) the statements

```
110 PRINT "DEPOSIT = ";
120 PRINT D
130 PRINT "BALANCE = ",
140 PRINT B
```

have the same effect as the two print statements shown in c) (Lines 120 and 140 do not initiate a new output line since the previous PRINT statements end with a semicolon and comma, respectively).

Exercise 1.6:   Write the seven print statements needed to print the TIC-TAC-TOE board configuration shown below.

```
      I      I
  X   I      I
  ---I---I---
      I O  I X
  ---I---I---
      I O  I
      I      I
```

1.5.2   More on READ and DATA Statements

The DATA statement is a nonexecutable statement. This means it is not translated into machine language and executed; instead, the compiler copies all items in each data list into a special area of memory as the program is translated. During execution, whenever a READ statement is encountered, the next group of data items is copied from this special area of memory into the variables specified in the input list.

Example 1.4:   As an example, consider the two sets of READ and DATA statements below:

```
100 READ H, R            100 READ H, R
110 DATA 30, 4.5         110 READ X, Y
120 READ X, Y            120 DATA 30, 4.5, 6.8, 1.5
130 DATA 6.8, 1.5
```

Both sequences of statements would cause the same values to be stored in memory

H	R	X	Y
30	4.5	6.8	1.5

We recommend the sequence on the left, even though it is longer, as each pair of data items appears directly below the READ statement that processes it.

1.5.3   Interactive Data Entry—the Input Statement

The program shown in Fig. 1.16 illustrates a second way in which data can be provided to a program: through the use of an INPUT statement. By using the INPUT statement, we can *interact* with a program while it is executing. It is not necessary to supply all of the problem data in advance; instead, we can supply data to the program as it is requested, during the running of the program.

If an *interactive program* is written properly, it will inform the user of important computational results, and *prompt* the user when it requires additional data. As shown in the program in Fig. 1.16, the PRINT statement can be used to print both results and prompting messages. A prompting message (lines 100, 130, 140) is printed each time additional information is needed by the program. The INPUT statement is then used to enter data items that are typed at the terminal. These data items are underlined in Fig. 1.16.

```
100 PRINT "HOW OLD ARE YOU";
110 INPUT A
120 PRINT A; "IS A GOOD AGE."
130 PRINT "HOW MANY BROTHERS AND SISTERS DO YOU HAVE?"
140 PRINT "TYPE NUMBER OF BROTHERS, A COMMA, AND NUMBER OF SISTERS"
150 INPUT B, S
160 LET T = B + S
170 PRINT "THAT MEANS YOU HAVE "; T ; "SIBLINGS."
180 END

RUN

HOW OLD ARE YOU? 25
 25 IS A GOOD AGE.
HOW MANY BROTHERS AND SISTERS DO YOU HAVE?
TYPE NUMBER OF BROTHERS, A COMMA, AND NUMBER OF SISTERS
? 3, 2
THAT MEANS YOU HAVE  5 SIBLINGS.
```

Fig. 1.16 Interactive data entry.

The INPUT statement is used exactly as a READ statement, except that data to be entered are typed at the terminal during program execution, rather than provided beforehand in a DATA statement as the program is initially typed. When an INPUT statement is executed by the computer, the running program is *interrupted*, a question mark is printed at the user's terminal, and the computer then waits for the user to supply the necessary data. As shown in Fig. 1.16, if the prompting message ends with a semicolon or comma (line 100), the question mark is printed on the same line as the prompt; otherwise, it is printed on the next output line (line 140). Once the data entry has been completed (usually indicated when the user presses the RETURN key), execution continues with the next statement in the program. The INPUT statement is described in the next display.

INPUT statement

BASIC form:

> INPUT list of variables

Interpretation: A question mark is printed and program execution is interrupted. As many data items should be typed in (separated by commas) as there are variables in the input list. After data entry is complete, the RETURN key should be pressed to resume program execution.

Note: A PRINT statement containing a relevant prompting message should precede each INPUT statement.

Exercise 1.7: Rewrite the programs in Fig. 1.13 and 1.15 as interactive programs.

1.6 SUMMARY

You have been introduced to the basic components of the computer: the memory, the central processor unit, and the input and output units. A summary of important facts about computers that you should remember follows.

1. A memory cell is never empty.
2. The current contents of a memory cell are destroyed whenever new information is placed in that cell (via an assignment, read, or input statement).
3. Programs must first be placed in the memory of the computer before they can be executed.
4. Data may not be manipulated by the computer without first being stored in memory.
5. The computer cannot think for itself, and must be instructed to perform a task in a precise and unambiguous manner, using a programming language.
6. Programming a computer can be fun—if you are patient, organized and careful.

You have also seen how to use the BASIC programming language to perform some very fundamental operations. You have learned how to instruct the computer to read information into memory, perform some simple computations and print the results of the computation. All of this has been done using symbols (punctuation marks, variable names and special operators such as *, − and +) that are familiar, easy to remember and easy to use. You needed to know virtually nothing about the computer you are using in order to understand and use BASIC. In Table 1.2, we have provided a summary of all of the BASIC statements introduced in this chapter. An example of the use of each instruction is also given. You should use these examples as guides to ensure that you are using the correct syntax in the program statements that you write.

Statement type and use	Examples
ASSIGNMENT: Computes or assigns a new value for a variable.	LET G = H * R
	LET T = 25
READ: Enters input data into a variable.	READ H, R
DATA: Provides a list of input data items.	DATA 35, 3.5
INPUT: Enters input data interactively during program execution.	INPUT B, S
PRINT: Displays the value of a variable or a string.	PRINT "GROSS = "; G
END: Terminates execution and informs the compiler that there are no more program statements to be translated.	END

Table 1.2   Summary of BASIC statements

The small amount of BASIC that you have seen is sufficient to enable you to solve many problems using the computer. However, many problems cannot be solved with just this limited BASIC subset. The more you learn about BASIC, the easier it will be for you to write programs to solve more complicated problems on the computer.

In the remainder of the text we will introduce you to more of the features of the BASIC language and provide precise descriptions of the rules for using these features. You must remember throughout that, unlike the rules of English, the rules of BASIC are quite precise and allow no exceptions. BASIC instructions formed in violation of these rules will cause syntax errors in your programs.

You should find the mastery of the rules of BASIC relatively easy. By far the most challenging aspect of your work will be the formulation of the logic and organization of your programs. For this reason, we will introduce you to a methodology for problem solving with a computer in the next chapter and continue to emphasize this methodology throughout the remainder of the book.

PROGRAMMING PROBLEMS

1.2   Write a program to read in the weight (in pounds) of an object, and compute and print its weight in kilograms and grams. [*Hint:* one pound is equal to 0.453592 kilograms or 453.59237 grams.]

1.3   A cyclist coasting on a level road slows from a speed of 10 miles/hr. to 2.5 miles/hr. in one minute. Write a computer program that calculates the cyclist's constant rate of acceleration and determines how long it will take the cyclist to come to rest, given his original speed of 10 miles/hr.
[*Hint:* Use the equation

$$a = \frac{v_f - v_i}{t}$$

where a is acceleration, t is time, v_i is initial velocity, and v_f is the final velocity.]

1.4   Write a program to read three data items into variables X, Y, and Z, and find and print their product and sum.

1.5 Eight track stars entered the mile race at the Penn Relays. Write a program that will read in the race time in minutes (M) and seconds (S) for any one of these runners, and compute and print the speed in feet per second (F) and in meters per second (M1). [*Hints:* There are 5280 feet in one mile and one meter equals 3.282 feet.] Test your program on one of the times (minutes and seconds) given below.

3.0 minutes 52.83 seconds	3.0 minutes 56.22 seconds	3.0 minutes 59.83 seconds
4.0 minutes 00.03 seconds	4.0 minutes 16.22 seconds	4.0 minutes 19.00 seconds
4.0 minutes 19.89 seconds	4.0 minutes 21.21 seconds	

1.6 You are planning to rent a car to drive from Boston to Philadelphia. Cost is no consideration, but you want to be certain that you can make the trip on one tankful of gas. Write a program to read in the miles-per-gallon (M) and tank size (T) in gallons for a particular rent-a-car, and print out the distance that can be travelled on one tank. Test your program for the following data:

miles-per-gallon M	tank size *(gallons)*
10.0	15.0
40.5	20.0
22.5	12.0
10.0	9.0

1.7 Write a program that prints your initials in large block letters. (*Hint:* Use a 6×6 grid for each letter and print six messages. Each message should consist of a row of *'s interspersed with blanks.)

PROBLEM SOLVING WITH THE COMPUTER

2.1   PROBLEM ANALYSIS

2.1.1   Introduction

Now that you have been introduced to the computer—what it is, how it works and what it can do—it is time to turn our attention to learning how to use the computer to solve problems.

Using the computer for problem solving is similar to trying to put a man on the moon in the late 1950's and 1960's. In both instances, there is a problem to be solved and a final "program" for solving it.

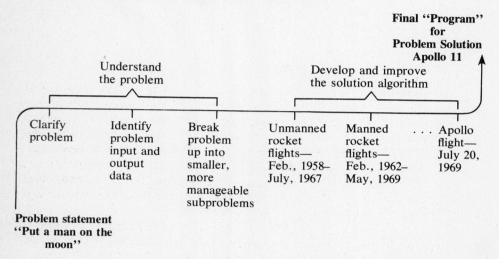

In the moon effort, the final goal was not achieved directly. Rather, it was brought about through the careful planning and organization of subtasks, each of which had to be completed successfully before the Apollo 11 flight could even be attempted.

Writing a computer program also requires careful planning and organization. It is rare, indeed, to see an error-free computer program written directly from the original statement of a problem. Usually, the final program is achieved only after a number of steps have been followed. These steps are the subject of this chapter.

2.1.2   Representation and Manipulation of Data

We stated earlier that the computer is a tool that can be used to represent and to manipulate data. It is, therefore, not too surprising that the first two steps in solving a problem on the computer require the definition of the data to be represented in the computer memory, and the formulation of an *algorithm*—a list that describes the desired manipulation of these data.

These two steps are not entirely unrelated. Decisions that we make in defining the data may be subject to numerous changes throughout the algorithm formulation. Nevertheless, it is absolutely essential that we perform the data definition in as complete and precise a fashion as possible before constructing the algorithm. Careless errors, or errors in judgment in deciding what information is to be represented, and what form this information is to take, can result in numerous difficulties in the later stages of solving a problem on the computer. Such mistakes can make the algorithm formulation extremely difficult, and sometimes even impossible.

Once the definition of the information to be represented in the computer has been made and a precise formulation of the problem statement is available, the algorithm for solving the problem can be formulated.

2.1.3 Understanding the Problem

The definition of the data to be represented in the computer memory requires a clear understanding of the stated problem. First, we must determine what information is to be computed and printed by the computer. Then it is necessary to identify the information that is to be given as input to the computer. Once the input and output data have been identified, we must ask if sufficient information is available to compute the required output from the given input. If the answer to this question is no, we must determine what additional information is needed and how this information can be provided to the program.

When identifying the data items associated with the problem, it is helpful to assign to each item a descriptive variable name that can be used to represent the computer memory cell containing the data item. (Recall from Chapter 1 that we do not have to be concerned with the actual memory cell associated with each variable name. The compiler will assign a unique memory cell to each variable name and it will handle all bookkeeping details necessary to retain this correspondence.)

To see how this process works, we will apply it to a specific problem.

Problem 2.1: Write a program to compute and print the sum and average of two numbers.

Discussion: The first step is to make certain that we understand the problem and to identify the input and output data for the problem. Then we can obtain a more precise formulation of the problem in terms of these input and output items.

All items of information to be used to solve a given problem should be listed in a *data table*, along with a description of the variable used to represent each data item. The data table for Problem 2.1 is given next. The entries shown describe the input and output data for the problem.

Data Table for Problem 2.1

Input variables	*Program variables*	*Output variables*
N1: First number to be used in computation		S: Sum of two numbers
N2: Second number to be used in computation		A: Average of two numbers

There are clearly two items of information required as output for this problem. They are the sum and the average of two numbers. In order to compute these values, we must be able to store the data items to be summed and averaged into the memory of the computer. In this example, we will use the variables N1 and N2 to represent these two data items.

The table form just illustrated will be used for all data tables in the text. Variables whose values are entered through read statements are listed as input variables; variables whose values represent final computational results required by the problem statement are listed as output variables. Other variables which may be used to store program constants or intermediate computational results are listed as program variables. (There are no program variables for Problem 2.1.) In all cases, it is important to include in the data table a short, concise description of how each variable is to be used in the program.

The data table is valuable not only during algorithm development but also as a piece of *program documentation*. It is a convenient reference document for associating variable names and their uses in the program. You should always prepare a data table, pay close attention to it during the algorithm development process, and save it along with your program listing. The data table may subsequently turn out to be your only reminder of how the variables in your program are being used.

A more precise formulation of Problem 2.1 is now possible: We must read two data items into the variables N1 and N2, find the sum and the average of these two items, and print the values of the sum and the average.

2.2 DESCRIPTION OF THE PROBLEM SOLUTION

2.2.1 Developing an Algorithm

At this point we should have a clear understanding of what is required for the solution of Problem 2.1. We can now proceed to organize the problem formulation into a carefully constructed list of steps—the algorithm—that will describe the sequence of manipulations to be performed in carrying out the problem solution.

Algorithm for Problem 2.1 (Level One)

STEP 1   Read the data items into the variables N1 and N2 and print the data.

STEP 2   Compute the sum of the data items in N1 and N2 and store the result in the variable S.

STEP 3   Compute the average of the data items in N1 and N2 and store the result in the variable A.

STEP 4   Print the values of the variables S and A.

STEP 5   Stop.

2.2.2 Algorithm Refinement

Note that this sequence of events closely mirrors the problem formulation given earlier. This is as it should be! If the problem formulation is complete, it should provide us with a general outline of what must be done to solve the problem. The purpose of the algorithm formulation is to provide a detailed and precise description of the individual steps to be carried out by the computer in solving the problem. The algorithm is essentially a *refinement* of the general outline provided by the original problem formulation. It is often the case that several *levels of refinement* of the general outline are required before the algorithm formulation is complete.

The key question in deciding whether or not further refinement of an algorithm step is required is this:

Is it clear precisely what BASIC instructions are necessary in order to tell the computer how to carry out the step?

If it is not immediately obvious what the BASIC instructions are, then the algorithm should be further refined.

What is obvious to some programmers may not be at all clear to others. The refinement of an algorithm is, therefore, a personal matter to some extent. As you gain experience in developing algorithms and converting them to BASIC programs, you may discover that you are doing less and less algorithm refinement. This may also happen as you become more familiar with the BASIC language.

If we examine the level one algorithm for Problem 2.1, we see that only Step 3 may require further refinement. We already know how to write BASIC instructions for reading, printing, adding and stopping. However, we may not know how to tell the computer to find the average of two numbers.

Refinement of Step 3

STEP 3.1 Divide the sum (stored in S) by the number of items (2) used to compute the sum.

We now have an algorithm that is refined to a level of detail that is sufficient for us to write the BASIC representation of the steps required to solve Problem 2.1 (see Fig. 2.1). We do this by implementing the algorithm on a step-by-step basis, using the variable names provided in the data table. The REM statements are explained in the next section.

```
100 REM  COMPUTE THE SUM AND AVERAGE OF TWO NUMBERS
110 REM
120 REM  READ AND PRINT DATA ITEMS
130      READ N1, N2
140      DATA 33, 55
150      PRINT "N1 = "; N1, "N2 = "; N2
160 REM
170 REM  COMPUTE SUM AND AVERAGE
180      LET S = N1 + N2
190      LET A = S / 2
200 REM
210 REM  PRINT RESULTS
220      PRINT "SUM = "; S, "AVERAGE = "; A
230 REM
240      END

RUN

N1 =  33        N2 =  55
SUM =  88       AVERAGE =  44
```

Fig. 2.1   BASIC program for Problem 2.1.

Exercise 2.1:   Write a data table and an algorithm to compute the sum and average of four numbers.

2.2.3   Use of REM Statements

The statements in Fig. 2.1 that start with REM are descriptive comments or remarks. They are ignored by the compiler during translation and are listed with the program statements to aid the programmer in identifying or documenting the purpose of each section of the program.

Each remark (REM) line describes the purpose of the program statements that follow it. There should be enough REM statements to clarify the intent of each section of your program; however, too many REM statements can clutter the program, make it difficult to read and waste time and space. A good rule of thumb is to use a REM statement to identify the BASIC implementation of each step in the level one algorithm as well as any other steps requiring further refinement. In this way, the correspondence between the algorithm and its BASIC implementation becomes obvious.

REM statements (along with the data table) can also aid in identifying the use of the important variables in each program segment. At least one REM statement should appear at the beginning of a program to summarize the program purpose.

2.2.4 Flow Diagram Representations of Algorithms

As problems become more complicated, precise English descriptions of algorithms for solving these problems become more complex and difficult to follow. It is, therefore, helpful if some kind of descriptive notation can be used to describe an algorithm. We will use one such descriptive notation, called a *flow diagram*, throughout this text.

Not everyone in the computer field believes that flow diagrams are useful and many experienced programmers do not always use them. However, we believe that flow diagrams are helpful because they provide a graphical, two-dimensional representation of an algorithm. Consistent use of the special flow diagram symbols and forms shown in the text will make algorithms easy to write, easy to refine and still easier to follow.

Flow diagram representations of two levels of the algorithm for Problem 2.1 are shown in Fig. 2.2. They contain a number of symbols that should be noted.

1. Ovals are used to indicate the starting and stopping points of an algorithm.
2. Rectangular boxes are used to indicate the manipulation of information in the memory of the computer.
3. A box in the shape of a computer card (with one corner cut off) is used to indicate the reading of information into the computer.

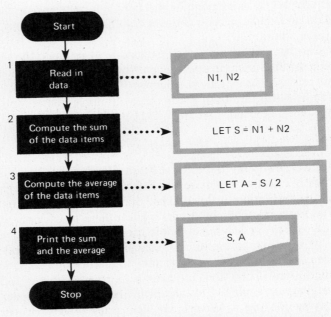

Fig. 2.2 Level one flow diagram and refinements for Problem 2.1.

4. A box with a wavy bottom is used to indicate the printing of information stored in the computer memory.
5. Arrows are used to indicate the "flow of control" of an algorithm from one step to another.

   You will find it convenient to represent all levels of algorithms with a flow diagram. The first level will often be quite general and imprecise. It will contain a summary, usually written in English, of the basic steps of an algorithm, as shown on the left side of Fig. 2.2. In some cases, usually when the step is very simple, these summaries may be precise and detailed. However, in most cases, one or more levels of refinement will be necessary before a sufficiently detailed and precise diagram is completed. A flow diagram for Problem 2.1, complete with refinements of steps 1, 2, 3, and 4, is shown in Fig. 2.2. The large dotted arrows point to the refinement for each of these steps. The solid arrows indicate the flow of control from one step to the next.

2.2.5   Problem Solving Principles

   Up to now we have presented a few suggestions for solving problems on the computer. These suggestions are summarized below.

1. Understand what you are being asked to do.
2. Identify all problem input and output data. Assign a variable name to each input or output item and list it in the data table.
3. Formulate a precise statement of the problem in terms of the input and output data and make certain there are sufficient input items provided to complete the solution.
4. State clearly the sequence of steps necessary to produce the desired problem output through manipulation of the input data; i.e., develop the algorithm and represent it as a flow diagram.
5. Refine this flow diagram until it can be easily implemented in the programming language to be used. List any additional variables required as program variables in the data table.
6. Transform the flow diagram to a program.

   Steps 4 and 5 are really the most difficult of the steps listed; they are the only truly creative part of this process. People differ in their degree of capability to formulate solutions to problems. Some find it easy to develop algorithms for the most complex problem, while others must work diligently to produce an algorithm for solving a simple problem.
   The ability to solve problems is fundamental to computer programming. The transformation of the refined algorithm to a working program (step 6) is a highly skilled clerical task that requires a thorough knowledge of the programming language available. This detailed knowledge can normally be acquired by anyone willing to devote the necessary effort. However, a flow diagram that correctly represents the necessary problem-solving operations and their relationship must first be developed.

In this book, we will provide many detailed solutions to sample problems. Examining these solutions carefully should enable you to become more adept at formulating your own solutions, because the techniques used for one problem may frequently be applied in a slightly different way to solve another. Often, new problems are simply expansions or modifications of old ones.

The process of outlining and refining problem solutions can be used to break a complex problem up into more manageable subproblems that can be solved individually. This technique will be illustrated in all of the problems solved in the text. We suggest you practice it in developing your own solutions to the programming problems.

2.3 ALGORITHMS INVOLVING DECISIONS AND LOOPS

2.3.1 Decision Steps and Conditions

Normally, the steps of an algorithm are performed in the order in which they are listed. In many algorithms, however, the sequence of steps to be performed is determined by the input data. In such cases, decisions must be made, based upon the values of certain variables, as to which sequence of steps is to be performed. Such decisions require the evaluation of a condition that is expressed in terms of the relevant variables. The result of the evaluation determines which algorithm steps will be executed next.

The algorithm step that describes the condition is called a *decision step*. The simplest kind of decision step involves the evaluation of a *logical condition*—that is, a condition that may have a value of either true or false.

A logical condition normally describes a particular relationship between a pair of variables or a variable and a constant. Examples of conditions are shown in Table 2.1.

Condition	BASIC form
G greater than M	G > M
X equal to S	X = S
X not equal to 0	X < > 0
C less than or equal to 10	C < = 10

Table 2.1   Examples of BASIC conditions

The value of each of the above conditions is true if the specified relationship holds for the current variable values; otherwise, the condition value is false.

The BASIC form of each condition follows the pattern

$$\text{operand}_1 \quad \text{relational-operator} \quad \text{operand}_2$$

where operand$_1$ is normally a variable and operand$_2$ is a variable or constant. The relational-operators in BASIC are described in Table 2.2. We will provide further details on the use of BASIC conditions in Chapter 3.

Relational-operator	Meaning
=	equal to
< >	not equal to
<	less than
>	greater than
< =	less than or equal to
> =	greater than or equal to

Table 2.2   BASIC relational-operators

We will illustrate the decision step by studying a modified form of the payroll problem discussed in Chapter 1.

Problem 2.2:   Compute the gross salary and net pay for an employee of a company, given the number of hours worked and the employee's hourly wage rate. Deduct a tax amount of $25 if the employee's gross salary exceeds $100.

The data table for this problem is shown below. The flow diagrams are drawn in Fig. 2.3.

Data Table for Problem 2.2

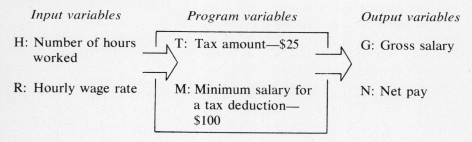

Input variables   *Program variables*   *Output variables*

H: Number of hours worked   T: Tax amount—$25   G: Gross salary

R: Hourly wage rate   M: Minimum salary for a tax deduction— $100   N: Net pay

In numbering flow diagrams and their refinements, we will use a scheme that is analogous to the numbering of sections in this text. For example, refinements of step 3 are numbered 3.1, 3.2, 3.3. If step 3.1 were to be refined further, its refinements would be numbered 3.1.1, 3.1.2, etc. All steps in a level one flow diagram will be numbered. Normally, only those refinement steps that are referred to in the text narrative will be numbered.

The decision step (3.1) describes the logical condition ("G greater than M") that is evaluated in order to decide which algorithm step should be executed next. If the condition is true, step 3.2 (deduct tax, T) is performed next. Otherwise, step 3.3 (set N to G) is performed next. In either case, step 4 will be carried out following the completion of the chosen step.

The decision step just discussed (3.1) involves a choice between two alternatives—a sequence of one or more steps to be executed if the condition is

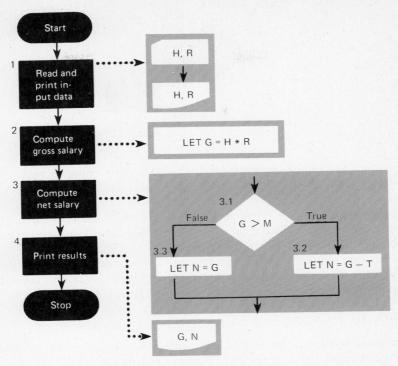

Fig. 2.3   Flow diagrams for modified payroll problem.

true (the True Task) and a sequence to be executed if the condition is false (the False Task). Such a decision step is called a *double-alternative decision step*. The general flow diagram pattern for this step is shown in Fig. 2.4.

Quite often, a decision step in an algorithm will involve only one alter-

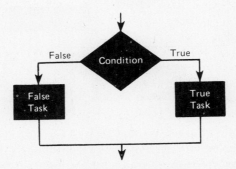

Fig. 2.4   Flow diagram pattern for the double-alternative decision step.

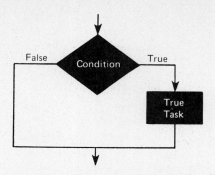

Fig. 2.5 Flow diagram pattern for the single-alternative decision step.

native: a sequence of one or more steps that will be carried out if the given condition is true, but skipped if the condition is false. The flow diagram pattern for this *single-alternative decision step* is shown in Fig. 2.5.

In the next chapter, we will see how to express decision steps in BASIC. We will see that the flow diagram-to-program conversion process is relatively easy, even when complicated decision steps are required.

Example 2.1:   Additional flow diagram patterns for decision steps

a)   If base earnings (B) exceed $5000 then set B equal to $5000. Otherwise, skip this step. Then compute the Social Security tax (S) for the base. The translation of the above yields the diagram shown next.

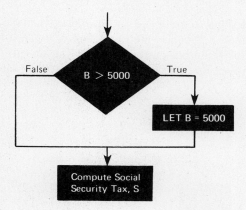

b)   If the amount of a check (C) is less than or equal to the balance (B) in an account, then recompute the balance by subtracting C from B. Otherwise, print an "account overdrawn" message and subtract $5 (for penalty) from B.

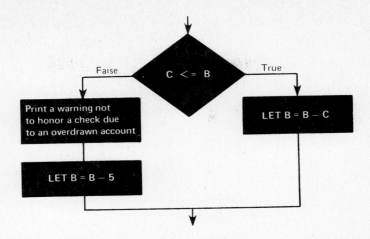

Example 2.2:   Finding the largest of three numbers.

Fig. 2.6 shows an algorithm for finding the largest of three numbers. After the numbers have been read into N1, N2, and N3 (step 1), the double-alternative decision step (step 2.1) stores the larger of N1 and N2 in L. The single

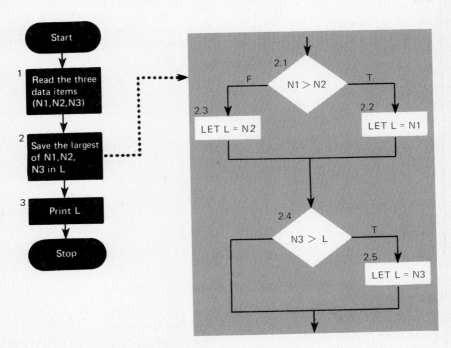

Fig. 2.6   Flow diagram for largest of three numbers

alternative decision step (step 2.4) then compares N3 to this value and copies N3 into L if N3 is larger. The data table is shown below.

Data Table for Example 2.2

Input variables	*Program variables*	*Output variables*
N1, N2, N3: used for storage of the original three numbers	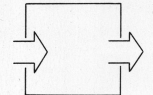	L: Used to contain the largest value

Exercise 2.2:   Write the flow diagram pattern to represent the following descriptions:

  a) If a data item (I) is not equal to 0, then multiply the product (P) by I. Otherwise, skip this step. In either case, then print the value of P.
  b) If I exceeds L, store the value of I in L. Otherwise skip this step. In either case, then print the value of I.
  c) If X is larger than 0, add X to the positive sum (S1). Otherwise, if X is smaller than 0, add X to the negative sum (S2). Otherwise, if X is equal to 0, add one to the count of zeros (C).

Exercise 2.3:   What values would be printed by the algorithm in Fig. 2.3 if H is 37.5 and R is 3.75? If H is 20 and R is 4? "Execute" the program yourself to determine the results.

Exercise 2.4:   What happens in Fig. 2.6 if N1 is equal to N2 or N3 is equal to L? Does the algorithm work for these cases?

Exercise 2.5:   Modify the flow diagram in Example 2.2 to find the largest of four numbers.

Exercise 2.6:   Draw a flow diagram for an algorithm that computes the absolute difference between two numbers. If X is greater than Y, the absolute difference is X−Y; if Y is greater than X, the absolute difference is Y−X.

2.3.2   The Motivation for Loops

In Section 2.2.1, we developed an algorithm for finding the sum and average of two numbers. Suppose, however, that we are asked to solve a slightly different problem.

Problem 2.3:   Write a program to compute and print the sum and average of 2000 data items.

Discussion: The first question to be answered now is whether or not the approach previously taken will be satisfactory for this problem too. The answer is clearly *no*! It is not that the approach won't work, but rather that no reasonable person is likely to have the patience to carry out this solution for 2000 numbers. Our difficulties would begin in attempting to produce a data table listing the differently named variables for each of the 2000 items involved (see the data table below). We can't even specify 2000 different variable names in BASIC. (How many can we specify?)

Data Table for Problem 2.3

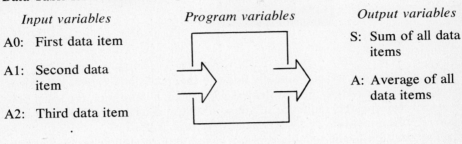

Input variables	Program variables	Output variables
A0: First data item		S: Sum of all data items
A1: Second data item		A: Average of all data items
A2: Third data item		

Even if we could name all 2000 variables, we would have quite a boring task describing the algorithm for solving the problem. Not even little children enjoy drawing pictures that much!

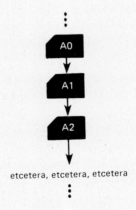

etcetera, etcetera, etcetera

A new approach is needed in order to solve this problem. Regardless of what this new approach involves, it will still be necessary to instruct the computer to read in and add together 2000 numbers. The essence of the problem is to find a way to do this without writing separate instructions for the reading and the addition of each of the 2000 data items needed to compute the sum. It would be ideal if we could write one step for reading, one step for accumulating the sum and then repeat these two steps for each of the 2000 items.

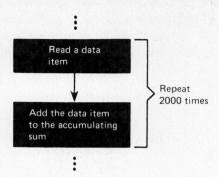

It happens that we can actually achieve this goal quite easily. All that is necessary is to (a) solve the problem of naming each data item, (b) learn how to describe a repeated sequence of steps in a flow diagram and (c) learn how to specify the repetition of a sequence of steps in BASIC.

The solution to the naming problem rests upon the following realization:

> Once a data item has been read into the computer memory and added to the sum, it is no longer needed in the computer memory.

Thus, each data item can be read into the same variable. After each item is entered, the value of this variable can be added to the sum and the next data item can be read into the same variable. This, of course, destroys the previous data item, but it is no longer needed for the computation.

To see how this works, consider what happens if we try to carry out an algorithm consisting solely of the repetition of the steps

   (i) Read a data item into a variable named X.
   (ii) Add the value of X to the accumulated sum (S) and store the result in S.

Initially, the memory cells X and S appear as shown below. S must be *initialized* to zero (set to an initial value of zero) or else the final sum will be off by whatever value is stored in S before the repetition of steps (i) and (ii) begins.

Let us assume that the first three data items are the numbers +10.5, −11.5 and +6.0. After steps (i) and (ii) are performed the first time, the variables X and S will be defined as follows:

Note that the number 10.5 has now been incorporated into the sum that we are computing and is no longer required for this problem. We may, therefore, read the next data item into the variable X. After the second execution of (i) and (ii), we have:

X	S
−11.5	−1.0

and upon completion of the third execution of (i) and (ii), we obtain:

X	S
+6.0	+5.0

This process continues for all 2000 items. During each execution of steps (i) and (ii), the data item just read in is processed and can then be replaced in memory by the next data item.

With this solution to the naming problem, the data table for Problem 2.3 can be rewritten with relative ease.

Revised Data Table for Problem 2.3

Input variables	*Program variables*	*Output variables*
X: Contains each data item as it is being processed	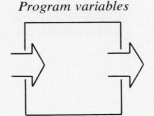	S: Contains the accumulated sum of the data items as they are processed—initial value zero A: Average of all data items

We can also write a level one version of the flow diagram for our algorithm (Fig. 2.7). This diagram reflects the three phases of an algorithm, the *initialization phase*, the *data manipulation phase*, and the *output phase*.

From this diagram, it is clear what is required in the initialization and output phases (steps 1 and 4) of the algorithm. However, part of the computation phase (step 2) requires further refinement before the program can be written.

In order to refine algorithm step 2, we need to have a flow diagram representation for a sequence of repeated steps. This representation, shown in Fig. 2.8, is called a *loop*.

The *loop body* is the sequence of steps that is to be repeated; it is connected to the rest of the flow diagram by an arrow drawn to the right of the loop control step. This arrow always points to the first step in the algorithm that is to be repeated in the indicated loop. In Problem 2.3, this is the step to

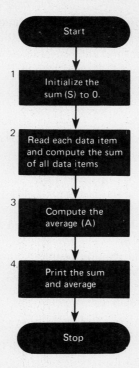

Fig. 2.7   Level one flow diagram for Problem 2.3.

read in a data item. The exit arrow always points to the first step in the algorithm that is to be carried out upon completion of the loop. The dotted line in
Fig. 2.8 labelled NEXT serves as a reminder that control returns to the loop

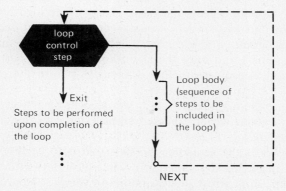

Fig. 2.8   Flow diagram pattern for a loop.

control step before each repetition of the loop body. This line is not part of the flow diagram and we shall omit it in later chapters.

How do we know when the loop is complete? More importantly, how can we tell the computer when it has completed the execution of the loop? A human might do it 10 or 100 times and then ask, "Am I done yet?" However, we are developing an algorithm that will eventually take the form of a sequence of steps to be performed by a computer—and the computer cannot think!! Therefore, if we want to tell it to repeat a sequence of steps, it is not enough to tell it what those steps are. We must also tell the computer how many times to repeat the loop and when to stop performing these steps. This information is provided by the *loop control step*.

For this problem, the loop control step should specify that 2000 repetitions of the loop are to be performed. We can guarantee the correct number of loop repetitions by introducing a new program variable that functions as a *repetition counter*. The counter is used to control loop repetition by counting the number of loop repetitions that are performed. The counter must be

(i)   Initialized to a value of 1 just before the first loop execution.
(ii) Incremented (increased) by one after each loop repetition.
(iii) Tested before each loop repetition. If the counter value is still less than or equal to 2000, the loop body should be repeated; otherwise, the loop exit should occur.

Additional program variable

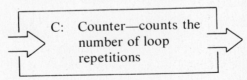

C: Counter—counts the number of loop repetitions

The flow diagram pattern for this *counter-controlled loop* is illustrated in Fig. 2.9. This is the refinement of step 2 in the level one flow diagram (Fig. 2.7). The variable C in the loop control step (2.1) is the counter. This step specifies that the loop is to be executed once for each integer value of C between 1 and 2000 inclusive; hence, the loop body (steps 2.2 and 2.3) will be repeated exactly 2000 times as required, once for each data item. The label, NEXT C, indicates that the counter, C, will be incremented and tested before the next loop repetition begins. With this refinement, the flow diagrams for Problem 2.3 are complete and are redrawn in Fig. 2.10.

Exercise 2.7:

a)   Draw a flow diagram for a counter-controlled loop that computes the sum of the first 10 integers.
b)   Draw a flow diagram for a counter-controlled loop that computes the product of the first 10 integers.

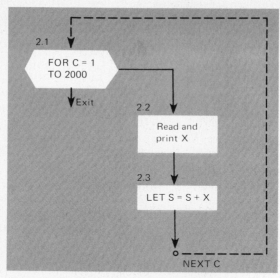

Fig. 2.9   Refinement of step 2 in Fig. 2.7.

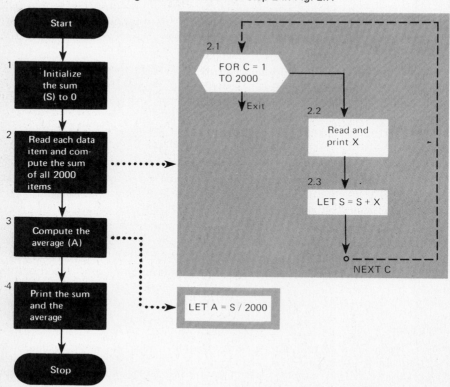

Fig. 2.10   Flow diagram for Problem 2.3.

2.3.3 Manual Simulation of a Flow Diagram

Once the algorithm and data table for a problem are complete, it is important to verify that the algorithm specifies the sequence of steps required to produce the desired results. This algorithm verification can be carried out by manually *simulating* or *tracing* the sequence of steps indicated by the algorithm. Such traces can often lead to the discovery of a number of logical errors in the flow diagram. The correction of these errors prior to writing the BASIC instructions can save considerable effort during the final checkout, or *debugging*, of the BASIC program.

Program traces must be done diligently, however, or they are of little use. The flow diagram must be traced carefully, on a step-by-step basis. Changes in variable values must be noted at each step and compared to the expected results of the program. This should be done for at least one carefully chosen set of test data for which the final and intermediate results can easily be determined. When decision steps are involved, it is desirable to follow every path in the flow diagram. To accomplish this, additional sets of test data will be required.

We will now provide an illustration of a program trace for the flow diagram shown in Fig. 2.10. It is clear that we cannot trace the algorithm in Fig. 2.10 for 2000 data items. However, we can perform a meaningful, informative test for three items. If the algorithm works properly for this limited case, it should work for 2000 data items as well.

The trace table is shown in Table 2.3. The algorithm step numbers are from the flow diagram in Fig. 2.10. Only the new value of the variable affected by an algorithm step is shown to the right of each step. All other variable values are unchanged. The values of all variables after the execution of step 1 are shown in the first line. The data items being tested are 12.5, 15 and −3.5.

When the loop is entered (first execution of step 2.1), C is initialized to 1. Each time the loop control step (2.1) is repeated, C is incremented by 1.The value of C is 3 during the last loop repetition. Step 3 is executed after the loop exit. In step 3, the value of S (24) divided by 3 is assigned to A; the variable A is undefined until then.

Algorithm Step	S	C	X	A
1	0	undefined	undefined	undefined
2.1		1		
2.2			12.5	
2.3	12.5			
2.1		2		
2.2			15	
2.3	27.5			
2.1		3		
2.2			−3.5	
2.3	24			
3				8

Table 2.3   Trace of algorithm in Fig. 2.10

The trace table shows that the loop is executed exactly three times. The final value accumulated in S is 24; the average, stored in A, is 8.

Exercise 2.8:   Carry out a complete trace of the flow diagram in Fig. 2.10 for the five data items shown below.

$$-12.5, 8.25, 0, -16.5, .25$$

Exercise 2.9:   Trace the algorithm drawn in Fig. 2.6, for N1, N2, N3 equal to 5, 20, 15 respectively.

2.4 IMPLEMENTING ALGORITHMS AS PROGRAMS

2.4.1 Solving the Most General Case of a Problem

Suppose that you are asked to solve Problem 2.3 for 20,000 data items instead of 2000; or for 1995 items; or for 10 data items. Will the approach just taken work here too? The answer, of course, is *yes!* In fact, the only change that we must make in each case is in those steps in which the constant 2000 is used. In Problem 2.3, there are two such steps (steps 2.1 and 3, shown in Fig. 2.10).

It is often advantageous to be able to develop algorithms and write programs in the fullest possible generality, so that any conceivable case of a problem can be solved using the program without any alteration whatsoever. In such full generality, the algorithm for Problem 2.3 would compute the sum and average for an arbitrary, but prespecified, number of data items. The number of items should be treated as an input variable, rather than a constant, to be read in by the program at the beginning of execution. In this way, a collection of data of arbitrary size may be processed by the same program, as long as the first item input to the computer is the *number of items* in this data collection.

To accomplish this, we add an additional variable N to the data table for Problem 2.3 and insert a step to read N in the level one flow diagram. The resulting data table is shown below; the new flow diagrams for Problem 2.3 are shown in Fig. 2.11.

Revised Data Table for Problem 2.3

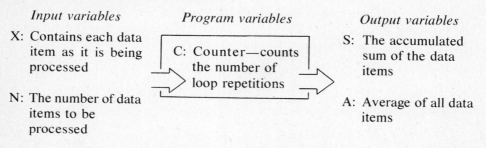

Input variables	*Program variables*	*Output variables*
X: Contains each data item as it is being processed	C: Counter—counts the number of loop repetitions	S: The accumulated sum of the data items
N: The number of data items to be processed		A: Average of all data items

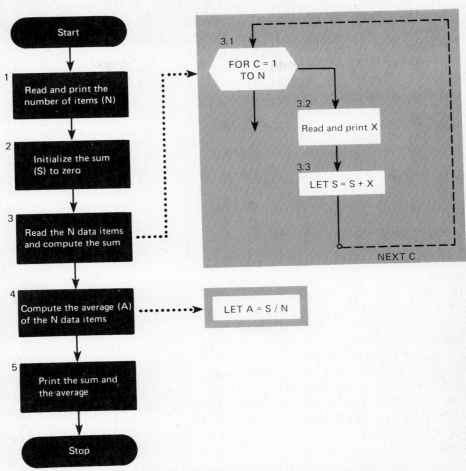

Fig. 2.11 Flow diagrams for the general case solution of Problem 2.3.

2.4.2 Implementing a Loop in BASIC

BASIC provides a special looping structure (called the *FOR loop*) for implementing counter-controlled loops. The BASIC implementation of the loop in Fig. 2.10 is shown next.

```
200 REM PROCESS 2000 DATA ITEMS
210     FOR C = 1 TO 2000
220         REM READ AND PROCESS NEXT ITEM
230         READ X
240         PRINT X
250         LET S = S + X
260     NEXT C
```

Lines 210 through 260 form a program unit called a *control structure*. We will introduce a number of control structures in the text for implementing flow diagram patterns such as decision steps and loops. Each control structure will consist of an easily recognizable first and last line (the *header* and *terminator* statements, respectively). Although it is not required, the body of the structure will be indented to aid in its recognition and to enhance program readability.

Line 210 is the loop header statement. It specifies that the loop will be executed 2000 times—or once for all integer values of C between 1 and 2000 inclusive. The loop body is represented by lines 220-250. In the loop body, line 240 echo prints each data item as it is read and line 250 adds each data item to S. Line 260 is the loop terminator; it simply marks the end of the loop with repetition counter C. A restricted version of the BASIC FOR loop (the counter-controlled loop) is summarized in the next display; we will describe the general form of the FOR loop in the next chapter.

Counter-Controlled Loop (Restricted form of the BASIC FOR Loop)

BASIC form:

```
FOR counter = 1 TO number of repetitions
   _____
   _____  } loop body
   _____
NEXT counter
```

Interpretation: The loop repetition is controlled by counter. The number of repetitions may be specified as a whole number or variable. After the required number of loop repetitions have been performed, execution continues with the first statement following NEXT counter.

In order to implement the general case algorithm shown in Fig. 2.11, the variable N (number of data items) should replace the constant 2000 in the loop header (line 210 above). The complete program is shown in Fig. 2.12 along with a sample run for N equal to 5.

Exercise 2.10:   Write the flow diagram and BASIC program to read in a collection of seven data items, compute the product of all items in the collection and print the final product. Check your flow diagram with a hand simulation.

Exercise 2.11:   Write the BASIC programs for Exercise 2.7.

2.5   DEBUGGING A BASIC PROGRAM

2.5.1   Introduction

It is very rare that a program runs correctly the first time it is typed in. Often one spends a considerable amount of time in removing errors or "bugs" from programs.

```
100 REM PROGRAM TO COMPUTE SUM AND AVERAGE OF N NUMBERS
110 REM
120 REM INITIALIZE N AND SUM S
130     READ N
140     DATA 5
150     PRINT "THERE ARE"; N; " DATA ITEMS"
170 REM COMPUTE SUM S
180     LET S = 0
190 REM
200 REM PROCESS N DATA ITEMS
210     FOR C = 1 TO N
220        REM PROCESS EACH ITEM
230        READ X
240        PRINT X
250        LET S = S + X
260     NEXT C
270     DATA 25, 16.2, -3, -27.8, 4
280 REM
290 REM COMPUTE AVERAGE AND PRINT RESULTS
300     LET A = S / N
310     PRINT "SUM = "; S, "AVERAGE = "; A
320 REM
330     END

RUN

THERE ARE 5 DATA ITEMS
 25
 16.2
-3
-27.8
 4
SUM = 14.4      AVERAGE = 2.88
```

Fig. 2.12 General sum and average program.

The process of removing errors or ''bugs'' from a program is called debugging. You will find that a substantial portion of the time you spend programming is used for debugging. The debugging time can be reduced if you follow the algorithm and program development steps outlined in this chapter accurately, without taking any shortcuts.

This approach requires a careful analysis of the problem description, the identification of the input and output data for the problem in a data table and the development of the flow diagrams for the problem solution. The algorithm development should proceed on a step-by-step basis, beginning with an outline of the algorithm in the form of a level one flow diagram. Additional algorithm detail (flow diagram refinements) should be provided as needed, until enough detail has been added so that writing the program is virtually a mechanical process. The data table should be updated during the refinement process, so that all variables introduced in the algorithm are listed and clearly defined in the table.

Once the algorithm and data table are complete, a systematic hand simulation (or trace) of the flow diagrams, using one or two representative sets of data, can help eliminate many bugs before they show up during the execution of your program. When the hand trace is complete, the program may be written, using the data table and the refined flow diagrams, and then entered at the terminal. Before running your program, you should request a listing and study it carefully to verify that there are no obvious errors in your typed program.

2.5.2   Syntax Errors

There are three general categories of errors that you may encounter when running programs:

> (i)   BASIC syntax errors
> (ii) run-time errors
> (iii) program logic errors

BASIC syntax errors are caused by BASIC statements that do not follow the precise rules of formation *(syntax rules)* of BASIC. These errors are detected by the compiler during the translation of a BASIC program. The compiler will identify lines containing most syntax errors by printing the error diagnostic

```
ILLEGAL STATEMENT AT LINE n
```

where n is the number of the statement in error. It is up to you to compare carefully the statement in error with those rules of BASIC that could apply in order to correct your errors.

Any typing mistakes are likely to cause syntax errors. An example of such an error would be mistyping a keyword (e.g., DATE instead of DATA). Other similar errors would be missing or extra commas, omission of a line number or typing an illegal variable name.

2.5.3   Run-Time Errors

Run-time errors are normally the result of programmer carelessness. They are not severe enough to prevent the compiler from translating the program; however, they will prevent the program from executing through to normal completion.

A common run-time error is caused by referencing a variable before its value has been defined. For example, if line 130 (READ N) in Fig. 2.12 were omitted, the value of N (number of data items) would not be entered and, therefore, would not be properly defined when the loop header statement (FOR C = 1 TO N) was reached. In this case, the loop would not be executed the required number of times.

Some BASIC compilers will print an error message and terminate program execution if an undefined variable is encountered. In other systems, all variables are initialized to zero and the "undefined variable" may go undetected or cause a different run-time error. For example, if the divisor N in line 300 of

Fig. 2.12 (LET A = S / N) is not properly defined before its use, a diagnostic error message may be printed indicating "illegal division by zero."

Another example of a run-time error would be the failure to provide enough data items to satisfy the data requirements for a program. If the number 4 in line 270 were missing, the last data item (−27.8) would be processed during the fourth execution of the loop and no data would remain for processing during subsequent loop repetitions. Hence, a diagnostic message of the form

```
END OF DATA AT LINE 230
```

(the READ X statement) would be printed during the fifth repetition of the loop and program execution would be terminated.

2.5.4 Program Logic Errors

Program logic errors are caused by mistakes that have been made in the logical organization of the steps in your program. Many of these errors can be avoided if a careful, reasoned approach is taken to problem solving and program development. Logic errors that do occur can often be more easily diagnosed if some care and discipline have been applied in the design and coding of the program.

The mistakes described as syntax errors will cause errors that are *fatal* to your program because the compiler will not be able to translate the program completely and the computer will not be able to begin executing it. Run-time errors will cause premature termination of the program (at the line in error); however, they will not prevent program execution from starting. Both categories of errors usually cause diagnostic error messages to be printed. Program logic errors are more insidious because the program may be completely translated and executed, but will compute incorrect results.

To verify that your program is indeed producing the correct results, it is useful to add extra print statements to print out intermediate results. These results should be compared against hand calculations for one or more representative sets of data in order to verify that they are correct. The extra print statements can be removed prior to making your final program runs.

If your program runs but doesn't produce the desired results, there may be an error in logic. If there was not enough output information printed in your first run, it is often worthwhile to make an extra debugging run in which all pertinent variable values are printed at different steps in the execution of your program. It is most important to print those variables used in decision and loop header statements. This will help in determining what is wrong and in pinpointing the location of an undefined variable or a logic error.

If there is a logic error, go back to your flow diagrams, modify the steps that you believe are in error and then completely retrace the execution of the modified algorithm. This last step is extremely important and one that is often overlooked. Each algorithm change may have important side effects that are difficult to anticipate. Making what seems to be an obvious correction in one step of the algorithm may introduce new errors into other algorithm steps. The only way to establish that there are no side effects is to systematically retrace the revised flow diagrams.

Once the revised flow diagrams have been checked out, write the new program statements that are needed and correct and rerun your program. There is always a temptation to save time and make your changes directly in the program without first going back to the flow diagrams. If you resist this temptation, you will normally be better off in the long run.

2.6 SUMMARY

In the first part of this chapter we outlined a method for solving problems on the computer. This method stresses six points:

1. Understand the problem given.
2. Identify the input and output data for the problem as well as other relevant data.
3. Formulate a precise statement of the problem.
4. Develop an *algorithm*.
5. *Refine* the algorithm.
6. Implement the algorithm in BASIC.

Algorithms consist of three phases: initialization of variables, manipulation of data and output of results. However, the data manipulation phase is most important. This phase can be started once the input data and desired problem outputs have been clearly defined in a *data table* and a precise understanding of the problem has been achieved. The initialization of variable values that is required often depends on the particular method chosen to perform the data manipulation.

Often, additional entries are made to the data table as the data manipulation phase progresses. For example, in Problem 2.3, the need for the program variable C (loop counter) was not readily apparent until the algorithm for manipulating the data was chosen.

Several guidelines for using program remarks were discussed. Well-placed and carefully worded remarks, combined with a complete and concise data table, can easily provide all of the documentation necessary for a program.

In the remainder of the chapter, we introduced the flow diagram representation of the various steps in an algorithm. *Flow diagrams* provide a graphical representation of an algorithm consisting of a number of specially shaped boxes and arrows, as well as several *patterns* of boxes and arrows used to describe *decision steps* and *loops*. These boxes and patterns are summarized in Fig. 2.13.

Flow diagrams also provide a convenient form of representation for the loop and decision steps of an algorithm. By using these patterns we can main-

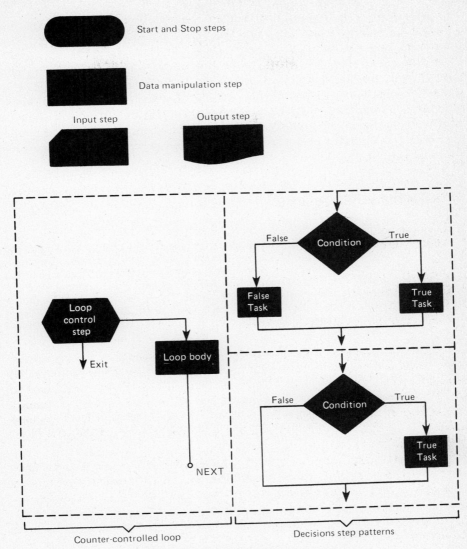

Start and Stop steps

Data manipulation step

Input step   Output step

Counter-controlled loop   Decisions step patterns

Fig. 2.13 Flow diagram symbols and patterns.

tain a clear separation between the relevant control information in a loop or decision structure and the steps to be carried out subject to this control.

The notion of a trace or simulation of an algorithm was also introduced in this chapter. These simulations, if carried out carefully, can often help uncover numerous algorithm logic errors even before a program is written. This can reduce program debugging time significantly.

We introduced the form of the condition in BASIC and also a restricted form of the BASIC FOR loop. We also described some common program errors and hints for debugging BASIC programs.

In the next chapter we will show how to implement general loop and decision structures based upon the flow diagram patterns just described. Use of these forms will enable us to translate our flow diagram representations of algorithms into BASIC programs with a minimum of effort. This will allow us to solve some relatively complex problems on the computer, using programs that reflect the careful planning and organization practiced in our algorithm development.

PROGRAMMING PROBLEMS

For all problems, a data table and flow diagram are required.

2.4 Given the bank balance in your checking account for the past month and all the transactions in your account for the current month, write a program for an algorithm to compute and print your checking account balance at the end of the current month. You may assume that the total number of transactions for the current month is known ahead of time. [*Hint:* Your first data item should be your checking account balance at the end of last month. The second item should be the number of transactions for the current month. All subsequent items should represent the amount of each transaction for the current month.]

2.5 Write a program for an algorithm to compute the factorial, N!, of a single arbitrary integer N. (N! = N × (N − 1) × · · · 2 × 1). Your program should read and print the value of N and print N! when done.

2.6 If N contains an integer, then we can compute X^N for any X, simply by initializing a variable V to 1 and multiplying it by X a total of N times. Write a program to read in a value of X and a value of N, and compute X^N via repeated multiplications. Check your program for

$$X = 6.0, N = 4$$
$$X = 2.5, N = 6$$
$$X = -8.0, N = 5$$

2.7 Continuation of Problem 2.6:

a) How many multiplications are required in your program for Problem 2.5 in order to compute X^9? Can you figure out a way of computing X^9 in fewer multiplications?

b) Can you generalize your algorithm for computing X^9 to compute X^N for any positive N?

c) Can you use your algorithm in part (b) to compute X^{-N} for any positive N? How?

2.8 Compute and print a table showing the first 15 powers of 2.

2.9 Redo the payroll program of Chapter 1 (Problem 1.1) so that a prespecified number of employees can be processed in a single run.

2.10 Redo Problem 1.5 so that all cases are processed in a single program run.

2.11 Redo Problem 1.6 so that all cases are processed in a single program run.

FUNDAMENTAL CONTROL STRUCTURES

3

3.1 INTRODUCTION TO CONTROL STRUCTURES

In Chapter 2, we introduced flow diagram patterns for decision structures and loops. We also introduced the BASIC condition and a restricted form of the FOR loop. In this chapter, we will discuss how general control structure patterns may be implemented and provide several examples of their use.

As you learn more of the features of BASIC, you will find it easier to solve more complicated problems. You will also see that the process of translating the flow diagram representation of an algorithm into a BASIC program will become easier because fewer levels of flow diagram refinement will be required for you to write your programs.

We will show that the development of correct, precise algorithms is an important part of using the computer to solve problems. Furthermore, the English descriptions of these algorithms are most critical, for if these descriptions are incorrect or imprecise, all further refinements as well as the resulting programs will reflect these maladies. Therefore, as we introduce new features of BASIC, we will continue to emphasize algorithm development through the use of the flow diagram.

3.1.1 Standard and Nonstandard BASIC

In Chapter 1 we mentioned that programs written in higher level languages such as BASIC are considerably more portable than machine-language programs. That is, they can be moved from one computer to another with relative ease provided the appropriate compiler is available on the new computer.

To help ensure a high degree of portability for BASIC programs, a standard has been developed for the BASIC language. This standard defines the syntax rules for a minimal set of BASIC features (often called *Minimal BASIC*) that must be available on all compilers. In addition, there are many *extended* versions of BASIC that support not only all standard features, but also a number of features not included in the standard.

These *nonstandard features* make it more convenient to program in BASIC. However, they also reduce the level of portability of any program in which they are used. This is because the nonstandard features are not implemented in the same way on all compilers and are not implemented at all in some. Because of this, we will introduce only those nonstandard features that we feel are most important and useful to programming in BASIC and we will clearly distinguish nonstandard features from the standard ones. Remember, the standard features found in Minimal BASIC will be available in all versions of BASIC; however, the features labelled as belonging to extended versions of BASIC are not part of standard (Minimal) BASIC and, hence, may not be available on your system.

One important extended version of BASIC is Dartmouth BASIC Edition 7 (or Dartmouth BASIC), which is used on the Dartmouth College Time-Sharing System. We believe that the control structures available in Dartmouth

BASIC provide a very natural and convenient means of writing programs. Another widely-used version of extended BASIC that will be discussed is BASIC-PLUS for Digital Equipment Corporation computers.

Since the BASIC-PLUS and Dartmouth BASIC structures are not available to many BASIC users, we will not rely on them exclusively. However, we will illustrate their use throughout the text by showing how to implement decision and loop structures in both of these extended versions of BASIC and in Minimal BASIC as well.

3.2 DECISION STRUCTURES

3.2.1 Double-Alternative Decision Structure—Dartmouth BASIC Form

In this section we will discuss the BASIC statements needed to represent the double-alternative flow diagram pattern in Section 2.3.1.

In the double-alternative decision structure (Fig. 3.1), if the indicated condition is true, the algorithm steps representing the True Task are carried out; otherwise, the steps representing the False Task are performed. Exactly one of the paths from the condition test is taken. Execution then continues at the point indicated by the arrow at the bottom of the diagram. The True and False Tasks may each consist of a number of different boxes and flow diagram patterns. In general, however, it is a good idea to keep these task descriptions simple and refine them in a separate diagram if additional details are needed.

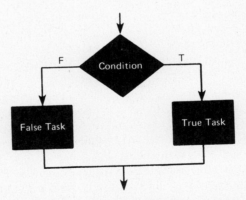

Fig. 3.1 The double-alternative decision pattern.

The double-alternative decision structure is implemented in many programming languages using a special control structure. The flow diagram and Dartmouth BASIC form of the double-alternative decision structure for the expanded payroll problem (Problem 2.2—see Fig. 2.3) are shown next.

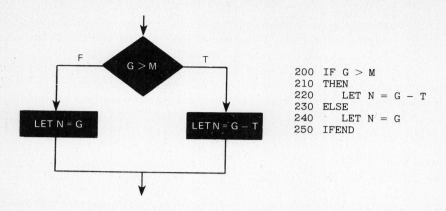

```
200  IF G > M
210  THEN
220      LET N = G - T
230  ELSE
240      LET N = G
250  IFEND
```

In the Dartmouth BASIC implementation, the statement

```
IF G > M
```

is called the *header statement*. The IFEND statement is called the *terminator statement*. These statements mark the beginning and end of a structure. Each header statement must be followed somewhere in the program by a matching terminator statement. The statement following the keyword THEN is the first statement in the True Task; the statement following the keyword ELSE is the first statement in the False Task. These points are shown in the next display.

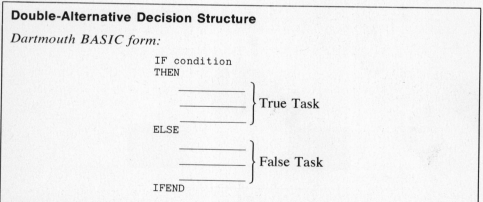

Double-Alternative Decision Structure

Dartmouth BASIC form:

```
IF condition
THEN

        ──────────
        ──────────  } True Task
        ──────────

ELSE

        ──────────
        ──────────  } False Task
        ──────────

IFEND
```

Interpretation: The condition is evaluated. If the condition is true, then the group of statements implementing the True Task is executed and the False Task is skipped. If the condition is false, the group of statements implementing the False Task is executed and the True Task is skipped.

Many other extended versions of BASIC provide a one line IF-THEN-ELSE statement that can be used whenever the True Task and False Task both consist of a single BASIC statement. In these systems, the IF-THEN-

ELSE statement

```
200 IF G > M THEN LET N = G - T ELSE LET N = G
```

would implement the double-alternative decision step from Fig. 2.3. Note that lines 200-240 of the Dartmouth BASIC form are compressed into one line. The IF-THEN-ELSE statement is described in the following display.

IF-THEN-ELSE Statement

Dartmouth BASIC and BASIC-PLUS form:

IF condition THEN statement$_T$ ELSE statement$_F$

Interpretation: The condition is evaluated. If the condition is true, statement$_T$ is executed. If the condition is false, statement$_F$ is executed instead.
Note: The True Statement and the False Statement can be any one of the BASIC statements described in Chapter 1 except DATA and END. In Section 3.2.2, we shall see that a line number may also be used.

Another example of the flow diagram and Dartmouth BASIC form of a double-alternative decision structure are:

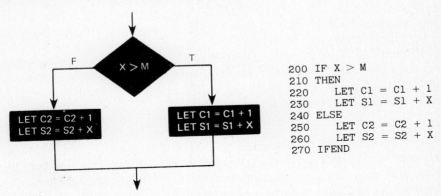

```
200 IF X > M
210 THEN
220     LET C1 = C1 + 1
230     LET S1 = S1 + X
240 ELSE
250     LET C2 = C2 + 1
260     LET S2 = S2 + X
270 IFEND
```

In this structure, any value of X greater than M is added to S1 and the count of such values (C1) is increased by one. Alternatively, S2 is used to accumulate the sum of values of X that are less than or equal to M, and C2 represents the count of these smaller items.

The Dartmouth BASIC decision structure is completely general in that the True and False Tasks can consist of any number of BASIC statements. However, the one line IF-THEN-ELSE statement can only be used when the True Task and the False Task are both single BASIC statements. In the next section we will discuss how to implement general decision structures in BASIC-PLUS and Minimal BASIC as well.

If you have Dartmouth BASIC, you might want to skim quickly through

Sections 3.2.3 and 3.2.4 just to become familiar with the other forms. If you don't have Dartmouth BASIC, you should carefully study the form of the decision structure you will use (either BASIC-PLUS or Minimal BASIC) and skim the material dealing with the other form. All students should read the first part of Section 3.2.2 dealing with transfer instructions.

Exercise 3.1: Write the complete program for Problem 2.2 (modified payroll problem).

Exercise 3.2: Write the program for Example 2.2 (largest of three values problem).

3.2.2 Transfer Instructions

In order to implement decision structures, we must first learn how to alter the flow of control through a program. Recall that the computer executes a program by starting with the first instruction and continuing to execute all instructions in sequence. In a decision structure, however, the value of a condition determines which of two alternative sequences of statements (the True Task or False Task) should be executed. The computer must be instructed to skip over one sequence and execute the other based on the condition value.

A *transfer instruction* modifies the order in which subsequent instructions are executed. For example, the *unconditional transfer* or *GOTO statement*

```
GOTO 130
```

causes an immediate transfer to line 130 of the program and execution will resume with that instruction.

On the other hand, a *conditional transfer* or *IF-THEN statement* causes a transfer only when a specified condition evaluates to true. If the condition evaluates to false, execution continues with the next statement in normal sequence. For the conditional transfer instruction

```
IF A > B THEN 200
```

a transfer of control to line 200 occurs only if "A is greater than B"; otherwise, no transfer occurs and the next instruction in normal sequence would be executed. The unconditional and conditional transfer instructions are described in the displays that follow. Since these statements are part of Minimal BASIC, they are available in all BASIC versions.

Unconditional Transfer (GOTO statement)

Minimal BASIC form:

```
GOTO line number
```

Interpretation: A transfer of control to the indicated line number occurs immediately.

Note: If no statement has that line number, an error is indicated.

Conditional Transfer (IF-THEN statement)

Minimal BASIC form:

```
IF condition THEN line number
```

Interpretation: The condition is evaluated. If it is true, control is transferred to the indicated line number. If the condition is false, execution resumes with the next instruction in normal sequence.
Note: If no statement has that line number, an error is indicated.

The Dartmouth BASIC compiler automatically inserts transfer and conditional transfer instructions during the translation of a decision structure, so that either the True Task or False Task is executed depending upon the value of the condition. In the next sections, we shall see how to use transfer instructions to implement decision structures in BASIC-PLUS and Minimal BASIC.

3.2.3 BASIC-PLUS Double-Alternative Decision Structure

The flow diagram and BASIC-PLUS form of the double-alternative decision structure are illustrated below. This form can be used in any BASIC system that supports the IF-THEN-ELSE statement described in Section 3.2.1.

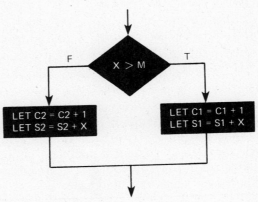

```
200       IF X > M THEN 210 ELSE 250
210 REM THEN
220           LET C1 = C1 + 1
230           LET S1 = S1 + X
240       GOTO 280
250 REM ELSE
260           LET C2 = C2 + 1
270           LET S2 = S2 + X
280 REM IFEND
```

The IF-THEN-ELSE statement is used as the structure header (line 200). It transfers control to either line 210 (the next line) or line 250, depending upon the value of the condition. Each of the REM statements has special significance: Line 210 is the start of the True Task; line 250 is the start of the False Task; line 280 is the structure terminator.

If the condition "X greater than M" is true, control is transferred to line 210 (the True Task). After the True Task is executed, the GOTO statement (line 240) transfers control to the structure terminator, thereby skipping over the False Task. On the other hand, if the condition evaluates to false, control is transferred to line 250 (the False Task), thereby skipping over the True Task.

The BASIC-PLUS form of the double-alternative decision structure is shown in the next display.

Double-Alternative Decision Structure

BASIC-PLUS form:

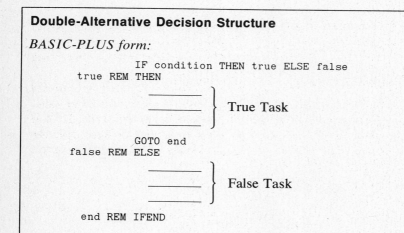

Interpretation: The labels true, false and end represent the line numbers of the THEN, ELSE and IFEND remark statements, respectively. The condition is evaluated. If the condition is true, control is transferred to line true (the next line) and the True Task is executed; after the True Task is completed, the GOTO statement transfers control to line end— the structure terminator. If the condition is false, control is transferred to line false, and the False Task is executed instead.

3.2.4   Minimal BASIC Double-Alternative Decision Structure

The flow diagram and Minimal BASIC form of the double-alternative decision structure are shown next. This form can be used in all BASIC systems, although we recommend the Dartmouth BASIC or BASIC-PLUS form if available.

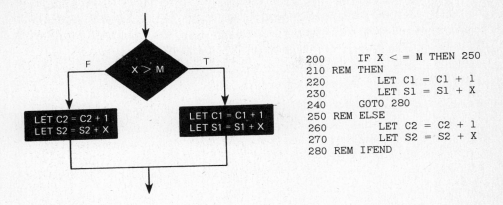

```
200        IF  X  < = M  THEN  250
210  REM  THEN
220            LET  C1  =  C1  +  1
230            LET  S1  =  S1  +  X
240        GOTO  280
250  REM  ELSE
260            LET  C2  =  C2  +  1
270            LET  S2  =  S2  +  X
280  REM  IFEND
```

The conditional transfer instruction (IF-THEN statement) is used as the structure header. Each of the REM statements has special significance: line 210 is the start of the True Task; line 250 is the start of the False Task; line 280 is the structure terminator.

If the condition in line 200 ("X less than or equal to M") is true, control is transferred to line 250 (the False Task), thereby skipping over the True Task. If this condition is false or "X greater than M" is true, the True Task is executed instead (starting at line 210). After the True Task is executed, the GOTO statement (line 240) transfers control to the structure terminator, thereby skipping over the False Task.

The condition "X less than or equal to M" is the *complement* or negation of the condition used in the other implementations and the flow diagram ("X greater than M"). The complement of a condition is true whenever the condition is false, and vice versa.

The complement of a condition is formed by prefixing the condition with the word "not." Thus, the complement of "X equal to Y" is "not (X equal to Y)" or "X not equal to Y." Similarly, the complement of "X greater than M" is "not (X greater than M)," or "X less than or equal to M." Table 3.1 shows all the BASIC relational operators and their complements.

Relational operator		Complement	
=	equal to	< >	not equal to
<	less than	> =	greater than or equal to
>	greater than	< =	less than or equal to
< >	not equal to	=	equal to
< =	less than or equal to	>	greater than
> =	greater than or equal to	<	less than

Table 3.1   BASIC relational operators and complements

Other than the difference in header statements, the Minimal BASIC form of the double-alternative structure is identical to the BASIC-PLUS form. The Minimal BASIC form is summarized in the next display.

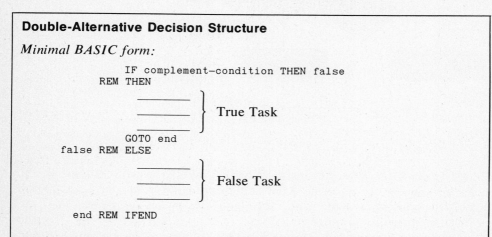

Double-Alternative Decision Structure

Minimal BASIC form:

```
            IF complement-condition THEN false
      REM THEN
```

True Task

```
            GOTO end
      false REM ELSE
```

False Task

```
      end REM IFEND
```

Interpretation: The labels false and end represent the line numbers of the ELSE and IFEND remark statements, respectively. The complement of the condition in the flow diagram pattern is evaluated. If the complement is true (the flow diagram condition is false), control is transferred to line false and the False Task is executed. If the complement is false (the flow diagram condition is true), the True Task is executed instead. After the True Task is completed, the GOTO statement transfers control to line end—the structure terminator.

Exercise 3.3: Use the decision structure implemented in this section to solve the following problem. We wish to examine a collection of data items and determine the number of values that exceed a specified value M and the number of values that do not. In addition, we wish to find the sum of all items in each category. Provide a data table, flow diagram, and program. (*Hint:* Assume the total number of items, N, and the boundary value, M, are provided as input data items.)

3.2.5   Single-Alternative Decision Structure

For the single-alternative decision structure (Fig. 3.2), there is no task to be carried out if the indicated condition is false. However, if the condition is true, the True Task is executed. In either case, the algorithm continues at the point indicated by the arrow at the bottom of the diagram. The single-alternative decision structure may be thought of as a special case of the double-alternative structure (no ELSE alternative) rather than a separate structure.

We illustrate the flow diagram and the three forms of this structure in Fig.

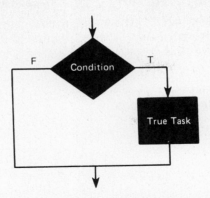

Fig. 3.2 The single-alternative decision pattern.

3.3. We suggest you study carefully the implementation that is available on your system and familiarize yourself with the others.

The Dartmouth BASIC form is the easiest to implement. The BASIC-PLUS form requires the use of line numbers in the header statement and the insertion of the word REM before the keywords THEN and IFEND. The Minimal BASIC version differs from the others in that it uses the complement of the condition. Since there is no False Task, the header statements for the

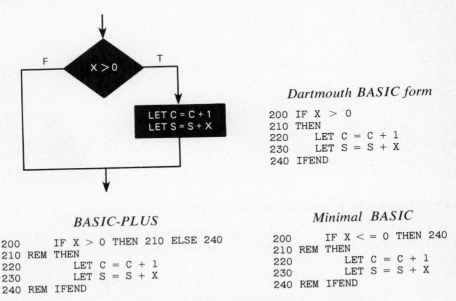

Dartmouth BASIC form

```
200 IF X > 0
210 THEN
220     LET C = C + 1
230     LET S = S + X
240 IFEND
```

BASIC-PLUS

```
200      IF X > 0 THEN 210 ELSE 240
210 REM THEN
220          LET C = C + 1
230          LET S = S + X
240 REM IFEND
```

Minimal BASIC

```
200      IF X < = 0 THEN 240
210 REM THEN
220          LET C = C + 1
230          LET S = S + X
240 REM IFEND
```

Fig. 3.3 Example of single-alternative decision structure.

BASIC-PLUS and Minimal BASIC versions transfer control to the structure
terminator (line 240) when ''X is less than or equal to 0.'' The general forms
of the single-alternative decision structure are shown in the display that follows.

Single-Alternative Decision Structure

Dartmouth BASIC form:

```
                    IF condition
                    THEN

                    _____
                    _____  } True Task
                    _____

                    IFEND
```

BASIC-PLUS form:

```
                    IF condition THEN true ELSE end
              true REM THEN

                    _____
                    _____  } True Task
                    _____

               end  REM IFEND
```

Minimal BASIC form:

```
                    IF complement—condition THEN end
                    REM THEN

                    _____
                    _____  } True Task
                    _____

               end  REM IFEND
```

Interpretation: The condition is evaluated. If the condition is true, then
the True Task is executed. If the condition is false, the True Task will
be skipped.

3.2.6 Special Extended BASIC Forms of Decision Structures*

If the True Task consists of a single BASIC statement, the IF-THEN-
ELSE statement can be used without the ELSE alternative. An example would
be the statement

```
            IF X > 10000 THEN PRINT "DATA ITEM TOO LARGE"
```

*This section is optional and may be omitted.

Some BASIC compilers (particularly those available on personal computers or microcomputers) permit multiple statements on a single line (BASIC-PLUS, Polymorphic BASIC, TINY BASIC). The single-alternative decision structure in Fig. 3.3 could be implemented on these systems as

```
200 IF X > 0 THEN LET C = C + 1: LET S = S + X
```

where we have used the colon to separate the statements in the True Task. (A reversed slash is used in BASIC-PLUS.) If the condition (X > 0) is true, all the statements following the keyword THEN would be executed in sequence. If the condition is false, these statements would be skipped and the next line would be executed instead.

On personal computers or microcomputers where storage space is at a premium, the multiple statement capability can be quite useful. The double alternative decision structure discussed in Section 3.2.2 can be implemented as follows:

```
200 IF X > M THEN LET C1 = C1 + 1: LET S1 = S1 + X: GOTO 220
210 LET C2 = C2 + 1: LET S2 = S2 + X
```

The True Task is listed on line 200 and the False Task on line 210. If the condition is true, line 200 is executed and the GOTO statement at the end of line 200 skips over the False Task. If the condition is false, the False Task on line 210 is executed instead.

An additional implementation form is available on the Radio Shack TRS-80 (Level II BASIC) using the one-line IF-THEN-ELSE statement.

```
200 IF X>0 THEN LET C1=C1+1: LET S1=S1+X: ELSE LET C2=C2+1: LET S2=S2+X
```

The above statement contains both the True Task and False Task. Obviously, these forms are not as readable or flexible as those presented earlier, and we do not recommend their use except where needed to conserve memory.

3.2.7   Comparison of Different Forms of Decision Structures

The advantages of the Dartmouth BASIC implementation of both decision structures should be obvious. There aren't any transfer instructions and, hence, no line number references. It is the function of the compiler to insert the required transfers when translating Dartmouth BASIC to machine language. The Dartmouth BASIC structures are, therefore, easier to write and to read—two important advantages of any programming language feature.

An important advantage of all extended BASIC versions over Minimal BASIC is that the condition from the corresponding flow diagram pattern is inserted directly into the structure header statement. In Minimal BASIC, the complement of this condition is used instead.

In both Dartmouth BASIC decision structures, the structure header and terminator statements bracket the structure, separating it from the rest of the program. The keyword THEN precedes the True Task and ELSE separates the True and False Tasks (when the False Task is present).

We believe that the clear delineation of decision structures from other portions of a program, and the separation of the True and False Tasks add considerably to the clarity of a program. Unfortunately, neither standard Minimal BASIC nor BASIC-PLUS provide these features of separation. We have, therefore, used remarks and indentation to provide the clearest separation possible. While this adds slightly to the length of the program, we feel that the benefits are worthwhile. We urge the reader who cannot use Dartmouth BASIC to follow this approach.

To further illustrate the use of the single- and double-alternative decision structures, we next present solutions to two simple problems.

3.2.8   Applications of Decision Structures

In the first problem, we illustrate the use of the single-alternative decision structure.

Problem 3.1:   Read two numbers into variables X and Y and compare them. Place the larger in X and the smaller in Y.

Data Table for Problem 3.1

Input variables	*Program variables*	*Output variables*
X,Y: Items to be compared	T: Temporary variable used in exchange	X: Larger item Y: Smaller item

Discussion: The flow diagram for this program is shown in Figure 3.4. As shown in the refinement of step 2, the contents of variables X and Y are exchanged only if the condition "Y greater than X" is true. In the completed program for this problem (shown in Fig. 3.5), this exchange is implemented using an additional variable, T, in which a copy of the initial value of X is saved.

To verify the need for T, we trace the program execution for the data list 3.5, 7.2. Only those statements that change the values of a variable are shown in the trace.

Program Trace	*Variables Affected*		
BASIC statements	X	Y	T
READ X, Y	3.5	7.2	
LET T = X			3.5
LET X = Y	7.2		
LET Y = T		3.5	

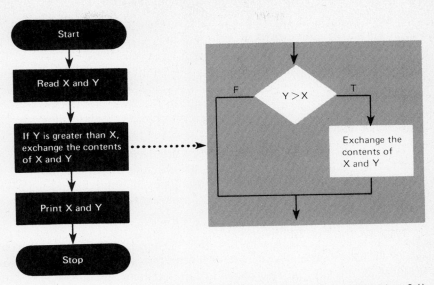

Fig. 3.4 Flow diagrams for determining the larger of two numbers (Problem 3.1).

```
100 REM LARGER OF TWO NUMBERS PROBLEM
110 REM
120 REM READ AND DISPLAY DATA
130     READ X, Y
140     DATA 3.5, 7.2
150     PRINT "X = "; X,  "Y = "; Y
160 REM
170 REM COMPARE X AND Y AND SWITCH IF NECESSARY
180     IF Y > X THEN 190 ELSE 240              [IF Y <= X THEN 240]
190 REM THEN
200         REM PERFORM SWITCH
210         LET T = X
220         LET X = Y
230         LET Y = T
240 REM IFEND
250 REM
260 REM PRINT RESULTS
270     PRINT
280     PRINT "LARGER = "; X,
290     PRINT "SMALLER = "; Y
300 REM
310     END

RUN

X =  3.5          Y =  7.2
LARGER =  7.2     SMALLER =  3.5
```

Fig. 3.5 BASIC program (with sample output) for Problem 3.1.

As indicated in the trace, the value 3.5 is no longer available in X following the execution of the statement

```
LET X = Y
```

Previously, copying X into T (using the statement LET T = X), prevents this value from being lost.

Program Form and Style

In Fig. 3.5, we have shown the BASIC-PLUS version of the program for Problem 3.1. We have tried to emphasize the structure of the program both by indenting and shading the decision structure. The shading is used to separate the function or purpose of the structure from its implementation details.

In shading the part of the structure that describes "what is happening," we also illustrate the Dartmouth BASIC form of the decision structure. As indicated, the special keywords THEN, IFEND and ELSE (if present) would be part of the Dartmouth BASIC decision structure without the introductory keyword REM. Finally, all references to line numbers and the GOTO statement (if present) would be omitted from the Dartmouth BASIC program.

We have also shown the decision structure header that should be used in Minimal BASIC to the right of line 180. This is the only change that would be required in order to implement this program in Minimal BASIC.

This practice will be followed in all complete programs in the text. The BASIC-PLUS version will be shown with any nonstandard structure shaded. The shaded portions will always correspond to Dartmouth BASIC. Any statements required in Minimal BASIC will be enclosed in brackets to the right of the statements that they would replace.

The part of the program before and after the decision structure would, of course, be the same in all BASIC systems.

Another example of the use of the double-alternative decision structure is shown in Problem 3.2.

Problem 3.2: Read two numbers into the variables X and Y and compute and print their quotient Q = X / Y.

Discussion: This is a problem that looks quite straightforward, but it has the potential for disaster hidden between the lines of the problem statement. In this case, as in many others, the potential trouble spot is due to unanticipated values of input data—values for which one or more of the data manipulations required by the problem are not defined.

In this problem, the quotient X / Y is not defined mathematically if Y equals 0. If we instruct the computer to perform the calculation X / Y in this case, it will either produce an unpredictable, meaningless result, or it will not even be able to complete the operation and will prematurely terminate or *abort* our program. Most computers will provide the programmer with a diagnostic message if division by zero is attempted, but some will not. In order to avoid the problem entirely, we will have our program test for a divisor of zero and print a message of its own if this situation should occur.

The data table for this problem follows; the flow diagrams are shown in Fig. 3.6, and the program in Fig. 3.7.

Data Table for Problem 3.2

Input variables	*Program variables*	*Output variables*
X: Dividend		Q: Quotient of X and Y
Y: Divisor		

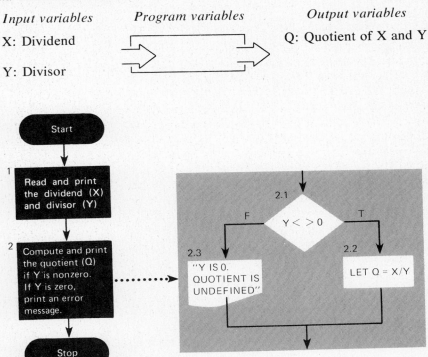

Fig. 3.6 Flow diagrams for quotient problem (3.2).

Exercise 3.4: Flow diagram and program the decisions stated below, using either single- or double-alternative decision structures.

a) Read a number into the variable N. If this number is positive, add one to the contents of P. If the number is not positive, add one to the contents of M.

b) Read a number into N. If N is zero, add one to the contents of Z.

c) This is a combination of the above. Read a number into N. If N is positive, add one to P; if N is negative, add one to M; and if N is zero, add one to Z.

```
110 REM QUOTIENT PROBLEM
120     PRINT "QUOTIENT PROBLEM"
130 REM
140 REM ENTER DATA AT THE TERMINAL
150     PRINT "ENTER DIVIDEND"
160     INPUT X
170     PRINT "ENTER DIVISOR"
180     INPUT Y
190 REM
200 REM COMPUTE QUOTIENT IF Y IS NON-ZERO
210     IF Y < > 0 THEN 220 ELSE 270                    [IF Y = 0 THEN 270]
220 REM THEN
230         REM COMPUTE QUOTIENT
240         LET Q = X / Y
250         PRINT "QUOTIENT = "; Q
260     GOTO 300
270 REM ELSE
280         REM QUOTIENT UNDEFINED
290         PRINT "Y IS 0. QUOTIENT UNDEFINED"
300 REM IFEND
310 REM
320     END

RUN

QUOTIENT PROBLEM
ENTER DIVIDEND
? 14
ENTER DIVISOR
? 2
QUOTIENT =  7
```

Fig. 3.7 BASIC program for Problem 3.2.

Exercise 3.5: The True Task in the decision structure of Fig. 3.5 contains three statements and uses an additional variable T. Could we have accomplished the same task with either set of statements below?

a) LET X = Y   or   b) LET T = Y
   LET Y = X   LET X = T
                         LET Y = X

What values would be stored in X and Y after each set of statements executes? Modify statement group (b) so that it works properly.

Exercise 3.6: Convert the following English descriptions of algorithms to flow diagrams and BASIC statements, using the single- and double-alternative decision structures.

a) If the remainder (R) is equal to zero, then print N.
b) If the product (P) is equal to N, then print the contents of the variable D and read a new value into N.
c) If the number of traffic lights (L) exceeds 25, then compute the gallons required (G) as total miles (M) divided by 14. Otherwise compute G as M divided by 22.5.

3.3 THE BASIC FOR LOOP

In Section 2.4.2 we introduced a restricted form of the BASIC FOR loop and used it to implement the flow diagram pattern below.

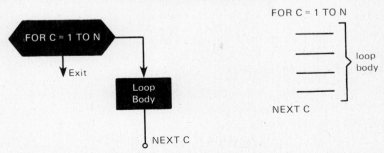

This loop is called a counter-controlled loop. The *loop control variable*, C, is a counter that is initialized to one and increased by one after each loop repetition. The loop body is executed N times or once for each value of C between 1 and N inclusive.

In general the initial value, final value, and step value for the loop control variable may be any legal BASIC expressions. As we shall see, it is even possible for the loop control variable to decrease in value after each repetition. The minimal BASIC FOR loop and its properties are described in the displays that follow.

FOR Loop

Minimal BASIC form:

```
FOR lcv = initval TO endval STEP stepval
```

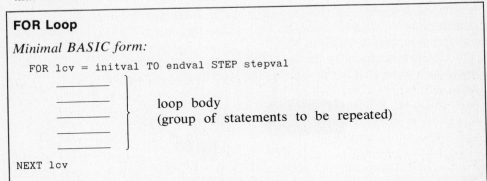

loop body
(group of statements to be repeated)

```
NEXT lcv
```

Interpretation: The loop control variable (lcv) must be a variable name. The *loop parameters* initval, endval, and stepval may be constants, variable names or expressions. In a FOR loop, the loop body is executed once for each value of the lcv, starting with the initial value (initval), and continuing in steps specified by the step value (stepval), until the end value (endval) is passed. When the end value is passed, execution continues with the first statement after the loop terminator (NEXT lcv).
Note: If the step value is one, then STEP 1 may be omitted from the loop header.

Properties of the FOR loop

1. Loop execution is terminated when the value of the loop control variable (lcv) passes the end value. If the loop header were

    FOR I = 3 TO 8 STEP 2

    the loop would be executed for values of I equal to 3, 5, and 7. If the loop header were FOR J = 8 TO 3 STEP −2 the loop would be executed for values of J equal to 8, 6 and 4.

2. If the loop parameters are such that the loop control variable initial value has already passed the end value parameter, the loop will not be executed at all. An example would be

    FOR I = 6 TO 4 STEP 1

    This means that if stepval > 0, then the loop will execute only if initval ≤ endval. If stepval < 0, then the loop will execute only if initval ≥ endval.

3. If stepval is 0 (or undefined), then an *infinite loop* will result. An infinite loop does not terminate until the program runs out of time or is aborted by the programmer.

Example 3.1:   In Fig. 3.8, the first loop computes the sum (S, initial value 0) of all odd integers less than or equal to N. After this value is printed, the second loop is used to compute the product (P, initial value 1) of all even integers less than or equal to N.

The flow diagram for the first FOR loop is shown below. In this diagram, the loop control step is the same as the loop header statement.

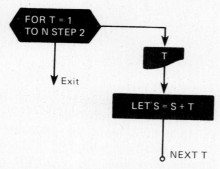

In both loops, T is used as the loop control variable, the end value expression is N, and the step value is 2. T is also used as an operand in the computations performed in the loops (lines 190 and 300).

Since the value of N is 10, the first loop executes for values of T equal to

```
110 REM COMPUTING SUM OF ODDS AND PRODUCTS OF EVENS
120 REM LESS THAN OR EQUAL TO 10
130 REM
140 REM COMPUTE SUM OF ODDS
150     LET N = 10
160     LET S = 0
170     FOR T = 1 TO N STEP 2
180         PRINT T; "       "
190         LET S = S + T
200     NEXT T
210 REM
220     PRINT "SUM OF ODD INTEGERS LESS THAN ";
230     PRINT "OR EQUAL TO "; N; " = "; S
240     PRINT
250 REM
260 REM COMPUTE PRODUCT OF EVENS
270     LET P = 1
280     FOR T = 2 TO N STEP 2
290         PRINT T; "       "
300         LET P = P * T
310     NEXT T
320 REM
330     PRINT "PRODUCT OF EVEN INTEGERS LESS THAN ";
340     PRINT "OR EQUAL TO "; N; " = "; P
350 REM
360     END

RUN

1       3       5       7       9
SUM OF ODD INTEGERS LESS THAN OR EQUAL TO  10  =  25

2       4       6       8       10
PRODUCT OF EVEN INTEGERS LESS THAN OR EQUAL TO  10  =  3840
```

Fig. 3.8 Computing with odd and even numbers.

1, 3, 5, 7 and 9, and the sum (25) is printed. The second loop executes for values of T equal to 2, 4, 6, 8 and 10, and the product (3840) is printed. You should trace both of these loops and verify that they indeed perform as described.

Example 3.2: The BASIC program in Fig. 3.9 computes and prints a table showing the conversion from degrees Celsius to degrees Fahrenheit for temperatures ranging from 0° C (value of I) to 100°C (value of H) in steps of 10°C (value of S). The formula

$$Fahrenheit = 1.8 \times Celsius + 32$$

is used to compute the equivalent Fahrenheit temperature, F, for each value of the loop control variable, C. This program can generate a conversion table for any desired range of Celsius values; all that is required is to change the values of I, H, and S entered at line 190. The data table is shown below.

```
110 REM PROGRAM TO PRODUCE A TABLE OF CELSIUS TO
120 REM FAHRENHEIT CONVERSIONS
130 REM
140      PRINT "CELSIUS TO FAHRENHEIT CONVERSION"
150      PRINT
160      PRINT "ENTER INITIAL CELSIUS TEMPERATURE,"
170      PRINT "HIGHEST TEMPERATURE, AND STEP VALUE"
180      PRINT "SEPARATED BY COMMAS";
190      INPUT I, H, S
200      PRINT "CELSIUS", "FAHRENHEIT"
210 REM
220      FOR C = I TO H STEP S
230         LET F1 = 1.8 * C
240         LET F = F1 + 32
250         PRINT C, F
260      NEXT C
270 REM
280      END

RUN


CELSIUS TO FAHRENHEIT CONVERSION

ENTER INITIAL CELSIUS TEMPERATURE,
HIGHEST TEMPERATURE, AND STEP VALUE
SEPARATED BY COMMAS ?0, 100, 10

CELSIUS        FAHRENHEIT
 0                32
 10               50
 20               68
 30               86
 40               104
 50               122
 60               140
 70               158
 80               176
 90               194
 100              212
```

Fig. 3.9 Celsius to Fahrenheit conversion program.

Data Table for Example 3.2

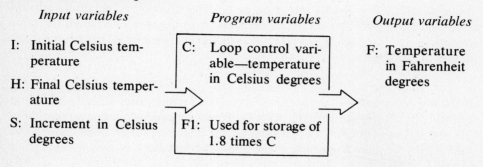

Input variables	Program variables	Output variables
I: Initial Celsius temperature	C: Loop control variable—temperature in Celsius degrees	F: Temperature in Fahrenheit degrees
H: Final Celsius temperature		
S: Increment in Celsius degrees	F1: Used for storage of 1.8 times C	

Line 200 in Fig. 3.9 is used to print two strings as column headings. The headings are printed before the FOR loop is executed; the numbers printed by the loop (line 250) will be aligned in two columns under these headings.

Example 3.3:   The program in Fig. 3.10 computes the factorial of a number. The factorial of a number, N, is defined to be the product of N and all positive integers less than N. It is denoted by the symbol N!.

$$N! = N \times (N-1) \times (N-2) \times \ldots 2 \times 1$$
$$\text{e.g. } 6! = 6 \times 5 \times 4 \times 3 \times 2 \times 1 = 720$$

The program contains a FOR loop with an expression $(N - 1)$ as the initial value parameter and a negative step value (-1).

Date Table for Example 3.3

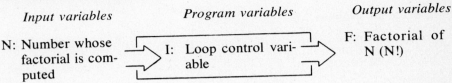

Input variables	Program variables	Output variables
N: Number whose factorial is computed	I: Loop control variable	F: Factorial of N (N!)

In this program, the output variable F is initialized to N. Each loop repetition causes the value stored in F to be multiplied by the next smaller integer. Hence, F equals $N \times (N - 1)$ after one repetition; F equals $N \times (N - 1)$

```
100 REM COMPUTE FACTORIAL OF N
110 REM
120 REM ENTER N - INITIALIZE FACTORIAL, F, TO N
130     PRINT "ENTER NUMBER FOR FACTORIAL COMPUTATION";
140     INPUT N
150     LET F = N
160     PRINT "FACTORIAL OF"; N; " = "; N;
170 REM
180 REM MULTIPLY F BY ALL INTEGERS LESS THAN N
190     FOR I = N - 1 TO 1 STEP -1
200         LET F = F * I
210         PRINT "*" ; I;
220     NEXT I
230 REM
240     PRINT "=" ; F
250 REM
260     END

RUN

ENTER NUMBER FOR FACTORIAL COMPUTATION ? 6
FACTORIAL OF 6 = 6 * 5 * 4 * 3 * 2 * 1 = 720
```

Fig. 3.10   Computation of N factorial.

× (N − 2) after two repetitions, etc. Eventually, F equals N × (N − 1) ×
(N − 2) ··· × 2 × 1 as desired.

The following problem also illustrates the use of the FOR loop.

Problem 3.3:   The banks in your area all advertise different interest rates for
various kinds of long-term savings certificates. Usually the advertisements
state the minimum investment period for the certificate (4 years, 6 years, etc.),
and the yearly interest rate. We will write an interactive program which, given
an investment period (P) in years, a yearly interest rate (R) in percent, and an
amount of deposit (D) in dollars and cents, will compute and print the yearly
interest amount (I) and the value of the certificate (V) at the end of each year
of the investment period.

Discussion: An initial data table for this problem is shown below. The level
one flow diagram appears on the left in Fig. 3.11.

Data Table for Problem 3.3

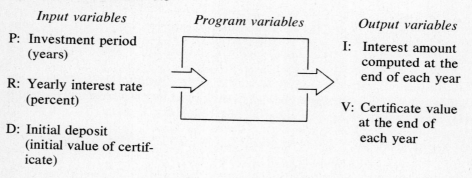

Input variables	*Program variables*	*Output variables*
P: Investment period (years)		I: Interest amount computed at the end of each year
R: Yearly interest rate (percent)		
D: Initial deposit (initial value of certif- icate)		V: Certificate value at the end of each year

From the level one flow diagram, it is clear that a repetition of a short
sequence of steps is needed in the refinement of step 2. The repetition can
easily be controlled by using a counter Y (for Year) that takes on successive
integral values from 1 (first year) through P (last year).

Additional Data Table Entry for Problem 3.3

Program variables

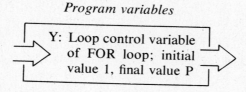

Y: Loop control variable
of FOR loop; initial
value 1, final value P

The refinement of step 2 is shown on the right in Fig. 3.11, and the BASIC
program is given in Fig. 3.12, along with sample output for P = 10 years, R =
7.25 percent and D = $3000.

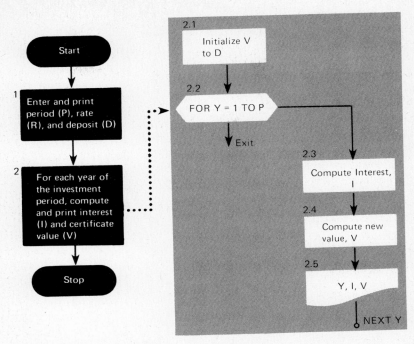

Fig. 3.11 Flow diagrams for bank certificate interest problem (3.3).

In the program, the interest rate (7.25%) is stored in R as the fraction .0725. The first statement in the loop (line 280) computes the interest, I, for the current year; the second statement increases the certificate value, V, by the interest amount.

Exercise 3.7: Assume the FOR loop is not available in your BASIC system. Show how it could be implemented using transfer and conditional transfer instructions.

Exercise 3.8: Modify Fig. 3.8 so that a single FOR loop is used to perform the computation. [*Hint:* Introduce a new variable E that is always one more than T.]

Exercise 3.9:
a) Modify the temperature-conversion program (Example 3.2) so that it will convert Fahrenheit temperatures to Celsius. Print out a table of conversions for temperatures ranging from 210°F down to −30°F in steps of −10°F.
b) Modify Example 3.2 to print a conversion table from Fahrenheit to Celsius degrees in steps of 20°F from 32°F to 212°F.

Exercise 3.10: Write a FOR loop to compute and print a table of square roots of positive integers between 1 and 50. (*Hint:* the square root of an integer K, written as $\sqrt{K}$ or $K^{\frac{1}{2}}$ may be computed in BASIC as

$$K \uparrow .5$$

where the symbol ↑ indicates *exponentiation or "raised to the power of."*)

```
110 REM BANK CERTIFICATE PROBLEM
120      PRINT "BANK CERTIFICATE PROBLEM"
130 REM
140 REM ENTER PERIOD, RATE AND DEPOSIT
150      PRINT "ENTER INVESTMENT PERIOD, RATE AND DEPOSIT,"
160      PRINT "SEPARATED BY COMMAS";
170      INPUT P, R, D
180 REM
190 REM INITIALIZE VALUE (V) TO INITIAL DEPOSIT
200      LET V = D
205      PRINT "INITIAL CERTIFICATE VALUE = $"; V
210 REM
220 REM PRINT TABLE HEADING
230      PRINT
240      PRINT "YEAR", "INTEREST", "VALUE"
250 REM
260 REM COMPUTE INTEREST AND VALUE AFTER EACH YEAR
270      FOR Y = 1 TO P
280          LET I = V * R
290          LET V = V + I
300          PRINT Y, I, V
310      NEXT Y
320 REM
330      END

RUN

BANK CERTIFICATE PROBLEM
ENTER INVESTMENT PERIOD, RATE AND DEPOSIT,
SEPARATED BY COMMAS ? 10, .0725, 3000
INITIAL CERTIFICATE VALUE = $ 3000
```

YEAR	INTEREST	VALUE
1	217.5	3217.5
2	233.269	3450.77
3	250.181	3700.95
4	268.319	3969.27
5	287.772	4257.04
6	308.635	4565.68
7	331.011	4896.69
8	355.01	5251.7
9	380.748	5632.45
10	408.352	6040.8

Fig. 3.12   Program for Problem 3.3.

3.4   THE WIDGET INVENTORY CONTROL PROBLEM

We will now turn our attention to the solution of a problem that illustrates the use of many of the structures introduced in the chapter.

Problem 3.4:   The Widget Manufacturing Company needs a simple program to help with the control of the manufacturing and shipping of widgets. Specifically, the program is to process orders for shipments of new widgets and check that there is sufficient inventory to fill the order. If an order can't be completely filled due to insufficient stock, the program should print the message "NOT FILLED" next to the shipment request; otherwise, the message "FILLED" should be printed. After all orders have been processed, the program should print out the final value of the inventory, the number of widgets shipped and the number of additional widgets that must be manufactured to fill all outstanding orders.

Discussion: The initial inventory value (I1) and the number of orders (N) must be entered prior to processing any order. As each order (R) is read in, it must be compared to the widget inventory. If the order amount is less than the inventory, it will be filled and the inventory reduced. If an order is too large to be completely filled, the number of widgets needed for unfilled orders (U) will be increased by the amount of this order. The data table follows; the flow diagrams are shown in Fig. 3.13.

Data Table for Problem 3.4

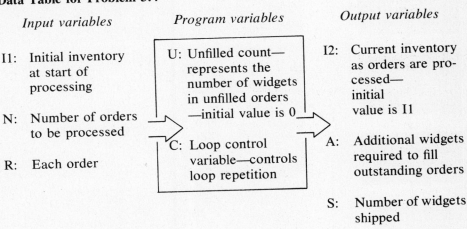

Input variables	*Program variables*	*Output variables*
I1: Initial inventory at start of processing	U: Unfilled count—represents the number of widgets in unfilled orders —initial value is 0	I2: Current inventory as orders are processed—initial value is I1
N: Number of orders to be processed	C: Loop control variable—controls loop repetition	A: Additional widgets required to fill outstanding orders
R: Each order		S: Number of widgets shipped

Besides printing each order as it is processed, the program output will show the final value of the widget inventory (I2), the number of widgets shipped (S), and the total number of widgets required to fill the outstanding orders (A). The number of widgets shipped is equal to the initial inventory minus the final inventory (I1 − I2). The value of A may be computed by subtracting the final inventory (I2) from the accumulated sum of unfilled orders (U). If there are no unfilled orders (U equal to 0), then no additional widgets are required.

We now have sufficient algorithm detail to write the program for the widget inventory problem. The BASIC-PLUS version is shown in Fig. 3.14. As before, the Dartmouth BASIC forms of the decision structures are shaded. The Minimal BASIC header statements are in brackets to the right.

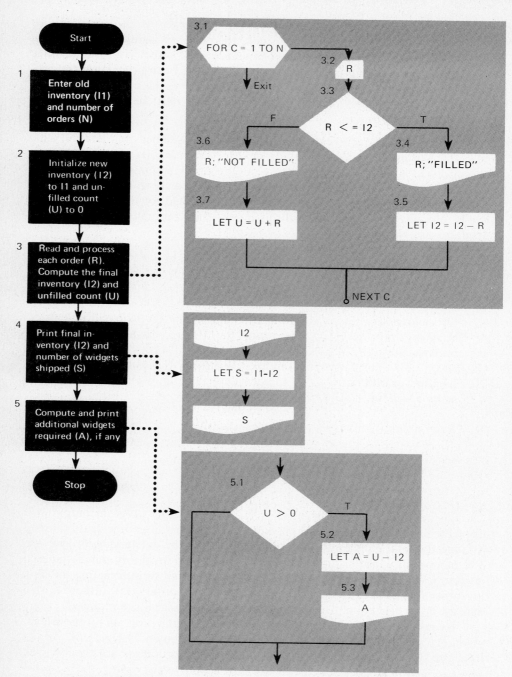

Fig. 3.13   Flow diagrams for the Widget inventory control problem (3.4).

```
100 REM WIDGET INVENTORY CONTROL PROBLEM
110     PRINT "WIDGET INVENTORY CONTROL PROBLEM"
120 REM
130 REM ENTER OLD INVENTORY (I1) AND NUMBER OF ORDERS (N)
140     PRINT "ENTER OLD INVENTORY";
150     INPUT I1
160     PRINT "ENTER NUMBER OF ORDERS";
170     INPUT N
175     PRINT
180 REM
190 REM INITIALIZATION OF NEW INVENTORY (I2)
200 REM AND UNFILLED COUNT (U)
210     LET I2 = I1
220     LET U = 0
230 REM
240 REM READ AND PROCESS EACH ORDER
250     FOR C = 1 TO N
260         PRINT "ENTER ORDER";
270         INPUT R
280         REM DECIDE IF ORDER CAN BE FILLED
290         IF R <= I2 THEN 300 ELSE 350        [IF R > I2 THEN 350]
300 REM     THEN
310             REM SUFFICIENT INVENTORY TO FILL ORDER
320             PRINT R; " FILLED"
330             LET I2 = I2 - R
340         GOTO 390
350 REM     ELSE
360             REM ORDER NOT FILLED, EXCEEDS INVENTORY
370             PRINT R; " NOT FILLED"
380             LET U = U + R
390 REM     IFEND
400     NEXT C
410 REM
420 REM PRINT FINAL INVENTORY COUNT
430     PRINT
440     PRINT "FINAL INVENTORY = "; I2
450 REM
460 REM COMPUTE AND PRINT NUMBER OF WIDGETS SHIPPED (S)
470 REM AND ADDITIONAL WIDGETS (A) IF NEEDED
480     LET S = I1 - I2
490     PRINT S; " WIDGETS SHIPPED"                [IF U <= 0 THEN 550]
500     IF U > 0 THEN 510 ELSE 550
510 REM THEN
520         REM ADDITIONAL WIDGETS NEEDED
530         LET A = U - I2
540         PRINT A; " NEW WIDGETS NEEDED"
550 REM IFEND
560 REM
570     END
```

Fig. 3.14   BASIC program for Problem 3.4.

A sample run is shown on the next page.

Exercise 3.11:   Is it possible for an order for widgets to be filled even if the one before it was not? Hand-trace the execution of this program for an initial inventory of 75 and orders for 20, 50, 100, 3, 15 and 12 widgets.

```
WIDGET INVENTORY CONTROL PROBLEM
ENTER OLD INVENTORY ? 300
ENTER NUMBER OF ORDERS ? 5

ENTER ORDER ? 54
 54 FILLED
ENTER ORDER ? 67
 67 FILLED
ENTER ORDER ? 99
 99 FILLED
ENTER ORDER ? 198
 198 NOT FILLED
ENTER ORDER ? 79
 79 FILLED

FINAL INVENTORY = 1
 299 WIDGETS SHIPPED
 197 NEW WIDGETS NEEDED
```

3.5 COMMENTS ON PROGRAM FORM AND PROGRAMMING STYLE

A program is a group of statements describing a task to be performed. Within a program, there are usually a number of *subtasks* to be carried out. For example, the body of a loop describes a particular subtask; the True Task of a decision step also describes a subtask.

It is important to be able to identify the individual subtasks within a program and to associate each group of statements with a particular task or subtask to be performed by the program. The identification of these tasks can be of considerable help in understanding a program, in correlating the program with the flow diagram and in finding and correcting logical errors that might exist. We believe that applying consistent rules of indentation and use of remarks, as demonstrated in this chapter, will help in the identification of logically meaningful groups of statements within your program.

The approach we have taken in numbering flow diagram steps should aid you in this identification. For example, in comparing the flow diagrams (Fig. 3.13) with the program (Fig. 3.14) for the widget inventory control problem, you will notice that the number of each flow diagram step is indicative of its relative position in the program. That is, the implementation of step 1 (lines 130–170) precedes the implementation of step 2 (lines 190–220). Similarly, the implementation of steps 3.4 and 3.5 (lines 310–330) precedes the implementation of steps 3.6 and 3.7 (lines 360–380). This correspondence will be reflected in all the flow diagrams and programs shown in the text.

The BASIC implementations of all decisions and FOR loop structures described in this chapter will make the logical organization of your program readily apparent. The use of these control structures should simplify the programming task, in addition to improving program readability.

With indentation and carefully chosen remarks summarizing the effect of each control structure or group of statements, the program should read from top to bottom as a linear sequence of level one subtasks. In Chapter 5, we will introduce a new loop structure (the WHILE loop) and an additional feature of BASIC (the subroutine) that will enable us to physically separate the detailed implementations of complicated subtasks from the level one outline of a program *(main program)*. This will make the main program and its parts even easier to write, read and modify.

3.6 COMMON PROGRAMMING ERRORS

In using the Minimal and BASIC-PLUS implementations of the decision structures, the major problem concerns the placement of the transfer statements required to provide the necessary transfers of control. Misplaced or missing GOTO's, or transfers to the wrong line number will usually all go undetected by the compiler and result in program logic errors. Often, the only indication of such errors is incorrect program results; hence, locating the error can be quite difficult. You should, therefore, take great care in the use and placement of all transfer statements. In particular, always check that you have a GOTO immediately following the True Task of a double-alternative decision. Also, double check to insure that line numbers have been included in all transfers and that these line numbers are correct. Finally, remember that the complement of the corresponding condition in the flow diagram should be used in the implementation of each Minimal BASIC decision structure—not the condition itself.

Of course, none of these errors of GOTO and line number misuse are likely if you are programming with the Dartmouth BASIC control structures. Nonetheless, errors can occur here too. The header and terminator statements of each control structure must satisfy the syntax rules. Care should be taken to ensure that header and terminator statements are included for each structure in a flow diagram and that the header and terminator match the structure used in the flow diagram (FOR loop or decision).

Missing loop terminators can be diagnosed easily by the compiler, which will print a diagnostic indicating that the terminator statement is missing. If the terminator statements for two nested control structures (a loop structure and a decision structure) are interchanged, the Dartmouth BASIC compiler will not be able to translate these structures properly and may provide a diagnostic indicating that the structures overlap. An example of improperly overlapping Dartmouth BASIC structures is shown in Fig. 3.15. Use of the wrong structure (for example, using a decision structure when a loop is required) will not be detected by the compiler, but will cause incorrect program results. It is advisable to adopt a set convention for translating flow diagrams into BASIC and to double-check the translation before typing the program.

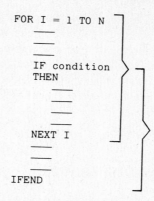

```
FOR I = 1 TO N
    ___
    ___
IF condition
THEN
    ___
    ___
    ___
NEXT I
    ___
    ___
IFEND
```

Fig. 3.15 Overlapping structures.

A common error in using loop structures involves the specification of too many or too few loop repetitions. You should check carefully that the initial, step and end values of all loop control variables are specified correctly. BASIC FOR loops that cause too few or too many repetitions of the loop body are most often the result of the incorrect specification of the end value. Also, when variables or expressions used for loop parameters are incorrectly defined prior to loop entry, the loop will not execute as expected. Printing critical loop parameter values can often be quite helpful during program debugging. Remember to end all FOR loops with a NEXT statement that includes the name of the loop control variable.

3.7 SUMMARY

In this chapter we have focused primarily on the control structures for implementing decisions and loops. Illustrations of the different ways of implementing the single- and double-alternative decision structures were provided. In addition, the FOR loop was described in some detail. The flow diagram patterns for the three structures are reviewed in Fig. 3.16.

The FOR loop and the Dartmouth BASIC decision structures are characterized by the lack of explicit transfer instructions. They all begin with a unique header statement and end with a special terminator. The header statement is used to distinguish each BASIC structure from the others and to indicate the type of the structure. The IF header indicates a decision structure; the FOR header indicates a loop. Each header has its own meaning and this meaning is defined by the way in which the structure is translated by the compiler into machine-language.

Terminator statements serve as end markers and indicate where the physical end of a structure is in the program. The IFEND indicates the physical end of a decision structure; the NEXT marks the end of a FOR loop.

Decision Structures

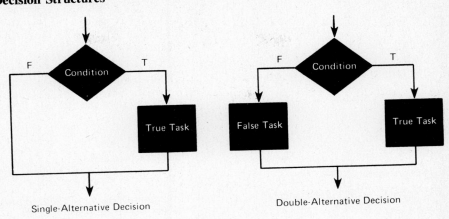

Single-Alternative Decision   Double-Alternative Decision

FOR Loop Structure

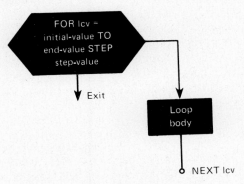

FOR Loop Structure

Fig. 3.16 Summary of structure flow diagram patterns.

Regardless of which structure implementations you use in writing a program, it is essential that you think in terms of the effect of each structure (not its implementation) in formulating your solution to a programming problem. The emphasis should be on how the structures affect what is to be done and not on the various transfers of control (if any) that might be needed in the implementation. To emphasize this point further, we urge you to review the interpretation of the structures, as given in Sections 3.2 and 3.3, and summarized next in Tables 3.2, 3.3 and 3.4.

Remember, the statements and structures available in Minimal BASIC

Statement	*Effect*

FOR loop

```
FOR I = 1 TO N STEP 2
   LET S = S + I
NEXT I
```
Accumulate the sum of all odd integers from 1 to N in S.

```
FOR I = N - 1 TO 1 STEP -1
   LET F = F * I
   PRINT I;
NEXT I
```
Multiply F by all integers less than N, starting with N − 1 and ending with 1, and print each integer.

Transfer statement

```
GOTO 200
```
Transfer to line 200.

Conditional transfer

```
IF X > 1000 THEN 320
```
If the condition X > 1000 is true, transfer to line 320.

Double-alternative decision

```
         IF R > I2 THEN 150
   REM THEN
         LET I2 = I2 - R
         PRINT R; "SHIPPED"
         GOTO 180
150 REM ELSE
         LET U = U + R
         PRINT R; "UNFILLED"
180 REM IFEND
```
If the condition R <= I2 is true, subtract R from I2 and print "SHIPPED"; otherwise, add R to U and print "UNFILLED."

Single-alternative decision

```
         IF X <= 0 THEN 130
   REM THEN
         LET S = S + X
         LET C = C + 1
130 REM IFEND
```
If X is positive (X > 0), add X to S and increment C by one.

Table 3.2   Summary of Minimal BASIC statements

may also be used in extended versions of BASIC. Consequently, the FOR loop, transfer statement and conditional transfer statement are only described in Table 3.2 even though they may appear in extended BASIC programs. The line in Table 3.2 separates those statements and structures that may be useful in all BASIC systems (above the line) from those that are likely to appear in Minimal BASIC programs only. The Minimal BASIC structure implementations have more convenient forms in BASIC-PLUS and in Dartmouth BASIC. If you are using BASIC-PLUS you should also study Table 3.3. If you are using Dartmouth BASIC, see Table 3.4.

Statement	*Effect*

IF-THEN-ELSE statement

```
IF A > B THEN LET M = A ELSE LET M = B
```
Store the larger of A and B in M.

IF-THEN statement

```
             IF X > 0 THEN PRINT "X POSITIVE"
```
If X is positive (X > 0), then print the message "X POSITIVE."

Double-alternative decision

```
             IF R <= I2 THEN 110 ELSE 150
110 REM  THEN
             LET I2 = I2 - R
             PRINT R; "SHIPPED"
         GOTO 180
150 REM  ELSE
             LET U = U + R
             PRINT R; "UNFILLED"
180 REM  IFEND
```
If the condition R <= I2 is true, subtract R from I2 and print "SHIPPED"; otherwise, add R to U and print "UNFILLED."

Single-alternative decision

```
             IF X > 0 THEN 110 ELSE 140
110 REM  THEN
             LET S = S + X
             LET C = C + 1
140 REM  IFEND
```
If X is positive (X > 0), add X to S and increment C by one.

Table 3.3   Summary of BASIC-PLUS statements

Statement	*Effect*

IF-THEN-ELSE statement

```
IF A > B THEN LET M = A ELSE LET M = B
```
Store the larger of A and B in M.

IF-THEN statement

```
             IF X > 0 THEN PRINT "X POSITIVE"
```
If X is positive (X > 0), then print the message "X POSITIVE."

Double-alternative decision

```
    IF R <= I2
    THEN
        LET I2 = I2 - R
        PRINT R; "SHIPPED"
    ELSE
        LET U = U + R
        PRINT R; "UNFILLED"
    IFEND
```
If the condition R <= I2 is true, subtract R from I2 and print "SHIPPED"; otherwise, add R to U and print "UNFILLED."

Single-alternative decision

```
    IF X > 0
    THEN
        LET S = S + X
        LET C = C + 1
    IFEND
```
If X is positive (X > 0), add X to S and increment C by one.

Table 3.4   Summary of Dartmouth BASIC statements

PROGRAMMING PROBLEMS

A data table and flow diagram should be provided for each problem.

3.5 Write a program to read in a list of integer data items and find and print the index of the first occurrence of the number 12. Your program should print an index value of 0 if the number is not found. (The index is the sequence number of the data item 12. For example, if the 8th data item read in is 12, then the index value 8 should be printed.)

3.6 Write a program to read in a collection of exam scores ranging in value from 1 to 100. Your program should count and print the number of outstanding scores (90-100), the number of satisfactory scores (60-89), and the number of unsatisfactory scores (1-59). Test your program on the following data:

63	75	72
72	78	67
80	63	75
90	89	43
59	99	82
12	100	

In addition, print each exam score and its category.

3.7 (Expanded payroll problem.) Write a program to process weekly employee time cards for all employees of an organization. Each employee will have three data items indicating an identification number (N, an integer), the hourly wage rate (R) and the number of hours (H) worked during a given week. Each employee is to be paid time-and-a-half for all hours worked over 40. A tax amount of 3.625 percent of gross salary (G) will be deducted. The program output should show the employee's number and net pay (P).

3.8 Suppose you own a beer distributorship that sells Piels (ID number 1), Coors (ID number 2), Bud (ID number 3), and Iron City (ID number 4) by the case. Write a program to (a) read in the case inventory for each brand for the start of the week; (b) process all weekly sales and purchase records for each brand; and (c) print out the final inventory. Each case transaction will consist of two data items. The first item will be the brand identification number (an integer). The second will be the amount purchased (a positive integer value) or the amount sold (a negative integer value). The weekly inventory for each brand (for the start of the week) will also consist of two data items—the identification and initial inventory—for that brand. For now, you may assume that you always have sufficient foresight to prevent depletion of your inventory for any brand. [*Hint:* Your data entry should begin with eight values representing the case inventory. These should be followed by the number of transactions and then all the transaction values.]

3.9 Write a program to read in an integer N and compute $L = \sum_{i=1}^{N} i = 1 + 2 + 3 + 4 + \cdots + N$ (the sum of all integers from 1 to N, inclusive). Then compute $F = (N \times (N + 1))/2$ and compare F and L. Your program should print both L and F and indicate whether or not they are equal. (You will need a loop to compute L and three arithmetic statements to compute F.) Which computation method is preferable?

To verify your hypothesis of the relationship between L and F, modify your program so that it will process a collection of numbers.

3.10 Write a program to find the largest value in a collection of N numbers, where the value of N will be the first data item read into the program.

3.11 Write a program to process a collection of checking account transactions (deposits or withdrawals) for Mr. Shelley's account. Your program should begin by reading in the previous account balance (B1), the number of transactions (N), and then process each transaction (T), computing the new balance (B2). Your output should appear in three columns, with withdrawals on the left, deposits in the middle and the new balance (after each transaction) on the right. Test your program with the following data.

Old balance = 325.50
Transactions: 25.00, −79.25, −60.00, 16.75, −259.47, 42.00, −5.50

3.12 Modify the data table, flow diagram and program of Problem 3.11 to compute and print the following additional information:
The number of withdrawals; the number of deposits; the number of transactions; the total sum of all withdrawals; the total sum of all deposits.

3.13 Following the processing of the transaction −259.47 in Problem 3.11 (or 3.12), the value of B2 was negative, indicating that Mr. Shelley's account was overdrawn. Modify your data table, flow diagram and program so that the resulting new program will test for withdrawal amounts that are not covered. Have your program completely skip processing each such withdrawal and, instead, use the following print statement to indicate an overdrawn account:

```
PRINT T, " ***WITHDRAWAL NOT COVERED AND NOT PROCESSED *** "
```

The value of B2 should not be altered by withdrawals that are not covered. Your program should count the number of such withdrawals and print a total at the end of execution. (Note that, in Problem 3.11 or 3.12, Mr. Shelley's final balance was positive. This indicates that he made a deposit during the current time period to cover the $259.47 withdrawal. What could be done to prevent such a transaction from being considered as overdrawn as long as the final account balance for the current period is positive?)

3.14 Write a program to compute and print the fractional powers of two ($\frac{1}{2}$, $\frac{1}{4}$, $\frac{1}{8}$, $\frac{1}{16}$, . . .) in decimal form. Your program should print two columns of information, as shown below:

Power	Fraction
1	0.5
2	0.25
3	0.125
4	0.0625
.	.
.	.
.	.

3.15 Modify the program for Problem 3.14 to accumulate and print the sum of the fractions computed *at each step*. Add a third column of output containing the accumulated sum.

> Sum
> 0.5
> 0.75
> 0.875
> 0.9375
> .
> .
> .

Explain the results in this column. Could this value ever reach 1?

3.16 The trustees of a small college are considering voting a pay raise for the 12 full-time faculty members. They want to grant a 5½ percent pay raise. However, before doing so, they want to know how much additional cash this will cost the college. Write a program that will provide this information. Test your program for the following salaries:

$12,500	$14,029.50
$16,000	$13,250
$15,500	$12,800
$20,000.50	$18,900
$13,780	$17,300
$14,120.25	$14,100

Have your program print the initial salary, raise and final salary for each faculty member as well as the total amounts for all faculty.

3.17 Modify your solution to 3.16 so that faculty earning $14,000 or less receive a raise of 4 percent; faculty earning $14,000–$16,500 receive a raise of 5½ percent; and faculty earning more than $16,500 receive a raise of 7 percent.

3.18 The assessor in the local township has estimated the value of all 14 properties in the township. Properties are assessed a flat tax rate of 125 mils per $100 of assessed value, and each property is assessed at only 28 percent of its estimted value. Write a program to compute the total amount of taxes that will be collected on the 14 properties in the township. (A mil is equal to 0.1 of a penny). The estimated values of the properties are:

$50,000	$48,000
$45,500	$67,000
$37,600	$47,100
$65,000	$53,350
$28,000	$58,000
$52,250	$48,000
$56,500	$43,700

4

EXPRESSIONS, STRINGS, AND BUILT-IN FUNCTIONS

4.1 INTRODUCTION

While writing earlier programs you may have thought about, and perhaps even written, BASIC assignment statements containing parentheses and more than one arithmetic operator. You may have also wondered whether or not BASIC could be used to instruct the computer to manipulate something other than numbers and, if so, how?

In this chapter, we shall see that BASIC can be used to manipulate strings of characters as well as numeric information. We will learn how to form BASIC assignment statements of greater complexity than those used so far in order to specify numeric computations, and we will introduce some simple character-string manipulations. All of these features will make it still more convenient to program in BASIC.

4.2 GENERALIZING THE ASSIGNMENT STATEMENT

4.2.1 Multiple Operators and Operands

In the first three chapters of the text, we used simple assignment statements containing expressions with, at most, one arithmetic operator (+, −, *, /). In Chapter 1 (Section 1.3.3) these statements were described as having the general form

```
LET result = operand₁ arithmetic-operator operand₂
LET result = operand
```

Obviously, the BASIC language would have a very limited mathematical capability if only expressions with a single operator were allowed. In fact, it is possible to represent almost any mathematical formula in BASIC using expressions with multiple operators and parentheses. The general form of the BASIC assignment statement is shown in the next display.

BASIC Assignment Statement

```
                    LET variable = expression
```
Interpretation: This statement is used to assign the value of the indicated expression to the variable on the left side of the assignment operator, "=".

In addition to the arithmetic operators described in Table 1.1 (+, −, *, /), there is one additional BASIC operator, ↑ (implemented as ∧ or ** in some BASIC systems). This is the exponentiation operator and it raises its first operand to the power indicated by the second operand. The operands can be variables, constants or expressions.

Example 4.1: In the assignment statement

```
                    LET Z = X ↑ 2
```

$X \uparrow 2$ is the BASIC representation of X^2 (X raised to the power of 2) or X multiplied by itself. If the value of X were 5, the number 25 would be assigned to Z.

Example 4.2:   In this example, the BASIC assignment statement

$$\texttt{LET X = A / (B + C)}$$

is evaluated assuming the variable values shown below. (X is initially undefined.)

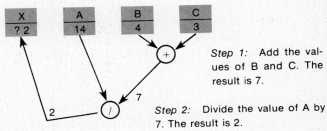

Step 1:   Add the values of B and C. The result is 7.

Step 2:   Divide the value of A by 7. The result is 2.

Step 3:   Store the value of the expression in X.

4.2.2   Evaluating BASIC Expressions

In order to be certain that the BASIC expressions we write produce the desired results, we must understand the way expressions are evaluated in BASIC. For example, in the expression A + B * C, is the multiplication performed before the addition or vice-versa? Is the expression X / Y * Z evaluated as (X / Y) * Z or X / (Y * Z)? We can formulate a set of *rules of evaluation of BASIC expressions*. These rules, which are based upon the conventional rules of *operator precedence*, are summarized in Table 4.1.

(a)   All parenthesized subexpressions must be evaluated first. Nested parenthesized subexpressions must be evaluated inside-out, with the innermost subexpression evaluated first.

(b)   Operators in the same subexpression are evaluated in the following order.
↑   first,
*, /   next,
+, −   last.

(c)   Operators in the same subexpression and at the same precedence level (such as + and −) are evaluated left to right.

Table 4.1   Rules of evaluation of arithmetic expressions

Example 4.3:   Consider the expression

$$\texttt{Y - (A + B / 2) * W ↑ 2}$$

The parenthesized *subexpression* (A + B / 2) is evaluated first beginning with B / 2. Once the value of B / 2 is determined, it can be added to A to obtain the value of (A + B / 2). Next the exponentiation operation is performed and the value for W ↑ 2 is determined. Then the value of (A + B / 2) is multiplied by W ↑ 2 and, finally, this product is subtracted from Y.

This sequence is illustrated in the diagram that follows. Each numbered circle shows the operator and the order in which it is evaluated. The lines connect each operator with its operands.

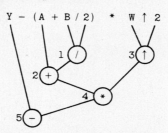

Example 4.4:   The formula for the area of a circle $a = \pi r^2$ may be written in BASIC as

$$\text{LET } A = 3.14159 \text{ * } R \uparrow 2$$

where π is represented by the constant 3.14159. The evaluation of this formula is shown below.

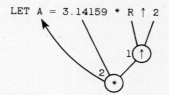

If R is 4, then A is $3.14159 * 4 \uparrow 2 = 3.14159 * 16 = 50.26544$.

Example 4.5:   The formula for computing the amount on deposit in a savings account after n days is given by

$$a = X(1 + r/365)^n$$

where X is the initial deposit, r is the yearly interest rate and interest is computed on a daily basis. This formula is written and evaluated in BASIC as

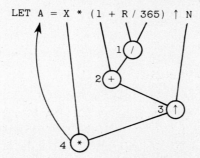

Example 4.6:   The formula for the average velocity v of a particle traveling on a line between points p_1 and p_2 in time t_1 to t_2 is

$$v = \frac{p_2 - p_1}{t_2 - t_1}$$

This formula may be written and evaluated in BASIC as shown below:

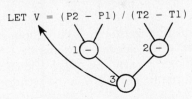

It should be obvious that inserting parentheses in an expression will affect the order of operator evaluation. If you are in doubt as to the order of evaluation that will be followed by the BASIC compiler, you should use parentheses freely to clearly specify the intended order of evaluation.

Example 4.7:   The diagrams that follow show how parentheses affect the order of operator evaluation and, thus, the value of the expression. Without parentheses, rule b of Table 4.1 would dictate the evaluation sequence as shown in the diagram on the left; the insertion of parentheses would result in the evaluation sequence shown on the right. If X were 3, the value of the expression without parentheses would be 10; the value of the expression with parentheses would be 0.1.

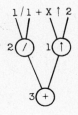

Equivalent mathematical formula:

$$1 + X^2$$

Equivalent mathematical formula:

$$\frac{1}{1 + X^2}$$

4.2.3   Writing BASIC Expressions

There are two inherent difficulties in representing a mathematical formula in BASIC; one concerns multiplication and the other concerns division. Multiplication can often be implied in a mathematical formula by writing the two items to be multiplied next to each other; e.g., a = bc. In BASIC, however, the * operator must always be used to indicate multiplication as in:

$$\text{LET } A = B * C$$

The other difficulty arises in formulas involving division. We normally write these with the numerator and denominator on separate lines:

$$m = \frac{y - b}{x - a}$$

In BASIC, all assignment statements must be written on a single line; consequently, parentheses are often needed to separate the numerator from the denominator, and to indicate clearly the order of evaluation of the operators in the expression. The formula above would be written as

$$\text{LET } M = (Y - B) / (X - A)$$

In BASIC expressions, it is illegal for two operators to appear side by side. Thus the mathematical formula

$$f = g^{-h}$$

must be written as

$$\text{LET } F = G \uparrow (-H)$$

where the left parenthesis separates the operators $\uparrow$ and $-$.

Example 4.8: This example illustrates how several mathematical formulas can be implemented in BASIC using expressions involving multiple operators and parentheses.

Mathematical formula	BASIC expression
a. $b^2 - 4ac$	B ↑ 2 - 4 * A * C
b. $a + b - c$	A + B - C
c. $\dfrac{a + b}{c + d}$	(A + B) / (C + D)
d. a^b	A ↑ B
e. $\dfrac{1}{1 + X^2}$	1 / (1 + X ↑ 2)
f. $xy - \dfrac{a}{d^5}$	X * Y - A / D ↑ 5
g. $1 + X^{-t}$	1 + X ↑ (-T)

The points just illustrated are summarized in the following list of *rules of formation* for BASIC expressions.

1. Always specify multiplication explicitly by using the operator * where needed (see Example 4.8a and f).

2. Use parentheses when required to control the order of operator evaluation (see Example 4.8c and e).
3. Never write two arithmetic operators in succession; they must be separated by an operand or parentheses (see Example 4.8g).

4.2.4 Scientific Notation and Summation Notation

As we have already seen, constants written with or without a decimal point may be used as operands anywhere in an expression. Constants may also be written in scientific notation. For example, the constant .0000053 (5.3×10^{-6} in scientific notation) may be written in BASIC as 5.3E$-$6, where the letter E is used to indicate multiplication times the base 10 raised to the indicated power. The indicated power must always be written without a decimal point. Commas are not allowed in constants.

Example 4.9: The average of a collection of N data items is computed by accumulating the sum, S1, of the data, and dividing by N. If each data item is read into the memory cell X, then S1 can be computed in BASIC as follows:

```
110     LET S1 = 0
120     FOR I = 1 TO N
130         PRINT "ENTER NEXT DATA ITEM";
140         INPUT X
150         LET S1 = S1 + X
160     NEXT I
```

This computation is often represented using the mathematical notation for summation. In this notation, the sum S1 would be written as

$$S1 = \Sigma X$$

where Σ is the Greek letter *sigma*; the average M can be expressed as

$$M = \frac{S1}{N} = \frac{\Sigma X}{N}$$

If N is 4 and the four values of X are 4, 5, 8, and 6, then $S1 = \Sigma X = 4 + 5 + 8 + 6 = 23$, and $M = {}^{23}/_4 = 5.75$.

Exercise 4.1: Write the mathematical equivalents of the following BASIC expressions

```
a)      (W + X) / (Y + Z)
b)      G * H - F * W
c)      A ↑ (B ↑ 2)
d)      (B ↑ 2 - 4 * A * C) ↑ .5
e)      (X * X - Y * Y) ↑ .5
f)      X * 2 + R / 365 ↑ N
g)      P2 - P1 / T2 - T1
```

Exercise 4.2: Let X = 2, Y = 3, and Z = 5. What are the values of the following BASIC expressions?

```
a)      (X + Y) / (X + Z)
b)      X + Z / X / Z
```

c)   X + Y * Z
d)   X / Y * Z
e)   X ↑ (Y − Z)
f)   X ↑ Y − Z

Exercise 4.3:   Write BASIC assignment statements (using LET) for the following:

a) $c = (a^2 + b^2)^{\frac{1}{2}}$

b) $y = 3x^4 + 2x^2 - 4$

c) $z = 3k^4 (7k + 4) - k^3$

d) $x = \dfrac{a^2(b^2 - c^2)}{bc}$

e) $d = (a^2 + b^2 + c^2)^{\frac{1}{2}}$

f) $z = \pi r^2$ (use $\pi = 3.14159$)

g) $r = 6.27 \times 10^{45} S$

h) $p = c_0 + c_1 x - c_2 x^2 - c_3 x^3 - c_4 x^4$

i) $b = a^{-5}$

Exercise 4.4:   Write a program that computes and prints the average M and standard deviation S of a collection of N data items. To compute S use the formula

$$S = \sqrt{\frac{S2}{N} - M^2}$$

where S2 is computed by accumulating the sum of the squares of each data item: S2 = ΣX^2. [*Hint:* If N is 4, and the four values of X are 4, 5, 8, and 6, then S2 = $4^2 + 5^2 + 8^2 + 6^2 = 141$.] A single loop can be used to compute S1 and S2.

4.3   STRING DATA AND STRING VARIABLES

Until now, we have used *string constants* (strings of characters enclosed in quotes) for annotating program output only. In addition to numeric variables, BASIC also has *alphabetic* or *string* variables. String variables are distinguished from numeric variables by the use of the symbol $ after the name of a variable. Any letter followed by a dollar sign is a legal string variable; for example: A$, C$, S$. Character strings consisting of single letters, words, phrases, sentences or any other combination of symbols available on a terminal keyboard may be stored in string variables only. Storage may be achieved through the use of simple assignment statements such as

```
LET G$ = "A"
LET V$ = "ZZZZZZ"
LET P$ = G$
```

or via the use of data entry statements, such as

```
READ C$
INPUT C$
```

Character string constants appearing in PRINT or assignment statements must be enclosed in quotes. However, string data that are entered via READ or INPUT statements do not have to be enclosed in quotes; although we recommend their use. If quotes are not used, any leading or trailing blanks will be ignored. It is also not permissible to enter string data containing a comma unless quotes are used. It is permissible to enter both string and numeric data using the same data entry statements.

Example 4.10:   The READ-DATA statements

```
100 READ X, T$, Y, F$
110 DATA 25.7, "TREE, APPLE  ", 9.37, BANANAS
```

would result in the following assignment of values:

where the symbol □ denotes the blank character.

Numeric operations on strings are not allowed; however, it is permissible to compare strings. This means that statements such as

```
IF C$ = "YES" THEN 400
IF A$ <> S$ THEN 500
```

are allowed in all BASIC systems. The first condition evaluates to true if the string constant "YES" is stored in the string variable C$; the second condition evaluates to true if the values of the string variables A$ and S$ are different.

With some restrictions, order comparisons on string variables can also be performed using the relational operators $<$, $<=$, $>$, $>=$. On most systems, character strings containing letters only (or digits only) may be compared. For strings of letters, the result of the order comparisons depends on the alphabetical order of the strings. For example, if the string stored in A$ would precede the string stored in S$ in a dictionary or telephone book, then the order comparisons

```
A$ < S$, A$ <= S$
```

would be true and the order comparisons

```
A$ > S$, A$ >= S$
```

would be false.

You should be extremely careful in performing order comparisons on any character strings containing mixtures of letters, numbers or special characters. While the order relations

```
"A" < "B" < "C" < ... < "Y" < "Z"
"0" < "1" < "2" ... < "8" < "9"
```

are guaranteed in all BASIC systems, other relations may vary.

Example 4.11:   The following relations on character strings are always true:

```
a)   "BART" < "BARTH"
b)   "HARP" <= "HART"    (< also holds)
c)   "K" > "E"
d)   "1234" >= "1222"    (> also holds)
e)   "56" > "55"
```

Exercise 4.5:   Indicate the effect of the following groups of statements. Identify any illegal statements.

```
a)    100 READ S$, H, R
      110 DATA "033-30-0785", 40, 5.63
      120 PRINT "SOCIAL SECURITY NUMBER", S$

b)    100 READ S, H, R
      110 DATA 033-30-0785, 40, 5.63
      120 PRINT "SOCIAL SECURITY NUMBER", S

c)    110     READ W$
      120     IF W$ < > "DONE" THEN 130 ELSE 160
      130 REM THEN
      135         PRINT W$
      140         READ W$
      150         GOTO 120
      160 REM IFEND
      170     DATA "FLOW", "ROSE", "THORN", "DONE", "CHART", "GREEN"

d)    100 READ X$, Y$
      110 LET S = X$
      120 LET T = S + X$
      130 DATA "AB", "35"
```

4.4   A SAMPLE PROBLEM—THE REGISTERED VOTERS LIST

Problem 4.1   For the local election next Tuesday, town officials have decided to use three clerks, Abraham, Martin and John, to verify that each resident wishing to vote is legally registered and, of course, votes only once. The officials decided that in order to distribute the registered voters fairly evenly among the three clerks, they would assign Abraham to check voters with last names beginning with A through I, Martin to check the voters with last names beginning with J through R, and John to check voters with last names beginning with S through Z.

We will write a program to print a complete voter list with the correct clerk assignment for each voter. The program should read the voter name, house number and street name for each registered voter in the township. The program will then print a master list with the house number and street name printed first, followed by the voter name, with the clerk assigned to the voter printed last. We will assume that all names are entered correctly, with the last names entered first. The number of voters assigned to each clerk should be printed at the end.

Discussion: The data table for this problem is shown below. The flow diagrams are drawn in Fig. 4.1a and 4.1b. N1, N2, and N3 represent the count of voters assigned to each of the three clerks and they must be initialized to zero (step 2 of Fig. 4.1a). Step 3 is the only step of the level one flow diagram needing refinement; its refinement consists of a loop in which the data for each voter is entered and the clerk is designated. The latter operation is performed by step 3.3 which is refined in Fig. 4.1b. Fig. 4.1b shows a *nested decision structure*. The first condition (V$ < "J") separates out all voter names that begin with the letters A-I; the second condition (V$ < "S") separates all other names into the remaining two categories (J-R) or (S-Z). The program and a sample run are shown in Figs. 4.2a and 4.2b.

Data Table for Problem 4.1

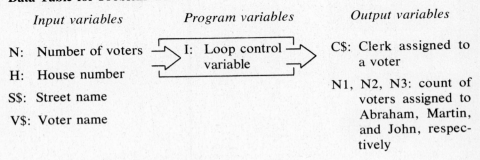

Input variables	*Program variables*	*Output variables*
N: Number of voters	I: Loop control variable	C$: Clerk assigned to a voter
H: House number		
S$: Street name		N1, N2, N3: count of voters assigned to Abraham, Martin, and John, respectively
V$: Voter name		

Program Form and Style

Lines 290-440 of Fig. 4.2a contain an example of a nested decision structure implemented in BASIC-PLUS. As in Chapter 3, we have used indentation and shading to clarify the structure of the program and to highlight the Dartmouth BASIC form as well. The Minimal BASIC header statements are shown on the right (lines 290 and 350).

The keyword REM is normally located directly to the right of the line number so that it does not clutter the decision structure. The only exception is for remarks that describe a True or False Task. In such cases, the keyword REM is indented along with the task (lines 300 and 410). We have also used the keyword REM by itself to separate the main sections of the program.

Exercise 4.6:   The flow diagram in Fig. 4.1b shows a nested decision structure consisting of two double-alternative decision steps. Redraw the flow diagram as a sequence of single-alternative decision steps instead.

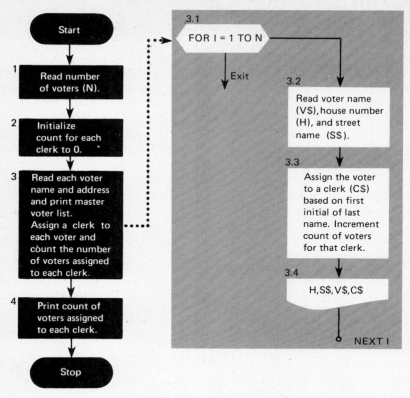

Fig. 4.1a Level one and two diagrams for voter registration (Problem 4.1).

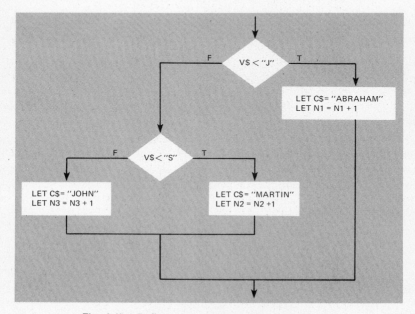

Fig. 4.1b Refinement of step 3.3 (from Fig. 4.1a).

```
110 REM TOWNSHIP VOTER/CLERK ASSIGNMENT LIST
120 REM PRINTS MASTER LIST OF EACH VOTER AND ASSIGNED CLERK
130 REM ALSO COUNTS NUMBER OF VOTERS ASSIGNED TO EACH CLERK
140 REM    VOTERS A-I ASSIGNED TO CLERK ABRAHAM (COUNT IN N1)
150 REM    VOTERS J-R ASSIGNED TO CLERK MARTIN (COUNT IN N2)
160 REM    VOTERS S-Z ASSIGNED TO CLERK JOHN (COUNT IN N3)
165 REM
170 REM READ IN AND PRINT NUMBER OF REGISTERED VOTERS.
175 REM INITIALIZE COUNTS
180     READ N
190     PRINT "THE NUMBER OF REGISTERED VOTERS IS "; N
195     PRINT
200     LET N1 = 0
210     LET N2 = 0
220     LET N3 = 0
230 REM
240 REM LOOP TO READ VOTER NAME (V$), HOUSE ADDRESS (H),
245 REM    AND STREET NAME (S$) FOR EACH VOTER. ASSIGN
250 REM    CLERK (C$) TO EACH VOTER, UPDATE COUNTER FOR
255 REM    THE CLERK, AND PRINT H, S$, V$, AND C$
260     PRINT "REGISTERED VOTER ADDRESS", "    NAME", " ", " CLERK"
270     FOR I = 1 TO N
280         READ V$, H, S$
290         IF V$ < "J" THEN 295 ELSE 340          [IF V$ >= "J" THEN 340]
295 REM     THEN
300             REM CLERK IS ABRAHAM
310             LET C$ = "ABRAHAM"
320             LET N1 = N1 + 1
330         GOTO 440
340 REM     ELSE
345             REM SEE IF CLERK IS MARTIN OR JOHN
350             IF V$ < "S" THEN 360 ELSE 400       [IF V$ >= "S" THEN 400]
360 REM         THEN
365                 REM CLERK IS MARTIN
370                 LET C$ = "MARTIN"
380                 LET N2 = N2 + 1
390             GOTO 435
400 REM         ELSE
410                 REM CLERK IS JOHN
420                 LET C$ = "JOHN"
430                 LET N3 = N3 + 1
435 REM         IFEND
440 REM     IFEND
450         PRINT H; S$, V$, C$
460     NEXT I
470 REM
480 REM PRINT COUNTS
485     PRINT
490     PRINT "THE NUMBER OF VOTERS ASSIGNED TO ABRAHAM IS ", N1
500     PRINT "THE NUMBER OF VOTERS ASSIGNED TO MARTIN IS ", N2
510     PRINT "THE NUMBER OF VOTERS ASSIGNED TO JOHN IS ", N3
520 REM
530 REM INITIAL VOTER LIST
535     DATA 6
540     DATA "ADAMS, JOHN        ",   125, "ABBOT ST.        "
550     DATA "ADAMS, MARY        ",   129, "ABBOT ST.        "
560     DATA "WASHINGTON, GEORGE",   137, "MOUNT VERNON AVE."
570     DATA "KING, MARTIN       ",   270, "PEACHTREE LANE  "
580     DATA "JONES, BILLY       ",   112, "XAVIER RD.       "
590     DATA "ICEMAN, JOE        ",   286, "ZOO AVE.         "
600 REM
610     END
```

Fig. 4.2a Voter registration program.

```
THE NUMBER OF REGISTERED VOTERS IS  6

REGISTERED VOTER ADDRESS              NAME                    CLERK
   125 ABBOT ST.                 ADAMS, JOHN             ABRAHAM
   129 ABBOT ST.                 ADAMS, MARY             ABRAHAM
   137 MOUNT VERNON AVE.         WASHINGTON, GEORGE      JOHN
   270 PEACHTREE LANE            KING, MARTIN            MARTIN
   112 XAVIER RD.                JONES, BILLY            MARTIN
   286 ZOO AVE.                  ICEMAN, JOE             ABRAHAM

THE NUMBER OF VOTERS ASSIGNED TO ABRAHAM IS 3
THE NUMBER OF VOTERS ASSIGNED TO MARTIN IS  2
THE NUMBER OF VOTERS ASSIGNED TO JOHN IS    1
```

Fig. 4.2b Sample run of voter registration program.

4.5 FUNCTIONS

The *function* is a feature of the BASIC language that is of considerable help in specifying numerically oriented computations that produce a single result. Functions are referenced directly in an expression; the value computed by the function is then substituted for the function reference.

Example 4.12: SQR is the name of a function that computes the square root of a non-negative value. Consider the BASIC statement

LET Y = 5.5 + SQR (20.25)

The value computed by the function reference SQR (20.25) is 4.5; the result of the evaluation of the addition operation is 10 (5.5 + 4.5), which is stored in the variable Y.

BASIC provides a number of standard mathematical functions, such as SQR, that are already defined in the BASIC system and may be referenced by

Name	Description of Computation
ABS	Absolute value of the argument
EXP	The value of e raised to the power of the argument
INT	The value of the largest integer less than or equal to the argument
LOG	The logarithm (to the base e) of the argument
RND	A random number between 0 and 1. (Some systems require any integer constant as an argument; others require no argument.)
SQR	The positive square root of the argument
SGN	The sign of the argument (+1 if the argument is positive; 0 if the argument is 0; −1 if the argument is negative)
ATN	The arctangent of the argument ⎫ the argument
COS	The cosine of the argument ⎬ must be
SIN	The sine of the argument ⎪ expressed
TAN	The tangent of the argument ⎭ in radians

Table 4.2   Eleven BASIC mathematical functions.

the programmer. The names and descriptions of these functions are given in Table 4.2. The function name is usually followed by its *argument* enclosed in parentheses as shown in Example 4.12 (argument is 20.25). Any legal BASIC expressions, including numeric constants and variables, may be used as arguments for these functions.

The following examples illustrate the use of some of these functions. Examples 4.14 and 4.15 require additional mathematical background in trigonometry. These examples may be skipped if you don't have this background.

Example 4.13: Square root (SQR), absolute value (ABS), sign (SGN) and integer (INT).

```
110 REM AN ILLUSTRATION OF SQR, ABS, SGN, AND INT
120     PRINT " X", "ABS (X)", "SQR(ABS(X))", "SGN(X)", "INT(X)"
130     FOR I = 1 TO 5
140         READ X
150         PRINT X, ABS(X), SQR(ABS(X)), SGN(X), INT(X)
160     NEXT I
170 REM
180     DATA -6.3, 0, -19, 7, 20.25
190 REM
200     END
RUN
```

X	ABS(X)	SQR(ABS(X))	SGN(X)	INT(X)
-6.3	6.3	2.50998	-1	-7
0	0	0	0	0
-19	19	4.3589	-1	-19
7	7	2.64575	1	7
20.25	20.25	4.5	1	20

Each line of the printout shows the value of X and four functions of X. In line 150, we see that it is permissable to include a function reference in the output list of a PRINT statement. (Actually, any valid BASIC expression can appear in an output list).

The third item in the output list of line 150, SQR (ABS(X)), is an example of a nested function reference. Since the square root of a negative number is mathematically undefined, we should first determine the absolute value of X before computing the square root.

The INT function determines the largest integer that is less than or equal to its argument; hence, the INT function simply *truncates* or removes the fractional part of a positive argument (INT(20.25) = 20). However, for a negative argument like −6.3, the integer formed by truncating the fractional part, −6, would be larger than the argument. Thus, the value of INT (−6.3) is −7, the "largest integer less than or equal to" −6.3.

Example 4.14: The trigonometric functions COS and SIN are illustrated in the program below.

```
110 REM AN ILLUSTRATION OF SIN AND COS
120 REM
130     PRINT "X (IN DEGREES)", "  SIN(X)", "  COS(X)"
140 REM DEFINE THE MATHEMATICAL CONSTANT PI TO 6 SIGNIFICANT DIGITS
150     LET P = 3.14159
160 REM
170     FOR X = 0 TO 180 STEP 15
180         PRINT X, SIN(X * P / 180),
190         PRINT COS(X * P / 180)
200     NEXT X
210 REM
220     END

RUN
```

X (IN DEGREES)	SIN(X)	COS(X)
0	0	1.
15	.258819	.965926
30	.5	.866026
45	.707106	.707107
60	.866025	.500001
75	.965925	.25882
90	1.	1.32679E−6
105	.965926	−.258818
120	.866026	−.499998
135	.707108	−.707105
150	.500002	−.866024
165	.258821	−.965925
180	2.65359E−6	−1.

It is important to remember that the input argument to the trigonometric functions SIN, COS, TAN, and ATN must be expressed in radians. To convert from degrees, a measure familiar to most of us, we take advantage of the fact that π radians is equal to 180 degrees. Using 3.14159 as an approximation of the value of π (accurate to five decimal places) we have

$$1 \text{ degree } = \pi/180 \text{ radians}$$
$$X \text{ degrees} = X \times \pi/180 \text{ radians}$$

as shown in the above program (P represents π in the program).

Example 4.14 provides an illustration of the use of an expression (X*P/180) as the argument of a function. The value of the expression is computed first and then the function is applied to this value. Since the expression is evaluated twice inside the loop (lines 180 and 190) it would be more efficient to assign the value 3.14159/180 to a variable R before entering the loop, and to compute Y = X * R as the first step in the loop body. This is left as an exercise (Exercise 4.7).

If you look closely at the output from the Example 4.14 program, you will note that neither the sine of 180 degrees nor the cosine of 90 degrees were computed to be identically zero. This is due to a loss of accuracy in the computations of these functions. Loss of accuracy is discussed in more detail in Section 4.7.

Example 4.15:   The next example illustrates the conversion of formulas from physics into BASIC statements. You need not be concerned if the formulas are unfamiliar. The main point of the example is to illustrate their application in a BASIC program.

Prince Valiant is trying to rescue Rapunzel by shooting an arrow with a rope attached through her tower window that is 100 feet off the ground. We will assume that the arrow travels at a constant velocity. The time it takes to reach the tower is given by the formula

$$T = \frac{D}{V \cos \theta}$$

where D is the distance Prince Valiant is standing from the tower, V is the velocity of the arrow and θ is its angle of elevation.

Our task is to determine whether or not the Prince's arrow goes through the window by computing its distance off the ground when it reaches the tower as given by the formula

$$H = VT \sin \theta - \frac{GT^2}{2}$$

where G is the gravitational constant. For the arrow to go through the window, H should be between 100 and 110 feet. We will print out an appropriate message to help Prince Valiant correct his aim.

The program and a sample run are shown in Fig. 4.3a, b.

Example 4.16:   There is one additional BASIC function, TAB, that appears only in PRINT statements and is used to control spacing across an output line. Whenever TAB is referenced, the value of its argument determines the column in which the next item to be printed begins. The first PRINT statement below would display the values of A1, A2, and A3 in three zones of width 10 (A2 starts in column 11, and A3 starts in column 21). In the second PRINT statement, the width of each zone depends on the value of N.

```
PRINT Al; TAB (11); A2; TAB (21); A3
PRINT Al; TAB (N); A2; TAB (2 * N); A3
```

The TAB function could be used to advantage in Fig. 4.2a. The PRINT statements

```
260    PRINT "REGISTERED VOTER ADDRESS";
265    PRINT TAB (35); "NAME"; TAB (62); "CLERK"
450    PRINT H; S$; TAB (31); V$; TAB (61); C$
```

would ensure that the voter name (V$) and clerk name (C$) were properly aligned in output columns, regardless of how they were typed in the DATA statements (lines 535-590).

Exercise 4.7:   Rewrite the program shown in Example 4.14. Compute and print the value R = 3.14159/180 before entering the loop. (This value is the decimal representation of the number of radians in one degree.) Then, inside the loop, compute Y = X * R

```
110 REM PRINCE VALIANT TAKES AIM AT RAPUNZEL
120 REM
130 REM PRINT INTRODUCTORY REMARKS
140     PRINT "DEAR PRINCE,"
150     PRINT "RAPUNZEL, LESS HER GOLDEN TRESSES, IS LOCKED"
160     PRINT "INSIDE THE HIGH TOWER BY THE WICKED WITCH."
170     PRINT "YOUR MISSION, PRINCE, SHOULD YOU CHOOSE TO ACCEPT IT."
180     PRINT "IS TO SHOOT AN ARROW, WITH ROPE ATTACHED, AT"
190     PRINT "SUCH AN ANGLE AND SUCH A SPEED AS TO SECURE"
200     PRINT "THE FAIR MAIDEN'S DESCENT."
210     PRINT
220 REM
230 REM INITIALIZE PROGRAM PARAMETERS
240 REM G IS GRAVITY (FT/SEC↑2)
250 REM P IS PI
260     LET G = 32.17
270     LET P = 3.14159
280 REM
290 REM REQUEST ENTRY OF DISTANCE (D), VELOCITY (V) AND
300 REM ANGLE OF ELEVATION (A) FOR ARROW
310     PRINT "ENTER YOUR DISTANCE (IN FEET) FROM YON TOWER,"
320     PRINT "THE SPEED OF THY ARROW (IN FEET/SEC),"
330     PRINT "AND ITS ANGLE OF FLIGHT (IN DEGREES)."
340     INPUT D, V, A
345     PRINT
```

Fig. 4.3a Prince Valiant rescues Rapunzel program. (Continued on page 117.)

and use Y as the argument of the functions SIN and COS. Compare your output to the results shown in Example 4.14. Which results are more accurate? Do you have any idea why?

Exercise 4.8:   The roots of an equation of the form

$$y = ax^2 + bx + c$$

where a, b, and c are real numbers may be computed as follows.

$$r1 = \frac{-b + \sqrt{b^2 - 4ac}}{2a}$$

$$r2 = \frac{-b - \sqrt{b^2 - 4ac}}{2a}$$

Write a program to read in three values a, b, and c, and determine and print r1 and r2. Test your program with the following values for a, b, and c.

a	b	c
1	1	−6
1	−8	16
1	0	−1
1	0	1
15	−2	−1
0	0	0

```
350 REM CONVERT DEGREES TO RADIANS
360     LET R = A * P / 180
370 REM
380 REM COMPUTE TRAVEL TIME (T) AND HEIGHT (H) OF ARROW
390     LET T = D / (V * COS(R))
400     LET H = V * T * SIN(R) - (G * T ↑ 2) / 2
410 REM
420 REM CHECK TO SEE IF ARROW HEIGHT AT BASE OF TOWER
430 REM IS BETWEEN 100 AND 110 FEET
440 REM PRINT APPROPRIATE MESSAGES
450     IF H < 100 THEN 460 ELSE 570              [IF H >= 100 THEN 570]
460 REM THEN
470         REM H < 100 -- ARROW FELL SHORT
480         IF H < 0 THEN 490 ELSE 520            [IF H >= 0 THEN 520]
490 REM     THEN
500             PRINT "BAD SHOT ARROW DIDN'T EVEN REACH THE TOWER"
510         GOTO 550
520 REM     ELSE
530             REM ARROW HIT TOWER BELOW WINDOW
540             PRINT "TOO LOW, PRINCE. HEIGHT WAS "; H
550 REM     IFEND
560     GOTO 670
570 REM ELSE
580         REM ARROW NOT SHORT, IS IT TOO HIGH?
590         IF H > 110 THEN 600 ELSE 630          [IF H <= 110 THEN 630]
600 REM     THEN
610             PRINT "TOO HIGH, PRINCE. HEIGHT WAS "; H
620         GOTO 660
630 REM     ELSE
640             REM H <= 110
650             PRINT "BULLS-EYE, PRINCE. LIVE HAPPILY EVER AFTER"
660 REM     IFEND
670 REM IFEND
680 REM
690     END
```

Fig. 4.3a   Completion of Prince Valiant rescues Rapunzel program.

```
DEAR PRINCE,
RAPUNZEL, LESS HER GOLDEN TRESSES, IS LOCKED
INSIDE THE HIGH TOWER BY THE WICKED WITCH.
YOUR MISSION, PRINCE, SHOULD YOU CHOOSE TO ACCEPT IT,
IS TO SHOOT AN ARROW, WITH ROPE ATTACHED, AT
SUCH AN ANGLE AND SUCH A SPEED AS TO SECURE
THE FAIR MAIDEN'S DESCENT.

ENTER YOUR DISTANCE (IN FEET) FROM YON TOWER,
THE SPEED OF THY ARROW (IN FEET/SEC),
AND ITS ANGLE OF FLIGHT (IN DEGREES).
 ? 100, 110, 55

BULLS-EYE, PRINCE. LIVE HAPPILY EVER AFTER
```

Fig. 4.3b   Sample output for program in Fig. 4.3a.

For each triple a, b, c, your program should test the value of the *discriminant* d = b²
− 4ac. If d is negative, print the message 'no real roots,' and omit the remaining
computation for the current values of a, b, c.

Exercise 4.9:   The numeric constant e is known as Euler's Number. It has had an
established place in mathematics alongside the Archimedean number π for over 200
years. The approximate value of e (accurate to 9 decimal places) is 2.71828183. Write
a BASIC program that prints EXP(X) and LOG(X) for integer values of X from 1 to
10.

Exercise 4.10:   Let N = 1000. Write a program to compute P = 0.1 * N and S =
$\sum_{i=1}^{N} 0.1$ (where $\sum_{i=1}^{N} 0.1$ is equal to 0.1 added to itself 1000 times). You will need a loop
to compute S. Following the loop, your program should print the values of S and P and
also print an appropriate message indicating whether or not S and P are equal.

Exercise 4.11:   The formula for the velocity of a body dropped from rest is v = gt,
where g is the acceleration due to gravity, and t is time (air resistance is ignored here).
Write a loop to compute v at 10-second intervals (starting with t = 0) for a pickle
dropped from a building that is 600 meters tall, with g = 9.81 meters/second. [*Hint:*
Use the formula t = $\sqrt{2s/g}$ to determine the time, T1, it takes for the pickle to hit the
ground (s equals 600). Use T1 to limit the number of repetitions of the loop that produces
the table.]

Exercise 4.12:   Modify the Prince and Rapunzel program (Fig. 4.3a) so that the velocity of the arrow will automatically be increased by 10 feet/sec if the arrow is too low
and decreased by 8 feet/sec if the arrow is too high. This repetition should terminate
when the arrow enters the window.

Exercise 4.13:   The modulus of two positive integers i and j is defined to be the
remainder obtained from dividing i by j. For example, if i is 5 and j is 3, then the
modulus of 5 and 3, written mod (5,3) is 2. Similarly, mod (9,3) = 0. Use the INT
function to write a BASIC statement to compute the modulus of any two positive
integers i and j.

Exercise 4.14:   Using the INT function, write a BASIC statement to round any positive real value X to the nearest two decimal places. [*Hint:* If the third decimal digit
in X is betwen 0 and 4, then round down by truncating (chopping off) all digits to the
right of the second digit. If the third digit is between 5 and 9, round up.]

4.6   THE PRIME NUMBER PROBLEM

The prime numbers have been studied by mathematicians for many years.
A *prime number* is an integer that has no divisors other than 1 and itself. The
following problem makes use of the INT function to determine if one number
is a divisor of another. In solving this problem, we introduce the notion of a
program flag.

Problem 4.2:   Find and print all exact divisors of an integer N other than 1
and N itself. If there are no divisors, print out the message "N is a prime
number." The value of N will be provided as a data item to be read in by the
program.

Discussion: The general approach we will take is to see whether we can find an integer, D, that divides N evenly (with no remainder). We shall examine all integers between 2 and N−1 and print any exact divisors.

The data table is shown below. The flow diagrams are shown in Fig. 4.4.

Data Table for Problem 4.2

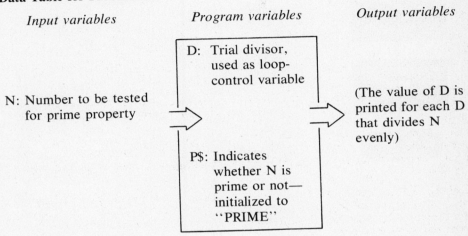

Input variables   *Program variables*   *Output variables*

D: Trial divisor, used as loop-control variable

N: Number to be tested for prime property

(The value of D is printed for each D that divides N evenly)

P$: Indicates whether N is prime or not— initialized to "PRIME"

The variable P$ is used as an indicator of whether or not N is prime. The value of P$ is initially set to "PRIME" (step 1.2) before the loop is entered. In the loop, each value of D is tested to see if it is a divisor of N; if a divisor of N is found, then D is printed and the value of P$ is redefined to be "NOT PRIME" (step 2.4). When step 3 is reached, the value of P$ is printed.

P$ is called a program flag. A *program flag* is a variable that is used to communicate to one program step the result of computations performed in another step. If a divisor is found, P$ is redefined in step 2, so that the program can determine at step 3 whether or not N was prime.

As shown in the flow diagram, the algorithm proceeds by checking all integers between 2 and N−1 inclusive as possible divisors of N (loop 2.1). The test for an exact divisor (step 2.2) is performed by evaluating the expression

$$INT \ (N \ / \ D) \ * \ D$$

and comparing it to N. If D is not an exact divisor of N, the INT function will truncate the remainder of N/D and multiplying by D will yield a value that is "not equal to" N. For example, if N = 9 and D = 2, a value of 8 would be computed as shown next.

$$INT \ (9 \ / \ 2) \ * \ 2 = 4 \ * \ 2 = 8$$

However, if D is an exact divisor of N, there will be no remainder to truncate

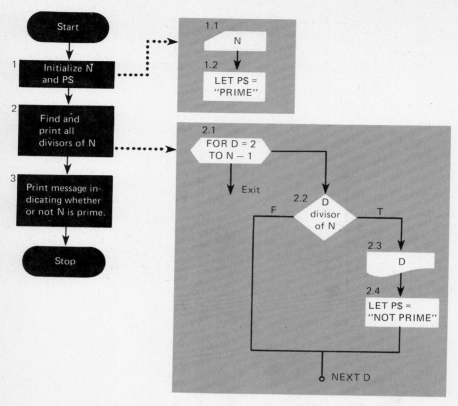

Fig. 4.4   Flow diagrams for prime number problem (4.2).

and the value computed will equal N. For example, if N = 9 and D = 3, a value of 9 would be computed:

$$INT \ (9 \ / \ 3) \ * \ 3 \ = \ 3 \ * \ 3 \ = \ 9$$

The program for Problem 4.2 is shown in Fig. 4.5.

Exercise 4.15:   (For the more mathematically inclined.) The program shown in Fig. 4.5 tests all integer values between 2 and N−1 inclusive to see if any of them divide N. This is, in fact, quite inefficient, for we need not test all of these values. Revise the algorithm shown in Fig. 4.4 to minimize the number of possible divisors of N that must be tested to determine whether or not N is prime. Make certain that your improved algorithm still works. [*Hints:* If 2 does not divide N, no other even number will divide N. If no integer value between 2 and N/2 divides N, then no integer value between N/2 + 1 and N − 1 will divide N. In fact, we can even compute a smaller maximum test value than N/2 using the SQR function. What is it?]

```
110 REM PRIME NUMBER PROBLEM
120     PRINT "PRIME NUMBER PROBLEM"
130     PRINT
140 REM
150 REM ENTER VALUE (N) TO BE TESTED FOR DIVISORS
160     PRINT "ENTER N";
170     INPUT N
180     PRINT "LIST OF DIVISORS OF "; N
190 REM
200 REM TEST ALL POSSIBLE DIVISORS OF N
210 REM IF ANY ARE FOUND, SET PRIME FLAG (P$) TO "NOT PRIME"
220 REM IF NO DIVISORS FOUND, P$ MUST BE "PRIME"
230 REM
240 REM ASSUME NO DIVISORS AT START
250     LET P$ = "PRIME"
260     FOR D = 2 TO N - 1
265         LET N1 = INT (N/D) * D
270         IF N1 = N THEN 275 ELSE 310 [IF N1 <> N THEN 310]
275 REM     THEN
280             REM D DIVIDES N, N NOT PRIME. PRINT D.
290             PRINT D
300             LET P$ = "NOT PRIME"
310 REM     IFEND
320     NEXT D
325 REM
330 REM PRINT WHETHER OR NOT N IS PRIME
340     PRINT; N; "IS "; P$
350 REM
360     END

RUN

PRIME NUMBER PROBLEM

ENTER N ? 12
LIST OF DIVISORS OF 12
  2
  3
  4
  6
 12 IS NOT PRIME
```

Fig. 4.5 Program for Problem 4.2.

4.7 NUMERICAL ERRORS*

All of the errors discussed in earlier chapters have been programmer errors. However, even if a program is correct, it still may compute the wrong answer, especially if extensive numerical computation is involved. The cause of error is the inherent inaccuracy in the internal representation of data having fractional parts (*real* values as opposed to *integer* values).

---

*This section may be omitted.

We stated earlier that all information is represented in the memory of the computer as a number. For most computers, data are represented using the binary number system (base 2), rather than the decimal system (base 10). Thus, the representation of information in the memory of the computer is in terms of binary digits (0's and 1's), rather than decimal digits (0-9). However, as shown in the next example, many decimal numbers do not have precise binary equivalents and, therefore, can only be approximated in the binary number system.

Example 4.17:   This example lists several binary approximations of the number 0.1. The precise decimal equivalent of the binary number being represented and the numerical error are also shown.

Number of binary digits	Binary approximation	Decimal equivalent	Numerical error
4	.0001	0.0625	0.0375
5–8	.00011000	0.09375	0.00625
9	.000110001	0.09765625	0.00234375
10	.0001100011	0.099609375	0.000390625

We can see from this example that, as the number of binary digits used to represent 0.1 is increased, the precise decimal equivalent represented by the binary number gets closer to 0.1. However, it is impossible to obtain an exact binary representation of 0.1, no matter how many digits are used. Unfortunately, the number of binary digits that can be used to represent a real number in the memory of the computer is limited by the size of a memory cell. The larger the cell, the larger the number of binary digits and the greater the degree of accuracy that can be achieved. (Is it possible to represent the fraction ⅓ exactly in the decimal number system?)

The effect of a small error can become magnified when a long sequence of computations is performed. For example, in determining the sine or cosine of an angle, many operations are performed by the computer on real numbers (see Example 4.14). The repeated execution of a relatively simple computation may also cause a magnification of round-off error as the inaccuracy in each individual computation is accumulated (see Exercise 4.10). Such magnification can sometimes be diminished through the use of special functions or a reordering of the computations. You should be aware that the problem of round-off error exists, and that it may cause the same BASIC program to produce different results when run on computers having memory cells of different sizes.

Example 4.18:

a)   The computation

```
SQR(X)
```

is likely to produce more accurate results than X ↑ .5 since most square root functions produce more accurate results than the computations required to evaluate $X \uparrow .5$.

b) If we have two real numbers A and B, whose difference is very small, and a third number C that is relatively large (compared with $A - B$), then the calculation

$$(A - B) * C$$

may produce results that are less accurate than

$$A * C - B * C.$$

This is because the percentage of error is greater in a very small number such as $(A - B)$, and additional inaccuracy is introduced when a very small number is multiplied by one that is much larger.

4.8 COMMON PROGRAMMING ERRORS

In working with expressions, especially complicated ones, a good deal of care is necessary. Some of the more common programming errors involving expressions and assignment statements are listed below, along with their remedies. The compiler diagnostics for these errors may be similar in wording to the short descriptions that are given here, or they may simply read "Unrecognizable Statement" or "Illegal Statement." In some cases, the error may not be detected, since it may result in a legal statement, although not the one intended.

1. *Mismatched or unbalanced parentheses*. The statement in error should be carefully scanned, and left and right parentheses matched in pairs, inside-out, until the mismatch becomes apparent. This error is often caused by a missing parenthesis at the end of an expression.

2. *Missing operator in an expression*. This error is usually caused by a missing multiplication operator, *. The expression in error must be scanned carefully, and the missing operator inserted in the appropriate position.

3. *String data used with arithmetic operator*. These errors are examples of *mixed-type* expressions; operators that can manipulate data of one type are being used with data of another type. It is senseless and illegal to do arithmetic on string operands. Attempts to store string data (through assignment or data input) in numeric variables (and vice versa) will result in "Illegal Statement" errors.

4. *Arithmetic underflow or overflow or division by zero attempted*. Another type of numerical error is caused by attempts to manipulate very large real numbers or numbers that are very close in value to zero. For example, dividing by a number that is almost zero may produce a number that is too large to be represented (*overflow*). You should check that the correct variable is being used as a divisor and that it has the proper value. On some compilers, a divisor that is undefined

would be set to zero and would cause a *division by zero* diagnostic to be printed. Arithmetic *underflow* occurs when the magnitude of the result is too small to be represented.

One type of programming error that can't be detected by a compiler involves the writing of expressions that are syntactically correct, but do not accurately represent the computation called for in the problem statement. All expressions, especially long ones, must be carefully checked for accuracy. Often, this involves the decomposition of complicated expressions into simpler subexpressions producing intermediate results. The intermediate results should be printed and compared with hand calculations for a simple, but representative data sample.

Care should be taken to ensure that the standard mathematical functions are not given illegal input arguments. The actual arguments that are accepted by these functions may vary according to computer. On some systems, taking the square root or logarithm of a negative argument will produce an error message. Attempts to compute the logarithm of 0, or the tangent of 90° or 270° will produce an error message on most systems. Program execution will terminate immediately after the error message is printed.

Remember that string variable names must end with a dollar sign, $, and that all strings used in a program must be enclosed in quotes. If you forget the closing quotation mark (on the right), your string will run on beyond its intended limit. When comparing string values, remember that the only orderings that are assured are that "A" < "B" < ... < "Z" and "0" < "1" < ... < "9". You should check your BASIC manual for the ordering of other characters on your system.

4.9 SUMMARY

The specification of multi-operator arithmetic assignment statements and the use of string data have been discussed. The rules of formation and evaluation of arithmetic expressions were summarized. The operations of addition (+), subtraction (−), multiplication (*), division (/) and exponentiation (↑) may be combined according to these rules to form complicated arithmetic expressions. These expressions may be used in assignment statements on the right-hand side of the assignment operator (=), in the list portion of a print statement, and as arguments in function references. None of these operators may be used with string operands, although strings may be compared for equality and, in a restricted way, for order. Character strings may also be stored in string variables using a read or simple assignment statement.

Eleven standard mathematical functions provided by BASIC, as well as the TAB function for carriage control, have been described. The mathematical functions are summarized in Table 4.2. Table 4.3 provides a summary of the new statements introduced in this chapter. They are all part of Minimal BASIC, hence they are included in BASIC-PLUS and Dartmouth BASIC as well.

Statement	Effect
String assignment	
LET A$ = "CAT" LET B$ = A$	Store the string "CAT" in A$. Copy the string stored in A$ into B$.
String comparison	
IF A$ = "RAT" THEN 100	Transfer to line 100 if the string "RAT" is stored in A$.
IF N$ < Q$ THEN 120	Transfer to line 120 if the string stored in N$ is alphabetically less than the string stored in Q$.
Reading strings	
READ N$, A DATA "JOE", 18	Enter the string "JOE" in N$ and the number 25 in A.
Referencing functions	
LET I = INT (20.25)	Remove the fractional part of 20.25 and store the result, 20, in I.
LET H = SQR (A ↑ 2 + B ↑ 2)	Store the square root of A^2 plus B^2 in H.

Table 4.3   Summary of Minimal BASIC statements

PROGRAMMING PROBLEMS

4.3   Write a program to compute the sum $1+2+3+4+\ldots+N$ for any positive integer N; use a FOR loop to accumulate this sum (S1). Then compute the value S2 by the formula

$$S2 = \frac{(N+1)N}{2}$$

Have your program print both S1 and S2, compare them, and print a message indicating whether or not they are equal. Test your program for values of N = 1, 7, 25.

4.4   The Hoidy Toidy baby furniture company has ten employees, many of whom work overtime (more than 40 hours) each week. They want a payroll program that reads the weekly time records (containing employee name, hourly rate (r), and hours worked (h) for each employee) and computes the gross salary and net pay as follows:

$$g = \text{gross salary} = \begin{cases} h \times r & (\text{if } h <= 40) \\ 1.5r(h - 40) + 40r & (\text{if } h > 40) \end{cases}$$

$$p = \text{net pay} = \begin{cases} g & (\text{if } g <= \$65) \\ g - (15 + .045g) & (\text{if } g > \$65) \end{cases}$$

The program should print a five column table listing each employee's name, hourly rate, hours worked, gross salary, and net pay. The total amount of the payroll should be printed at the end. It can be computed by summing the gross salaries for all employees. Test your program on the following data:

name	rate	hours
IVORY HUNTER	3.50	35
TRACK STAR	4.50	40
SMOKEY BEAR	3.25	80
OSCAR GROUCH	6.80	10
THREE BEARS	1.50	16
POKEY PUPPY	2.65	25
FAT EDDIE	2.00	40
PUMPKIN PIE	2.65	35
SARA LEE	5.00	40
HUMAN ERASER	6.25	52

4.5   Write a program to read in a collection of integers and determine whether each is a prime number. Test your program with the four integers 7, 17, 35, 96.

4.6   Let n be a positive integer consisting of up to 10 digits, $d_{10}d_9 \ldots d_1$. Write a program to list in one column each of the digits in the number n. The rightmost digit d_1 should be listed at the top of the column. [*Hint:* If n = 3704, what is the value of *digit* as computed according to the following formula?

digit = n − INT(n/10) * 10

Test your program for values of n equal to 6, 3704, and 170498.]

4.7   An integer N is divisible by 9 if the sum of its digits is divisible by 9. Use the algorithm developed for Problem 4.6 to determine whether or not the following numbers are divisible by 9.
  N = 154368
  N = 621594
  N = 123456

4.8   Each month a bank customer deposits $50 in a savings account. The account earns 6.5 percent interest, calculated on a quarterly basis (one-fourth of 6.5 percent each quarter). Write a program to compute the total investment, total amount in the account, and the interest accrued, for each of 120 months of a 10-year period. You may assume that the rate is applied to all funds in the account at the end of a quarter regardless of when the deposits were made.

The table printed by your program should begin as follows:

MONTH	INVESTMENT	NEW AMOUNT	INTEREST	TOTAL SAVINGS
1	50.00	50.00	0.00	50.00
2	100.00	100.00	0.00	100.00
3	150.00	150.00	2.44	152.44
4	200.00	202.44	0.00	202.44
5	250.00	252.44	0.00	252.44
6	300.00	302.44	4.91	307.35
7	350.00	357.35	0.00	357.35

Keep all computations accurate to two decimal places. How would you modify your program if interest were computed on a daily basis?

4.9 Compute a table of values of $X/(1 + X^2)$ for values of $X = 1,2,3,...,50$. Your table of values should be accurate to four decimal places and should begin as follows:

X	$X / (1 + X^2)$
1	.5000
2	.4000
3	.3000
4	.2353
5	.1923
.	.
.	.
.	.

4.10 The interest paid on a savings account is compounded daily. This means that if you start with X dollars in the bank, then at the end of the first day you will have a balance of

$$X \times (1 + rate/365)$$

dollars, where rate is the annual interest rate (0.06 if the annual rate is 6 percent). At the end of the second day, you will have

$$X \times (1 + rate/365) \times (1 + rate/365)$$

dollars, and at the end of N days you will have

$$X \times (1 + rate/365)^N$$

dollars. Write a program that will process a set of data records, each of which contains values for X, rate, and N and compute the final account balance. Round your interest computation to the nearest two decimal places.

4.11 Write a data table, flow chart, and computer program to solve the following problem:
Compute the monthly payment and the total payment for a bank loan, given:
1. the amount of the loan (L),
2. the duration of the loan in months (M),
3. the interest rate for the loan (R).

Your program should read in one record at a time (each containing a loan value, months value, and rate value), perform the required computation and print the values of the loan, months, rate, and the monthly payment (P1), and total payment (P2). P1 and P2 should be rounded to two decimal places.
Test your program with at least the following data (and more if you want).

Loan	Months	Rate
16000	300	6.50
24000	360	7.50
30000	300	9.50
42000	360	8.50
22000	300	9.50
300000	240	9.25

Don't forget to first read in a value indicating how many data records you have.

Notes.
i) The formula for computing monthly payment is

$$mpaymt = \left[\frac{rate}{1200.} \times \left(1. + \frac{rate}{1200.}\right)^{months} \times loan \right] \Big/ \left[\left(1. + \frac{rate}{1200.}\right)^{months} - 1. \right]$$

ii) The formula for computing the total payment is

$$totpmt = mpaymt \times months$$

Also, you may find it helpful to introduce additional variables defined below in order to simplify the computation of the monthly payment. You can print the values of ratem and expm to see whether your program's computations are accurate.

ratem = rate/1200.
expm = (1. + ratem)^{months}

4.12 The rate of radioactive decay of an isotope is usually given in terms of the half-life, H (the time lapse required for the isotope to decay to one-half of its original mass). For the strontium 90 isotope (one of the products of nuclear fission), the rate of decay is approximately .60/H. The half-life of the strontium 90 isotope is 28 years. Compute and print, in table form, the amount remaining after each year for up to 50 years from an initial point at which 50 grams are present. [*Hint:* For each year, the amount of isotope remaining can be computed using the formula

r = amount * C$^{(Year/H)}$

where amount is 50 grams (the initial amount), and C is the constant $e^{-0.693}$ (e = 2.71828).]

4.13 Write a program that will read a data record containing two words and store them in the variables F\$ and L\$. The program will then process a collection of data items, each consisting of a single word, and print that word in field 1 if it precedes F\$, field 2 if it lies between F\$ and L\$, and field 3 if it follows L\$. At the end, print the count of all words in each field.

4.14 An examination with nine questions is given to a group of 28 students. The exam is worth 10 points and everyone turning in an answer sheet receives at least 1 point. Each problem is graded on a no credit, half credit, full credit basis. An exam score (S) and name (N\$) is entered for each student. Write a program to determine the rank for each score and print a three column list containing the name, score and rank of each student. The ranks are determined as follows:

Score	Rank
9.0-10.0	GOOD
6.0-8.5	FAIR
1.0-5.5	POOR

The program should also print the number of scores in each rank and the total number of scores.

4.15 Write a program to simulate the tossing of a coin. Use the random number generator RND, and consider any number less than 0.5 to represent tails, and any number greater than or equal to 0.5 to represent heads. Print the number produced by RND and its representation (heads or tails). [*Hint:* Repeat the call to RND—50 or 100 times. At the end, print a count of the number of heads versus the number of tails.]

THE WHILE LOOP, TOP-DOWN PROGRAMMING AND SUBROUTINES

5

5.1   INTRODUCTION

One of the most fundamental ideas of computer programming and problem solving concerns the subdivision of large and complicated problems into smaller, simpler and more manageable subproblems. Once these smaller tasks have been identified, the solution to the original problem can be specified in terms of these tasks; and the algorithms and programs for the smaller tasks can be developed separately.

We have tried to emphasize this technique of programming in all earlier examples through the use of algorithm refinement. In this process, each major part of a problem was identified in a level one flow diagram, and then broken down further into smaller problems during successive stages of refinement. A number of special control structures were introduced that enabled us to implement the solution to each of these subproblems in terms of clearly defined groups of BASIC statements.

One of these structures, the FOR loop, has been used extensively to specify the repetition of a group of statements where the repetition is controlled by a counter. Yet there are many programming problems requiring the use of loops in which the repetition can't be conveniently controlled by a counter. For this reason, many BASIC systems now support a more general loop construct as an extension of the FOR loop. This structure, often called a *conditional* or *WHILE loop structure*, is described in the first part of this chapter.

BASIC has still another feature, called a *subroutine*, which facilitates solving problems in terms of their more manageable parts. Through the use of the subroutine, we can write BASIC programs in much the same way as we refine flow diagrams. That is, we list the sequence of tasks that must be performed at a particular level, and then provide the implementation details for tasks requiring extensive refinement in separate *program modules* called subroutines. The subroutine and its application in the *top-down* approach to programming is the subject of the second portion of this chapter. The top-down technique will be illustrated through the use of several completely solved problems.

5.2   THE WHILE LOOP STRUCTURE

5.2.1   Introduction to the WHILE Loop

There is a large collection of programming problems whose solution requires the use of loops that are not conveniently controlled by a counter. For some of these loops, repetition is controlled through the use of a condition involving a test of one or more values that are computed in the body of the loop. For example, many problems of numerical approximation require the repetition of a computation until the difference between two consecutive computed values becomes very small, say, less than .000001 or 10^{-6}.

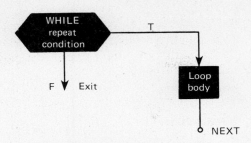

Fig. 5.1   The WHILE loop pattern.

A second kind of loop repetition control involves the use of a special input data value, called a *sentinel value*, as a signal to terminate loop repetition. In this case, loop repetition continues as long as the sentinel value has not yet been read.

Both of the above cases are characterized by the fact that the number of loop repetitions required is not known beforehand. Thus, a counter could not be used to control the repetition. In this section and the next, we will illustrate the use of a structure called the *conditional* or *WHILE loop*, in which the loop repetition specification can be independent of a counter. The flow diagram for this loop pattern is shown in Fig. 5.1.

The *repeat condition* is evaluated prior to the execution of the loop body. As long as the condition is true, the loop body is repeated. Once the condition becomes false, loop execution terminates and the algorithm continues at the point marked exit. It is important to remember that the loop repetition test for the WHILE loop structure is at the beginning of the loop. The loop body will not be executed at all if the repeat condition is false the first time that the repetition test is encountered.

Example 5.1:   The WHILE loop in Fig. 5.2 computes and prints all powers of two that are less than 1000, starting with 2^0 or 1. The last value assigned to P would be 1024; however, the last value printed would be 512.

In Fig. 5.2, the variable P is used as the loop control variable; its value controls the loop repetition process. The behavior of the loop control variable in a WHILE loop is similar to that of the FOR loop control variable; it is

  (i)   set to an initial value (step 1);
  (ii)   tested before each loop repetition (step 2);
  (iii) updated after each repetition (step 4).

However, unlike the FOR loop, these loop control steps must be explicitly shown in the WHILE loop flow diagram.

The general flow diagram pattern for the WHILE loop is shown in Fig. 5.3; it illustrates how the loop control variable (lcv) is used to control loop repetition.

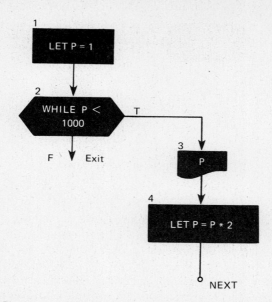

Fig. 5.2 WHILE loop for powers of 2 less than 1000.

In the next sections (5.2.2 and 5.2.3), we will discuss the implementation of the WHILE loop. We recommend that you carefully study the specific implementation available on your system. It will be helpful to become generally familiar with the other forms, although you won't have to use them.

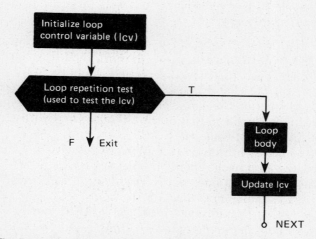

Fig. 5.3 The WHILE loop pattern illustrating the use of the lcv.

5.2.2 Dartmouth BASIC and BASIC-PLUS WHILE Loop

Unfortunately, Minimal BASIC does not have a special structure for writing WHILE loops. However, a number of extended BASIC systems, including Dartmouth BASIC and BASIC-PLUS, do support such a structure. The Dartmouth BASIC and BASIC-PLUS forms are shown in the next display.

WHILE Loop Structure

Dartmouth BASIC form: *BASIC-PLUS form:*

```
DO WHILE condition                    WHILE condition
 _____                           _____
 _____ } loop body               _____ } loop body
 _____                           _____
LOOP                                  NEXT
```

Interpretation: The condition in the header statement is evaluated first. If the condition is true, then the loop body is executed. This sequence is repeated as long as the condition evaluates to true. If the condition is false, the loop body is skipped, and execution continues with the first statement following the loop. The keyword NEXT (or LOOP) is the structure terminator.
Note: The BASIC-PLUS form shown is only available in a special version of BASIC-PLUS called BASIC-PLUS-2. The general BASIC-PLUS form is given in Section 5.2.4.

The loop in Fig. 5.2 is implemented below.

BASIC-PLUS [Dartmouth BASIC]

```
190 LET P = 1
200 [DO] WHILE P < 1000
210    PRINT P,
220    LET P = P * 2
230 [LOOP] NEXT
240 END

RUN

1          2          4          8          16
32         64         128        256        512
```

The BASIC-PLUS form is shown with the changes required for Dartmouth BASIC indicated in brackets: the keyword DO must be inserted before WHILE in the loop header and the loop terminator is LOOP (not NEXT). The three loop control steps are line 190 (lcv initialization), line 200 (lcv test) and line 220 (lcv update).

5.2.3   Minimal BASIC WHILE Loop

If your system does not support a special WHILE loop structure, then we suggest that you use transfer and conditional transfer instructions to implement a WHILE loop. The Minimal BASIC implementation of Fig. 5.2 is shown next.

```
190       LET P = 1
200 REM WHILE P < 1000
210       IF P > = 1000 THEN 250
220          PRINT P,
230             LET P = P * 2
240       GOTO 200
250 REM
```

The general form of the Minimal BASIC WHILE loop is shown in the next display.

WHILE loop

Minimal BASIC form:

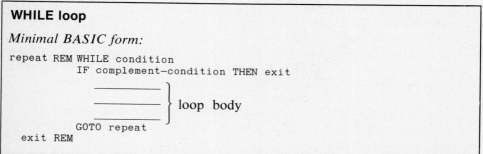

Interpretation: The labels repeat and exit represent the numbers of the statements immediately preceding and following the loop, respectively. The complement of the loop repetition condition is evaluated first. If the complement is false (loop repetition condition true), the loop body is executed. This sequence is repeated as long as the complement evaluates to false. When the complement evaluates to true (loop repetition condition false), the loop body is skipped and execution resumes with the first statement following the loop.

Example 5.2:   The programs shown below read character strings into the string variable C$ and then print the contents of C$. These steps are repeated as long as the string that is read is not equal to "DONE". If these programs were run with the data

```
DATA "FUN", "SUN", "ONE", "NONE", "DONE"
```

the output would appear as

```
FUN SUN ONE NONE
```

BASIC-PLUS Program [*Dartmouth BASIC*]

```
110 READ C$
120 [DO] WHILE C$ < > "DONE"
130    PRINT C$;
140    READ C$
150 [LOOP] NEXT
```

Minimal BASIC Program

```
110     READ C$
120 REM WHILE C$ < > "DONE"
130     IF C$ = "DONE" THEN 170
140        PRINT C$;
150        READ C$
160     GOTO 120
170 REM
180     END
```

Example 5.3: Since the WHILE loop is a general looping structure, we should be able to implement a FOR loop using a WHILE loop. This process is illustrated in Fig. 5.4 for a loop that computes the sum of all odd numbers from 1 through N. The WHILE loop implementation is understandably longer as separate statements must be provided for the initialization (line 140), test (line 150), and update (line 170) of the loop control variable I.

```
100     PRINT "ENTER N"
105     INPUT N
110 REM
120 REM COMPUTE SUM OF ODD NUMBERS FROM 1 TO N
130     LET S = 0
140     FOR I = 1 TO N STEP 2
150        LET S = S + I
160     NEXT I
170 REM
180     PRINT "SUM = "; S
190     END
```

```
100     PRINT "ENTER N"
105     INPUT N
110 REM
120 REM COMPUTE SUM OF ODD NUMBERS FROM 1 TO N
130     LET S = 0
140     LET I = 1
150     [DO] WHILE I <= N
160        LET S = S + I
170        LET I = I + 2
180     [LOOP] NEXT
190 REM
200     PRINT "SUM = "; S
210     END
```

Fig. 5.4 FOR loop (top) implemented by a WHILE loop (bottom).

In Section 5.3, we illustrate the design and implementation of algorithms involving the use of the WHILE loop structure. Two completely solved problems are presented: one illustrates the use of a sentinel value for loop control; the other shows how values computed in the loop body may be used to control loop repetition.

Exercise 5.1:   List the values printed as the loops below are executed.

a.
```
110 FOR I = 5 TO -5 STEP -2
120     PRINT I
130 NEXT I
```

b.
```
110 READ P$
120 [DO] WHILE P$ <> "ME"
130     PRINT P$
140     READ P$
150 [LOOP] NEXT
160 DATA "I", "HIM", "HER", "IT", "YOU", "ME"
```

c.
```
110 LET N = 77
120 LET D = 3
130 [DO] WHILE D <= SQR (N)
140     PRINT D
150     LET D = D + 2
160 [LOOP] NEXT
```

Exercise 5.2:   Write a WHILE loop to read a collection of character strings into the string variable C$ and print C$ if it begins with the letters A-H. Loop repetition should continue as long as C$ is not equal to ".".

Exercise 5.3:   Write a WHILE loop to read a collection of numbers into the variable V, multiply each V by the next power of 2 (P), and print P, V, and the computed result, R. (The first value of V is to be multiplied by 2^0; the second value by 2^1, the third by 2^2, and so on.) Repeat the loop as long as R is less than 100,000.

Exercise 5.4:   Use a WHILE loop structure and write the flow diagram and program for a loop that will find the largest cumulative product of the numbers 1, 2, 3, 4, ... that is smaller than 10,000.

5.2.4   Additional Extended Form of the WHILE Loop

In many versions of BASIC-PLUS and in UBASIC (developed for Sperry-Univac computers), the WHILE loop header is simply an expanded form of the FOR loop header. The implementation of Example 5.1 is shown next using this form of WHILE loop.

```
100 LET P = 1
110 FOR Z9 = 0 WHILE P < 1000
120     PRINT P,
130     LET P = P * 2
140 NEXT Z9
150 END
```

As in the other implementations, the value of P controls loop repetition (WHILE P < 1000). The counter variable Z9 is initialized to zero and increased by one after each repetition, however, its value has no effect on loop behavior.

We will continue to use the BASIC-PLUS-2 form described in Section 5.2.2. If you have BASIC-PLUS and not BASIC-PLUS-2, remember to change the loop header and terminator as shown above.

5.3 ILLUSTRATIONS OF ALGORITHM DEVELOPMENT USING THE WHILE LOOP STRUCTURE

5.3.1 Use of the Sentinel Value

Often we don't know exactly how many data items there are to be processed until just before running a program. We might be handed a collection of data items and asked to count them in order to determine the value of a variable such as N (number of items).

One way to avoid this trying task is to insert a sentinel value at the end of the data collection. A sentinel value can be used to signal the program that all of the data items have been read into the computer memory and processed. A sentinel value is a number or string that would not normally occur as a data item for the program. When that value is read, it can be recognized by the program as an indication that all of the actual data items have been processed.

The concept of a sentinel value can be incorporated in the WHILE loop pattern as shown in Fig. 5.5. (See also Example 5.2.)

The variable into which each data item is read acts as a loop control variable. It must be initialized using a read step (step 1) prior to the first test

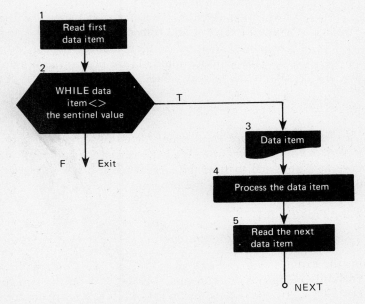

Fig. 5.5 Use of the sentinel value in WHILE loop pattern.

of the repeat condition, and its value must be updated during each execution of the loop body, using a second read (step 5). This is normally the last step in the loop, and is executed after all other processing of the current value has been performed. We illustrate these and other points concerning the use of the sentinel value in the following problem.

Problem 5.1:   Write a program that will read all of the scores for a course examination and compute and print the largest of these scores.

Discussion: In order to gain some insight into a solution of this problem, we should consider how we would go about finding the largest of a long list of numbers without the computer. Most likely we would read down the list of numbers, one at a time, and remember or "keep track of" the largest number that we had found at each point. If, at some point in the list, we should encounter a number, S, that is larger than the largest number found prior to that point, then we would make S the new largest number, and remember it rather than the previously found number.

An example of how this might proceed is given in the monologue shown in Fig. 5.6.

Test scores	Effect of each score
35	"Since 35 is the first number, we will consider it to be the largest number initially."
12	"12 is smaller than 35, so 35 is still largest."
68	"68 is larger than 35. Therefore, 35 cannot be the largest item. Forget it and remember 68."
8	"8 is smaller than 68, so 68 is still the largest."
−1	"−1 is the sentinel value. There are no more numbers, so 68 is the largest value."

Fig. 5.6   Finding the largest of four numbers (a monologue).

We can use this procedure as a model for constructing an algorithm for solving Problem 5.1 on the computer. We will instruct the computer to process a single score at a time and to save the largest score it has processed at any given point during the execution of the program in the variable L.

Data Table for Problem 5.1

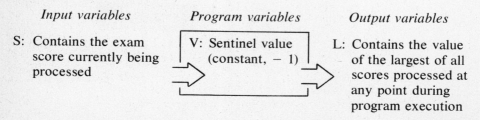

Input variables	Program variables	Output variables
S: Contains the exam score currently being processed	V: Sentinel value (constant, − 1)	L: Contains the value of the largest of all scores processed at any point during program execution

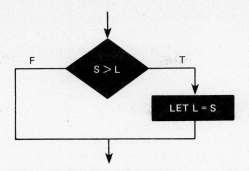

Fig. 5.7   Updating current largest score (L).

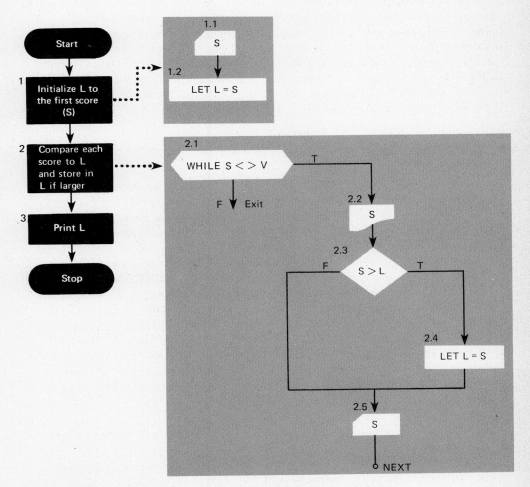

Fig. 5.8   Flow diagrams for largest score problem (5.1).

Fig. 5.7 shows the flow diagram representation of the algorithm step to compare each new score to L and change L if a new largest score is found. This constitutes the main task to be performed and it will have to be repeated once for each score entered.

In order to terminate the loop repetition, we will use a sentinel value of − 1, which is not within the possible range of scores for the exam. The use of the sentinel value is required since we do not know how many test scores are to be processed.

Figure 5.8 shows the flow diagrams for this problem. Note that L is initialized to the first score entered (step 1.2) since, in the beginning, this is the largest, and only, score processed. In this algorithm, it is assumed that at least one valid data item is entered before the sentinel value.

From the flow diagrams, we see that S is the loop control variable. Each time a score is read in, it must first be compared to the sentinel value, V, in order to determine when loop execution is complete. The repeat condition in this solution is "score not equal to sentinel value." Prior to performing this test for the first time, we must initialize the loop control variable S via an INPUT statement (step 1.1). Finally, at the end of the loop, we must update S (also via an INPUT statement, step 2.5). The BASIC program for this problem and a sample run are shown in Fig. 5.9.

Program Form and Style

In Fig. 5.9, we have shown the BASIC-PLUS version of the program for Problem 5.1. (The material in brackets is not part of the BASIC-PLUS implementation.) Shading and indentation are used to emphasize the structure of the program. As before, shading is used to separate the function or purpose of each control structure from its implementation details and to highlight the Dartmouth BASIC form.

The changes required for the Dartmouth BASIC WHILE loop are indicated in brackets: the keyword DO should be inserted before WHILE in the loop header, and the terminator should be LOOP instead of NEXT. To implement the Minimal BASIC WHILE loop, lines 240 and 330 should be replaced as shown on the right.

In the program in Fig. 5.9, a single-alternative decision structure is nested inside the WHILE loop. The Minimal BASIC header statement is shown to the right of line 250. If the remark is omitted, this structure could be implemented in Dartmouth BASIC or BASIC-PLUS as

```
IF S > L THEN LET L = S
```

Exercise 5.5: What would happen in the execution of the largest value program (Fig. 5.9) if we accidentally omitted all data except the sentinel value?

```
110 REM FIND THE LARGEST OF A COLLECTION OF EXAM SCORES
120     PRINT "LARGEST VALUE PROBLEM"
130 REM
140 REM DEFINE PROGRAM PARAMETERS (SENTINEL VALUE)
150     LET V = -1
160 REM
170 REM INITIALIZE. L TO FIRST SCORE
180 REM
190     PRINT "ENTER FIRST SCORE"
200     INPUT S
210     LET L = S
220 REM
230 REM WHILE SCORE IS NOT SENTINEL VALUE (V), PROCESS SCORE
240     [DO] WHILE S < > V                [IF S = V THEN 340]
250         IF S > L THEN 260 ELSE 290    [IF S <= L THEN 290]
260 REM     THEN
270             REM REDEFINE LARGEST VALUE
280             LET L = S
290 REM     IFEND
300         PRINT "ENTER NEXT SCORE OR -1"
310         INPUT S
330     [LOOP] NEXT                       [GOTO 230]
340 REM
350 REM ALL SCORES PROCESSED. PRINT LARGEST
355     PRINT
360     PRINT "LARGEST EXAM SCORE = "; L
370 REM
380     END

RUN

LARGEST VALUE PROBLEM
ENTER FIRST SCORE
?75
ENTER NEXT SCORE OR -1
?86
ENTER NEXT SCORE OR -1
?97
ENTER NEXT SCORE OR -1
?56
ENTER NEXT SCORE OR -1
?66
ENTER NEXT SCORE OR -1
?-1

LARGEST EXAM SCORE =  97
```

Fig. 5.9 Program and sample output from largest value program.

Exercise 5.6: Modify the data table, flow diagram and program for the largest value problem, to count and print the number of scores processed.

Exercise 5.7: In Problem 5.1, we could have initialized L to 0 instead of the first exam score; however, initializing L to 0 would not always work. Provide a sample set of data for which initializing L to 0 would cause the program to produce the wrong answer.

Exercise 5.8:   Modify the largest value problem flow diagrams and data table so that the smallest score (M) and the largest score are found and printed. Also, compute the range, R, of the scores (R = L − M).

Exercise 5.9:   On January 1, the water supply tank for the town of Death Valley contained 10,000 gallons of water. The town used 183 gallons of water a week and it expected no rain in the near future. Write a loop to compute and print the amount of water remaining in the tank at the end of each week. Your loop should terminate when there is insufficient water to last a week.

5.3.2   Controlling Loop Repetition with Computational Results

The WHILE loop structure is well suited for loops in which the repetition condition involves a test of values that are computed in the loop body. For example, in processing checking account transactions, we might want to continue processing transactions as long as the account balance is positive or zero, and stop and print a message when the balance becomes negative.

In problems of this sort, the loop control variable serves a dual purpose: it is used for storage of a computational result as well as for controlling loop repetition. Occasionally, more than one computed value will be involved in the repetition test as illustrated in the following problem.

Problem 5.2:   Two cyclists are involved in a race. The first has a headstart because the second cyclist is capable of a faster pace. We will write a program to print out the distance from the starting line that each cyclist has travelled. These distances will be printed for each half hour of the race, beginning when the second cyclist departs, and continuing as long as the first cyclist is still ahead.

Data Table for Problem 5.2

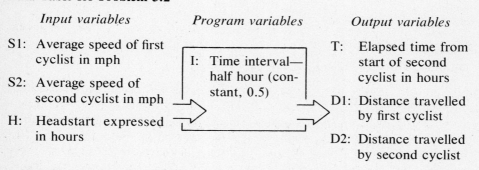

Input variables	*Program variables*	*Output variables*
S1: Average speed of first cyclist in mph	I: Time interval— half hour (constant, 0.5)	T: Elapsed time from start of second cyclist in hours
S2: Average speed of second cyclist in mph		D1: Distance travelled by first cyclist
H: Headstart expressed in hours		D2: Distance travelled by second cyclist

Discussion: This problem illustrates the use of the computer to *simulate* what would happen in a real world situation. We can get an estimate of the progress of the cyclists before the race even begins and perhaps use this information to set up monitoring or aid stations.

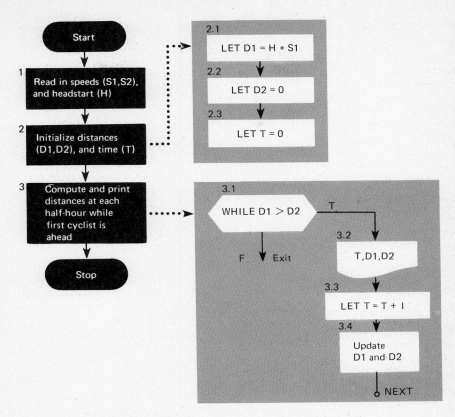

Fig. 5.10   Flow diagrams for cycle race (Problem 5.2).

The loop-repetition test will involve a comparison of the total distances travelled by each cyclist. We will make use of the formula

$$\text{distance} = \text{speed} \times \text{elapsed time}$$

in the computation of distance travelled. We will have to compute the distance travelled by the first cyclist before the second cyclist departs and the incremental distance travelled by each cyclist during each subsequent half hour.

The level one flow diagram and first refinement are shown in Fig. 5.10. The initial value of D1 (first cyclist's headstart) is computed as the product of speed (S1) and the duration of the headstart (H). D2 is initially zero. The loop-repetition test involves a comparison of the two output variables D1 and D2, both of which are updated at the end of the loop (step 3.4).

To refine step 3.4, we must compute the incremental distance travelled in each time interval and add it to the distance traveled prior to the current time interval. This computation can be described as

$$distance = distance + incremental\ distance$$

where

$$incremental\ distance = speed \times time\ interval$$

To carry out these computations for each cyclist, we must introduce two new program variables I1 and I2.

```
110 REM CYCLE RACE PROBLEM
120     PRINT "CYCLE RACE PROBLEM"
130 REM DEFINE PROGRAM PARAMETERS
135     LET I = 0.5
140 REM
150 REM READ DATA ITEMS
160     READ S1, S2, H
170     DATA 12, 15, 1
180 REM
190     PRINT "FIRST CYCLIST SPEED = "; S1
200     PRINT
210     PRINT "SECOND CYCLIST SPEED = "; S2
220     PRINT
230     PRINT "FIRST CYCLIST'S HEADSTART IN HOURS = "; H
240     PRINT
250 REM
260 REM COMPUTE DISTANCE INCREMENTS
270     LET I1 = S1 * I
280     LET I2 = S2 * I
290 REM
300 REM PRINT TABLE HEADING
310     PRINT
320     PRINT "TIME", "DISTANCE 1", "DISTANCE 2"
330 REM
340 REM INITIALIZATION FOR LOOP
350     LET D1 = S1 * H
360     LET D2 = 0
370     LET T = 0
380 REM
390 REM WHILE D1 > D2
400 REM COMPUTE DISTANCES PER HALF HOUR
410     [DO] WHILE D1 > D2                    [IF D1 <= D2 THEN 470]
420         PRINT T, D1, D2
430         LET T = T + I
440         LET D1 = D1 + I1
450         LET D2 = D2 + I2
460     [LOOP] NEXT                           [GOTO 390]
470 REM
480     PRINT "CYCLIST 2 PASSES CYCLIST 1 DURING NEXT HALF HOUR"
490 REM
500     END
```

Fig. 5.11a Program for Problem 5.2.

5.3   **Illustrations of algorithm development**   **145**

Program variables

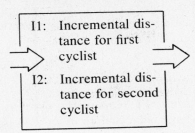

I1:   Incremental distance for first cyclist

I2:   Incremental distance for second cyclist

Given these variables, we can refine step 3.4 as follows:

```
LET I1 = S1 * I
LET D1 = D1 + I1
LET I2 = S2 * I
LET D2 = D2 + I2
```

At this point we note that the value of I1 and I2 will never vary while the loop is repeated. They remain the same because S1 and S2 never change and I is a program constant. There is consequently no reason to continually recompute the values of I1 and I2 for each execution of loop 3.1. This pair of computations should be removed from the loop and performed prior to loop entry rather than in step 3.4.

This change in the algorithm is reflected in the final program for Problem 5.2, shown in Fig. 5.11a. (Sample output is shown in Fig. 5.11b.) The computation of I1 and I2 immediately follows the definition of the variables S1 and S2. The technique of removing computations from the body of a loop yields

```
CYCLE RACE PROBLEM
FIRST CYCLIST SPEED = 12

SECOND CYCLIST SPEED = 15

FIRST CYCLIST'S HEADSTART IN HOURS = 1

TIME          DISTANCE 1        DISTANCE 2
0             12                0
.5            18                7.5
1             24                15
1.5           30                22.5
2             36                30
2.5           42                37.5
3             48                45
3.5           54                52.5
CYCLIST 2 PASSES CYCLSIT 1 DURING NEXT HALF HOUR
```

Fig. 5.11b Sample output for program 5.11a.

a faster-executing program because the multiplications required to compute I1 and I2 are performed only once, instead of many times. In general, any computations producing the same result for each repetition of a loop should be removed from the loop in this manner.

5.3.3   Program Parameters

The program parameter, 0.5, representing the time interval between measurements could easily have been written *in-line* whenever it was referenced; for example, we could have written

$$270 \ LET \ I1 = S1 * 0.5$$

rather than

$$270 \ LET \ I1 = S1 * I$$

However, we used a program variable, I, to represent this parameter in order to make any subsequent program modification easier. If we later decide to take measurements every 20 minutes (one-third of an hour), we need only change one line

$$135 \ LET \ I = 1 / 3$$

instead of all lines which use the value of I (lines 270, 280, and 430).

5.3.4   Reminders for Algorithm Development Using the WHILE Loop

The flow diagram pattern for the loops used in Problems 5.1 and 5.2 are identical to the pattern shown in Fig. 5.3. In addition, the steps leading to the construction of the WHILE loops seen so far are the same. These steps are summarized in the following list.

1. Complete a description of what must be done in the loop (the loop body).
2. Identify the loop control variable. This variable may already be a part of the loop body such as S in Problem 5.1, Fig. 5.8, or it may need to be added for the specific purpose of loop control.
3. Set up the loop control variable test to be performed before each execution of the loop.
4. Initialize the loop control variable just prior to the test.
5. Update the loop control variable as the last step of the loop.

Not all loops will fit the category just described by the above pattern and loop construction steps. However, a significant percentage of the loops you will write do fit this category, so you should familiarize yourself with both the pattern and the construction steps.

5.4 TOP-DOWN PROGRAMMING

5.4.1 Top-Down Programming and Subroutines

Early in Chapter 2, we indicated that a desirable goal in problem solving was to break a complicated problem into independent subproblems and work on these subproblems separately. We have practiced this technique of problem decomposition throughout the text by drawing a level one flow diagram outlining the subproblems to be solved. We have then separately refined each of these subproblems to fill in the details of an algorithm, subdividing each subproblem still further when necessary. This technique of specifying algorithms through successive refinement is often referred to as *top-down programming*.

Up to now, the logic, or flow of control in the sample programs was relatively straightforward and easy to follow. Most programs consisted of short sequences of structures with little or no nesting. We now have the tools and the skills to write more complex programs involving several levels of nesting. Such programs can become quite cumbersome and difficult to follow unless proper procedures are followed in their design and implementation.

We have seen how the practice of top-down programming can aid in the description of the flow of control in programs; we have used this technique in designing the algorithms in the text by drawing level one flow diagrams and successive refinements. Unfortunately, we have not been able to carry this top-down process through to the implementation of our programs. What we would like to do is implement our programs in the same manner in which the flow diagram was designed. This involves writing an initial program segment (the *main program*) that looks much like a level one flow diagram. Within the main program, each of the subproblems to be solved may be referenced by line number. The specific program statements corresponding to each subproblem are written together as a separate program module called a *subroutine*. The subroutine is provided in a separate section at the end of the main program rather than being imbedded within the main program itself. If further problem subdivision is necessary, each of the subproblem program segments may be written top-down as well.

To be able to write programs in the manner just described, we must have a structure available for designating sequences of statements that are to be treated as subroutines. We must also have a statement that can be used to request the execution of a subroutine.

In BASIC, there are three different structures available for writing subroutines. One of these structures is actually called a *subroutine*; the others are the *user-defined function* and the *subprogram*. In the next section, we will describe and illustrate the use of the BASIC subroutine; in Chapter 8 we will provide an in-depth discussion of subprograms and user-defined functions.

5.4.2   Use of Subroutines

In order to illustrate the top-down approach to programming and the use of subroutines, we will reexamine the widget inventory control problem from Chapter 3 (Problem 3.4). The level one flow diagram from Fig. 3.13 is redrawn in Fig. 5.12a and the main program is shown in Fig. 5.12b.

The main program parallels the level one flow diagram in that it lists the sequence in which the major subtasks of the program are to be carried out. Each of these subtasks is either written as part of the main program (steps 1,

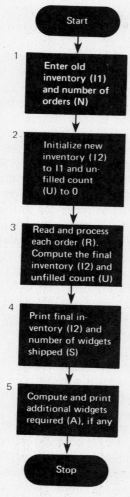

Fig. 5.12a   Level one flow diagram for Problem 3.4.

```
110 REM WIDGET INVENTORY CONTROL PROBLEM (WITH SUBROUTINES)
120     PRINT "WIDGET INVENTORY CONTROL PROBLEM"
130 REM
140 REM ENTER OLD INVENTORY (I1) AND NUMBER OF ORDERS (N)
150     PRINT "ENTER OLD INVENTORY ";
160     INPUT I1
170     PRINT "ENTER NUMBER OF ORDERS ";
180     INPUT N
185     PRINT
190 REM
200 REM INITIALIZATION OF NEW INVENTORY (I2)
205 REM AND UNFILLED COUNT (U)
210   , LET I2 = I1
220     LET U = 0
230 REM
240 REM READ AND PROCESS EACH ORDER
250     GOSUB 1010
260 REM
270 REM PRINT FINAL INVENTORY COUNT
280     PRINT
290     PRINT "FINAL INVENTORY = "; I2
295 REM
300 REM COMPUTE AND PRINT NUMBER OF WIDGETS SHIPPED (S)
310 REM AND ADDITIONAL WIDGETS (A) IF NEEDED
320     LET S = I1 - I2
330     PRINT S; "WIDGETS SHIPPED"
340     IF U > 0 THEN 350 ELSE 380            [IF U <= 0 THEN 380]
350 REM THEN
355         REM ADDITIONAL WIDGETS NEEDED
360         LET A = U - I2
370         PRINT A; " NEW WIDGETS NEEDED"
380 REM IFEND
390 REM
400     STOP
```

Fig. 5.12b Main program with subroutine calls for Problem 3.4.

2, 4 and 5) or implemented as a separate program module or *subroutine* (step 3) and referenced or *called* in the main program. Normally, only subtasks that are complicated enough to require refinement are implemented as subroutines.

5.4.3 Subroutines in BASIC

A subroutine in BASIC is a sequence of statements grouped together as a separate unit or *module* within a BASIC program. The *entry*, or transfer of control to a subroutine, is accomplished through the execution of a *subroutine call* or GOSUB statement (line 250 of Fig. 5.12b). The line number (1010) indicated in the GOSUB statement specifies the location of the first statement of the subroutine. After the subroutine is executed, control is returned to the first statement in the main program following the subroutine call.

The subroutine for the new version of the widget inventory control problem is provided in Fig. 5.13. These statements should be typed immediately

```
1010 REM SUBROUTINE TO READ AND PROCESS EACH ORDER (R)
1020 REM FILL ORDER IF INVENTORY SUFFICIENT
1030 REM OTHERWISE, INDICATE NOT FILLED
1031 REM
1040 REM PROCESS EACH OF THE N ORDERS
1045     FOR C = 1 TO N
1050     PRINT "ENTER AN ORDER"
1060     INPUT R
1080        REM DECIDE IF THE ORDER CAN BE FILLED
1090        IF R <= I2 THEN 1095 ELSE 1140          [IF R > I2 THEN 1140]
1095 REM    THEN
1100            REM SUFFICIENT INVENTORY TO FILL ORDER
1110            PRINT R; " FILLED"
1120            LET I2 = I2 - R
1130        GOTO 1170
1140 REM    ELSE
1145            REM ORDER NOT FILLED. EXCEEDS INVENTORY
1150            PRINT R; " NOT FILLED"
1160            LET U = U + R
1170 REM    IFEND
1180     NEXT C
1190 REM
1200     RETURN
1210 REM
1220 REM END OF PROGRAM
1230     END
```

Fig. 5.13 Subroutine called by main program in Fig. 5.12 (Problem 3.4).

following the statements in Fig. 5.12b as they are part of the same BASIC program. You should compare the new program (Figs. 5.12b and 5.13) with the original program (Fig. 3.14) and the flow diagram from which it was derived (Fig. 3.13).

As illustrated in Fig. 5.13, a BASIC subroutine must be terminated by a RETURN statement (line 1200). The group of statements from the first line of a subroutine (line 1010) through the RETURN constitutes the *subroutine definition*.

The statement GOSUB 1010, causes an immediate transfer of control to the subroutine at line 1010. Following this transfer, the subroutine is executed; exit from the subroutine occurs when the subroutine RETURN statement is executed. RETURN causes an immediate transfer back to the first statement following the subroutine call (line 260).

The actual sequence of statement execution in the program is listed below.

1.   Main program: lines 110–250.
     Steps 1 and 2 of the flow diagram (Fig. 5.12a) are performed and the subroutine is called.

2. Subroutine: lines 1010–1200.
   Step 3 of the flow diagram is performed and control is returned to the main program.
3. Main program: lines 260–400.
   Steps 4 and 5 of the flow diagram are performed. Program execution is terminated at line 400.

In Fig. 5.13, the END statement is the last statement in the BASIC program as always. However, in this case, the END statement only serves to indicate to the BASIC compiler that the last program statement has been processed; the STOP statement in the main program (line 400) actually terminates program execution.

The STOP Statement

Minimal BASIC form:

STOP

Interpretation: Terminates execution of the program.

5.4.4   Review of Subroutines

The use of subroutines enables the programmer to implement a flow diagram in a modular fashion. Each subtask requiring refinement may be implemented as a separate subroutine that is called or referenced in the main program. The decision as to whether a subtask in the level one flow diagram should be included as part of the main program or implemented separately as a subroutine depends on the complexity of the refinement. Step 3 of Fig. 5.12a was implemented as a subroutine since its refinement consists of a FOR loop with an IF-THEN-ELSE nested in the loop body; step 5 was implemented directly in the main program since its refinement is a relatively straightforward decision step.

As we indicated earlier, each subroutine is a separate program module that can only be entered through execution of a GOSUB statement. Consequently, all subroutines must be defined following a STOP, a RETURN or a GOTO statement. The first statement of each subroutine definition will follow the last statement of the main program or the preceding subroutine definition. The END statement comes after the last subroutine RETURN statement.

The rules for defining and referencing a subroutine in BASIC are summarized in the following display.

Subroutine: Definition, Entry, and Exit

Minimal BASIC form:

Subroutine Definition—a group of BASIC statements that is entered only through the use of a GOSUB statement and exited only through the use of a RETURN. The first statement of the subroutine must be preceded by a STOP, RETURN, or unconditional transfer (GOTO) statement, which serves to isolate the subroutine from the rest of the program.

The Minimal BASIC Subroutine Call (for subroutine entry)

```
GOSUB line
```

This statement causes an immediate transfer of control to the indicated line, the first statement in the subroutine.

The Minimal BASIC Subroutine Return (for subroutine exit)

```
RETURN
```

This statement causes an immediate transfer of control to the first statement following the GOSUB that was used for subroutine entry.

Exercise 5.10:   Implement Problem 4.1 (see Fig. 4.2a) using the top-down approach. Step 3 in the level one flow diagram should be implemented as a subroutine.

5.5 APPLICATION OF TOP-DOWN PROGRAMMING

In this section, we will further illustrate top-down programming and the use of subroutines by studying two sample programs.

5.5.1 A Simple Computer-Aided Instruction (CAI) Program

Example 5.4:   Figures 5.14a and b show an example of a program that provides an interactive question and answer facility for students practicing multiplication. A WHILE loop (loop control variable G$) is used to control loop repetition. In this program, the INT and random number (RND) functions are used to determine two random integers (M1 and M2) between 0 and 99 (see lines 300 and 310). (Recall that RND produces a random value between 0 and 1. Multiplying by 100 moves the decimal point two positions to the right and INT removes the fractional part of a positive number.) These integers are then printed at the terminal; the student is asked to compute and type in the product (R) of these integers. The subroutine at line 1010 then computes the actual answer (A), compares it to R, and informs the student whether or not the response (R) is correct. A sample run is shown in Fig. 5.14c.

```
110 REM  A CAI PROGRAM FOR MULTIPLICATION DRILL
120       PRINT "THIS IS A PROGRAM TO AID YOU IN IMPROVING"
130       PRINT "YOUR MULTIPLICATION SKILLS"
140       PRINT
150       PRINT "THE COMPUTER WILL TYPE TWO INTEGERS BETWEEN 0 AND 99,"
160       PRINT "AND THEN PROMPT YOU FOR AN ANSWER. IF YOUR ANSWER"
170       PRINT "IS WRONG, THE COMPUTER WILL GIVE YOU THE CORRECT ANSWER"
180       PRINT
190       PRINT "YOU MAY CONTINUE THIS DRILL AS LONG AS YOU WISH BY"
200       PRINT "TYPING 'YES' WHEN ASKED IF YOU WISH TO CONTINUE."
210       PRINT "WHEN YOU DECIDE TO STOP, TYPE 'NO'."
220       PRINT
230 REM
240 REM  LOOP FOR REPEATING THE DRILL
260       LET G$ = "YES"
270 REM  WHILE G$ = "YES" CONTINUE DRILL
280       [DO] WHILE G$ = "YES"              [IF G$ <> "YES" THEN 430]
290           REM DETERMINE NUMBERS TO BE MULTIPLIED
300           LET M1 = INT (100 * RND)
310           LET M2 = INT (100 * RND)
320           REM PRINT OUT NUMBERS AND GET STUDENT RESPONSE
330           PRINT "WHAT IS THE VALUE OF "; M1; " * "; M2;
340           INPUT R
350           REM COMPUTE M1 * M2 AND COMPARE TO R
370           GOSUB 1010
380           REM ASK TO CONTINUE OR NOT
385           PRINT
390           PRINT "DO YOU WISH TO CONTINUE";
400           INPUT G$
410       [LOOP] NEXT                        [GOTO 270]
430 REM
440       PRINT "END OF DRILL. BYE NOW."
450 REM
460       STOP
```

Fig. 5.14a   Main program for CAI example.

```
1010 REM  SUBROUTINE TO COMPUTE ACTUAL ANSWER (A)
1020 REM  COMPARE A TO STUDENT RESPONSE (R) AND
1030 REM  INDICATE IF RESPONSE IS CORRECT
1040 REM
1050       LET A = M1 * M2
1060       IF A = R THEN 1065 ELSE 1100      [IF A <> R THEN 1100]
1065 REM  THEN
1070           REM A = R —— ANSWER IS CORRECT
1080           PRINT "CORRECT"
1090       GOTO 1120
1100 REM  ELSE
1105           REM ANSWER IS WRONG
1110           PRINT "INCORRECT. "; M1; " * "; M2; "="; A
1120 REM  IFEND
1130 REM
1140       RETURN
1150 REM
1160       END
```

Fig. 5.14b   Subroutine for CAI example.

```
RUN

THIS IS A PROGRAM TO AID YOU IN IMPROVING
YOUR MULTIPLICATION SKILLS

THE COMPUTER WILL TYPE TWO INTEGERS BETWEEN 0 AND 99,
AND THEN PROMPT YOU FOR AN ANSWER. IF YOUR ANSWER
IS WRONG, THE COMPUTER WILL GIVE YOU THE CORRECT ANSWER

YOU MAY CONTINUE THIS DRILL AS LONG AS YOU WISH BY
TYPING 'YES' WHEN ASKED IF YOU WISH TO CONTINUE.
WHEN YOU DECIDE TO STOP, TYPE 'NO'.

WHAT IS THE VALUE OF 6 * 39 ?200
INCORRECT. 6 * 39 = 234

DO YOU WISH TO CONTINUE ?YES
WHAT IS THE VALUE OF 90 * 17 ? 1530
CORRECT

DO YOU WISH TO CONTINUE ?NO
END OF DRILL. BYE NOW.
```

Fig. 5.14c   Sample output for CAI example.

Programs such as this, which provide computer-aided instruction (CAI), can be effective tools for classroom use in any educational environment requiring the development of fundamental skills through repetitive drill.

Exercise 5.11:   Revise the subroutine shown in Fig. 5.14b to give the student three chances to produce the correct answer. For each incorrect answer, have the program give the student a prompting message indicating that the answer was "TOO LARGE" or "TOO SMALL," and encourage the student to try again. After the third try, print the correct answer.

5.5.2 Checking Account Transaction Problem

Problem 5.3:   Write a program to process the checks and deposit slips for a single checking account at the close of each month. The date, amount and type of each transaction should be printed out along with information that summarizes the monthly transactions.

Discussion: Before developing the algorithm, we must first identify the input information that will be available and determine the desired form of the printout. The input to our program will be in the form of a sequence of *records* of information. For each account to be processed, the records are as follows:
  1. month record
  2. header record (one for each account, containing three data items)
        account number
        depositor name
        starting balance

3. one or more transaction records for each account (each transaction
    record contains four data items)
        account number
        transaction type code
            "C" for check transaction
            "D" for deposit transaction
            "Z" for sentinel transaction
        amount of transaction
        date of transaction
    A sample data collection is shown in Figure 5.15. The month, the depos-
itor's name, the transaction type code and the transaction date are all treated
as strings.

```
DATA "SEPTEMBER"           (month record)
DATA 11385, "GREG LUZINSKI", 85.67          (header record)
DATA 11385, "C", 79.15, "9/9"    ⎫
DATA 11380, "D", 200.00, "9/10"  ⎬  (transaction records)
DATA 11385, "D", 3.57, "9/11"    ⎪
DATA 11385, "C", 125.67, "9/12"  ⎭
DATA 11385, "Z", 0, "0"          (sentinel transaction record)
```

Fig. 5.15 Sample collection of data records for Problem 5.3.

For each depositor, the final printout should list all transactions in column
form with summary statistics, as shown below:

```
CHECKING ACCOUNT PROBLEM
GREG LUZINSKI ACCOUNT NO. 11385
TRANSACTION RECORD FOR SEPTEMBER

DATE           CHECK        DEPOSIT      PENALTY
9/9            79.15
9/11                        3.57
9/12           125.67                    5 (OVERDRAFT)

STARTING BALANCE  85.67     FINAL BALANCE  5.09
NO. OF CHECKS PAID  1       NO. OF DEPOSITS  1
NO. OF OVERDRAWN CHECKS  1
INVALID TRANSACTION PRESENT
```

This printout indicates that checks were written on the 9th and 12th of the
month and a deposit was made on the 11th. Furthermore, the check on Sep-
tember 12 was for more money than the account balance; consequently, it was
not paid and a $5 penalty was assessed. The message shown in the last line is
printed when one or more transaction cards containing incorrect data (such as
an invalid account number or type code) have been read; all such transaction
cards are ignored (e.g., the transaction record for 9/10 in Fig. 5.15 contains
the wrong account number).

    The data table is shown next, and the flow diagrams are shown in Figs.
5.16a and b.

Data Table for Problem 5.3

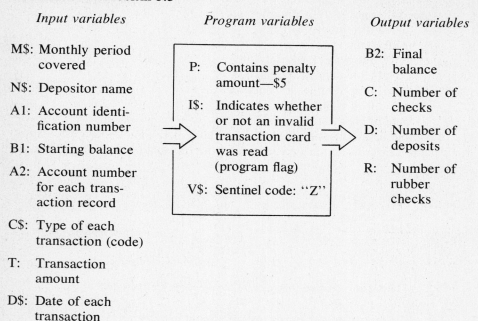

Input variables	Program variables	Output variables
M$: Monthly period covered	P: Contains penalty amount—$5	B2: Final balance
N$: Depositor name	I$: Indicates whether or not an invalid transaction card was read (program flag)	C: Number of checks
A1: Account identification number		D: Number of deposits
B1: Starting balance		R: Number of rubber checks
A2: Account number for each transaction record	V$: Sentinel code: "Z"	
C$: Type of each transaction (code)		
T: Transaction amount		
D$: Date of each transaction		

The string variable I$ is used as a program flag; that is, the value of I$ is used to communicate the result of some prior data manipulation to a decision step that is executed later. The string constant "VALID" is initially stored in I$. If an invalid account number or transaction type code appears on a transaction card, I$ will be reset to "INVALID" (in step 3.4.8 or 3.4.9). By later testing I$ (step 4.2), the program can determine whether an invalid account number or type code was encountered during the earlier execution of step 3 and print out a warning message.

Step 3.4 is a nested decision structure with four conditions. Step 3.4.1 validates the transaction account number, A2. Step 3.4.2 separates the checks from other transactions. Step 3.4.3 differentiates between proper checks and overdrafts. Step 3.4.6 "flags" any invalid transaction codes. Steps 3.4.4, 3.4.5 and 3.4.7 in Fig. 5.16b need no explicit refinement; the account balance (B2) should be updated, the appropriate counter (C, D or R) increased by one, and the transaction printed.

The program for this problem is shown in Fig. 5.17a, b, and c. We have used two subroutines in writing the program: one for step 3 of the level one flow diagram, and a separate subroutine for processing a single transaction (step 3.4). The latter subroutine is called by the subroutine that performs step 3. This should cause no confusion; BASIC allows one subroutine to call another.

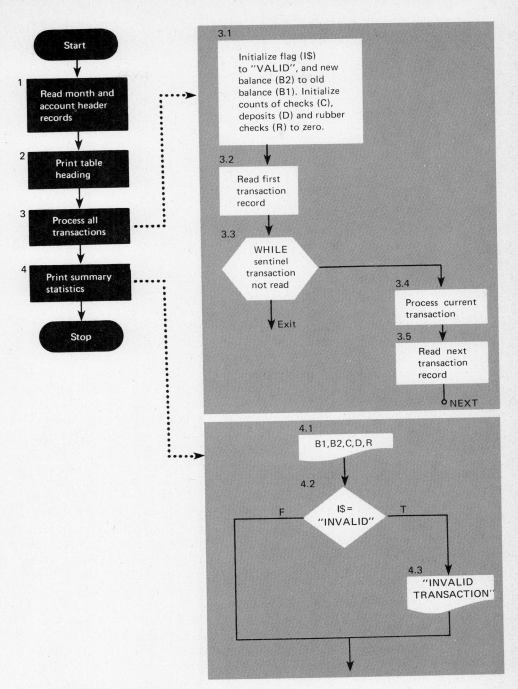

Fig. 5.16a Level one and two flow diagrams for Checking Account Problem 5.3.

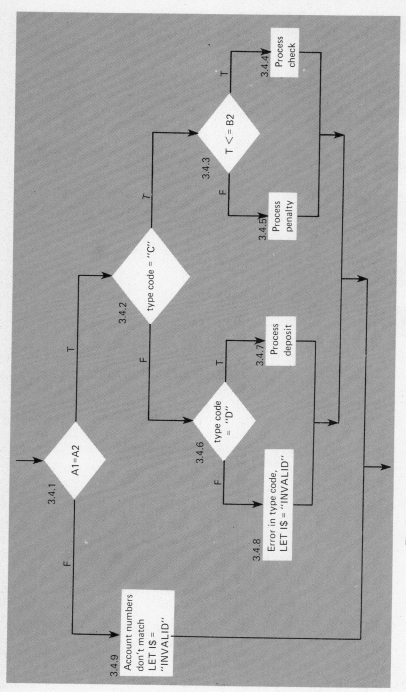

Fig. 5.16b Refinement of Step 3.4 (Fig. 5.16a), Checking Account Problem 5.3.

```
110 REM CHECKING ACCOUNT PROBLEM
120      PRINT "CHECKING ACCOUNT PROBLEM"
130 REM
140 REM INITIALIZE PROGRAM PARAMETERS FOR SENTINEL VALUE AND PENALTY
150 REM
160      LET V$ = "Z"
170      LET P = 5
180 REM
185 REM READ MONTH AND ACCOUNT HEADER RECORD
190      READ M$
200      READ A1, N$, B1
210 REM
220 REM PRINT TABLE HEADER
230      PRINT N$, "ACCOUNT NO. "; A1
240      PRINT "TRANSACTION RECORD FOR "; M$
250      PRINT
260      PRINT "DATE", "CHECK", "DEPOSIT", "PENALTY"
270 REM
280 REM PROCESS ALL ACCOUNTS AND TRANSACTIONS
290      GOSUB 3010
300 REM
310 REM PRINT SUMMARY STATISTICS
320      PRINT
330      PRINT "STARTING BALANCE "; B1, "FINAL BALANCE "; B2
340      PRINT "NO. OF CHECKS PAID "; C, "NO. OF DEPOSITS "; D
350      PRINT "NO. OF OVERDRAWN CHECKS "; R
360      IF I$ = "INVALID" THEN 370 ELSE 390 [IF I$ <> "INVALID" THEN 390]
370 REM THEN
380          PRINT "INVALID TRANSACTION PRESENT"
390 REM IFEND
400 REM
410      STOP
420 REM
430      DATA "SEPTEMBER"
440      DATA 11385, "GREG LUZINSKI", 85.67
450      DATA 11385, "C", 79.15, "9/9"
460      DATA 11380, "D", 200.00, "9/10"
470      DATA 11385, "D", 3.57, "9/11"
480      DATA 11385, "X", 123.45, "9/11"
490      DATA 11385, "C", 125.67, "9/12"
500      DATA 24077, "Z", 0, "0"
```

Fig. 5.17a Main program for Problem 5.3.

Exercise 5.12: In the Checking Account Problem, simply indicating the presence of invalid transactions would provide the bank with very little information concerning the transactions in error. Modify the program and subroutine for this problem to
a) print each transaction as it is read
b) indicate with an appropriate error message which transactions contain illegal account numbers and which have illegal transaction codes
c) count the number of transactions with illegal accounts and the number with illegal transaction codes
d) after printing the summary statistics, print the counts of illegal transactions.

```
3010 REM  SUBROUTINE TO PROCESS ALL TRANSACTIONS FOR THIS ACCOUNT
3040 REM
3050 REM  INITIALIZE PROGRAM FLAG, COUNTERS AND CURRENT BALANCE
3060      LET I$ = "VALID"
3070      LET B2 = B1
3080      LET C = 0
3090      LET D = 0
3100      LET R = 0
3110 REM
3120 REM  READ FIRST TRANSACTION
3130      READ A2, C$, T, D$
3140 REM  WHILE TRANSACTION NOT SENTINEL VALUE, PROCESS ALL TRANSACTIONS
3150      [DO] WHILE C$ < > V$                        [IF C$ = V$ THEN 3200]
3160           REM PROCESS A SINGLE TRANSACTION.
3170           GOSUB 5010
3180           READ A2, C$, T, D$
3190      [LOOP] NEXT                                 [GOTO 3140]
3200 REM
3210      RETURN
```

Fig. 5.17b   Subroutine to process all transactions.

Program Form and Style

The BASIC-PLUS implementations of the subroutines are shown in Fig. 5.17b and c. As before, we have used shading in each structure to separate "what is happening" from the implementation requirements. The shaded portion of Fig. 5.17c shows a rather complex nest of four double-alternative decision structures with three levels of nesting. We shall see a more straightforward way of implementing this nest in chapter 7.

It is worth noting the relative simplicity of the main program and the subroutine in Fig. 5.17b compared to the subroutine in Fig. 5.17c. The top-down approach to program design enables us to implement each of these program segments independently without introducing unnecessary complications. Therefore, we can implement the main program and subroutine for step 3 (Fig. 5.16a and Fig. 5.17b) first, and postpone the implementation of step 3.4 (Fig. 5.16b and Fig. 5.17c) until the very end.

The Dartmouth BASIC implementations of all structures are shaded in Fig. 5.17a, b, c. The Minimal BASIC implementations use the structure header statements shown on the right.

Exercise 5.13:   Modify the flow diagrams and program so that a number of different accounts can be processed in sequence. The records for each account will have the form shown in Fig. 5.15. There must be a final sentinel record to indicate the end of all data as well as a sentinel transaction record for each account. [*Hint:* For each account, a new header must be read. Then, steps 2, 3, and 4 in Fig. 5.16a are repeated as long as the header card read is not the final sentinel record.]

```
5010 REM SUBROUTINE TO PROCESS EACH TRANSACTION
5020 REM
5030 REM CHECK FOR VALID ACCOUNT NUMBER
5040     IF A1 = A2 THEN 5045 ELSE 5320        [IF A1 < > A2 THEN 5320]
5045 REM THEN
5050         REM VALID ACCOUNT -- PROCESS TRANSACTION
5060         IF C$ = "C" THEN 5065 ELSE 5185   [IF C$ < > "C" THEN 5185]
5065 REM     THEN
5070             REM PROCESS CHECK
5080             IF T <= B2 THEN 5085 ELSE 5130 [IF T > B2 THEN 5130]
5085 REM         THEN
5090                 REM CHECK IS OK
5100                 LET B2 = B2 - T
5110                 LET C = C + 1
5120                 PRINT D$, T
5125                 GOTO 5170
5130 REM         ELSE
5135                 REM CHECK IS OVERDRAWN, DEDUCT PENALTY
5140                 LET B2 = B2 - P
5150                 LET R = R + 1
5160                 PRINT D$, T, TAB(45); P; " (OVERDRAFT)"
5170 REM         IFEND
5180             GOTO 5300
5185 REM     ELSE
5190             IF C$ = "D" THEN 5200 ELSE 5260 [IF C$ < > "D" THEN 5260]
5200 REM         THEN
5210                 REM PROCESS VALID DEPOSIT
5220                 LET B2 = B2 + T
5230                 LET D = D + 1
5240                 PRINT D$, TAB(30); T
5250             GOTO 5290
5260 REM         ELSE
5270                 REM INVALID TRANSACTION TYPE
5280                 LET I$ = "INVALID"
5290 REM         IFEND
5300 REM     IFEND
5310         GOTO 5350
5320 REM ELSE
5330         REM BAD ACCOUNT NUMBER
5340         LET I$ = "INVALID"
5350 REM IFEND
5360 REM
5370     RETURN
5380 REM
5390     END
```

Fig. 5.17c Subroutine to process a single transaction.

5.6 COMMON PROGRAMMING ERRORS

The most common errors in writing WHILE loops are syntax errors in the header statement, failure to provide the proper terminator statement (NEXT or LOOP), or failure to initialize or update the loop control variable.

You must always be certain that your WHILE loop header and terminator

Statement	Effect
Subroutine call or reference	
GOSUB 1000	Transfers control to the subroutine starting at line 1000.
Subroutine terminator	
RETURN	Indicates the end of a BASIC subroutine. Transfers control to the first statement following the subroutine reference (call) in the calling program.
STOP statement	
STOP	Terminates program execution.

Statement	Effect
WHILE loop	
``` 100 REM WHILE A$ = "YES" 110 IF A$ <> "YES" THEN 160 120 GOSUB 2010 130 PRINT "TRY AGAIN"; 140 INPUT A$ 150 GOTO 100 160 REM ```	The loop body is repeated as long as A$ is equal to "YES." For each loop repetition, the subroutine starting at line 2010 is executed, a prompting message is printed, and data are entered into A$ and tested.

Table 5.1   Summary of Minimal BASIC statements

Statement	Effect
WHILE loop	

``
WHILE A$ = "YES"
    GOSUB 2010
    PRINT "TRY AGAIN";
    INPUT A$
NEXT
``
	The loop body is repeated as long as A$ is equal to "YES." For each loop repetition, the subroutine starting at line 2010 is executed, a prompting message is printed, and data are entered into A$ and tested.

Table 5.2   Summary of BASIC-PLUS WHILE loop

Statement	Effect

``
DO WHILE A$ = "YES"
    GOSUB 2010
    PRINT "TRY AGAIN";
    INPUT A$
LOOP
``
	The loop body is repeated as long as A$ is equal to "YES". For each loop repetition, the subroutine starting at line 2010 is executed; a prompting message is printed, and data are entered into A$ and tested.

Table 5.3   Summary of Dartmouth BASIC WHILE loop

statements conform to the syntax rules of your BASIC system. If you are not sure of the form of the WHILE loop in your system, consult the BASIC manual.

Failure to initialize and update the WHILE loop lcv will not be detected by the compiler. Failure to initialize the lcv may cause a loop to be skipped entirely; failure to update the lcv will likely cause the loop to execute "forever"; that is, until your program runs out of data, or exceeds a time limit or some other system constraint causing the loop to stop execution.

When writing subroutines in BASIC, it is essential to ensure that all of these modules are properly terminated and that the only means of entry to a module is through an explicit call or reference. Remember that subroutines must terminate with a RETURN and that subroutines may be defined anywhere in a BASIC program. However, they must be immediately preceded by a GOTO, a STOP or a RETURN, in order to guarantee entry through explicit reference only.

5.7 SUMMARY

We have introduced and illustrated the use of WHILE loops and subroutines. Both of these BASIC constructs are of considerable help in implementing programs in a modular fashion that is consistent with the top-down algorithm development process. Subroutines are also helpful in writing programs in which certain operations are performed more than once. These operations can be specified once as a subroutine, and then referenced as often as needed in the program. In Chapter 8 we will study additional, more powerful features of user-defined functions and subprograms which can be used in the same way, but with greater flexibility.

A summary of the forms of the new statements is given in Tables 5.1 through 5.3. You should study the statements in Table 5.1 above the dotted line and the WHILE loop form that is appropriate for your BASIC system.

PROGRAMMING PROBLEMS

5.4 Do Problem 4.4 (Chapter 4) using a sentinel value to terminate loop repetition (rather than a count of employees). Have your program keep a tally T of the number of employees, and print this count at the end. *Hint:* As the last DATA record in your input list use

name	*rate*	*hours*
ZZZZ ZZZZ	0.00	0

5.5 Do Problem 4.5 using a sentinel value to determine when all the numbers have been read and processed. [*Hint:* Use 0 as the sentinel value.]

5.6 Do Problem 4.6 for any positive integer n, regardless of the number of digits it contains.

5.7   Do Problem 4.11 using a sentinel value to determine when all of the data have been read and processed.

5.8   Do Problem 4.14 for a class whose size is unknown. Use a sentinel value to mark the end of the input.

5.9   Write a program that will read in a positive real number and determine and print the number of digits to the left of the decimal point. [*Hint:* Repeatedly divide the number by 10 until it becomes less than 1.] Test the program with the following data:

4703.62	0.01
0.47	5764
10.12	40000

5.10   Write a program that uses subroutines to find the range of values in a data collection (largest value − smallest value) and the mean value.

5.11   The function SIN(X) increases in value starting at X = 0 radians. Write a program to determine the value of X for which SIN(X) begins to decrease. [*Hint:* Calculate the value of SIN(X) beginning at X = 0 for intervals of .01 radians, and watch for a decrease.] Print a two-column table of X and SIN(X) as long as the increase continues. At the point of decrease, simply print X and stop.

5.12   The Small Time Company has three employees, all of whom earn $4 an hour. The company keeps a daily record of the hours worked by each employee. Write a program to read the daily time cards for each employee, and compute the total hours worked and gross pay for the employee. For each employee, print a three-column table entry containing employee name, total hours and gross pay (gross pay = $4 × hours worked). At the end, print the total hours and the total gross pay. Test your program on the following data. (Assume that the time records for each employee are entered consecutively.)

SMALL FRY	8
SMALL FRY	8
SMALL FRY	6
SMALL FRY	4
SMALL FRY	8
SHORT PERSON	8
SHORT PERSON	8
SHORT PERSON	6
THIN MAN	8
THIN MAN	8
THIN MAN	2
THIN MAN	8
THIN MAN	8
THIN MAN	5

5.13   The Norecall Auto Company keeps sales records for each employee. Each time an automobile is sold the following data are entered into the record:

name of salesperson   make of car   date of sale   amount of sale

For example:

LITTLE NELL	CADILLAC	6/6	$4532.67

Each month the company must collect the sales records for each employee, add up the number of sales and the sales amount, and compute the employee commission as follows:

For sales up to $30,000,	five percent commission
For sales between $30,000–$50,000,	five percent commission on first $30,000 eight percent commission on the rest
For sales over $50,000,	five percent of first $30,000 eight percent of next $20,000 fifteen percent of the rest

Write a program to perform these computations. For each employee, your program should print employee name, total sales count, total dollar amount of sales, and total commission. At the end, print grand totals of sales count, dollar amount, and commissions. Test your program on the following data.

LITTLE NELL	CADILLAC	6/6	$4500.00
LITTLE NELL	BUICK	6/7	$3200.00
LITTLE NELL	CADILLAC	6/9	$5200.00
LITTLE NELL	BUICK	6/12	$3900.00
LITTLE NELL	BUICK	6/12	$3700.00
LITTLE NELL	CADILLAC	6/18	$5100.00
LITTLE NELL	CADILLAC	6/24	$6000.00
BIG SIS	BUICK	6/8	$3800.00
BIG SIS	BUICK	6/20	$4100.00
BIG SIS	OLDS	6/30	$4900.00
MODERN MILLIE	CADILLAC	6/1	$6500.00
MODERN MILLIE	CADILLAC	6/3	$7300.00
MODERN MILLIE	CADILLAC	6/4	$5200.00
MODERN MILLIE	CADILLAC	6/8	$7800.00
MODERN MILLIE	BUICK	6/12	$3200.00
MODERN MILLIE	OLDS	6/14	$4200.00
MODERN MILLIE	CADILLAC	6/15	$5200.00
MODERN MILLIE	CADILLAC	6/18	$4700.00
MODERN MILLIE	BUICK	6/20	$5500.00
MODERN MILLIE	OLDS	6/22	$4900.00

Use a subroutine to compute the commission.

5.14 Extend the CAI program (Fig. 5.14a and b) to provide drill for addition, subtraction, and division, as well as multiplication. Write three additional subroutines similar to the multiplication subroutine (see Fig. 5.14b) to compute the actual answer for subtraction, addition and division drills, respectively. [*Hint:* Each time the student decides to continue, your main program should ask if the next drill is to be subtraction ("SUB"), addition ("ADD"), division ("DIV") or multiplication ("MUL"), and then call the appropriate subroutine to check the student solution.]

5.15 Write a program to read in a collection of positive integers and print all divisors of each, except for 1 and the number itself. If the number has no divisors, print a message indicating that it is prime. Use a subroutine to determine all of the divisors of each integer read. This subroutine should set a flag, P$, to indicate whether or not an integer is prime. The main program should test the flag to decide whether or not to print the prime message (see Problem 4.2). Use a sentinel value of 0 to terminate the execution of the loop that reads each data item.

5.16 Do Problem 5.12 using a subroutine to process each employee time card. Include computation and output steps for each employee in the subroutine.

ARRAYS AND SUBSCRIPTS

6

6.1 INTRODUCTION

In many applications, we are faced with the problem of having to store and manipulate large quantities of data in memory. In our problems so far, it has been necessary to use only a few memory cells to process relatively large amounts of data. This is because we have been able to process each data item separately and then re-use the memory cell in which that data item was stored.

For example, in Problem 5.1 we computed the maximum value of a set of exam scores. Each score was read into the same memory cell, named S, and then completely processed. This score was then lost when the next score was read into memory. This approach allowed us to process a large number of scores without having to allocate a separate memory cell for each one. However, once a score was processed, it was impossible to reexamine it later.

There are many applications in which we may need to save data items for subsequent reprocessing. For example, we might wish to write a program that computes and prints the average of a set of exam scores and also the difference between each score and the average. In this case, all scores must be processed and the average computed before we can calculate the differences requested. We must, therefore, be able to examine the list of student exam scores twice, first to compute the average and then to compute the differences. Since we would rather not have to read in the exam scores twice, we will want to save all of the scores in memory during the first step, for re-use during the second step.

In entering each data item, it would be extremely tedious to have to reference each memory cell by a different name. If there were 100 exam scores to process, we would need a long sequence of READ statements in which every variable name was listed once. We would also need 100 assignment statements in order to compute the difference between each score and the average.

In this chapter, we will learn how to use a new feature of BASIC, called an *array*, for storing a collection of related data items. Use of the array will simplify the task of naming and referencing the individual items in the collection. Through the use of arrays, we will be able to enter an entire collection of data items using a single read statement inside a loop. Once the collection is stored in memory, we will be able to reference any of these items as often as we wish without ever having to reenter that item into memory.

6.2 DECLARING ARRAYS

In all prior programming discussed in this text, each symbolic name used in a program has always been associated with a single memory cell, whether the name represented a number or a character string. The compiler automatically associated each name with a memory cell as soon as it encountered the name in our program.

   An *array* is a collection of two or more adjacent memory cells, called
array elements, that are associated with a single symbolic name. Whenever we
want to tell the compiler to associate two or more memory cells with a single
name, we must use an *array declaration statement* in which we state the name
to be used and the number of elements to be associated with this name.

   For example, the array declaration statement

DIM X(8)

instructs the compiler to associate eight memory cells (array elements) with
the name X. Each element of X is assumed to contain a numeric value.

   The association of a collection of memory cells with one variable name
poses a problem. How can we refer to the individual elements in the collection
if they are all associated with the same name? After all, the computer can
manipulate only one data item at a time. Consequently, in writing a program
to tell the computer how to manipulate an array of data, we must be able to
refer to each and every item in the array. This is accomplished through the
use of an array subscript.

   For example, if X is an array with eight elements, then we may refer to
the elements of the array X as shown in Fig. 6.1.

X(1)	X(2)	X(3)	X(4)	X(5)	X(6)	X(7)	X(8)
16	12	6	−2.5	−12	−24	−38	−54.6

First   Second   Third   . . .   Eighth
element element element   element

Fig. 6.1   The eight elements of the array X.

The *subscripted variable* X(1) can be used to reference the first element of the
array X, X(2) the second element, and X(8) the eighth element. The integer
enclosed in parentheses is the *array subscript*.

Example 6.1:   Let X be the array shown in Fig. 6.1 Then the statement

LET S = S + X(4)

will cause the value −2.5 (the contents of the memory cell designated by X(4)
to be added to S.

   In the next section, we will study subscripts in more detail and we will
see that integer constants are not the only form of a subscript that is allowed
in BASIC. However, first we will describe the complete syntax and interpretation of the BASIC array declaration.

Array Declaration

Minimal BASIC form:

```
DIM name (range)
```

Interpretation: The compiler will associate a collection of memory cells (array elements) with the variable indicated by name. The individual array elements will be referenced by the subscripted variables name(1), name(2), . . ., name (range) where the largest legal subscript value is range. The number range must be an integer. The name of a numeric array must be a single letter only.

Notes: The declaration of an array should precede any reference to the array in a program.

In some BASIC systems, there is also an element name(0).

In many extended BASIC systems, string arrays are also permitted. The name of a string array must be a single letter followed by a $.

Example 6.2: More than one array may appear in a declaration statement. For the declaration

```
DIM C(5), P(6)
```

the largest legal subscript values are five for array C, and six for array P.

Example 6.3: The declaration

```
DIM F$(20), L$(20), P$(15)
```

will allocate three arrays for storage of string data. The largest legal subscript value is 20 for string arrays F$ and L$, and 15 for string array P$.

It is permissible in BASIC to reference a numeric array without explicitly declaring that array. In this case, the compiler will assume that the largest legal subscript value is ten. However, we strongly recommend that you provide an explicit declaration for each array.

Some BASIC compilers allocate an additional memory cell with a subscript value of zero for each array. In these systems, the array declaration

```
DIM C(5), P(6)
```

would cause six array elements to be assigned to the array C (C(0), C(1), . . ., C(5)) and seven to the array P (P(0), P(1), . . ., P(6)). We will not make use of the array element with subscript zero in this chapter; consequently, all programs and examples will run correctly regardless of what convention your compiler uses.

6.3 ARRAY SUBSCRIPTS

In the preceding section, we introduced the array subscript as a means of differentiating the individual elements of an array. We showed that an array element can be referenced by specifying the name of the array followed by a pair of parentheses enclosing a subscript.

In general, BASIC allows any arithmetic expression to be used as the subscript of an array. The compiler can determine the particular array element referenced by evaluating the *subscript expression* and using the result of this evaluation to indicate the element to be referenced. The rules for the specification and evaluation of array subscripts are summarized below.

Array Subscripts

Minimal BASIC form:

name(subscript)

Interpretation: The subscript may be any arithmetic expression. If necessary, the value of each subscript is rounded to the nearest integer. For example, subscript values ≥ 9.5 and < 10.5 would reference the tenth element of an array. The range of permissible values is between 1 (0 on some compilers) and the largest legal subscript value for that array (as specified in the declaration).

Note: Some compilers truncate (remove the fractional part) of the subscript value rather than round. For this reason, it is always preferable to use integer subscript values.

Example 6.4: Let I be a memory cell containing the value 3, and let X be the array declared below.

DIM X(10)

Then: X(I) refers to the 3rd element of the array X;
          X(2*I) refers to the 6th element of the array X;
          X(5*I−6) refers to the 9th element of the array X;
          X(I+3) refers to the 6th element of the array X.

As shown above, we will write subscript expression without blanks around the arithmetic operators.

Exercise 6.1:   In Example 6.4, which elements in the array X are referenced if I is equal to 4 rather than 3?

Exercise 6.2:   Let I contain the integer 6 and let X be the array in Example 6.4. Which of the following references to elements of X are within the range of X?

a)	X(I)	e)	X(4*I − 12)
b)	X(3*I−20)	f)	X(I − 2*I)
c)	X(4+I)	g)	X(30)
d)	X(I*3−12)	h)	X(I*I − 1)

6.4   MANIPULATING ARRAYS

6.4.1   Manipulating Individual Array Elements

Array elements may be manipulated just as other variables are manipulated in BASIC statements. Each use of an array name in a BASIC statement must be followed by a subscript.

It is important to understand the distinction between the array subscript, the value of the subscript (sometimes called an *index* to the array) and the contents of the array element. The subscript is enclosed in parentheses following the array name. Its value is used to select one of the array elements for manipulation. The contents of that array element is either used as an operand or modified as a result of executing a BASIC statement.

Example 6.5:   Let G be an array of 10 elements as shown below.

G(1)	G(2)	G(3)	G(4)	G(5)	G(6)	G(7)	G(8)	G(9)	G(10)
−11.2	12	−6.1	4.5	8.2	1.3	−.7	8.3	9	−3.3

According to this representation of the array G, the following statements can be made:

a) The contents of the 2nd element (subscript value 2) in the array is 12.

b) The contents of the 4th element (subscript value 4) is 4.5.

c) The contents of the 10th element (subscript value 10) is −3.3.

Remember, the subscript value is used to select a particular array element, but it does not, by itself, tell us what is stored in that element.

Example 6.6:   Let G be the array shown in Example 6.5. Then the sequence of instructions

```
10 LET J = 1
20 LET I = 4
30 LET G(10) = 10
40 LET G(I) = 400
50 LET G(2*I) = G(I) + G(J)
```

Statement	Subscript	Subscript Value	Effect
30 LET G(10) = 10	10	10	Store 10 in G(10). Destroy old value, −3.3.
40 LET G(I) = 400	I	4	Store 400 in G(4). Destroy old value, 4.5.
50 LET G(2*I) = G(I) + G(J)	I J 2 * I	4 1 8	Add contents of G(4) and G(1) (400 + (−11.2)). Store result (388.8) in G(8). Destroy old value, 8.3.

Table 6.1   Manipulating the array G

will alter the contents of the 10th, 4th, and 8th elements of G, as shown in Table 6.1. Three distinct elements of the array G are referenced in line 50: the new value of G(I), or G(4) is added to G(J), or G(1); the result is stored in G(2*I), or G(8). The new array G is shown in Fig. 6.2.

Exercise 6.3:   Given the array G as shown in Fig. 6.2:
a)   What is the contents of G(2)?
b)   If I = 3, what is the contents of G(2*I−1)?
c)   What is the value of the condition G(I) < > 8.2 if I is equal to 3; if I is equal to 5?
d)   What will be the value of the variable F after the statements below are executed?

```
10 LET F = 0
20 FOR I = 1 TO 10
30     IF G(I) = 388.8 THEN LET F = 1
40 NEXT I
```

e)   What will the array G look like after the following statements are executed?

```
10 FOR I = 1 TO 5
20     LET G(I) = 2 * I
30 NEXT I
40 FOR I = 6 TO 10
50     LET G(I) = 2 * G(I-5)
60 NEXT I
```

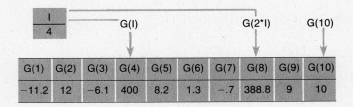

Fig. 6.2 New array G.

f) Describe how the array G would be changed by the following sequences of statements. Assume the array is reset to Fig. 6.2 before each sequence executes.

```
10 FOR I = 1 TO 4          10 FOR I = 10 TO 2 STEP -1
20    READ G(I)            20    G(I) = G(I-1)
30 NEXT I                  30 NEXT I
40 DATA 12, 18, 22, -9.3   40 G(1) = 0
```

g) What would happen to array G if the loop header for the righthand loop in (f) were FOR I = 2 TO 10? Would the answer be the same?

6.4.2   Initialization of Arrays

Most compilers will automatically initialize all elements of a numeric array to zero and a string array to blanks (the null string) when the array declaration is processed. However, it is best to initialize all array elements explicitly before they are referenced either through assignment statements or data entry (READ/ INPUT) statements.

Example 6.7:   The program segment below initializes all elements of the array P to zero and Q to one.

```
10 DIM P(100), Q(100)
20 FOR I1 = 1 TO 100
30    LET P(I1) = 0
40    LET Q(I1) = 1
50 NEXT I1
```

The FOR loop is repeated 100 times. Each time, an element of P is set to zero and the corresponding element of Q is set to one: first P(1), Q(1), then P(2), Q(2), and finally P(100), Q(100).

Example 6.8:   The program segment below creates an array of squares. The value I^2 is stored in the array element with subscript I.

```
10 DIM S(10)
20 FOR I = 1 TO 10
30    LET S(I) = I * I
40 NEXT I
```

S(1)	S(2)	S(3)		S(10)
1	4	9	$\cdots$	100

Example 6.9:   The statements

```
10 DIM X(9)
20 FOR I1 = 1 TO 5
30    LET X(I1) = 200
40 NEXT I1
50 FOR I2 = 6 TO 8
60    LET X(I2) = 300
70 NEXT I2
```

would initialize the array X as shown below.

X(1)	X(2)	X(3)	X(4)	X(5)	X(6)	X(7)	X(8)	X(9)
200	200	200	200	200	300	300	300	?

Example 6.10:   In compilers that allow string arrays, the statements

```
10 DIM A$(4)                            10 DIM A$(4)
20 LET A$(1) = "MY"                     20 FOR I = 1 TO 4
30 LET A$(2) = "AGE"        or          30    READ A$(I)
40 LET A$(3) = "IS"                     40 NEXT I
50 LET A$(4) = "97"                     50 DATA MY, AGE, IS, "97"
```

will cause the four elements of the array A$ to be initialized as shown below.

A$(1)	A$(2)	A$(3)	A$(4)
MY	AGE	IS	97

Exercise 6.4:   Use a FOR loop for parts b) — d)
a) Declare and initialize an array called A$ that contains each letter of the alphabet in consecutive elements.
b) Declare and initialize an array S of size 10 in which the value of each element is the same as its subscript; i.e., $S(1) = 1$, $S(2) = 2$, . . ., $S(10) = 10$.
c) Declare and initialize an array T of size 10 for which $T(1) = 10$, $T(2) = 9$, . . ., $T(10) = 1$.
d) Declare and initialize an array U of size 10 in which the value of each element is the cube of its subscript; i.e., $U(1) = 1$, $U(2) = 8$, . . ., $U(10) = 1000$.

6.4.3   Reading and Printing Array Elements

In Chapter 10, we will introduce additional BASIC operations that will enable us to enter data into an entire array or print all the values stored in an array. For the time being, however, we will read and print array elements one at a time. Subscripts will be used to specify which array element is being defined or printed.

The program shown in Fig. 6.3, reads two separate arrays of data and prints both arrays in tabular form. The first loop reads in all elements of the string array N$; the second loop reads in all elements of the array Y. In the third loop, the output list for the print statement (line 220) references a pair of array elements with subscript I3. As the value of I3 goes from 1 to 5, the contents of these arrays will be printed in two columns, as shown in the output portion of Fig. 6.3.

If the input data had been prepared so that each president's name was followed by his first year in office, a single FOR loop could be used to enter

```
110        DIM N$(5), Y(5)
120        FOR I1 = 1 TO 5
130            READ N$(I1)
140        NEXT I1
150        DATA "WASHINGTON", "ADAMS", "JEFFERSON", "MADISON", "MONROE"
155 REM
160        FOR I2 = 1 TO 5
170            READ Y(I2)
180        NEXT I2
190        DATA 1789, 1797, 1801, 1809, 1817
195 REM
200        PRINT " NAME", "FIRST YEAR IN OFFICE"
210        FOR I3 = 1 TO 5
220            PRINT N$(I3); TAB(23) ; Y(I3)
230        NEXT I3
235 REM
240        END

RUN

 NAME              FIRST YEAR IN OFFICE
WASHINGTON               1789
ADAMS                    1797
JEFFERSON                1801
MADISON                  1809
MONROE                   1817
```

Fig. 6.3 A program, with sample output, for reading and printing two arrays.

all data. In this case, the statements that follow would replace lines 110 through 190 of Fig. 6.3. The resulting program would be more efficient.

```
110        DIM N$(5), Y(5)
120        FOR I1 = 1 TO 5
130            READ N$(I1), Y(I1)
140        NEXT I1
150        DATA "WASHINGTON", 1789, "ADAMS", 1797, "JEFFERSON", 1801
160        DATA "MADISON", 1809, "MONROE", 1817
```

Exercise 6.5: Declare an array P consisting of ten elements. Prepare a data statement and read statement for entering the first ten prime numbers into the array P.

Exercise 6.6: Write a program segment to display the index and the contents of each element of the array P in the tabular form shown below. (See Exercise 6.5.)

N	PRIME(N)
1	1
2	2
3	3
4	5
.	.
.	.
.	.
10	23

6.4.4   Computing a Table of Fibonacci Numbers

Problem 6.1:   The Fibonacci series is a sequence of numbers with the property that each number in the sequence represents the sum of the two preceding numbers (the first two numbers in the sequence are assumed to be one). Write a flow diagram and a program that computes, stores and prints the first fifteen Fibonacci numbers in the array F; e.g.,

```
F(1) = 1
F(2) = 1
F(3) = F(1) + F(2) = 1 + 1 = 2
F(4) = F(2) + F(3) = 1 + 2 = 3
F(5) = F(3) + F(4) = 2 + 3 = 5
F(6) = F(4) + F(5) = 3 + 5 = 8
                .
                .
                .
```

The Fibonacci series has been shown to model the growth pattern of a rabbit colony. Starting with one pair of baby rabbits, there should be 610 pairs of rabbits at the end of 15 months, assuming it takes two months for a rabbit to mature, and that each mature pair produces a new pair of baby rabbits every month.

Discussion: Each Fibonacci number (besides the first and second) can be computed from the previous two Fibonacci numbers by use of the formula

$$F(n) = F(n-2) + F(n-1), \qquad n \geq 3$$

We will use this formula in a BASIC program that computes each Fibonacci number, saves it in the appropriate element of an array F and uses this value in the computation of the next two Fibonacci numbers. The data table for this problem follows; the flow diagrams are given in Fig. 6.4.

Data Table for Problem 6.1

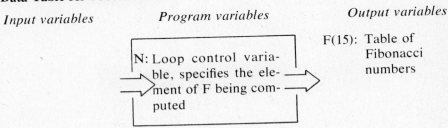

Input variables	Program variables	Output variables
	N: Loop control variable, specifies the element of F being computed	F(15): Table of Fibonacci numbers

The program and its output are shown in Fig. 6.6. A single program statement (line 260) is used to compute each of the Fibonacci numbers from F(3) through F(15). The effect of this statement when N equals 6 is illustrated in Fig. 6.5.

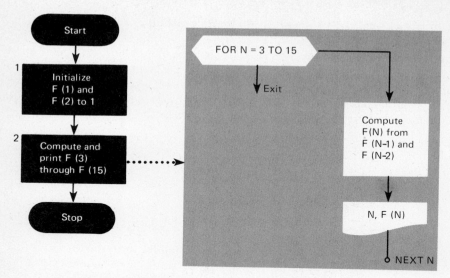

Fig. 6.4 Flow diagrams for Fibonacci number program.

The statement at line 270 is used to display each new Fibonacci number. The final contents of the array F would be:

F(1)	F(2)	F(3)	F(4)	F(5)	F(6)	F(7)	F(8)	F(9)	F(10)	F(11)	F(12)	F(13)	F(14)	F(15)
1	1	2	3	5	8	13	21	34	55	89	144	233	377	610

It is important to realize that the loop control variable N, in the program of Fig. 6.6, determines which array element is assigned a value during each loop repetition. This use of the loop control variable of a FOR loop is very common in manipulating array elements since it allows us to easily specify the

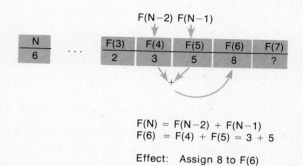

$$F(N) = F(N-2) + F(N-1)$$
$$F(6) = F(4) + F(5) = 3 + 5$$

Effect: Assign 8 to F(6)

Fig. 6.5   Illustration of the computation of F(6) (line 260 of Fig. 6.6).

```
110 REM PROGRAM TO COMPUTE THE FIRST FIFTEEN FIBONACCI NUMBERS
120 REM
130      PRINT "FIRST 15 FIBONACCI NUMBERS"
135      PRINT
140 REM
150      DIM F(15)
160 REM
165      PRINT " N", "NTH FIBONACCI NUMBER"
170 REM INITIALIZE AND PRINT F(1) AND F(2)
180      LET F(1) = 1
190      LET F(2) = 1
220      PRINT 1; TAB(24) ; F(1)
230      PRINT 2; TAB(24) ; F(2)
235 REM
240 REM COMPUTE AND PRINT F(3) THROUGH F(15)
250      FOR N = 3 TO 15
260          LET F(N) = F(N-2) + F(N-1)
270          PRINT N; TAB(24) ; F(N)
280      NEXT N
290 REM
300      END

RUN

FIRST 15 FIBONACCI NUMBERS

  N              NTH FIBONACCI NUMBER
  1                    1
  2                    1
  3                    2
  4                    3
  5                    5
  6                    8
  7                   13
  8                   21
  9                   34
 10                   55
 11                   89
 12                  144
 13                  233
 14                  377
 15                  610
```

Fig. 6.6 Program for Problem 6.1, with sample output.

sequence in which the elements of an array are to be manipulated. Each time the loop control variable is increased, the next array element is automatically selected.

Exercise 6.7: Rewrite the Fibonacci program from the flow diagram in Fig. 6.4, using a subroutine to implement step 2.

Exercise 6.8: What would be stored in the array F if line 260 were incorrectly written as

$$\text{LET } F(N) = (N-2) + (N-1)$$

Exercise 6.9: The factorial of a number is often used in formulas for computing the probability that a given event will occur. The factorial of a number N (written as N!) is defined to be the product of N and all integers smaller than N.

$$N! = N \times (N-1) \times (N-2) \times \ldots \times 2 \times 1$$

Since

$$(N-1)! = (N-1) \times (N-2) \times \ldots \times 2 \times 1$$

the formula for N! can be rewritten as

$$N! = N \times (N-1)!$$

where 0 is defined to be 1. Compute and print a table of factorials for the integers 1 through 7 and accumulate the sum of the factorials. Use an array for storage of all factorials computed.

6.4.5   Partially Filled Arrays—The Grading Program

In many problems, we may want to manipulate only a portion of an array, with the exact number of elements involved determined during each execution of the program. In this case, we should declare the size of the array to be large enough to accommodate the largest possible set of data items.

In addition to the array element values themselves, a very important piece of data is a count of the number of array elements to be processed. This is normally the first data item read since it is used as the end value parameter in all loops that read and manipulate the array elements as illustrated next.

Problem 6.2: A number of faculty members at the New University have requested an interactive grading program that can be used at a terminal to determine letter grades for their classes. The faculty members would like to be able to enter each student's name and exam score and have the class average printed out. Using the class average as a guide, the faculty member would next specify the exam score ranges for the letter grades A, B and C by entering the minimum score for grades of A and B into the computer (only grades of A, B and C are given at the New University). The program would then display the distribution of grades (number of A's, B's and C's).

The faculty member could continue to reenter new minimum scores for grades of A and B until he or she is satisfied with the resulting grade distribution. At this point, the program would list each student's name, exam score and final letter grade. The maximum class size at the New University is 100.

Discussion: The variable C indicates the number of students receiving grades. We will read each student name and exam score into corresponding elements of the arrays N$ and S respectively. The class average, A, can then be computed and the minimum exam scores for a grade of A and B read in to L1 and L2 respectively. Once this information has been provided, tentative letter grades for each student can be computed and stored in the array G$; a running total of the number of A's (N1), B's (N2), and C's (N3) should be maintained as the letter grades are being determined.

The data table follows and the flow diagrams are shown in Fig. 6.7.

Data Table for Problem 6.2

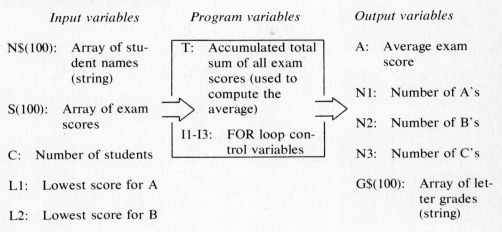

Input variables	Program variables	Output variables
N$(100): Array of student names (string)	T: Accumulated total sum of all exam scores (used to compute the average)	A: Average exam score
S(100): Array of exam scores		N1: Number of A's
	I1-I3: FOR loop control variables	N2: Number of B's
C: Number of students		N3: Number of C's
L1: Lowest score for A		G$(100): Array of letter grades (string)
L2: Lowest score for B		

The refinements of steps 1, 2 and 4 are relatively straightforward. In step 1, a FOR loop is used to enter each pair of data items (a student name and exam score) into corresponding elements of the arrays N$ and S; in step 4, a FOR loop is used to display corresponding values of the arrays N$, S, and G$ in three columns across a line of output. In the refinement of step 2, the variable T is used to accumulate the total of all exam scores (T = S(1) + S(2) + ... + S(C)). After exiting from loop 2, T is divided by C to find the average, A.

In step 3, the grade boundaries may be reset as many times as desired; hence, a WHILE loop is needed. We will introduce a new variable, D$, to control loop repetition. As long as the faculty member desires a new grade distribution (D$ equal to "YES"), the loop will be repeated. The new program variable is listed below; the flow diagram for step 3 is shown in Fig. 6.8.

Additional program variable

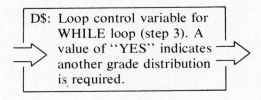

D$: Loop control variable for WHILE loop (step 3). A value of "YES" indicates another grade distribution is required.

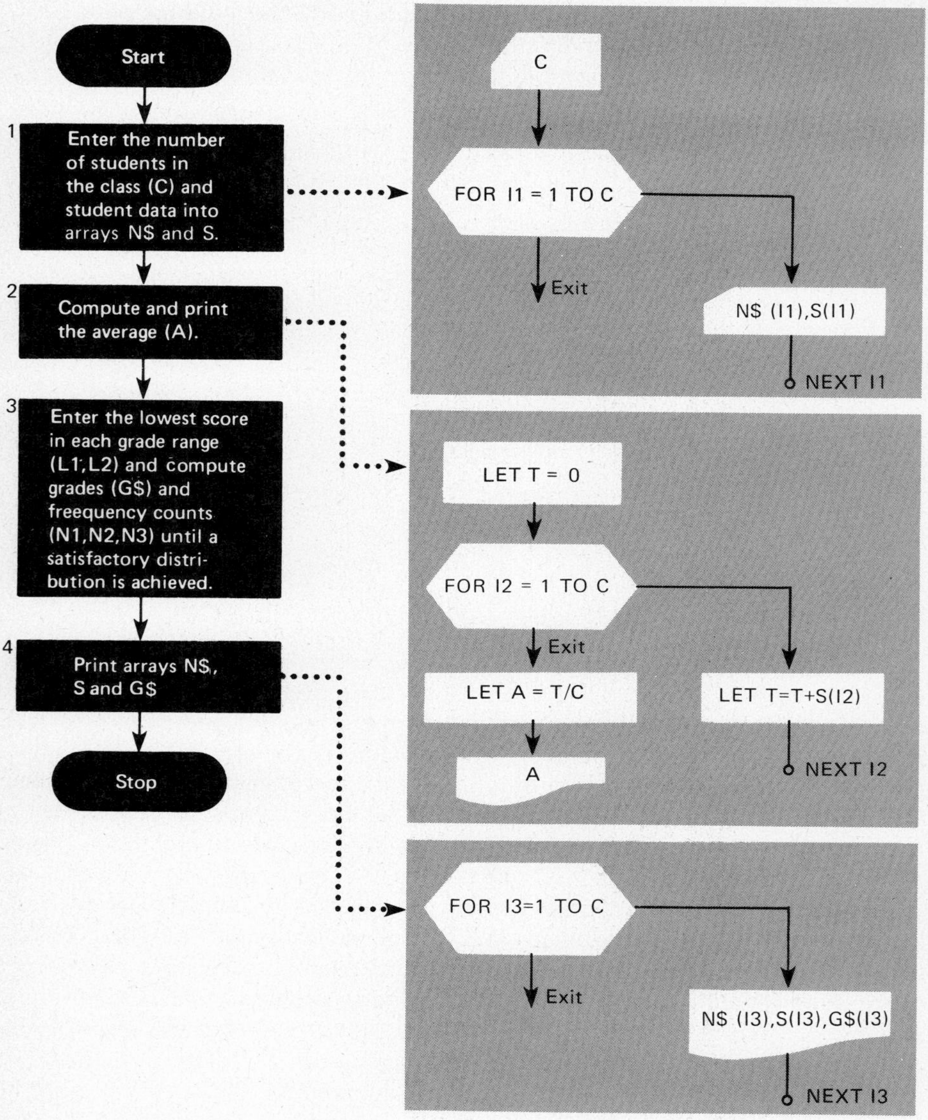

Fig. 6.7 Flow diagrams for grade problem (6.2).

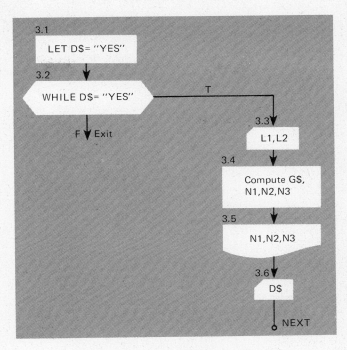

Fig. 6.8 Refinement of step 3 of Fig. 6.7.

Within the WHILE loop, the new lowest scores for each grade are entered (step 3.3), the grade distribution is determined (step 3.4), and the frequency counts are displayed (step 3.5). Next, the faculty member is asked whether a new grade distribution is desired (step 3.6); if the answer is not "YES", the loop is exited and the final results are printed (step 4). The determination of letter grades for each student (array G$) and of the frequency counts N1, N2, N3 (step 3.4) requires additional refinement (shown in Fig. 6.9). (The loop control variable, I4, should also be added to the data table.)

Additional program variable

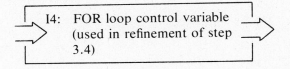

I4:   FOR loop control variable (used in refinement of step 3.4)

The main program for this problem is given in Figure 6.10a. The data entry and print refinements are simple enough that they are implemented directly in the main program. The subroutines are shown in Fig. 6.10b and 6.10c.

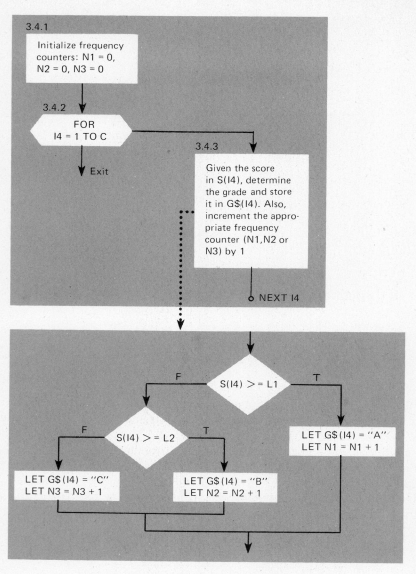

Fig. 6.9 Refinement of step 3.4 in grade problem.

```
110 REM INTERACTIVE GRADE DISTRIBUTION PROGRAM
120 REM MAXIMUM CLASS SIZE OF 100
130     PRINT "GRADE DISTRIBUTION PROGRAM"
135 REM
140     DIM N$(100), S(100), G$(100)
145 REM
150 REM ENTER NUMBER OF STUDENTS AND THE EXAM RECORDS FOR EACH
160     PRINT "HOW MANY STUDENTS TOOK THE EXAM ";
170     INPUT C
175     PRINT
180     PRINT "FOR EACH STUDENT, ENTER THE NAME (IN QUOTES) "
190     PRINT "FOLLOWED BY A COMMA AND THE EXAM SCORE"
200     FOR I1 = 1 TO C
210         INPUT N$(I), S(I)
220     NEXT I1
230 REM
240 REM COMPUTE AND PRINT CLASS AVERAGE
245     PRINT
250     GOSUB 2010
260 REM
270 REM ENTER A AND B GRADE RANGE MINIMA UNTIL SATISFACTORY
280 REM DISTRIBUTION IS ACHIEVED
290     GOSUB 3010
300 REM
310 REM DISTRIBUTION IS ADEQUATE, PRINT RESULTS
320     PRINT
330     PRINT "FINAL LIST OF GRADES"
340     PRINT
350     PRINT "STUDENT", "SCORE", "GRADE"
360     FOR I3 = 1 TO C
370         PRINT N$(I), S(I), "  "; G$(I)
380     NEXT I3
390 REM
400     STOP
```

Fig. 6.10a   Main program for Problem 6.2

```
2010 REM SUBROUTINE TO COMPUTE AND PRINT AVERAGE
2020 REM
2030     LET T = 0
2040     FOR I2 = 1 TO C
2050         LET T = T + S(I)
2060     NEXT I2
2065 REM
2070     LET A = T / C
2080     PRINT "THE CLASS AVERAGE IS "; A
2090 REM
2100     RETURN
2110
2120
3010 REM SUBROUTINE TO ALLOW ENTRY OF A AND B GRADE RANGE MINIMA
3020 REM      AND COMPUTE STUDENT GRADES AND FREQUENCY COUNTS
3030 REM
3040 REM INITIALIZE LCV TO GUARANTEE AT LEAST ONE LOOP REPETITION
3050     LET D$ = "YES"
3060 REM WHILE D$ EQUALS YES, READ RANGE MINIMA AND DETERMINE
```

Fig. 6.10b   Level two subroutines for Problem 6.2 (Continued on next page.)

```
3070 REM    GRADES AND FREQUENCY COUNTS
3080    [DO] WHILE D$ = "YES"                        [IF D$ < > "YES" THEN 3200]
3085        PRINT "ENTER MINIMUM A AND B GRADES SEPARATED BY COMMA";
3090        INPUT L1, L2
3095 REM
3100        REM DETERMINE STUDENT GRADES AND FREQUENCY COUNTS
3110        GOSUB 5010
3115 REM
3120        REM PRINT COUNTS
3125        PRINT
3130        PRINT "GRADE", "NUMBER"
3135        PRINT "  A", N1
3140        PRINT "  B", N2
3150        PRINT "  C", N3
3155        PRINT
3160 REM
3165        REM CHECK IF ANOTHER DISTRIBUTIONS IS DESIRED
3170        PRINT "DO YOU DESIRE ANOTHER DISTRIBUTION";
3180        INPUT D$
3190    [LOOP] NEXT
3200 REM                                            [GOTO 3060]
3210        RETURN
```

Fig. 6.10b Continuation of level two subroutines for Problem 6.2

```
5010 REM SUBROUTINE TO DETERMINE LETTER GRADES AND FREQUENCY COUNT
5020 REM
5030 REM INITIALIZE COUNTS
5040        LET N1 = 0
5050        LET N2 = 0
5060        LET N3 = 0
5065 REM
5070 REM FOR EACH STUDENT, DETERMINE LETTER GRADE (A, B, OR C)
5080 REM AND UPDATE APPROPRIATE FREQUENCY COUNTER
5090        FOR I4 = 1 TO C
5100        IF S(I4) >= L1 THEN 5105 ELSE 5150 [IF S(I4) < L1 THEN 5150]
5105 REM    THEN
5110            REM S(I4) >= L1, GRADE IS A
5120            LET G$(I4) = "A"
5130            LET N1 = N1 + 1
5140        GOTO 5250
5150 REM    ELSE
5155            REM S(I4) < L1, GRADE IS B OR C
5160            IF S(I4) >= L2 THEN 5165 ELSE 5210
                                            [IF S(I4) < L2 THEN 5210]
5165 REM        THEN
5170                REM L2 <= S(I4) < L1, GRADE IS B
5180                LET G$(I4) = "B"
5190                LET N2 = N2 + 1
5200            GOTO 5240
5210 REM        ELSE
5215                REM GRADE IS C
5220                LET G$(I4) = "C"
5230                LET N3 = N3 + 1
5240 REM        IFEND
5250 REM    IFEND
5260        NEXT I4
5270 REM
5280        RETURN
5290 REM
5300        END
```

Fig. 6.10c Level three subroutine for Problem 6.2.

A sample of the output produced from the execution of the program shown in Fig. 6.10 is illustrated below.

```
RUN

GRADE DISTRIBUTION PROGRAM
HOW MANY STUDENTS TOOK THE EXAM ? 5

FOR EACH STUDENT, ENTER THE NAME (IN QUOTES)
FOLLOWED BY A COMMA AND THE EXAM SCORE
?"BACH", 82
?"FIEDLER", 75
?"BRAHMS", 63
?"BEETHOVEN", 52
?"BACHARACH", 99

THE CLASS AVERAGE IS 74.2
ENTER MINIMUM A AND B GRADES SEPARATED BY COMMA ?85, 60

GRADE          NUMBER
  A              1
  B              3
  C              1

DO YOU DESIRE ANOTHER DISTRIBUTION ? NO

FINAL LIST OF GRADES

STUDENT        SCORE        GRADE
BACH            82            B
FIEDLER         75            B
BRAHMS          63            B
BEETHOVEN       52            C
BACHARACH       99            A
```

Exercise 6.10: It may be desirable to use an array of counters to keep track of the number of grades in each category where N(1) would represent the count of A's, N(2) the count of B's, etc. Show what modifications would be required to Fig. 6.10.

Exercise 6.11: In Problem 6.2, the value of C (the number of students) should be checked after the first input statement to verify that it lies between 1 and 100. Write an IF structure to perform the necessary test on C and print appropriate diagnostics if C is out of the range 1 to 100. (The program execution should terminate if C is out of range.) Why is this test so important?

Exercise 6.12: Rewrite the program in Fig. 6.10 using a pair of sentinel values to indicate the end of student data rather than entering the number of students beforehand. [*Hints:* Use a WHILE loop and read the data into two temporary cells (one of which is the loop control variable). If these temporary cells do not contain the sentinel values, copy them into the next elements of N$ and S. Count the number of students entered in this fashion.]

Exercise 6.13: In determining a reasonable grade distribution, many instructors might wish to know the standard deviation, D, of the class exam scores, as well as the average, A. Modify the grade program to compute the standard deviation.

Also print out both A and D, and the values of A + D, and A − D. *Hint:* To compute D use the formula

$$D = \sqrt{\frac{\Sigma S^2}{C} - A^2}$$

where ΣS^2 is the sum of the squares of each score. For example, given the scores 63, 47, 82

$$\Sigma S^2 = 63^2 + 47^2 + 82^2 = 3969 + 2209 + 6724 = 12902.$$
$$\frac{\Sigma S^2}{C} = 4300.67$$

Then: $A = \dfrac{\Sigma S}{N} = \dfrac{63 + 47 + 82}{N} = \dfrac{192}{3} = 64,$

so $D = \sqrt{4300.67 - 64^2} = \sqrt{204.67} \approx 14.31$

You only need to alter one subroutine to compute and print the desired results.

6.5 SEARCHING AN ARRAY

A very common problem in working with arrays of data items is the need to *search* an array to determine whether a particular data item, called a *key*, is in the array. We might also want to know how many times the key is present and where in the array each copy of the key is located. The following problem requires an array search in order to determine the index of an array element containing a specified key.

Problem 6.3:   Write an interactive program that could be used by a small bank (maximum of 20 depositor accounts) to process the daily transactions (deposits and withdrawals) against each account and maintain an up-to-date record of the balance for each account.

Discussion: For each (depositor) account, the bank keeps a record of depositor name, starting balance and current balance. We will use three arrays (N$— for depositor names, S—for starting balances, and B—for current balances) of size 20 to store this data. The initial data for N$ and S will be read in at the start of the program. The current balance for each depositor account will initially be equal to the starting balance. At the end of the day, the current balance array will contain the final balance for that day for each account.

Once the initial account information has been processed, all transactions for the day will be entered at the terminal. Each transaction record will specify the depositor name (A$) and transaction amount (T); a positive transaction amount indicates a deposit, and a negative amount indicates a withdrawal. At the end of the day, when there are no more transactions to be processed, the data entry operator at the terminal can obtain a printout of the starting and final balance for each account simply by typing the sentinel record "DONE", 0.

The data table for this program follows and the flow diagrams are shown in Fig. 6.11.

Data Table for Problem 6.3

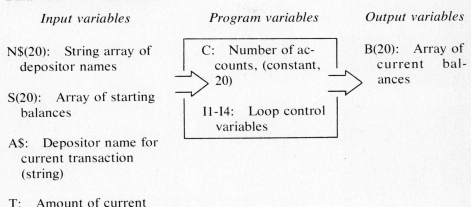

Input variables	*Program variables*	*Output variables*
N$(20): String array of depositor names	C: Number of accounts, (constant, 20)	B(20): Array of current balances
S(20): Array of starting balances	I1-I4: Loop control variables	
A$: Depositor name for current transaction (string)		
T: Amount of current transaction		

The array of current balances, B, must be initially the same as the array of starting balances, S. Hence, each individual element of S should be copied into the corresponding element of B. A FOR loop is used to accomplish this in the refinement of step 2.

The refinement of step 3 consists of the WHILE loop used to process all transactions. Each transaction is completely processed before the next transaction is entered; hence, only two variables (A$ and T) are needed to store the depositor name and transaction amount for the current transaction. When the sentinel transaction ("DONE", 0) is entered, the WHILE loop is exited and execution continues at step 4. The actual processing of each transaction (step 3.3) is discussed next.

It is important to realize that the transactions do not follow any particular order and that there may be zero, one, or many transactions during the day for each depositor's account. In order to process the current transaction, each transaction amount, T, must be added to the current balance for the proper account. In other words, T must be added to a particular element of the array, B—namely, that element that contains the current balance for the depositor name, A$.

The value of A$ is the key that must be found in N$ (array of depositor names). Each element of N$ is examined in sequence until the element that matches the key is found. The corresponding element of B (same index as the key) is then updated.

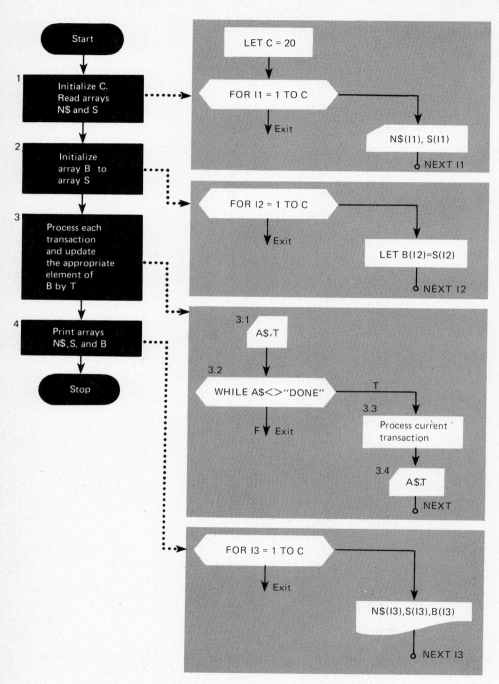

Fig. 6.11 Flow diagrams for savings account update program.

For example, consider the arrays N$ and B and the depositor name A$ shown below (A$ equals "KLEIN"). The key is "KLEIN," and the index of the element of N$ that matches the key is 3; hence B(3) should be updated.

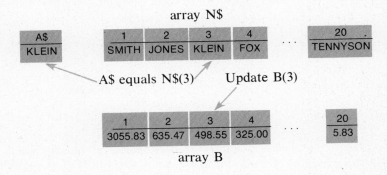

This process of examining each element in N$ to find a key is called an *array search*. The implementation of the search is shown in Fig. 6.12. In this diagram, the FOR loop control variable I4 is used to select each element of N$ in sequence to 6.35.

If an array element N$(I4) matches A$, the count of matches, M, is increased by one and the index of the key, X, is set to I4. After the loop is exited, the transaction amount, T, is added to B(X) provided there was exactly

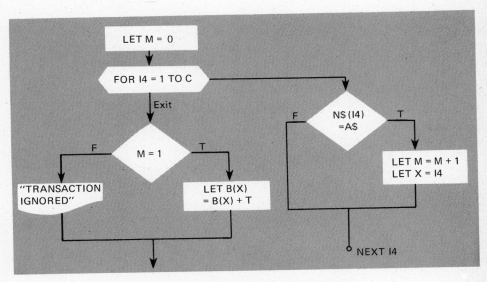

Fig. 6.12 Refinement of Step 3.3 of Fig. 6.11.

one occurrence of the key in N$ (M equal to 1). If M is equal to zero (A$ not found) or M is greater than one (multiple occurrences of A$), an error message is printed instead. The additions to the data table follow.

Additional program variables

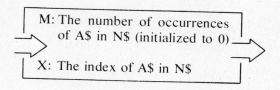

> M: The number of occurrences of A$ in N$ (initialized to 0)
>
> X: The index of A$ in N$

The program is shown in Fig. 6.13. As in earlier programs, short refinements (in this case, for steps 2 and 4) were not implemented as separate subroutines.

```
110 REM SMALL BANK SAVINGS ACCOUNT UPDATE PROBLEM
120     PRINT "SAVINGS ACCOUNT UPDATE PROGRAM"
130 REM TWENTY DEPOSITORS
140 REM
150 .   DIM N$(20), S(20), B(20)
160 REM
170 REM INITIALIZE PROGRAM PARAMETER FOR NO. OF ACCOUNTS (C)
180 REM AND READ INITIAL DATA
190     GOSUB 1010
200 REM
210 REM INITIALIZE CURRENT BALANCES (B) TO STARTING BALANCES (S)
220     FOR I2 = 1 TO C
230         LET B(I2) = S(I2)
240     NEXT I2
250 REM
260 REM PROCESS ALL TRANSACTIONS
270     GOSUB 3010
280 REM
290 REM WHEN TRANSACTION PROCESSING IS COMPLETE, DISPLAY FINAL
300 REM   RESULTS FOR THE DAY
310     PRINT
320     PRINT "TOTALS FOR TODAY"
330     PRINT
340     PRINT "ACCOUNT", "START", "FINAL"
350     PRINT "NAME", "BALANCE", "BALANCE"
355     PRINT
360     FOR I3 = 1 TO C
370         PRINT N$(I3), S(I3), B(I3)
380     NEXT I3
390 REM
400     STOP
```

Fig. 6.13a   Main program for Problem 6.3.

```
1010 REM INITIALIZATION SUBROUTINE. DEFINE NO. OF ACCOUNTS (C)
1020 REM    AND INITIAL DATA
1030 REM
1040      LET C = 20
1050      FOR I1 = 1 TO C
1060         READ N$(I1), S(I1)
1070      NEXT I1
1080 REM
1090      RETURN
1100 REM
1110 REM ACCOUNT NAMES AND INITIAL BALANCES
1120      DATA "SMITH", 3055.83
1130      DATA "JONES", 635.47
1140      DATA "KLEIN", 498.55
1150      DATA "FOX", 325.00
1160      DATA "O'HARA", 4567.98
1170      DATA "FITZGERALD", 532.76
1180      DATA "FRY", 45.90
1190      DATA "LESSING", 1345.70
1200      DATA "JONG", 789.05
1210      DATA "DATES", 7040.88
1220      DATA "GARDNER", 890.54
1230      DATA "EVERT", 33.99
1240      DATA "ROTH", 668.90
1250      DATA "STEINBECK", 1087.43
1260      DATA "ROSNER", 55.78
1270      DATA "BRONTE", 888.77
1280      DATA "CARMICHAEL", 66.43
1290      DATA "BROWN", 7869.00
1300      DATA "PHILLIPS", 546.88
1310      DATA "TENNYSON", 5.83
1320
1330
3010 REM SUBROUTINE TO PROCESS ALL TRANSACTIONS
3020 REM
3030 REM ENTER FIRST TRANSACTION
3040      PRINT
3050      PRINT "ENTER ACCOUNT NAME FOLLOWED BY A COMMA AND A"
3060      PRINT "TRANSACTION AMOUNT"
3070      PRINT "POSITIVE AMOUNT REPRESENTS A DEPOSIT"
3080      PRINT "NEGATIVE AMOUNT REPRESENTS A WITHDRAWAL"
3090      PRINT "WHEN DONE, ENTER 'DONE' AND A ZERO"
3095 REM
3100      INPUT A$, T
3110 REM WHILE SENTINEL VALUE ("DONE") NOT READ, PROCESS
3120 REM    EACH TRANSACTION
3130      [DO] WHILE A$ < > "DONE"              [ IF A$ = "DONE" THEN 3220]
3150         REM SEARCH ARRAY N$ FOR A$
3160         REM IF A$ FOUND, UPDATE PROPER ELEMENT OF N$
3170         GOSUB 5010
3180         REM ENTER NEXT TRANSACTION
3190         PRINT "ENTER ACCOUNT NAME AND NEXT TRANSACTION"
3200         INPUT A$, T
3210      [LOOP] NEXT                           [GOTO 3110]
3220 REM
3230      RETURN
```

Fig. 6.13b Level two subroutines for Problem 6.3.

```
5010 REM SEARCH SUBROUTINE. FIND A$ IN N$
5020 REM IF FOUND ONCE, UPDATE CORRESPONDING BALANCE;
5030 REM OTHERWISE, PRINT AN ERROR MESSAGE
5040 REM
5050 REM INITIALIZE COUNT M TO ZERO
5060     LET M = 0
5065 REM
5070 REM SEARCH FOR A$ IN N$
5080     FOR I4 = 1 TO C
5090        IF N $(I4) = A$ THEN 5100 ELSE 5140    [IF N$(I4) <> A$ THEN 5140]
5100        THEN
5110           REM A$ FOUND AT ELEMENT I4
5120           LET M = M + 1
5130           LET X = I4
5140        IFEND
5150     NEXT I4
5160 REM
5170 REM UPDATE BALANCE IF A$ FOUND ONCE
5180     IF M = 1 THEN 5190 ELSE 5220          [IF M <> 1 THEN 5220]
5190     THEN
5200        LET B(X) = B(X) + T
5210     GOTO 5250
5220     ELSE
5230        PRINT "TRANSACTION IGNORED-";
5240        PRINT "THERE WERE"; M; "OCCURRENCES OF"; A$
5245        PRINT
5250     IFEND
5260 REM
5270     RETURN
```

Fig. 6.13c Level three subroutine for Problem 6.3.

We have placed the initial account information at the very end of the subroutine that reads these data (lines 1120-1310). These DATA statements will all be processed by the READ statement on line 1060. In Chapter 11, we will learn how to use another BASIC feature, the file, to simplify this process. None of the transaction data need be provided as the transactions will be entered interactively as the program executes (lines 3100 and 3200).

The final output for this program consists of the three columns of summary information for each account (produced by lines 360-380) of the main program. A sample run of the program is given in Fig. 6.14.

Exercise 6.14: A common error in implementing the search (Fig. 6.13) is to place the "TRANSACTION IGNORED" message in the false branch of the decision structure inside the loop instead of after the loop exit. Explain what effect this error would have on the program output.

Exercise 6.15: Reexamine Exercise 6.3 part (d). What does that program segment do?

Exercise 6.16: The withdrawal of $99 for Tennyson should not have been allowed as it exceeded the account balance. Modify the search subroutine so this is prevented.

Exercise 6.17: It would be desirable to keep track of the number of deposits

```
SAVINGS ACCOUNT UPDATE PROGRAM

ENTER ACCOUNT NAME FOLLOWED BY A COMMA AND A
TRANSACTION AMOUNT
POSITIVE AMOUNT REPRESENTS A DEPOSIT
NEGATIVE AMOUNT REPRESENTS A WITHDRAWAL
WHEN DONE, ENTER 'DONE' AND A ZERO

?KLEIN, 88.60
ENTER ACCOUNT NAME AND NEXT TRANSACTION
?FOX, 38.40
ENTER ACCOUNT NAME AND NEXT TRANSACTION
?TENNYSON, -99.00
ENTER ACCOUNT NAME AND NEXT TRANSACTION
?CARMICHAEL, -44.00
ENTER ACCOUNT NAME AND NEXT TRANSACTION
?WILSON, 33.00
TRANSACTION IGNORED-THERE WERE 0 OCCURRENCES OF WILSON

ENTER ACCOUNT NAME AND NEXT TRANSACTION
?BROWN, -1000.00
ENTER ACCOUNT NAME AND NEXT TRANSACTION
?DONE, 0

TOTALS FOR TODAY

      ACCOUNT          START            FINAL
       NAME            BALANCE          BALANCE

      SMITH            3055.83          3055.83
      JONES            635.47           635.47
      KLEIN            498.55           587.15
      FOX              325              363.4
      O'HARA           4567.98          4567.98
      FITZGERALD       532.76           532.76
      FRY              45.9             45.9
      LESSING          1345.7           1345.7
      JONG             789.05           789.05
      DATES            7040.88          7040.88
      GARDNER          890.54           890.54
      EVERT            33.99            33.99
      ROTH             668.9            668.9
      STEINBECK        1087.43          1087.43
      ROSNER           55.78            55.78
      BRONTE           888.77           888.77
      CARMICHAEL       66.43            22.43
      BROWN            7869             6869
      PHILLIPS         546.88           546.88
      TENNYSON         5.83             -93.17
```

Fig. 6.14 Sample run of savings account transaction program.

and withdrawals for each account during the day as well as the total number
of deposits and withdrawals. Explain how this information could be determined
and displayed.

6.6 ADDITIONAL TECHNIQUES FOR PROCESSING SELECTED ARRAY ELEMENTS

In Problem 6.3, the array N$ was used as a *search array* in order to determine the index of the element of array B that was to be processed. The array N$ was searched for a key A$; if A$ was found at N$(I), then B(I) was the element of B that was to be processed. The following example illustrates how the judicious use of arrays can simplify otherwise cumbersome or impractical solutions to problems. In this example, two additional techniques for selecting array elements are introduced.

Example 6.11: In many problems, we are provided with a table of class boundary values and we must determine in which class a particular item belongs. For example, Table 6.2 lists the salary ranges for a set of tax brackets. In order to compute the income tax due on a particular salary, we must first determine the tax bracket associated with that salary by comparing the salary to the table entries. We could then compute the tax due by selecting tax amounts and tax percentages appropriate to that bracket. (See Problem 6.7.)

The salary, S, could be compared to each of the tax table boundary values in an elaborate nested decision structure; however, it is much easier to simply store the tax table boundary values in order in an array, T. The elements of T should be examined in sequence until the first element, T(I), is found such that T(I) is greater than S. The index of this element, I, corresponds to the tax bracket. This process is illustrated in Fig. 6.15. The first four array element values would be compared to S (salary of $1750); the tax bracket, B, would be set to four.

A BASIC subroutine to find the tax bracket, B, is given in Fig. 6.16. Once B has been set, the loop is exited immediately (GOTO 1100) and B is returned to the calling program for further processing. (For example, the tax bracket, B, might be used to select corresponding tax amounts and percentages from companion arrays provided as input data.) For salaries outside the range of values listed in the table, the loop will be exited normally, an error message

Salary Range	Tax Bracket
less than $500	1
$500–$999.99	2
$1000–$1499.99	3
$1500–$1999.99	4
$2000–$3999.99	5
$4000–$5999.99	6
$6000–$7999.99	7
$8000–$9999.99	8
$10000–$11999.99	9
$12000–$13999.99	10

Table 6.2   Hypothetical salary ranges for ten tax brackets

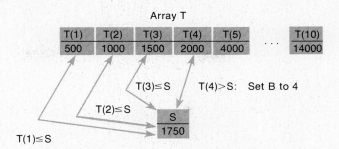

Fig. 6.15 Determining tax bracket (B).

will be printed (line 1085) and B will be set to zero (to indicate failure) before returning to the calling program.

An alternate approach to selecting the tax bracket is direct computation of the index as shown in Fig. 6.17. Direct computation is more convenient and efficient than array search if there is a constant increment between table items. In Fig. 6.17, the statement at line 1040

$$\text{LET B} = \text{INT (S / 500)} + 1$$

correctly computes the tax bracket, B, for all values of S less than $2000. (There is a constant increment of $500 for the tax table entries in this range.) The statement at line 1100

$$\text{LET B} = \text{INT (S / 2000)} + 4$$

correctly computes the tax bracket for all other salaries in the range of Table 6.2 (constant increment of $2000).

```
1000 REM SUBROUTINE TO SEARCH FOR TAX BRACKET - B
1005 REM
1010      FOR I = 1 TO 10
1020          IF T(I) > S THEN 1025 ELSE 1060      [IF T(I) <= S THEN 1060]
1025 REM     THEN
1030              REM BRACKET IS I - SET B AND EXIT
1040              LET B = I
1050              GOTO 1100
1060 REM     IFEND
1070      NEXT I
1075 REM
1080 REM BRACKET NOT FOUND
1085      PRINT "SALARY" ; S; "EXCEEDS TABLE VALUES"
1090      LET B = 0
1100 REM
1110      RETURN
```

Fig. 6.16 Subroutine to search for tax bracket (B).

```
1000  REM SUBROUTINE TO COMPUTE TAX BRACKET - B
1005  REM
1010      IF S < 2000 THEN 1020 ELSE 1060        [IF S >= 2000 THEN 1060]
1020  REM THEN
1030          REM S < 2000
1040          LET B = INT (S / 500) + 1
1050      GOTO 1170
1060  REM ELSE
1070          IF S < 14000 THEN 1080 ELSE 1120   [IF S >= 14000 THEN 1120]
1080          THEN
1090              REM S BETWEEN $2000 AND $14000
1100              LET B = INT (S / 2000) + 4
1110          GOTO 1160
1020  REM     ELSE
1130              REM BRACKET NOT FOUND - S > 14000
1140              PRINT "SALARY"; S; "EXCEEDS TABLE VALUES"
1150              LET B = 0
1160  REM     IFEND
1170  REM IFEND
1180  REM
1190      RETURN
```

Fig. 6.17 Subroutine to compute tax bracket (B).

Exercise 6.18:   Implement the subroutine in Fig. 6.16 using a WHILE loop.

Exercise 6.19:   Verify by hand simulation that the above formulas for B are correct. Test the following values of S:

$250, $1275, $2750, $4000, $11700, $23000.

Exercise 6.20:   Write program segments to show how the tax table boundary values could be used to find B using
a) nested double-alternative decision structures
b) a sequence of single-alternative decision structures

Exercise 6.21:   For an exam with the grade ranges

A: 90–100
B: 80–89
C: 70–79
D: 60–69
F: 0–59

Write a subroutine that determines and prints each student grade. Use both the array search and direct computation techniques. *Hint:* Store the lower grade boundaries in an array G and the letter grades in an array G$. For the direct computation technique, use decision structures to take care of the grades 100 and 0 through 49, and use direct computation to process grades between 50 and 99 inclusive.

6.7 COMMON PROGRAMMING ERRORS

There are two very common programming errors associated with arrays. One involves the failure to declare a name that is to be used to represent an array and the other involves the use of subscripts with values that are too small or too large.

1. Failure to Declare an Array

The use of a subscript reference with a symbolic name that has not been declared as an array (via a DIM statement) may result in error diagnostics. Some BASIC compilers permit the "implicit declaration of arrays," however, the largest legal subscript value for all such arrays is always assumed to be ten. If you reference an element with a subscript value greater than ten, you will get an out-of-range error diagnostic as described in the next section.

2. Out-of-Range Subscript Values

Out-of-range subscript values (subscripts that are less than one or exceed the largest legal subscript value for an array) are often caused by errors in subscript computation (such as the computations described in Section 6.6) or by loops that do not terminate properly. These are not syntax errors and can't be diagnosed during compilation. If they go undetected during program execution then unpredictable changes might occur in the program's data or even in the program itself. In either case, before considerable time is spent in debugging, all suspect subscript calculations should be carefully checked for out-of-range errors. This can most easily be done by inserting diagnostic output statements in your program, in order to print subscript values that might be out of range.

Some compilers automatically provide such a subscript checking facility. This facility will print a message indicating an out-of-range subscript, the line number of the program statement at which the error occurred and the value of the subscript. For example, the message

```
SUBSCRIPT RANGE ERROR AT LINE NO. 120 FOR ARRAY B, I = -1
```

indicates that the subscript I in the reference to array B at line 120 has value -1. When such errors occur, the statement used to define the value of I must be corrected in order to produce the proper in-range value.

6.8 SUMMARY

In this chapter we introduced a special *data structure* called an array, which is a convenient facility for naming and referencing a collection of like items. We discussed how to inform the compiler that an array of elements is to be allocated (by using the DIM statement), and we described how to reference an individual array element by placing a parenthetical expression, called a subscript, following the array name. A summary of statements that manipulate arrays is provided in Table 6.3

The FOR loop was shown to be a convenient structure for referencing each array element in sequence. We have used this structure to initialize arrays, read and print arrays, and to control the manipulation of array elements.

Statement	Effect
Array Declaration	
DIM X(15)	Allocate storage for array elements X(1), X(2), ..., X(15) (and also X(0) in some systems).
Array Manipulation	
LET R = X(15) - X(1)	Subtract the value of array element X(1) from array element X(15). Store the difference in R.
Array Assignment	
LET X(2) = A + B	Store the sum of A and B in array element X(2).
Array Read and Print	

FOR I = 1 TO N
  READ X(I)
  PRINT X(I);
NEXT I
	Enter data into elements X(1), X(2), ... X(N). Echo print each value read.

Table 6.3   Summary of BASIC statements

6.8.1   Referencing Array Elements—Review

In the examples we have seen, there have been two methods used to select an array element for manipulation. The first involved the use of a FOR loop to reference all elements of an array in sequence; the second involved setting an index through a search process or computation in order to select a single array element for update.

The first approach to scanning through an array has been used many times in program solutions. We have read information into array elements in sequential order (Problems 6.2 and 6.3); we have searched array elements in sequential order to find a specific data item (Problem 6.3), etc. For each of these operations, a FOR loop was used in which the loop control variable also served as the subscript of the array being scanned.

Both approaches were used in Problem 6.3. In this problem, the loop control variable I4 was used to scan through an array of depositor names to find a desired name (the key). The location of the key was used as the index to a different array, the array of account balances, in order to select the corresponding account balance for update.

6.8.2   Categorizing a Data Item

In Example 6.11, we showed that the problem of categorizing a data item could be simplified through the use of arrays. If an ordered list of boundary values for tax brackets were stored in an array, the tax bracket corresponding to a particular salary could be easily determined through an array search. If there were a constant increment between boundary values, direct computation could be used to conveniently determine the appropriate category (tax bracket). Once the bracket was defined, it could be used as an index to select elements from other arrays for further processing in subsequent program steps.

The arrays discussed in this chapter are often called *linear arrays* or *lists*. These arrays are "one dimensional," in that a single subscript is used to uniquely identify each array element. In Chapter 10, we shall examine a more complex data structure—an array with two dimensions (called a matrix).

PROGRAMMING PROBLEMS

6.4 Instructor X has given an exam to a large lecture class of students. The grade scale for the exam is 90–100(A), 80–89(B), 70–79(C), 60–69(D), 0–59(F). Instructor X needs a program to perform the following statistical analysis of the data:
   i) Count the number of A's, B's, C's, D's, and F's.
   ii) Determine the averages of the A, B, C, D, and F scores, computed on an individual basis—i.e., the average A score, the average B score, . . ., the average F score.
   iii) Find the total number of students taking the exam.
   iv) Compute the average and standard deviation for all of the scores (see Exercise 6.13 for the formula for the standard deviation)

6.5 Let A be an array consisting of 20 elements. Write a program to read a collection of up to 20 data items into A, and then find and print the subscript of the largest item in A.

6.6 The Department of Traffic Accidents each year receives accident count reports from a number of cities and towns across the country. To summarize these reports, the Department provides a frequency-distribution printout that gives the number of cities reporting accident counts in the following ranges: 0-99, 100-199, 200-299, 300-399, 400-499, 500 or above.The Department needs a computer program to read the number of accidents for each reporting city or town and to add one to the count for the appropriate accident range. After all the data has been processed, the resulting frequency counts are to be printed.

6.7 Write a program which, given the *taxable income* for a single taxpayer, will compute the income tax for that person. Use Schedule X shown in Fig. 6.18. Assume that "line 47," referenced in this schedule, contains the taxable income.

Example: If the individual's taxable income is $8192, your program should use the tax amount and percent shown in column 3 of line 7 (arrow). The tax in this case is

$$\$1590 + .25(8192. - 8000) = \$1638.$$

For each individual processed, print taxable earnings and the total tax. *Hint:* Set up three arrays, one for the base tax (column 3), one for the tax percent (column 3), and the third for the excess base (column 4). Your program must then compute the correct index to these arrays, given the taxable income (see Example 6.11).

6.8 Assume for the moment that your computer has the very limited capability of being able to read and print only single decimal digits at a time; and to add

Tax Rate
Schedules

SCHEDULE X—Single Taxpayers Not Qualifying for Rates in Schedule Y or Z

Use this schedule if you checked the box on Form 1040, line 1—

If the amount on Form 1040, line 47, is:		Enter on Form 1040, line 16a:	
Not over $500...14% of the amount on line 47.			
Over—	But not over—		of the amount over—
$500	$1,000	$70+15%	$500
$1,000	$1,500	$145+16%	$1,000
$1,500	$2,000	$225+17%	$1,500
$2,000	$4,000	$310+19%	$2,000
$4,000	$6,000	$690+21%	$4,000
$6,000	$8,000	$1,110+24%	$6,000
$8,000	$10,000	$1,590+25%	$8,000
$10,000	$12,000	$2,090+27%	$10,000
$12,000	$14,000	$2,630+29%	$12,000
$14,000	$16,000	$3,210+31%	$14,000
$16,000	$18,000	$3,830+34%	$16,000
$18,000	$20,000	$4,510+36%	$18,000
$20,000	$22,000	$5,230+38%	$20,000
$22,000	$26,000	$5,990+40%	$22,000
$26,000	$32,000	$7,590+45%	$26,000
$32,000	$38,000	$10,290+50%	$32,000
$38,000	$44,000	$13,290+55%	$38,000
$44,000	$50,000	$16,590+60%	$44,000
$50,000	$60,000	$20,190+62%	$50,000
$60,000	$70,000	$26,390+64%	$60,000
$70,000	$80,000	$32,790+66%	$70,000
$80,000	$90,000	$39,390+68%	$80,000
$90,000	$100,000	$46,190+69%	$90,000
$100,000	....	$53,090+70%	$100,000

Fig. 6.18   Schedule X (from IRS Form 1040).

together two integers consisting of one decimal digit each. Write a program to read in two ten-digit integers, add these numbers together, and print the result. Test your program on the following numbers.

$$X = 1487625$$
$$Y = 12783$$

$$X = 60705202$$
$$Y = 30760832$$

$$X = 1234567890$$
$$Y = 9876543210$$

Hints: Store the numbers X and Y in two arrays X, Y, of size 10, one decimal digit per element. If the number is less than 10 digits in length, enter enough *leading zeros* (to the left of the number) to make the number 10 digits long.

X

1	2	3	4	5	6	7	8	9	10
0	0	0	1	4	8	7	6	2	5

Y

1	2	3	4	5	6	7	8	9	10
0	0	0	0	0	1	2	7	8	3

You will need a loop to add together the digits in corresponding array elements. You must start with the element with subscript value 10 and work toward the left. Do not forget to handle the carry, if there is one!

Use a variable, C, to indicate if a carry occurred in adding together X(1) and Y(1). C is set to 1 if a carry occurs here; otherwise, C will be 0.

6.9 Write a data table, flow diagram, and a program for the following problem. You are given a collection of scores for the last exam in your computer course. You are to compute the average of these scores, and then assign grades to each student according to the following rule.

If a student's score S is within 10 points (above or below) of the average, assign the student a grade of SATISFACTORY. If S is more than 10 points higher than the average, assign the student a grade of OUTSTANDING. If S is more than 10 points below the average, assign the student a grade of UNSAT- ISFACTORY. Test your program on the following data:

> "RICHARD LUGAR" 62
> "FRANK RIZZO" 31
> "DONALD SCHAEFFER" 84
> "KEVIN WHITE" 93
> "JAMES RIEHLE" 74
> "ABE BEAME" 70
> "TOM BRADLEY" 84
> "WALTER WASHINGTON" 68
> "RICHARD DALEY" 64
> "RICHARD HATCHER" 82

Hint: If your compiler does not allow the use of the string array, then use student numbers instead of names. The output from your program should consist of a labelled three-column list containing the name, exam score, and grade of each student.

6.10 Write a program to read N data items into each of two arrays X and Y of size 20. Compare each of the elements of X to the corresponding element of Y. In the corresponding element, of a third array Z, store:

> +1 if X is larger than Y
> 0 if X is equal to Y
> −1 if X is less than Y

Then print a three-column table displaying the contents of the arrays X, Y, and Z, followed by a count of the number of elements of X that exceed Y, and a count of the number of elements of X that are less than Y. Make up your own test data, with N less than 20.

6.11 The results of a true-false exam given to a Computer Science class has been coded for input to a program. The information available for each student consists of a student identification number and the students' answers to 10 true-false questions. The available data is as follows:

Student identification	Answers (1 = true; 0 = false)									
0080	0	1	1	0	1	0	1	1	0	1
0340	0	1	0	1	0	1	1	1	0	0
0341	0	1	1	0	1	1	1	1	1	1
0401	1	1	0	0	1	0	0	1	1	1
0462	1	1	0	1	1	1	0	0	1	0
0463	1	1	1	1	1	1	1	1	1	1
0464	0	1	0	0	1	0	0	1	0	1
0512	1	0	1	0	1	0	1	0	1	0
0618	1	1	1	0	0	1	1	0	1	0
0619	0	0	0	0	0	0	0	0	0	0
0687	1	0	1	1	0	1	1	0	1	0
0700	0	1	0	0	1	1	0	0	0	1
0712	0	1	0	1	0	1	0	1	0	1
0837	1	0	1	0	1	1	0	1	0	1
9999	0	0	0	0	0	0	0	0	0	0 sentinel record

The correct answers are   0 1 0 0 1 0 0 1 0 1

Write a program to read the data records, one at a time, and compute and store the number of correct answers for each student in one array, and store the student ID number in the corresponding element of another array. Determine the best score, B. Then print a three-column table displaying the ID number, score and grade for each student. The grade should be determined as follows: If the score is equal to B or B − 1, give an A; if it is B − 2 or B − 3, give a C. Otherwise, give an F.

6.12 Write a program to read N data items into two arrays X and Y of size 20. Store the product of corresponding elements in X and Y in a third array Z, also of size 20. Print a three-column table displaying the arrays X, Y, and Z. Then compute and print the square root of the sum of the items in Z. Make up your own data, with N less than 20.

6.13 The results of a survey of the households in your township have been made available. Each record contains data for one household, including a four-digit integer identification number, the annual income for the household, and the number of members of the household. Write a program to read the survey results into three arrays and perform the following analyses:
  i)   Count the number of households included in the survey and print a three-column table displaying the data read in. (You may assume that no more than 25 households were surveyed.)
  ii) Calculate the average household income, and list the identification number and income of each household that exceeds the average.
  iii) Determine the percentage of households having incomes below the poverty level. The poverty level income may be computed using the formula
$$p = \$3750.00 + \$750.00 * (m - 2)$$
where m is the number of members of each household.

Test your program on the following data.

Identification number	Annual income	Household members
1041	$12,180	4
1062	13,240	3
1327	19,800	2
1483	22,458	8
1900	17,000	2
2112	18,125	7
2345	15,623	2
3210	3,200	6
3600	6,500	5
3601	11,970	2
4725	8,900	3
6217	10,000	2
9280	6,200	1

6.14 Write a program to simulate the tossing of a pair of dice. Use RND and INT to obtain the number on each die:

```
LET D1 = INT(6 * RND)+1
LET D2 = INT(6 * RND)+1
```

and·add these two values together.

Repeat the computation until 1000 tosses have been made and print a frequency table containing a list of die values and the number of times each occurred. Compare this table to the table of expected frequencies shown below.

die value	expected frequency	die value	expected frequency
2	28	7	167
3	56	8	139
4	83	9	111
5	111	10	83
6	139	11	56
		12	28

6.15 Let V be the value of a long-term savings certificate available at your local bank, let T be the term of the certificate (in years), and let R be the yearly interest rate. Write a program which, given V, T, and R, will compute and print the interest amount I (rounded to two decimal places), and the accumulated certificate value for each of the years of the term. Your program should print out V, T and R, and a three-column table containing the year (1, 2, 3, . . ., T), the interest for that year, and the accumulated value. Test your program for V = $5000, T = 10 years, and R = 7¼ percent.

6.16 It can be shown that a number is prime if there is no smaller prime number that divides it. Consequently, in order to determine whether N is prime, it is sufficient to check only the prime numbers less than N as possible divisors (see Problem 4.2). Use this information to write a program that stores the first one hundred prime numbers in an array. Have your program print the array after it is done.

6.17 Write a program that plays the game of HANGMAN. Read each letter of the word to be guessed into successive elements of the string array W$. The player must guess the letters belonging to W$. The program should terminate when either all letters have been guessed correctly (player wins) or a specified number of incorrect guesses have been made (computer wins). *Hint:* Use a string array S$ to keep track of the solution so far. Initialize each element of S$ to the symbol "*". Each time a letter in W$ is guessed, replace the corresponding "*" in array S$ with that letter.

NESTED AND MULTIPLE-ALTERNATIVE STRUCTURES

7.1 INTRODUCTION

In Chapters 2, 3, and 5 we introduced four fundamental control structures to be used in computer programming. We presented flow diagram patterns and described several forms of these structures. We illustrated the application of these structures in the solution to a number of problems, some of which utilized *nests of control structures*.

In this chapter, we will examine the use of nested control structures in some detail and provide some guidelines that should help reduce the potential for error in using nested structures. We will also introduce the logical operators AND and OR, which will enable you to implement decisions more conveniently. In addition, several forms of decision structures with multiple (more than two) alternatives will be presented. Throughout the chapter, a number of examples and solved problems illustrating the nesting of structures will be provided.

You may already be applying some of the guidelines discussed in this chapter in your programming. Nonetheless, we believe that a careful consideration of these guidelines will be useful in clearing up any confusion concerning the use of control structures; it might also provide some new insights as to how these structures can be used to solve a variety of problems.

7.2 NESTED STRUCTURES

7.2.1 Introduction

We have already seen examples of programs that contain nested control structures. For example, Problems 4.1, 4.2 and 6.2 all contain examples of decision structures nested within a loop. In implementing nested structures, one must be careful not to *overlap* the structures. That is, the inner structure(s) in a nest must be wholly contained *(nested)* within the outer structure(s).

Example 7.1:   The program segment in Fig. 7.1 contains two improperly nested *(overlapping)* FOR loops. The terminator for the inner loop (NEXT J) should precede the outer loop terminator (NEXT I).

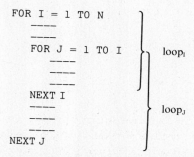

Fig. 7.1 Improper overlapping of FOR loops.

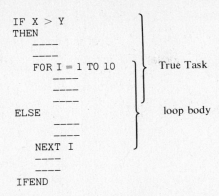

Fig. 7.2 Improper overlapping within a decision structure.

A further constraint is imposed if the outer structure of a nest is a decision structure with two or more alternatives. In this case, each inner structure must be wholly contained within a single alternative of the outer structure. In the program segment in Fig. 7.2, the FOR loop improperly overlaps both alternatives of an IF-THEN-ELSE structure. In order to execute the False Task, an illegal transfer into the middle of the FOR loop would be required.

If you carefully draw your level one flow diagram and then refine each step separately, it is impossible to draw a flow diagram that contains overlapping structures. However, if you are careless in converting your flow diagrams to BASIC program statements, or neglect to draw a flow diagram, you may end up with overlapping structures in your program.

7.2.2 Structure Entry and Exit

There is one important rule to follow when using the structures that have been presented in the text. This rule covers the manner in which these structures should be entered.

All structures should be entered only "through the top." That is, *no statement within a structure should be executed without prior execution of the header statement of the structure.* Transfers into the middle of a structure from outside the structure should be avoided because unpredictable program behavior may result.

Transfers of control within a structure or out of a structure are acceptable, although you should have little use for them except in specific situations. We have used the GOTO statement following the True Task of a double-alternative decision structure (in BASIC-PLUS and Minimal BASIC implementations) to transfer to the structure terminator. We have also used the GOTO statement to "exit" from a FOR loop (see Fig. 6.16). The Minimal BASIC implementa-

```
200 FOR I = 1 TO N
  .     ----
  .     ----
  .     ----
300     IF X + Y = Z THEN 310 ELSE 500
310       ----
  .       ----
  .       ----
400     NEXT I
  .     ----
  .     ----
  .     ----
500 IFEND
```

Fig. 7.3   Improperly nested structures.

tion of the WHILE loop uses both a conditional transfer statement and a GOTO statement for loop control.

Exercise 7.1:   What is wrong with the nest of structures depicted in Fig. 7.3? Rearrange the statements to produce a proper structure nesting.

Exercise 7.2:   Provide a flow diagram and BASIC program for the following problem: Find the index I of the first negative data item in the array X of size 20. If all items are non-negative, print an informative message.

7.2.3   AND and OR Logical Operators

There are many situations in which the execution of a task is dependent upon two or more conditions instead of just a single condition. For example, we might want a program to print the name, N$, of all male employees under 21 as illustrated in Fig. 7.4.

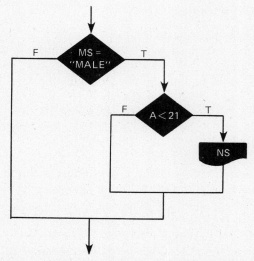

Fig. 7.4   Flow diagram for printing males under 21.

There are two *logical operators* (AND, OR) in Dartmouth BASIC and BASIC-PLUS that can be used to combine conditions to form *compound conditions*. In the statement:

```
IF M$ = "MALE" AND A < 21
```

the *logical AND operator* is used to form a compound condition that is true only when both condition$_1$ (M\$ = "MALE") *and* condition$_2$ (A < 21) are true. The compound condition would, therefore, be true only for males under 21. If we use the *logical OR operator* instead:

```
IF M$ = "MALE" OR A < 21
```

the compound condition is true if either condition$_1$ *or* condition$_2$ is true. Thus, the compound condition would be true for every male as well as for females under 21. The AND and OR logical operators are described in the next display.

Logical Operators AND, OR

Dartmouth BASIC and BASIC-PLUS form:

condition$_1$ AND condition$_2$

Interpretation: The compound condition above is true only if both condition$_1$ and condition$_2$ are true. If either condition is false, the compound condition is false.

condition$_1$ OR condition$_2$

Interpretation: The compound condition above is true if either condition$_1$ or condition$_2$ is true. The compound condition is false only when both conditions are false.

Example 7.2:   The decision structures in Fig. 7.5 might be used inside a loop to print each data item (X) with value in the range 5 to 10 inclusive. The variable I is increased by one if X is in this range.

   If X is within the desired range, both condition$_1$ (X > = 5) and condition$_2$ (X < = 10) must be true, so X will be printed. In the Minimal BASIC implementation, a transfer to the structure terminator (line 160) occurs if either the complement of condition$_1$ (X < 5) or the complement of condition$_2$ (X > 10) is true. In this case, X is outside the desired range and should not be printed.

   It is often tempting to write a condition of the form

```
X > = 5 AND < 10
```

to identify values of X within the range 5 to 10. This is an illegal compound condition as the symbols "< 10" do not represent a valid BASIC condition.

Example 7.3:   The decision structures in Fig. 7.6 could be used inside a loop to print each data item (X) that falls outside the range 5 to 10 inclusive. The variable C is increased by one if X falls outside this range.

BASIC-PLUS

```
100      IF X > = 5 AND X < = 10 THEN 110 ELSE 150
110 REM THEN
120          REM X IN RANGE 5 TO 10
130          PRINT X
140          LET I = I + 1
150 REM IFEND
```

Dartmouth BASIC

```
100      IF X > = 5 AND X < = 10
110      THEN
120          REM X IN RANGE 5 TO 10
130          PRINT X
140          LET I = I + 1
.50          IFEND
```

Minimal BASIC

```
100      IF X < 5 THEN 160
110      IF X > 10 THEN 160
120 REM THEN
130          REM X IN RANGE 5 TO 10
140          PRINT X
150          LET I = I + 1
160 REM IFEND
```

Fig. 7.5 Examples of AND operator.

BASIC-PLUS

```
200      IF X < 5 OR X > 10 THEN 210 ELSE 250
210      THEN
220          REM X OUTSIDE RANGE 5 TO 10
230          PRINT X
240          LET C = C + 1
250          IFEND
```

Dartmouth BASIC

```
200      IF X < 5 OR X > 10
210 REM THEN
220          REM OUTSIDE RANGE 5 TO 10
230          PRINT X
240          LET C = C + 1
250          IFEND
```

Minimal BASIC

```
200      IF X < 5 THEN 220
210      IF X < = 10 THEN 260
220 REM THEN
230          REM X OUTSIDE RANGE 5 TO 10
240          PRINT X
250          LET C = C + 1
260 REM IFEND
```

Fig. 7.6 Examples of OR operator.

If X falls outside the range 5 to 10, either condition$_1$ (X < 5) or condition$_2$ (X > 10) must be true, so X will be printed. In the Minimal BASIC implementation, a transfer to the True Task (line 220) occurs if condition$_1$ is true and X will be printed as its value is less than 5. If condition$_1$ is false, the value of condition$_2$ determines whether or not X is printed. If condition$_2$ is also false, its complement (X < = 10) is true and a transfer to the structure terminator (line 260) occurs; if condition$_2$ is true, no transfer occurs and X will be printed as its value is greater than 10.

Example 7.4:   The program in Fig. 7.7 shows that the AND and OR operators may also be used to control WHILE loop repetition. The WHILE loop below prints the first divisor of N only. Loop repetition continues as long as D is in the range of trial divisors ($2 \le D \le \sqrt{N}$) and a divisor has not yet been found (P\$ = "PRIME"). Compare this with the loop in Problem 4.2.

```
100        LET P$ = "PRIME"
110        LET D = 2
120        [DO] WHILE D <= SQR(N) AND P$ = "PRIME"
130            IF INT(N/D) * D = N THEN 140 ELSE 170
140  REM    THEN
145            REM D DIVIDES N EXACTLY
150            PRINT D
160            LET P$ = "NOT PRIME"
170  REM    IFEND
180            LET D = D + 1
190        [LOOP] NEXT
```

Fig. 7.7   AND operator in a WHILE loop.

Exercise 7.3:   Write a decision structure that prints the name (N\$) of all female employees between 25 and 35 inclusive.

Exercise 7.4:   Implement the following using the AND and OR logical operators.
a)   Write a program to search an array X of size 100 and print the index of every item in X that falls outside the range 50 to 100 inclusive.
b)   Write a program to search an array X of size 50 and print the index of every item in X that falls inside the range 50 to 100 inclusive.

7.3   THE MULTIPLE-ALTERNATIVE DECISION AND SELECT STRUCTURE

7.3.1   Introduction

The problems we have encountered so far have usually involved the execution of at most one or two separate decision steps. The solutions to many problems require rather complicated sequences or nests of decision in order to determine what program statements are to be executed. As can be seen from the BASIC program for Problem 5.3 (Fig. 5.17c), nested decision struc-

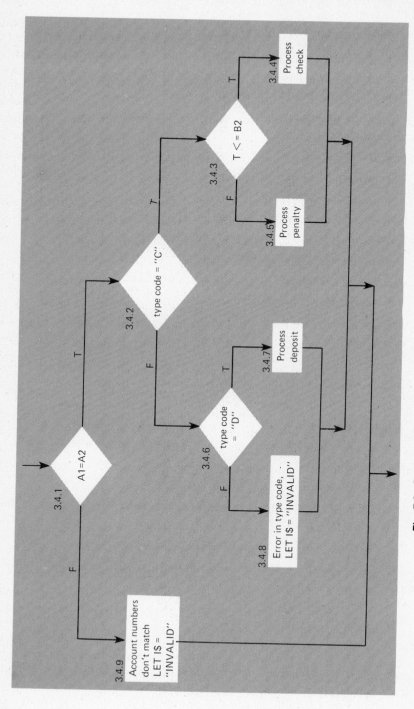

Fig. 7.8 Decision structure for checking account problem (Fig. 5.16b).

tures can be quite difficult to program and to read. For this reason, we will introduce a new flow diagram pattern, the *multiple-alternative decision structure*, which will enable us to more easily implement a complicated nest of decision structures.

7.3.2   Flow Diagram of Multiple-Alternative Decision Structure

In the checking account transaction problem from Chapter 5 (Problem 5.3), we distinguished between each of the following transaction types:

1. Transactions with invalid account numbers
2. Deposits
3. Legitimate checks
4. Rubber checks (insufficient account balance)
5. Unidentifiable transaction type (code neither "C" nor "D")

The nested decision structure we used is redone in Fig. 7.8.

This is a decision structure nest of considerable complexity, which is not particularly easy to follow, much less program. The necessary decisions for this problem can be more easily written if we generalize the flow diagram pattern for the IF-THEN-ELSE (double-alternative decision) into a multiple-alternative decision structure, so that more than two alternatives may be represented in a single structure. The flow diagram pattern for the multiple-alternative decision structure is shown in Fig. 7.9, along with an example of the structure defined for the checking account problem. (The conditions tested in Fig. 7.9 are not the same as those in Fig. 7.8. The changes were made in order to make optimum use of the multiple alternative structure.)

This flow diagram pattern implies the following program action:

a) The conditions are evaluated from top to bottom.
b) If condition$_i$ is the first condition to evaluate to true, then the corresponding task, Task$_i$, is executed. Structure exit occurs immediately after the completion of Task$_i$.
c) If no condition evaluates to true, Task$_D$ is performed.

Thus, the steps in exactly one of the tasks will be performed. More than one condition may actually be true, but only the topmost task will be executed because of the top-to-bottom order of evaluation of conditions. The structure exit immediately follows the execution of the task corresponding to the first true condition.

The bottom task, Task$_D$, may be omitted from this pattern. If this is done, all possible cases must be accounted for in the set of conditions provided. The descriptions of the tasks in a multiple-alternative decision pattern should be kept short, and refined, if necessary, in separate flow diagrams.

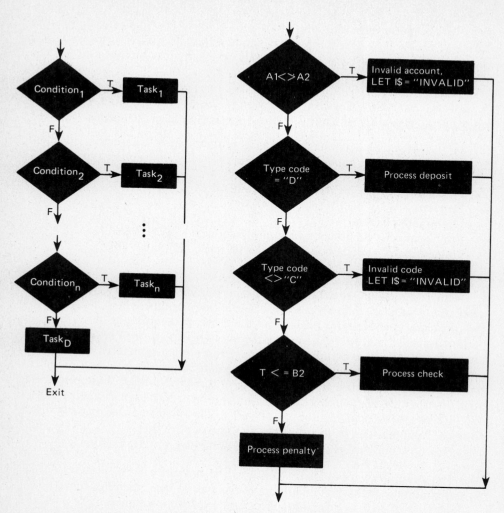

Fig. 7.9   Multiple-alternative decision pattern, general form (left) and example (right).

7.3.3   SELECT Structure

Dartmouth BASIC provides a special SELECT structure that is extremely convenient for implementing the multiple-alternative decision pattern. This structure is described in Fig. 7.10. The Minimal BASIC and BASIC-PLUS forms are shown in Figs. 7.11 and 7.12 respectively. Neither of these versions provide a special implementation structure for the multiple-alternative; we have provided an implementation form for both that we believe is relatively easy to write and read, although certainly not as nice as the Dartmouth BASIC SELECT structure.

SELECT Structure

Dartmouth BASIC Form:

SELECT
CASE condition$_1$

$\left.\begin{array}{c} \underline{\quad} \\ \underline{\quad} \end{array}\right\}$ Task$_1$

CASE condition$_2$

$\left.\begin{array}{c} \underline{\quad} \\ \underline{\quad} \end{array}\right\}$ Task$_2$

    .
    .
    .

CASE condition$_n$

$\left.\begin{array}{c} \underline{\quad} \\ \underline{\quad} \end{array}\right\}$ Task$_n$

DEFAULT

$\left.\begin{array}{c} \underline{\quad} \\ \underline{\quad} \end{array}\right\}$ Task$_D$

SELECTEND

Interpretation: Condition$_1$, condition$_2$, etc. are tested until a condition is reached that evaluates to true. If condition$_i$ is the first to evaluate to true, then Task$_i$ is executed. If none of the conditions evaluates to true, Task$_D$ is executed. Regardless of which task is carried out, execution next resumes with the first instruction following SELECTEND. If there is no Task$_D$ in the flow diagram, the DEFAULT alternative should be omitted.

Fig. 7.10   Dartmouth BASIC SELECT structure.

SELECT Structure

BASIC-PLUS Form:

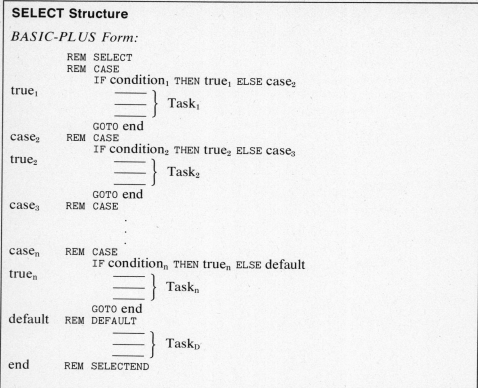

Interpretation: The label $true_i$ represents the line number of the first statement of $Task_i$; the label $case_i$ represents the line number of the REM CASE statement preceding $condition_i$; the label default represents the start of $Task_D$; the label end represents the line number of the structure terminator. The interpretation of the SELECT structure is the same as for the Dartmouth BASIC form.

Fig. 7.11   BASIC-PLUS SELECT structure.

SELECT Structure

Minimal BASIC Form:

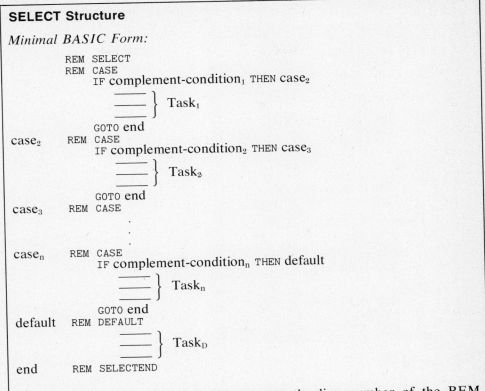

Interpretation: The label $case_i$ represents the line number of the REM CASE statement preceding the complement of $condition_i$; the label default represents the line number of the statement preceding $Task_D$; the label end represents the line number of the structure terminator. The interpretation of the SELECT structure is the same as for the Dartmouth BASIC form.

Fig. 7.12   Minimal BASIC SELECT structure.

```
5010 REM SUBROUTINE TO PROCESS EACH TRANSACTION
5020 REM
5030 REM SELECT
5040 REM CASE
5050     IF A1 < > A2 THEN 5060 ELSE 5090          [IF A1 = A2 THEN 5090]
5060         REM INVALID ACCOUNT
5070         LET I$ = "INVALID"
5080     GOTO 5300
5090 REM CASE
5100     IF C$ = "D" THEN 5110 ELSE 5150           [IF C$ <> "D" THEN 5150]
5110         REM PROCESS DEPOSIT
5120         LET B2 = B2 + T
5130         PRINT D$, TAB(30); T
5140     GOTO 5300
5150 REM CASE
5160     IF C$ < > "C" THEN 5170 ELSE 5200         [IF C$ = "C" THEN 5200]
5170         REM INVALID CODE
5180         LET I$ = "INVALID"
5190     GOTO 5300
5200 REM CASE
5210     IF T <= B2 THEN 5220 ELSE 5260            [IF T > B2 THEN 5260]
5220         REM PROCESS CHECK
5230         LET B2 = B2 - T
5240         PRINT D$, T
5250     GOTO 5300
5260 REM DEFAULT
5270         REM PROCESS PENALTY
5280         LET B2 = B2 - P
5290         PRINT D$, T; TAB(45) ; P
5300 REM SELECTEND
5310 REM
5320     RETURN
```

Fig. 7.13   BASIC program for Fig. 7.9.

The BASIC implementation of the multiple-alternative decision in Fig. 7.9 is given in Fig. 7.13.

Program Form and Style

The BASIC-PLUS form of the SELECT structure is shown in Fig. 7.13. As before, we have used shading to separate "what is happening" from the implementation requirements; consequently, the shaded portion corresponds to the Dartmouth BASIC form. However, in Dartmouth BASIC, the keyword CASE should be on the same line as the condition that follows. Also, the extra REM's and the GOTO statements are not needed.

The Minimal BASIC form could be obtained by substituting the conditional transfer statements on the right for the corresponding IF-THEN-ELSE statements.

Exercise 7.5:   You are writing a program to print grade reports for students at the end of each semester. After computing and printing each student's grade point average

P (maximum 4) for the semester, you are supposed to use the grade point average to make the following decision:

> If P is 3.5 or above, print DEANS LIST;
> If P is above 1 and less than or equal to 1.99, print PROBATION WARNING;
> If P is less than or equal to 1, print YOU ARE ON PROBATION NEXT
> SEMESTER

Draw a flow diagram and write the BASIC program segment for this decision. Use a multiple-alternative decision structure.

Exercise 7.6:   Replace the nested decision structures in Exercise 5.12 with a multiple-alternative decision structure.

7.4   THE BOWLING PROBLEM

The next problem makes use of the SELECT structure.

Problem 7.1:   Write a program that will compute a person's tenpin bowling score for one game, given the number of balls rolled, N, and the number of pins knocked down per ball. Print the score for each frame, as well as the cumulative score at the end of each frame.

Discussion: A bowling game consists of 10 *frames*. In tenpin bowling, a maximum of two balls may be rolled in each of the first nine frames, and two or three balls may be rolled in frame ten. Each frame is scored according to the following rules:

1.   If the first ball rolled in a frame knocks down all 10 pins, called a *strike*, then the score for the frame is equal to 10 + (the total score on the next two balls rolled). Since all ten pins are down, no other balls are rolled in the current frame.
2.   If the two balls rolled in the frame together knock down all 10 pins, called a *spare*, then the score for the frame is equal to 10 + (the score on the next ball rolled).
3.   If the two balls rolled knock down fewer than 10 pins (no mark), then the frame score is equal to the number of pins knocked down.

It is immediately clear that a loop will be needed to control the processing of each of the ten frames. The control variable for this loop (F) will simply serve to count each frame as it is processed. The array S (size 10) will be used to save the score for each frame.

The number of pins knocked down by each ball (pin count) will be read into an array called P. The variable I will serve as an index to this array. As such, it will be used to select particular elements of P—the elements whose values represent the number of pins knocked down by the first ball rolled in each frame. I should be increased by 1 each time a strike is bowled; otherwise, I should be incremented by 2. (Why?)

Frame	I	Frame score	Effect
1	1	10 + 7 + 3 = 20	STRIKE: Only one ball rolled in frame 1
2	2	10 + 5 = 15	SPARE: Two balls rolled in frame 2
3	4	5 + 3 = 8	NO MARK: Two balls rolled in frame 3
4	6	.	

Table 7.1   Processing array P

A sample of array P is given below.

P(1)	P(2)	P(3)	P(4)	P(5)	...
10	7	3	5	3	

This array shows that 10 pins were knocked down by the first ball, seven by the second, etc. The processing of this array is shown in Table 7.1.

Since P(1) is 10, a strike was bowled in the first frame. The frame score (20) is computed by adding together 10, P(2), and P(3); I is then set to 2. In the second frame, balls 2 and 3 are needed to knock down all 10 pins. Adding in the pins knocked down by the next ball, P(4), gives a frame score of 15; the index I is then set to 4. Two balls are rolled in the third frame (balls 4 and 5). The frame score is 8, and I is set to 6.

The data table is shown below; the flow diagrams are shown in Fig. 7.14a, b.

Data Table for Problem 7.1

Input variables

P(21): Array containing the number of pins knocked down by each ball rolled

N: The number of balls actually rolled

Program variables

I: Index which selects the number of pins knocked down by the first ball of each frame

F: Loop control variable, indicates number of frame

C: Loop control variable used in reading pin counts

Output variables

S(10): The score in each frame

T: The total score accumulated

In Fig. 7.14a, the loop control variable F serves as an index to the array S in steps 2 and 3. Note that the subscript expressions I, I + 1, I + 2, are used to select elements of the array P for testing or for the frame score computation. Since I represents the first ball bowled in each frame (anywhere from 1 to 19), I + 1 and I + 2 represent the next two balls rolled. The elements in P with these indices represent the number of pins knocked down by each ball in the sequence.

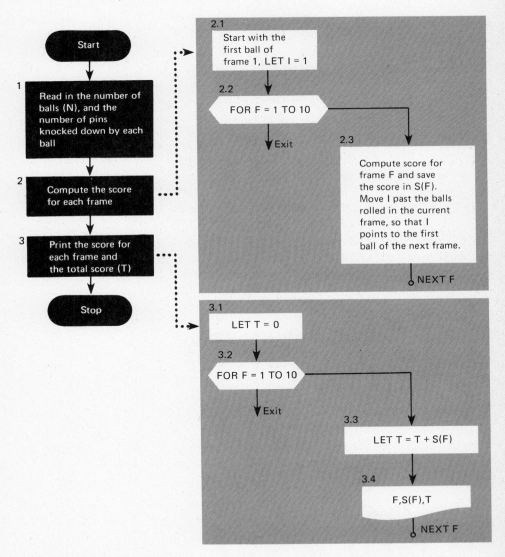

Fig. 7.14a   Level one and two flow diagrams for the bowling problem (7.1).

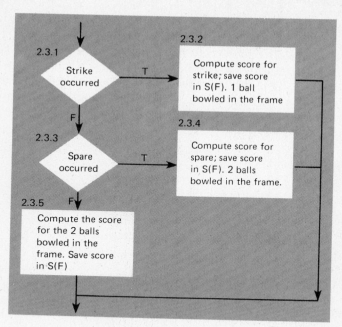

Fig. 7.14b   Refinement of step 2.3 of Fig. 7.14a.

We will now implement the program for the bowling problem (Fig. 7.15a, b) using subroutines for the refinements of each of the major steps (1, 2 and 3) as well as the refinement of step 2.3. A sample run of the program is shown in Fig. 7.15c.

```
110   REM BOWLING PROBLEM
120       PRINT "BOWLING PROBLEM"
130   REM
140       DIM P(21), S(10)
150   REM
160   REM ENTER NUMBER OF BALLS, N AND SCORES FOR EACH BALL IN P
170       GOSUB 1010
180   REM
190   REM COMPUTE SCORE FOR EACH FRAME
200       GOSUB 2010
210   REM
220   REM COMPUTE TOTAL SCORE AND PRINT RESULTS
230       GOSUB 3010
240   REM
250       STOP
260
270
1010  REM SUBROUTINE TO ENTER DATA
1020  REM ENTER NUMBER OF BALLS, N, AND SCORE FOR EACH IN P
1030  REM
1040      PRINT "HOW MANY BALLS WERE BOWLED";
```

Fig. 7.15a   Main program and level two subroutines for Problem 7.1. (Continued)

```
1050      INPUT N
1060      PRINT "ENTER PIN COUNTS FOR EACH BALL"
1070      FOR C = 1 TO N
1080         PRINT "BALL"; C;
1090         INPUT P(C)
1100      NEXT C
1110 REM
1120      RETURN
1130
1140
2010 REM SUBROUTINE TO COMPUTE FRAME SCORES
2020 REM BALL 1 IS FIRST BALL OF FRAME 1
2030 REM
2040      LET I = 1
2050      FOR F = 1 TO 10
2060         REM COMPUTE SCORE FOR FRAME F AND INCREMENT I
2070         GOSUB 4010
2080      NEXT F
2090 REM
2095      RETURN
2097
3000
3010 REM SUBROUTINE TO COMPUTE TOTAL SCORE, T, AND PRINT RESULTS
3020 REM
3030      LET T = 0
3035      PRINT
3040      PRINT "FRAME", "SCORE", "TOTAL SCORE"
3050      FOR F = 1 TO 10
3060         REM ADD IN SCORE FOR FRAME F
3070         LET T = T + S(F)
3080         PRINT F, S(F), T
3090      NEXT F
3100 REM
3110      RETURN
```

Fig. 7.15a Continuation of main program and level two subroutines for Problem 7.1.

```
4010 REM SUBROUTINE TO COMPUTE THE SCORE FOR THE CURRENT FRAME, F,
4020 REM AND INCREMENT I
4030 REM
4040 REM SELECT
4050 REM CASE
4060      IF P(I) = 10 THEN 4070 ELSE 4110              [IF P(I) <> 10 THEN 4110]
4070         REM PROCESS STRIKE
4080         LET S(F) = 10 + P(I+1) + P(I+2)
4090         LET I = I + 1
4100      GOTO 4210
4110 REM CASE
4120      IF P(I)+P(I+1) = 10 THEN 4130 ELSE 4170
                                          [IF P(I)+P(I+1) <> 10 THEN 4170]
4130         REM PROCESS SPARE
4140         LET S(F) = 10 + P(I+2)
4150         LET I = I + 2
4160      GOTO 4210
4170 REM DEFAULT
4185         REM NO MARK
5190         LET S(F) = P(I) + P(I+1)
4200         LET I = I + 2
4210 REM SELECTEND
4220 REM
4230      RETURN
4240      END
```

Fig. 7.15b Level three subroutine for Problem 7.1.

```
BOWLING PROBLEM
HOW MANY BALLS WERE BOWLED ? 19
ENTER PIN COUNTS FOR EACH BALL
BALL 1 ?6
BALL 2 ?4
BALL 3 ?7
BALL 4 ?2
BALL 5 ?10
BALL 6 ?3
BALL 7 ?0
BALL 8 ?9
BALL 9 ?0
BALL 10 ?8
BALL 11 ?2
BALL 12 ?10
BALL 13 ?4
BALL 14 ?2
BALL 15 ?6
BALL 16 ?1
BALL 17 ?8
BALL 18 ?2
BALL 19 ?6
```

FRAME	SCORE	TOTAL SCORE
1	17	17
2	9	26
3	13	39
4	3	42
5	9	51
6	20	71
7	16	87
8	6	93
9	7	100
10	16	116

Fig. 7.15c   Sample run of the bowling problem (7.1).

Exercise 7.7:   They do things a little differently in Massachusetts where Dr. Koffman grew up. The bowling pins (called candlepins) are narrow at the top and bottom and wider in the middle. The balls are about the size of a softball. The rules for a strike and a spare are the same; however, the bowler gets to roll a third ball in each frame if needed. Modify the bowling program to score a candlepin game. (Any pins that fall on the lane are not cleared away in candlepins. This can help the bowler but should not affect your program).

7.5   THE ON-GOTO AND ON-GOSUB STATEMENTS

7.5.1   ON-GOTO Statement

There is a special BASIC statement, the ON-GOTO, that can sometimes be used to speed up the process of determining which alternative to execute. Instead of evaluating a sequence of conditions, an index value is computed and used to select the next instruction (or task) for execution. The ON-GOTO is described in the next display.

ON-GOTO Statement

Minimal BASIC form:

```
ON expression line-list
```

Interpretation: The expression is first evaluated and rounded, if necessary, to obtain an integer. This integer value is then used to select one line number from the list of line numbers provided in line-list. The line numbers are indexed from left to right starting with 1; hence, if the expression value is 3, control would be transferred to the third line number in the list. If the expression value is less than 1 or greater than the number of line numbers in the list, an error message will be printed.

Notes: Some versions of BASIC truncate a noninteger expression value rather than round.

In some versions of BASIC, the next statement after the ON-GOTO will be executed if the expression value is out-of-range, i.e., too big or less than one, and no diagnostic will be printed.

Example 7.5:   Figure 7.16 provides an example of the use of an ON-GOTO structure (lines 170-290) to implement a multiple-alternative decision pattern. This program segment could be part of a CAI (computer-assisted instruction) drill.

```
100 REM ASK THE QUESTION
105 REM
110     PRINT "WHO INVENTED THE COTTON GIN"
120     PRINT "1 - ROBERT FULTON"
130     PRINT "2 - GEORGE WASHINGTON"
140     PRINT "3 - ELI WHITNEY"
145     PRINT "TYPE 1, 2 OR 3" ;
150     INPUT A
155 REM
160     PRINT A PROMPTING MESSAGE
170     ON A GOTO 180, 220, 260
180 REM A EQUAL 1
190         PRINT "NO. HE INVENTED THE STEAM BOAT"
200         LET W = W + 1
210     GOTO 290
220 REM A EQUAL 2
230         PRINT "NO. HE WAS THE FIRST PRESIDENT"
240         LET W = W + 1
250     GOTO 290
260 REM A EQUAL 3
270         PRINT "CORRECT"
280         LET R = R + 1
290 REM ON-GOTOEND
```

Fig. 7.16 ON-GOTO structure in a CAI program.

The multiple-choice question is printed (lines 110-140) and the student's answer is read into A. Depending upon the student's answer (1, 2, or 3) one of the three messages in the ON-GOTO structure will be printed (line 190, 230, or 270) and the count of wrong answers, W, or right answers, R, will be increased by one. Execution will resume with the first statement following line 290, the structure terminator.

Example 7.6:
a) If the value of D is three, execution of the statement

```
ON 2 * D - 1 GOTO 60, 70, 80, 90, 100, 110
```

will cause control to be transferred to the fifth line number, or line 100

b) Execution of the statements

```
READ X
ON X GOTO 200, 170, 150, 160, 200
DATA 3, 3, 2, 4, 1
```

in a loop would cause control to be transferred to lines 150 (line$_3$), 150 (line$_3$), 170 (line$_2$), 160 (line$_4$), and 200 (line$_1$) in that order.

You can list as many line numbers following the GOTO as are needed for your program. Line numbers do not have to be listed in order according to numeric value, and may occur more than once as is the case with line number 200 in Example 7.6b.

Exercise 7.8:   Explain why the multiple-alternative decision structure on the right of Fig. 7.9 could not be implemented using the ON-GOTO statement.

Exercise 7.9:   Write an ON-GOTO structure that would execute a different task for each of the cases listed below and print an error message if X is out-of-range.

$$\text{Case 1:} \quad 0 \le X < 5$$
$$\text{Case 2:} \quad 5 \le X < 10$$
$$\text{Case 3:} \quad 10 \le X < 15$$
$$\text{Case 4:} \quad 15 \le X < 20$$

7.5.2 ON-GOSUB Statement

BASIC-PLUS and Dartmouth BASIC have an ON-GOSUB statement that is similar to the ON-GOTO. The differences are:
1. Control is transferred to the subroutine indicated by the list of line numbers.
2. After returning from the subroutine, the next statement following the ON-GOSUB is executed.

Example 7.7:   The ON-GOSUB statement

```
ON E GOSUB 1000, 2000, 3000
```

will cause the subroutine starting at line 2000 to be executed if the value of E is two.

7.6   NESTED LOOPS

Nested loops, especially nested FOR loops, are perhaps the most difficult of all nested structures to write, read and debug. For this reason, we will examine some programs involving nested loops that should help clarify the relationship among the loops involved.

A flow diagram of a pair of nested FOR loops is shown in Fig. 7.17. The refinement of step 3 is itself a loop. This means that during each repetition of the outer loop, the inner loop must also be entered and executed until loop exit occurs. The number of times each loop is repeated depends upon its respective loop control parameters. Each time the inner loop is reentered, its loop control variable (J) is reinitialized. (In this case, it is set to the current value of A.)

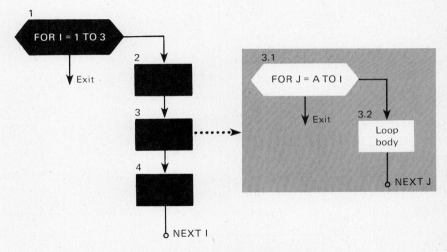

Fig. 7.17   Flow diagram of nested loops.

It is permissible to use the loop control variable of the outer loop as a parameter in the initialization, update or test of an inner loop control variable. However, the same variable should never be used as the loop control variable of both an outer loop and an inner loop in the same nest.

Example 7.8:   Fig. 7.18 shows a sample run of a program with two nested FOR loops. The number of repetitions of the inner loop is determined by the value of the outer loop control variable.

Example 7.9:   The program in Fig. 7.19a plots the contents of the array F in the form of a bar graph. Array F and the data table appear on the next page. The bar graph is shown in Fig. 7.19b.

```
20        LET A = 1
30        PRINT " ", " I", " J"
40        FOR I = 1 TO 3
50            PRINT "OUTER", I
60            FOR J = A TO I
70                PRINT "INNER", I, J
80            NEXT J
90        NEXT I
95 REM
98        END
RUN
```

	I	J
OUTER	1	
INNER	1	1
OUTER	2	
INNER	2	1
INNER	2	2
OUTER	3	
INNER	3	1
INNER	3	2
INNER	3	3

Fig. 7.18 Sample run with nested FOR loops.

Array F

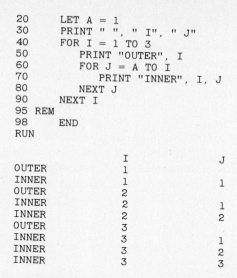

Data Table for Example 7.9

Input variables

F(10):   Array to be plotted

N: Number of elements of F to be plotted

Program variables

J: Loop control variable, serves as index to F

I: Inner loop control variable (for printing each bar)

V: Temporary variable for storage of each element of F

Output variables

F(10):   Array in form of a bar graph

The length of each line in the bar graph indicates the number of occurrences or frequency of a particular class. For example, the second line shows that class two was the most popular with 32 occurrences.

```
110   REM PLOT THE ARRAY F AS A BAR GRAPH
120   REM
130       DIM F(10)
140   REM
150   REM READ NUMBER OF ELEMENTS, N, AND ARRAY F
160       GOSUB 1010
170   REM
180   REM DRAW BAR GRAPH
190       GOSUB 2010
200   REM
210       STOP
220
230
1010  REM SUBROUTINE TO READ DATA (N ITEMS) INTO F
1020  REM
1030      READ N
1040      FOR J = 1 TO N
1050         READ F(J)
1060      NEXT J
1070  REM
1080      DATA 5, 8, 32, 24, 16, 3
1090  REM
1100      RETURN
1110
1120
2010  REM SUBROUTINE TO DRAW BAR GRAPH
2020  REM
2030      PRINT "CLASS", "FREQUENCY PLOT"
2040  REM
2050      FOR J = 1 TO N
2060         REM START NEW BAR
2065         PRINT
2070         PRINT "   "; J; " I";
2080         LET V = F(J)
2090         REM PRINT V STARS ON CURRENT BAR
2100         FOR I = 1 TO V
2110            PRINT "*";
2120         NEXT I
2130      NEXT J
2135      PRINT
2140      PRINT "        I----I----I----I----I----I----I----I"
2150  REM
2160      RETURN
2170  REM
2180      END
```

Fig. 7.19a Program and subroutines for bar graph example (7.9).

```
CLASS              FREQUENCY PLOT
    1  I********
    2  I******************************
    3  I***********************
    4  I****************
    5  I***
       I----I----I----I----I----I----I----I
```

Fig. 7.19b Bar graph printed by program in 7.19a.

This program has three FOR loops. The first loop (subroutine 1010) is used for reading data into F. The nested pair of loops (subroutine 2010) is used to draw the frequency plot. J is the outer loop control variable and is used to cycle through the elements of the array F. I is the loop control variable for the inner loop of the nested pair.

The statement

```
PRINT "*";
```

repeated in the inner loop at line 2110 instructs the computer to print a string of asterisks on each output line. The number of asterisks printed is determined by the value, V, of the element of F being represented on each output line (V is equal to F(J)).

Exercise 7.10:   Write out each line of the printout for the following program.

```
110 FOR I = 1 TO 2
120    PRINT "OUTER", I
130    FOR J = 1 TO 4 STEP 2
140        PRINT "INNER J", I, J
150    NEXT J
160    FOR K = 2 TO 4 STEP 2
170        PRINT "INNER K", I, K
180    NEXT K
190 NEXT I
```

7.7   SORTING AN ARRAY

The problem that follows is an example of the use of nested loops in sorting, or rearranging in numerical order, the data stored in an array. Sorting programs are used in a variety of applications and the program developed here could be easily modified to sort alphanumeric data, such as last names, stored in a string array. In this example, we will sort numeric data in ascending numerical order (smallest value first); however, it would be just as easy to sort the data in descending order (largest value first).

Problem 7.2:   Write a program to sort, in ascending order, an array of integer values.

Discussion: There are many different algorithms for sorting. We will use one of the simplest of these algorithms, the Bubble Sort. The Bubble Sort is so named because it has the property of "bubbling" the smallest items to the top of a list. The algorithm proceeds by comparing the values of adjacent elements in the array. If the value of the first of these elements is larger than the value of the second, these values are exchanged, and then the values of the next adjacent pair of elements are compared. This process starts with the pair of elements with indices 1 and 2 and continues through the pair of elements with indices n − 1 and n, in an array containing n data items. Then this sequence of comparisons, called a *pass*, is repeated, starting with the first pair of elements again, until the entire array of elements is compared without an exchange being made. At this point, the array must be sorted.

As an example, we will trace through the sort of the integer array M as shown in Fig. 7.20. In this sequence of diagrams, diagram 1 shows the initial arrangement of the data in the array; the first pair of values are out of order and they are exchanged. The result is shown in diagram 2. The new value of M(2), 60, is next compared to 83, the value of M(3). In this case, no exchange is required and M(3) is next compared to M(4). Since M(3) is less than M(4), these values would be exchanged as indicated in diagrams 2 and 3.

The sequence in Fig. 7.20 shows all exchanges that would be made during each pass through the adjacent pairs of array elements. After pass one, we see that the array is finally ordered except for the value 25 (see diagram 4). Subsequent passes through the array will "bubble" this value up one array element at a time until the sort is complete. In each pass through M, the elements are compared in the following order: M(1) and M(2); M(2) and M(3); M(3) and

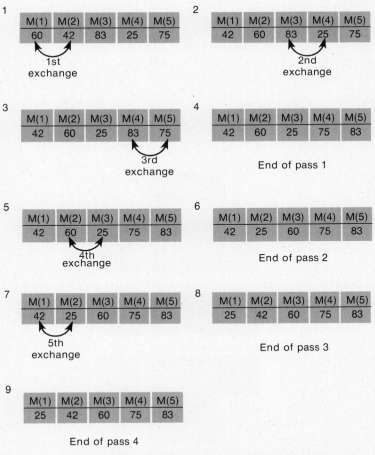

Fig. 7.20   Bubble sort trace on small array.

M(4); M(4) and M(5). Note that even though the array is sorted at the end of pass 3, it will take one more pass through the array without any exchanges to complete the algorithm.

Now that we have a general idea of how the algorithm works, we can write the data table and the flow diagrams (Figs. 7.21a and 7.21b) for the Bubble Sort.

Data Table for Problem 7.2

Input variables	*Program variables*	*Output variables*
M(20): Array containing the data to be sorted	P$: Program flag—a value of "MORE" indicates more passes through the data are required; a value of "NOMORE" indicates no exchanges made yet	M(20): At the conclusion of the program, this array will contain the data sorted in ascending order
N: Contains the number of array elements	T: Temporary storage cell required for the exchange	
	I: Loop control variable and array index	

Fig. 7.21a   Level one flow diagram for Bubble Sort Problem 7.2.

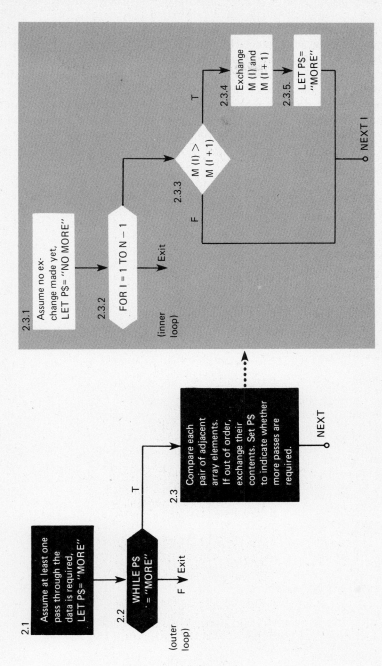

Fig. 7.21b. Successive refinements of step 2 in Fig. 7.21a.

Fig. 7.21b shows two levels of refinement for the sort step (step 2) shown in the level one diagram (Fig. 7.21a). As shown, the program flag P$ is tested in the outer loop to determine whether or not more passes are required. Since at least one pass through the data must be made, P$ is initialized to "MORE" before entering the outer loop. P$ is reset to "NOMORE" before each entry to the inner loop. If no exchange takes place, P$ will still equal "NOMORE" after completion of the inner loop and the outer loop will be exited with the array M sorted. If at least one pair of elements is out-of-order, P$ will be set to "MORE" (step 2.3.5) and the outer loop will be repeated after completion of the inner loop.

```
110  REM BUBBLE SORT PROGRAM
120      PRINT "BUBBLE SORT"
130  REM
140      DIM M(20)
150  REM
160  REM READ AND PRINT COUNT (N) AND ARRAY M
170      GOSUB 1010
180  REM
190  REM SORT ARRAY M
200      GOSUB 2010
210  REM
220  REM PRINT ARRAY M
230      GOSUB 3010
240  REM
250      STOP
260
270
1010 REM SUBROUTINE TO READ AND PRINT COUNT, N, AND ARRAY M
1020 REM
1030     READ N
1040     PRINT "NUMBER OF ITEMS TO BE SORTED IS "; N
1050     PRINT "ORIGINAL UNSORTED LIST"
1060     FOR I = 1 TO N
1070        READ M(I)
1080        PRINT M(I)
1090     NEXT I
1100 REM
1110     DATA 5, 60, 42, 83, 25, 75
1120 REM
1130     RETURN
1140
1150
2010 REM BUBBLE SORT SUBROUTINE
2020 REM
2030     LET P$ = "MORE"
2050 REM WHILE P$ = "MORE" MAKE ANOTHER PASS THROUGH M
2060     [DO] WHILE P$ = "MORE"              [IF P$ <> "MORE" THEN 2090]
2070        GOSUB 4010
2080     [LOOP] NEXT                         [GOTO 2050]
2090 REM
2100     RETURN
```

Fig. 7.22a   Main program and first two subroutines for Problem 7.2.

   As indicated in step 2.3 (Fig. 7.21b), if a pair of array elements is out of order, their values must be exchanged (step 2.3.4). We will use a temporary storage cell, T, to hold one of these values to facilitate the exchange. Note that I always points to the first array element of any pair being compared; consequently, the end value expression for the inner loop must be $N - 1$.

   The program for the Bubble Sort is shown in Figs. 7.22a, b.

```
3010 REM SUBROUTINE TO PRINT SORTED ARRAY M
3020 REM
3030      PRINT "FINAL SORTED LIST"
3040      FOR I = 1 TO N
3050         PRINT M(I)
3060      NEXT I
3070 REM
3080      RETURN
3090
3100
4010 REM SUBROUTINE TO PASS THROUGH M
4020 REM
4030 REM ASSUME NO MORE PASSES NEEDED AFTER THIS ONE
4040      LET P$ = "NOMORE"
4050 REM
4060 REM COMPARE PAIRS OF ADJACENT ELEMENTS, FROM FIRST PAIR TO LAST
4070      FOR I = 1 TO N - 1
4080          IF M(I) > M(I+1) THEN 4085 ELSE 4140
                                   [IF M(I) <= M(I+1) THEN 4140]
4085 REM      THEN
4090              REM M(I) > M(I+1) -- EXCHANGE VALUES AND RESET P$
4100              LET T = M(I)
4110              LET M(I) = M(I+1)
4120              LET M(I+1) = T
4130              LET P$ = "MORE"
4140 REM      IFEND
4150      NEXT I
4160 REM
4170      RETURN
4180 REM
4190      END

RUN

BUBBLE SORT
NUMBER OF ITEMS TO BE SORTED IS 5
ORIGINAL UNSORTED LIST
 60
 42
 83
 25
 75
FINAL SORTED LIST
 25
 42
 60
 75
 83
```

Fig. 7.22b Additional subroutines and sample output for Problem 7.2.

Exercise 7.11:   In Fig. 7.20, note that after pass k the kth largest value is in element M(N−k+1). Hence, it is only necessary to examine elements with indices less than N−k+1 during the next pass. Modify the algorithm to take advantage of this.

Exercise 7.12:   Modify the Bubble Sort program to sort the array M in descending order (largest number first). Trace the execution of your program on the initial array shown in Fig. 7.20.

Exercise 7.13:   Modify the Bubble Sort program so that the median or middle item of the final sorted array is printed out. If N is even, the median should be the average of the two middle values, i.e., the average of the elements with indices N/2 and N2 + 1. If N is odd, the median is simply the value of the array element with index N/2 + 1. A number is even if it is divisible by 2. (See Exercise 4.13.)

Exercise 7.14:   A different technique for sorting consists of searching the entire array to find the location of the smallest element that is then exchanged with the first element. Next, elements 2 through N are searched and the next smallest element is exchanged with the second array element. This process continues until only elements N − 1 and N are left to search. Flow diagram the algorithm. *Hint:* Use a pair of nested FOR loops.

7.7.2   Nested Loops—A Final Note

Whenever nested loops are used, the inner loop is executed from start to finish for each repetition or *iteration* of an outer loop. In the Bubble Sort program, the inner loop will be executed for all values of I between 1 and N − 1 for each execution of the outer loop.

This kind of repetition can be quite difficult to understand, much less to program. It is, therefore, often helpful to outline the logic of each loop separately, putting the loops together only at the final stage of writing the program. This can be done by simply summarizing the activity of any loop nested within another (see 2.3 in Fig. 7.21b), and then providing the details of execution of the inner loop in a separate place, possibly on another page.

7.8   COMMON PROGRAMMING ERRORS

7.8.1   Structure Nesting Errors

Structure nesting errors are among the most common programming errors that are made. Such errors are more likely to occur when nested decision structures or multiple-alternative decision structures with lengthy statement groups for each alternative are used.

To aid in obtaining the proper structure nesting, we urge you to faithfully follow the process of flow diagram refinement illustrated in the text. Refine each nested structure as a separate entity, and then carefully implement the refined flow diagram as a BASIC program. To retain the proper structure nesting, go back to the flow diagram when making any nontrivial changes to the algorithm. Rearranging structure components in the program without referring to the flow diagram may introduce unexpected logic errors.

7.8.2 Multiple-Alternative Decision (SELECT) Structure Errors

Care must be taken in listing the conditions to be used in a multiple-alternative decision or SELECT structure. If the conditions are not *mutually exclusive* (that is, if more than one of the conditions can be true at the same time), then the condition sequence must be carefully ordered to ensure the desired results.

It is always a good idea to include a DEFAULT subtask group in every multiple-alternative decision structure. Even if the condition list is constructed so as to "guarantee" that the DEFAULT subtask can never be executed, it is still a good practice to print a warning message, should the unexpected happen during the execution of your program.

7.8.3 ON-GOTO Errors

The most common ON-GOTO error is caused by the failure to ensure that the expression e falls within the range 1 to n, where n is the number of line numbers in the statement:

$$\text{ON } e \text{ GOTO line}_1, \text{ line}_2, \ldots, \text{ line}_n$$

If your BASIC system does not print a diagnostic message, you should insert your own error message just after the ON-GOTO statement.

7.8.4 Nested Loop Errors

The most common errors in using FOR loops involve the incorrect definition of loop parameters in the header statement. If the parameter expressions used in a FOR loop header are invalid expressions, you will get a diagnostic message. If they are valid but compute the wrong values, you will likely receive no diagnostics. Incorrect expressions will result in the wrong number of loop repetitions being performed. This error, in turn, may cause you to run out of data items and could result in an INSUFFICIENT DATA diagnostic message. If the loop control variable is being used in an array subscript expression, you may get a SUBSCRIPT-OUT-OF-RANGE diagnostic if the loop parameters are incorrect. It is often helpful to print the value of the loop control variable if you suspect it is not being manipulated properly.

Whenever practical, you should completely simulate the execution of each loop to ensure that the number of repetitions is correct. At a minimum, you should test the "boundary conditions"; i.e., verify that the initial and final values of the loop control variable are correct. Furthermore, you should verify that all array references that use the loop control variable in subscript computations are within range at the loop control variable boundary values.

When using nested loops, make sure that the loop terminators are in the correct order so that the loops do not overlap. Also, remember that a different loop control variable must be used with each loop in the nest.

7.9 SUMMARY

With this chapter, we conclude the discussion of the loop and decision control structures. Six structures have been presented in the text:

Single-alternative decision structure: Chapter 3,
Double-alternative decision structure: Chapter 3,
Multiple-alternative decision (SELECT) structure: Chapter 7,
The ON-GOTO statement and ON-GOTO structure: Chapter 7,
WHILE loop structure: Chapter 5,
FOR loop structure: Chapter 2 and Chapter 3.

Of these structures, only the FOR loop and the ON-GOTO are available as part of Minimal BASIC (and, therefore, can be expected to be available in all versions of BASIC). The implementation forms of the other four structures

Statement	Effect
ON-GOTO statement	

`170      ON A GOTO 180, 220, 260`
`180 REM  A EQUAL 1`
`190         PRINT "NO. HE INVENTED ..."`
`200         LET W = W + 1`
`210      GOTO 290`
`220 REM  A EQUAL 2`
`230         PRINT "NO. HE WAS THE ..."`
`240         LET W = W + 1`
`250      GOTO 290`
`260 REM  A EQUAL 3`
`270         PRINT "CORRECT"`
`280         LET R = R + 1`
`290 REM  ON-GOTOEND`
	If A is one, lines 180-210 are executed; if A is two, lines 220-250 are executed; if A is three, lines 260-280 are executed. Execution resumes with the first statement following line 290.

SELECT structure	

`100 REM  SELECT`
`110 REM  CASE`
`120      IF X >= 60 THEN 170`
`130         REM UNSATISFACTORY GRADE`
`140         PRINT "GRADE IS F"`
`150         LET F = F + 1`
`160      GOTO 270`
`170 REM  CASE`
`180      IF X >= 80 THEN 230`
`190         REM SATISFACTORY GRADE`
`200         PRINT "GRADE IS C"`
`210         LET C = C + 1`
`220      GOTO 270`
`230 REM  DEFAULT`
`240         REM EXCELLENT GRADE`
`250         PRINT "GRADE IS A"`
`260         LET A = A + 1`
`270 REM  SELECTEND`
	If X is less than 60, a grade of F is assigned; if X is between 60 and 80, a grade of C is assigned; if X is greater than or equal to 80, a grade of A is assigned. Execution resumes with the first statement following line 270.

Table 7.2   Summary of Minimal BASIC statements

depend upon the version of the BASIC system that you are using. We have illustrated BASIC-PLUS, Dartmouth BASIC and Minimal BASIC implementations of these structures.

The multiple-alternative decision structure introduced in this chapter is extremely useful in describing algorithms containing decisions for which there are more than two alternatives. Such situations could be described using nests of single- and double-alternative decision structures, but these can be extremely difficult to organize. Dartmouth BASIC provides the SELECT structure for the convenient implementation of multiple-alternative decisions. The forms of the multiple-alternative implementations in BASIC-PLUS and Minimal BASIC are patterned after the Dartmouth BASIC SELECT. In special cases where the choice of alternatives depends solely upon the value of a single expression, e, the Minimal BASIC statement

$$\text{ON } e \text{ GOTO line}_1, \text{ line}_2, \dots, \text{ line}_n$$

may be used to select the alternative to be executed instead of a sequence of conditions.

Examples of the new structures introduced in this chapter are provided in Tables 7.2, 7.3 and 7.4. The ON-GOTO in Table 7.2 should be studied along with the table appropriate for your version of BASIC.

All six structures that we have seen may be used in a BASIC program and any of them may be nested inside another. It is essential, however, that any structure nested inside another structure begin and end within the same state-

Statement	Effect
SELECT structure	
100 SELECT 110 CASE X < 60 120 REM UNSATISFACTORY GRADE 130 PRINT "GRADE IS F" 140 LET F = F + 1 150 CASE X < 80 150 REM SATISFACTORY GRADE 170 PRINT "GRADE IS C" 175 LET C = C + 1 180 DEFAULT 190 REM EXCELLENT GRADE 200 PRINT "GRADE IS A" 205 LET A = A + 1 210 SELECTEND	If X is less than 60, a grade of F is assigned; if X is between 60 and 80, a grade of C is assigned; if X is greater than or equal to 80, a grade of A is assigned. Execution resumes with the first statement following line 210.
ON-GOSUB statement	
ON I GOSUB 1000, 2000, 3000	If I is 1, the subroutine at line 1000 is called; if I is 2, the subroutine at line 2000 is called; if I is 3, the subroutine at line 3000 is called.

Table 7.3 Summary of Dartmouth BASIC statements

Statement	Effect
SELECT structure	

```
100 REM  SELECT
110 REM  CASE
120      IF X < 60 THEN 130 ELSE 170
130          REM UNSATISFACTORY GRADE
140          PRINT "GRADE IS F"
150          LET F = F + 1
160      GOTO 270
170 REM  CASE
180      IF X < 80 THEN 190 ELSE 230
190          REM SATISFACTORY GRADE
200          PRINT "GRADE IS C"
210          LET C = C + 1
220      GOTO 270
230 REM  DEFAULT
240          REM EXCELLENT GRADE
250          PRINT "GRADE IS A"
260          LET A = A + 1
270 REM  SELECTEND
```

If X is less than 60, a grade of F is assigned; if X is between 60 and 80, a grade of C is assigned; if X is greater than or equal to 80, a grade of A is assigned. Execution resumes with the first statement following line 270.

ON-GOSUB statement

```
ON I GOSUB 1000, 2000, 3000
```

If I is 1, the subroutine at line 1000 is called; if I is 2, the subroutine at line 2000 is called; if I is 3, the subroutine at line 3000 is called.

Table 7.4   Summary of BASIC-PLUS statements

ment group of the outer structure. Thus, a loop that begins in one alternative of a decision structure must terminate within that same alternative.

All structures must be entered via the execution of the header statement. Transfers into the middle of a structure are highly undesirable and should be avoided.

The Bubble Sort program shown in Fig. 7.22 illustrates, among other things, how complicated nests of structures can be greatly simplified through the use of subroutines. For example, this program actually requires the use of a single-alternative decision structure nested inside a FOR loop, which is itself nested inside a WHILE loop. However, the FOR loop and decision structure were coded as a separate subroutine (line 4010), as suggested by the stepwise development of the sort algorithm. The WHILE loop, therefore, contains only a transfer to the subroutine. This makes the program easier to code, to debug, to read and to maintain.

This kind of algorithm simplicity is one of the principal advantages of the top-down approach to problem solving. Specifying the algorithm for solving a problem in terms of a carefully chosen collection of subtasks guarantees a relatively simple structure for the algorithm produced. As has already been pointed out, the benefits of this approach are substantial.

PROGRAMMING PROBLEMS

7.3 *Frequency-distribution problem.* An instructor has just given an exam to a very large class and has punched the grades onto cards, one grade per card. The grading scale is 90-100 (A), 80-89 (B), 70-79 (C), 60-69 (D), 0-59 (F). The instructor wants to know how many students took the exam, what the average and standard deviation were for the exam and how many A's, B's, C's, D's, and F's there were. Write a program using a loop and a multiple-alternative decision structure to help the instructor obtain this information. Also, plot the frequency distribution as a bar graph.

7.4 A tax table is used to determine the tax rate for a company employee, based on weekly gross salary and number of dependents. The tax table has the form shown below. An employee's net pay can be determined by multiplying gross salary times the tax rate and subtracting this product from the gross salary. Write a program to read in the identification number, number of dependents and gross salary for each employee of a company, and then determine the net salary to be paid to each employee. Your program should also print out a count of the number of employees with gross salary in each of the ranges shown. [*Hint:* Use a multiple-alternative decision structure to "implement" this table. Note that the increase in rate for each column is constant (0.1 for 0-100, 0.12 for 100-200, 0.13 for ≥200.]

		Gross salary		
		0-100	100-200	≥200
Number of	0	0.2	0.28	0.38
dependents	1	0.1	0.16	0.25
	≥2	0.0	0.04	0.12

Tax rate table

7.5   The equation of the form

$$1. \quad mx + b = 0$$

(where m and b are real numbers) is called a linear equation in one unknown, x. If we are given the values of both m and b, then the value of x that satisfies this equation may be computed as

$$2. \quad x = -b/m.$$

Write a program to read in N different sets of values for m and b and compute x. Test your program for the following five sets of values:

m	b
−12.0	3.0
0.0	18.5
100.0	40.0
0.0	0.0
−16.8	0.0

[*Hint:* There are three distinct possibilities concerning the values of x that satisfy the equation mx + b = 0.
1. As long as m ≠ 0, the value of x that satisfies the original equation 1 is given by equation 2.
2. If both b and m are 0, then any real number that we choose satisfies mx + b = 0.
3. If m = 0 and b ≠ 0, then no real number x satisfies this equation.]

7.6   Each year the legislature of a state rates the productivity of the faculty of each of the state-supported colleges and universities. The rating is based on reports submitted by each faculty member indicating the average number of hours worked per week during the school year. Each faculty member is ranked, and the university also receives an overall rank.

The faculty productivity rank is computed as follows:

i) faculty members averaging over 55 hours per week are considered "highly productive";

ii) faculty members averaging between 35 and 55 hours a week, inclusive, are considered "satisfactory";

iii) faculty members averaging fewer than 35 hours a week are considered "overpaid".

The productivity rating of each school is determined by first computing the faculty average for the school:

$$\text{Faculty average} = \frac{\Sigma \text{ hours worked per week for all faculty}}{\text{Number of faculty reporting}}$$

and then comparing the faculty average to the category ranges defined in (i), (ii), and (iii).

Use the multiple-alternative decision structure and write a program to rank the following faculty:

HERM	63
FLO	37
JAKE	20
MO	55
SOL	72
TONY	40
AL	12
ZZZZ	0 (Sentinel value)

Your program should print a three-column table giving the name, hours and productivity rank of each faculty member. It should also compute and print the school's overall productivity ranking.

7.7   Write a savings account transaction program that will process the following set of data

"ADAM"	1054.37	
"W"	25.00	
"D"	243.35	group 1
"W"	254.55	
"Z"	0	
"EVE"	2008.24	
"W"	15.55	group 2
"Z"	0	
"MARY"	128.24	
"W"	62.48	
"D"	13.42	group 3
"W"	84.60	
"Z"	0	
"SAM"	7.77	group 4
"Z"	0	

"JOE"	15.27	
"W"	16.12	
"D"	10.00	group 5
"Z"	0	
"BETH"	12900.00	
"D"	9270.00	group 6
"Z"	0	
"ZZZZ"	0	(Sentinel record)

The first record in each group (header) gives the name for an account and the starting balance in the account. All subsequent records show the amount of each withdrawal (W) or deposit (D) that was made for that account followed by a sentinel record ("Z" 0). Print out the final balance for each of the accounts processed. If a balance becomes negative, print an appropriate message and take whatever corrective steps you deem proper. If there are no transactions for an account, print a message so indicating.

7.8 *Variation on the mortgage interest problem—Problem 4.11.* Use FOR loops to write a program to print tables of the following form.

Home loan mortgage interest payment tables

Amount_____ Loan duration (Months)_____

Rate (Percent)	Monthly payment	Total payment
6.00		
6.25		
6.50		
6.75		
7.00		
7.25		
7.50		
.		
.		
.		
10.00		
10.25		
10.50		
10.75		
11.00		

Your program should produce tables for loans of 30, 40, and 50 thousand dollars, respectively. For each of these three amounts, tables should be produced for loan durations of 240, 300 and 360 months. Thus, nine tables of the above form should be produced. Your program should contain three nested loops, some of which may be inside separate subroutines, depending upon your solution. Be careful to remove all redundant computations from inside your loops, especially from inside the innermost loop.

7.9 *Quadratic-equation problem.* The equation of the form

$$(1)\ ax^2 + bx + c = 0\ (a, b, c\ \text{real numbers, with}\ a \neq 0)$$

is called a quadratic equation in x. The real *roots* of this equation are those values of x for which

$$ax^2 + bx + c$$

evaluates to zero. Thus, if $a = 1$, $b = 2$, and $c = -15$, then the real roots of

$$x^2 + 2x - 15$$

are $+3$ and -5, since

$$(3)^2 + 2(3) - 15 = 9 + 6 - 15 = 0$$

and

$$(-5)^2 + 2(-5) - 15 = 25 - 10 - 15 = 0$$

Quadratic equations of the form (1) have either 2 real and different roots, 2 real and equal roots, or no real roots. The determination as to which of these three conditions holds for a given equation can be made by evaluating the discriminant d of the equation, where

$$d = b^2 - 4ac.$$

There are three distinct possibilities:
1.   If $d > 0$, then the equation has two real and unequal roots.
2.   If $d = 0$, the equation has two real and equal roots.
3.   If $d < 0$, the equation has no real roots.

Write a program to compute and print the real roots of quadratic equations having the following values of a, b, and c.

a	b	c
1.0	2.0	−15.0
1.0	−1.25	−9.375
1.0	0.0	1.0
1.0	−80.0	−900.0
1.0	−6.0	9.0

If the equation has no real roots for a set of a, b and c, print an appropriate message and read the next set. *Hint:* If the equation has two real and equal roots, then the root values are given by the expression

$$\text{Root 1} = \text{Root 2} = -b/2a.$$

If the equation has two real and unequal roots, their values may be computed as

$$\text{Root 1} = \frac{-b + \sqrt{d}}{2a},$$

$$\text{Root 2} = \frac{-b - \sqrt{d}}{2a}.$$

7.10 Write a program to solve the following problem:
Read in a collection of N data items, each containing one integer between 0 and 9, and count the number of consecutive pairs of each integer occurring in the data set. Your program should print the number of consecutive pairs of 0's, of 1's, 2's, . . ., and the number of consecutive pairs of 9's found in the data.

7.11 Write a program that will provide change for a dollar for any item purchased that costs less than one dollar. Print out each unit of change (quarters, dimes, nickels, or pennies) provided. Always dispense the biggest-denomination coin possible.

For example, if there are 37 cents left in change, dispense a quarter, which leaves 12 cents in change, then dispense a dime, and then two pennies. You may wish to use a multiple-alternative decision structure in solving this problem. However, you can also use a four-element array (to store each denominational value 25, 10, 5, and 1).

7.12 *Statistical measurements with functions—a simple linear-curve fit problem.* Scientists and engineers frequently perform experiments designed to provide measurements of two variables X and Y. They often compute measures of central tendency (such as the mean) and measures of dispersion (such as the standard deviation) for these variables. They then attempt to decide whether or not there is any relationship between the variables, and, if so, to express this relationship in terms of an equation. If there is a relationship between X and Y that is describable using a linear equation of the form

$$Y = aX + b,$$

the data collected is said to *fit a linear curve*.

For example, the ACE Computing Company recently made a study relating aptitude test scores to programming productivity of new personnel. The six pairs of scores shown below were obtained by testing 6 randomly selected applicants and later measuring their productivity.

Applicant	Aptitude score (Variable X)	Productivity (Variable Y)
1	$x_1 = 9$	$y_1 = 46$
2	$x_2 = 17$	$y_2 = 70$
3	$x_3 = 20$	$y_3 = 58$
4	$x_4 = 19$	$y_4 = 66$
5	$x_5 = 20$	$y_5 = 86$
6	$x_6 = 23$	$y_6 = 64$

ACE wants to find the equation of the line that they can use to predict the productivity of workers tested in the future. They are also interested in obtaining means and standard deviations for the variables X and Y. The required computations can be performed as follows:

1. Compute
   SUMX $= \Sigma X$ $= x_1 + x_2 + \cdots + x_6$
   SUMY $= \Sigma Y$ $= y_1 + y_2 + \cdots + y_6$
   SUMXY $= \Sigma X \cdot Y$ $= x_1 y_1 + x_2 y_2 + \cdots + x_6 y_6$
   SUMXSQ $= \Sigma X^2$ $= x_1^2 + x_2^2 + \cdots + x_6^2$
   SUMYSQ $= \Sigma Y^2$ $= y_1^2 + y_2^2 + \cdots + y_6^2$

2. Compute
   MEANX $=$ SUMX/N   where   N = 6
   MEANY $=$ SUMY/N

3. Compute
   STDDVX $= \sqrt{\text{SUMXSQ}/N - \text{MEANX}^2}$
   STDDVY $= \sqrt{\text{SUMYSQ}/N - \text{MEANY}^2}$

4. Compute a and b in $Y = aX + b$ using the equation

$$a = \frac{\text{SUMXY} - N \times \text{MEANX} \times \text{MEANY}}{\text{SUMXSQ} - N \times \text{MEANX}^2}$$

$$b = \text{MEANY} - a \times \text{MEANX}$$

Write subroutines to carry out the above computations. Test your program on the aptitude/productivity data just shown.

LARGER PROGRAMS: USER-DEFINED FUNCTIONS, SUBROUTINES AND SUBPROGRAMS

8.1   INTRODUCTION

In Chapter 5, we introduced the subroutine structure of BASIC and showed how this feature could be used to help us construct nicely modularized programs that reflected the top-down, level-by-level refinement process that was used in the design of algorithms. We also indicated that subroutines are helpful in writing programs in which it is necessary to perform certain operations (sequences of steps) more than once.

BASIC provides two additional features, the *user-defined function*, and the *subprogram*, which facilitate the solution of problems in terms of their more manageable parts. The user-defined function is supported in all versions of BASIC; the subprogram feature is currently provided in only a few versions of BASIC, including BASIC-PLUS-2 and Dartmouth BASIC. For this reason, we will concentrate more on user-defined functions in this chapter. In the next section, we describe the user-defined function in detail, providing numerous short examples. Following this, we illustrate how user-defined functions and subroutines can be used to implement a reasonably complicated problem involving the computation of several statistical measures. Finally, we introduce the notion of the subprogram, illustrate its use in the statistics problem and discuss some of the important differences between subroutines, user-defined functions and subprograms.

8.2   USER-DEFINED FUNCTIONS

8.2.1   Function Definitions

In addition to the standard mathematical functions discussed in Section 4.6, BASIC provides a facility for programmers to introduce function definitions of their own. The Minimal BASIC standard allows for a maximum of up to 26 such functions, and restricts function definition to a single line, and at most a single, numeric argument. However, most versions of BASIC, including BASIC-PLUS and Dartmouth BASIC, support multiple-argument and multi-line function definitions. We will, therefore, describe all function forms (single line, multi-line, and single- and multiple-argument) in this chapter. You are urged to consult your BASIC manual for the function definition features supported at your installation.

Example 8.1:   The *single-line function* FNR defined as

```
DEF FNR(X) = INT(X * 1E2 + 0.5) / 1E2
```

can be used to round any positive number (represented by X) to the nearest two decimal places (1E2 is 100 in BASIC scientific notation). FNR is an example of a single-line function. Single-line functions are defined by prefixing the *function description* with the letters DEF. The statement

```
LET Z = FNR(30.9864)
```

calls the function FNR. The number 30.9864 is substituted for X and the value 30.99 would be assigned to Z.

Recall that BASIC prints numbers with fractional parts to six significant digits of accuracy. Therefore, functions such as FNR can be extremely useful if answers accurate to fewer decimal places (such as dollars and cents) are required.

Example 8.2: We can define a *multiple line function*, named FNM, which determines which of two data items has the larger value:

```
110 REM MAXIMUM VALUE FUNCTION FOR TWO VARIABLES, X AND Y
115 REM
120     DEF FNM(X, Y)
130     IF X >= Y THEN 140 ELSE 170
140 REM THEN
150         LET FNM = X
160     GOTO 190
170 REM ELSE
180         LET FNM = Y
190 REM IFEND
195 REM
200     FNEND
```

The statement

```
LET M = FNM(20, 35)
```

calls the function FNM. The number 20 is substituted for X and 35 for Y; the value 35 would be assigned to M.

In a multiple-line function, the DEF statement starts the definition, and the statement FNEND marks the end of the function definition. The statements between are all considered to be part of the *function description*. The variables listed in the DEF statement (X and Y in this case) are called the *dummy arguments* or *parameters* of the function.

The statements

```
150 LET FNM = X
180 LET FNM = Y
```

in the function description define the value of the function. At least one statement that assigns a value to the function name must be executed each time the function is used. In this example, the first of these statements is executed if the number represented by X is the larger; otherwise, the second one is executed.

The rules of definition for functions are summarized in the following displays.

Single-Line Function Definition

Minimal BASIC form:

```
         DEF FNX = expression
    or DEF FNX (parameter) = expression
```

Interpretation: FNX is the function name where X is a letter of the alphabet. When the function is called, the expression is evaluated and its value is returned. If the function has a parameter, the argument value is substituted for the parameter. The parameter must be a simple numeric variable as array parameters are not permitted.

Multiple-Line Function Definition

Dartmouth BASIC and BASIC-PLUS form:

```
        DEF FNX
   or DEF FNX (parameter-list)
        ─────
        ─────  } function description
        ─────
        FNEND
```

Interpretation: FNX is the function name where X is a letter of the alphabet. The function description is carried out when the function is called. At least one statement of the form

```
      LET FNX = expression
```

in the function description must be executed each time the function is called.

The argument-list appearing in the function call must be the same length as the parameter-list; each argument value is substituted for the corresponding parameter. The parameters must be simple variables as array parameters are not permitted. If a string parameter is used, its corresponding argument must be a string variable or constant.

Exercise 8.1: Show how the function FNM could be used to find the largest of four variables A, B, C and D. Use a single BASIC statement.

Exercise 8.2:
a) Define a one-argument function FNA that calculates the absolute value of its argument without using the ABS function.
b) Define a one-argument function FNS that performs the same computation as SGN, but do not use SGN in the definition.
c) Write a program to check the equivalency of FNA and ABS as well as FNS and SGN.

8.2.2 Function Parameters and Global Variables

The parameters appearing in a function definition are used in the description of the action of the function. They are not, themselves, manipulated;

rather, they represent the data that is actually to be used in the computation. At each call of the function the values of the *actual arguments* appearing in the function reference are substituted for the parameters in the definition. The data manipulation is then performed on the actual argument values, and the result is assigned as the value of the function.

Any legal BASIC expression may be used as an actual argument in a function reference. The order and number of the arguments in a function reference must correspond exactly to the order and number of the parameters in the definition.

Example 8.3:   Let FNM(X, Y) be the maximum value function (with two parameters X and Y) defined in Example 8.2.

a) The value of Z following the execution of the statements

```
210 LET A = 35.5
220 LET Z = FNM(A, 30) + 10
```

is 45.5. In the reference to FNM at statement 220, the value of the variable A (value 35.5) is substituted for X, and 30 is substituted for Y. This correspondence between actual arguments and parameters is illustrated below.

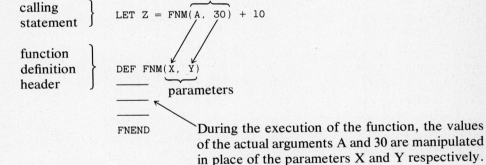

b) The value of P following the execution of the statements

```
210 LET A = 22
220 LET B = 30
230 LET P = FNM(A + 10, 30)
```

is 32. When the function FNM is referenced, the expression A + 10 is evaluated first and the result, 32, is substituted for the parameter X. The value 30 is substituted for the parameter Y.

c) We could use the pair of statements below:

```
260 LET Z1 = FNM(A, B)
270 LET Z = FNM(Z1, C)
```

to find the largest of three variables A, B, and C. In this example, the larger of A and B is first assigned to Z1, and then the larger of Z1 and C is assigned to Z. In the first function reference, A is substituted for X and B for Y; in the second function reference, Z1 is substituted for X and C for Y.

These two statements could be combined as the single statement:

260 LET Z = FNM(FNM(A, B), C)

This statement contains a nested function reference. The value of the first (inner) reference, FNM(A, B), is used as an actual argument in the second (outer) reference.

Example 8.4: The formula for computing interest compounded annually on a principle amount P is

$$A = P(1+r)^n$$

where r is the interest rate, and n is the number of years. The program below uses a single-line function statement (line 120) to compute the amount of money that would be on deposit after n, 2n and 3n years, given P = \$100 and r = 6.5 percent. This function is referenced three times in line 160 and each value returned is printed.

```
110 REM VALUE OF P DOLLARS INVESTED AT RATE R AFTER N YEARS
115 REM
120     DEF FNA(N) = P * (1 + R) ↑ N
125 REM
130     READ P, R, N
140     DATA 100, .065, 5
145 REM
150     PRINT "AMOUNT INVESTED = "; P; " DOLLARS"
155     PRINT "TERM = ", N, 2 * N, 3 * N, "YEARS"
160     PRINT "AMOUNT = ", FNA(N), FNA(2*N), FNA(3*N), "DOLLARS"
165 REM
170     END

RUN

AMOUNT INVESTED = 100 DOLLARS
TERM =          5              10             15        YEARS
AMOUNT =     137.009        187.714        257.184      DOLLARS
```

The function FNA defined in line 120 has a single parameter N. The function definition also contains two variables, P and R, which must be defined prior to the function call. When the function FNA is referenced (line 160) the values used for P and R are those entered via the read statement at line 130 (P = 100, R = .065). These same values are used in all three of the calculations specified at line 160; variables defined outside the function are called *global variables*.

The symbolic name N is used both as a function parameter (line 120) and as a variable outside this function (lines 130, 155, 160). In this case, the external variable N and the parameter N are treated as separate entities.

The value of the external variable, N, would not be affected by any change in the value of the parameter N. For example, in line 160, the value of the external variable N (N equal to 5) is first substituted for the parameter N. In the second call to FNA, the value of the expression 2*N or 10 is substituted for the parameter N. Even though the value associated with the parameter N (inside the function) is doubled by this substitution, the value of the external variable N (outside the function) is still 5. Consequently, in the third call to FNA, the value substituted for the parameter N is 3*5 or 15 and not 30.

These points are summarized below.

Parameters and Global Variables in Function Definitions

Variables used in a function definition, but not included in the parameter list, are global variables. They are identical to the variables of the same name that appear outside the function definition.

Any parameter of a function is distinct from any variable with the same name used outside the function definition.

Note that it is possible for a function, when called, to change the values of global variables. These changes are often called the *side effects* of a function.

Because of the importance of the parameters and global variables to user-defined functions, we will describe these items in a special way when defining multiple-line functions as illustrated next.

Example 8.5: A function to calculate a college student's tuition charge given the number of semester credit hours is shown in Fig. 8.1. According to the college rules, any student enrolled in 12 or more semester hours is charged a flat rate of \$450. Students enrolled for less than 12 hours are charged at the rate of \$40 per credit hour.

In this example, we have included a few comment lines to describe the

```
110 REM FUNCTION TO COMPUTE STUDENT TUITION
120 REM
130      DEF FNT(H)
140 REM
150 REM PARAMETER DEFINITIONS
160 REM      H - NUMBER OF HOURS STUDENT IS ENROLLED
170 REM
180 REM DETERMINE TUITION CHARGE
190      IF H >= 12 THEN 195 ELSE 225        [IF H < 12 THEN 225]
195 REM THEN
200          REM CHARGE FLAT RATE
210          LET FNT = 450
220      GOTO 250
225 REM ELSE
230          REM COMPUTE CHARGE
240          LET FNT = H * 40
250 REM IFEND
260 REM
270      FNEND
```

Fig. 8.1 Function for computing tuition cost.

use of the parameter, H, in the function FNT. The value returned by the
function is H * 40 if the actual argument is less than 12; otherwise, the value
is 450.

If the IF-THEN-ELSE statement is available, the function description
(lines 190-250) could be written in a single line as

```
IF H >= 12 THEN LET FNT = 450 ELSE LET FNT = H * 40
```

Example 8.6: An algorithm for determining the largest of a collection
of N data items in an array X (N > 1) is shown in Fig. 8.2.

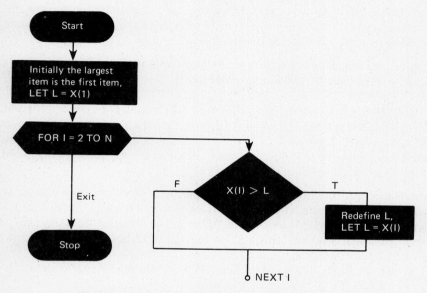

Fig. 8.2 Algorithm to find largest item, L, in array X.

This algorithm can be implemented as a multiple-line function FNL (see lines
250-450 in Fig. 8.3). FNL is a function having one parameter, N, which represents the number of input data items. The array X is a global variable used
to provide input data to the function. We have described X ( ) as an input
global variable (IN). This is because the array X is used to provide input data
to the function only; there are no modifications made to the array X during
the execution of the function. If the data were initially stored in another array,
it would have to be copied into X before FNL was called.

It would be most convenient if we could write FNL as a two-parameter
function with the first parameter being the name of the array containing the
list of data, and the second being the number of items in the list. Then the
name of the array in which the data was stored could be specified at each call
of FNL, and the actual argument array name would be substituted for the

```
        210 REM FUNCTION TO DETERMINE THE LARGEST OF A COLLECTION OF
        220 REM N DATA ITEMS IN AN ARRAY X
        225 REM
        230     DIM X(20)
        240 REM
       ┌250     DEF FNL(N)
        260 REM
        270 REM PARAMETER DEFINITIONS
        280 REM    N - NUMBER OF ITEMS IN X
        285 REM
        290 REM GLOBAL VARIABLES
        300 REM    IN: X( ) - ARRAY TO BE SEARCHED
        310 REM
        320 REM OTHER VARIABLES CHANGED - L
        330 REM
        340 REM INITIALIZE LARGEST VALUE L
        350     LET L = X(1)
        360 REM CHECK FOR LARGER VALUES THAN L
function 370     FOR I = 2 TO N
definition 380     IF X(I) > L THEN 385 ELSE 410      [IF X(I) <= L THEN 410]
        385 REM   THEN
        390           REM REDEFINE L
        400           LET L = X(I)
        410 REM   IFEND
        420     NEXT I
        430 REM
        440     LET FNL = L
        445 REM
       └450     FNEND
        460 REM
        465 REM
       ┌470 REM MAIN PROGRAM
        475 REM
        480 REM INITIALIZE ARRAY X
        490     READ N
        500     FOR I = 1 TO N
        510        READ X(I)
main    520     NEXT I
program 530     DATA 10, 67, 4, 35, 89, 765, 22, 134, 17, 33, 1
        535 REM
        540 REM FIND LARGEST ITEM
        550     LET B = FNL(N)
        560     PRINT "THE LARGEST VALUE IS", B
        570 REM
       └580     END
```

Fig. 8.3 The definition and call of a function to compute the largest value
in array X.

array parameter. Unfortunately, BASIC does not permit the use of arrays as parameters, so we were forced to treat X as a global variable to the function FNL.

The use of the additional variable L is required for storage of the largest value encountered so far. Since the function name, FNL, must be set to the largest value before completing the function (line 440), we might consider using FNL everywhere in place of L. However, within the function definition, the name of the function may be used only to the left of the equal sign in an assignment statement. Thus FNL could not have been used (in place of L) in the IF statement at line 380.

We have listed L as a variable whose value is changed by the function (line 320). This is to inform the user of function FNL that the value of L changes as FNL executes. This change in L is a side effect of FNL that could cause unexpected results if L is used elsewhere in any program that references FNL.

The main program starts at line 470 of Fig. 8.3, and the first statement to be executed is at line 490. The first subtask (lines 490-530) reads the input data into N and the array X. The function FNL is called at line 550, and the result is printed at line 560.

Minimal BASIC requires that function definitions occur at lower numbered lines than the references to the function. If your version of BASIC enforces this rule, then you should place function definitions at the beginning of the program in which they are used (following the declaration of any arrays referenced in the function). All functions must be entered and executed in accordance with the rules summarized in the following display.

Execution and Transfer Rules for Functions

1. A function cannot be executed unless it is referenced by name in an expression. If control is passed to a definition statement or to the definition header of a multiple-line function in some other fashion, then the statement immediately following the function definition will be the next one executed—the entire function definition is skipped.

2. Transfer of control to a line within a function definition from outside is not permitted; transfer to a line outside a function from within (other than through a reference to another function) is also not permitted.

Exercise 8.3:   Let B (an array of size 20) and N (a variable) be defined as follows:

N
16

Array B

1	2	3	4	5	6	7	8	9	10	11	12	13	14	15	16	17	18	19	20
0	1	1	0	1	0	0	0	1	1	0	1	1	0	1	0	?	?	?	?

a) Consider the following function:

```
110      DEF FNC(K, N)
120      LET C = 0
130      FOR I = 1 TO N
140          IF B(I) = K THEN 150 ELSE 170      [IF B(I) < > K THEN 170]
150 REM      THEN
160              LET C = C + 1
170 REM      IFEND
180      NEXT I
185 REM
190      LET FNC = C
195 REM
200      FNEND
```

i) What are the global variables used as input in FNC? Document the function parameters and global variables as in Example 8.6

ii) What is the value of L after execution of the statement

$$\text{LET L = FNC(0, N)}$$

iii) What is the value of L after execution of the statement

$$\text{LET L = FNC(1, N)}$$

iv) What are the values of N, K and L after execution of the statements

$$\text{LET K = 5}$$
$$\text{LET L = FNC(6–K, 12)}$$

v) What is the value of L after the execution of the statement

$$\text{LET L = FNC(B(10), B(10)+10)}$$

b) Write a sequence of BASIC statements that use the function FNC to count the number of occurrences of a value V in an array X(12) containing M elements (M ≤ 12). You may destroy the contents of B if necessary.

c) Redo part b for an array Y(12) containing K elements (K ≤ 12).

d) Write a function FNP of three arguments K, F and L, which counts the number of occurrences of K in the array B between the Fth and Lth elements of B inclusive. (Assume F is always less than or equal to L. F and L are indices to the array B.)

Exercise 8.4:   Write a function FNR(X, N) of two arguments that will round a value X to the nearest N decimal places for any integer N greater than or equal to zero (See Example 8.1).

Exercise 8.5:   Rewrite Example 4.14 using the function FNR to round both the computer sine and cosine to the nearest three decimal places before printing. Run the new program at the terminal.

Exercise 8.6:

a) Write a function FND(I, J) to compute mod(i, j) the remainder in the division of the positive integer i by the positive integer j. (See also Exercise 4.13). Rewrite the IF statement (line 270) of the prime number program (Fig. 4.5) to use this function to determine if D is a divisor of N.

b) Write a function FNF(X) that removes the integral part of X [thus FNF(−27.851) is −.851]

c) Write a function FNI(X) that removes the fractional part of X. [FNI(−27.85) = − 27]

d) Write a function FNC(X) that computes the smallest integer that is greater than X. [FNC(27.851) = 28, FNC(−27.851) = −27]

8.3   SOLVING A LARGER PROBLEM—THE SIMPLE STATISTICS PROBLEM

8.3.1   Program System Charts

As algorithms and programs become larger and more complicated and the number of modules used in a program begins to grow, it becomes increasingly important to maintain complete and concise documentation to illustrate the functional relationships and information flow among the modules. In this section we provide the solution to a simple statistics problem, illustrating the use of user-defined functions (hereafter referred to simply as functions) and subroutines. In the process, we illustrate some conventions of programming style and documentation that we believe are helpful in describing the flow of information into and out of each module of a program.

Problem 8.1:   Given a collection of N real numbers stored in an array, compute the range, mean (average), and median for this collection.

The initial data table is shown below; the level one flow diagram for this problem is shown in Fig. 8.4. Each box in the diagram represents a major step in the problem solution. Additional lower level subproblems may be identified within each of the steps 2, 3 and 4. Each of these subtasks represents a refinement of a task shown at a higher level. We can represent the functional relationship among the main problem and all of the subproblems using a *program system chart* (Fig. 8.5).

Data Table for Problem 8.1

Input variables	*Program variables*	*Output variables*
N: Number of data items to be processed		R: Range of the data (Difference between the largest and smallest values)
X(20): Array containing the data		
		A: Average of the data
		M: Median of the data

The program system chart identifies the major subproblems of the original problem and illustrates the relationship among them. The solutions to the subproblems shown at one level in the chart can be specified in terms of the

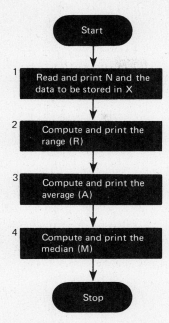

Fig. 8.4   Level one flow diagram for Statistics Problem 8.1.

connected subproblems at the next lower level. For example, the program system chart indicates that the solution of the subproblem "compute median" may be specified in terms of the solution to the subproblems "sort data" and "compute middle value of sorted data." Similarly, in order to find the average, we must first solve the subproblem "compute sum."

Once the data table, level one flow diagram and program system chart have been completed, we can begin to add data flow information to the program system chart and to work on the lower level refinements shown in the chart. In considering the refinements, it is necessary to decide which subtasks should be implemented as subroutines or functions and which should be implemented as part of the solution of the task above it in the program system chart. In general, a subtask should be implemented using a function or subroutine unless it occurs only once in the program system chart and is rather trivial. The subtasks "read and print," "compute range," and "compute middle value" fall in this category.

The decision as to whether to write a subroutine or a function depends upon the number of values to be returned. Functions are most convenient when a single value is to be computed. Such is the case in the subtasks for computing the largest value, the smallest value, the average, and the median. The sort task, however, rearranges an entire array of information (it does not compute a single value) and is, therefore, written as a subroutine. (Further discussion concerning functions and subroutines appears in Section 8.4.)

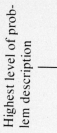

Highest level of prob-
lem description

Toward lower levels
of problem descrip-
tion (refinements of
higher levels)

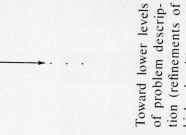

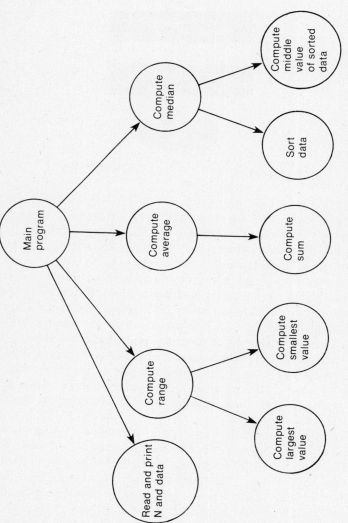

Fig. 8.5   Program system chart for statistics problem (8.1).

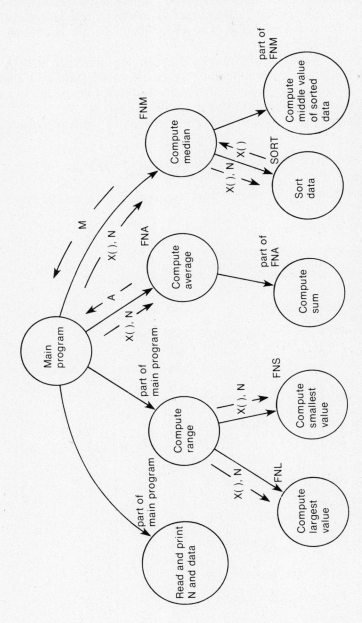

Fig. 8.6 Program system chart with data flow and function designation for statistics problem (8.1).

Fig. 8.6 shows a program system chart (updated from Fig. 8.5) that reflects the decisions just discussed. In addition, we have added a description of the information flow between the various program modules. For example, the array X and its size N are provided as input to FNM; the median value, M, is returned by FNM.

At this point, we are ready to write the main program (Fig. 8.7). As was the case with the largest value function FNL (see Example 8.6), we treat FNS, FNA and FNM as functions of one argument. Additional input data to all four of these functions is passed through the global variable X.

This program (Fig. 8.7) represents the step-by-step implementation of the

```
110   REM SIMPLE STATISTICS PROBLEM - MAIN PROGRAM
120       PRINT "SIMPLE STATISTICS PROBLEM"
130   REM
140   REM COMPUTE THE RANGE, MEAN AND MEDIAN OF A COLLECTION
145   REM OF N DATA ITEMS
150   REM
160       DIM X(20)
165   REM
170   REM FUNCTIONS REFERENCED -
180   REM    FNL, FNS, FNA, FNM
190   REM FUNCTION DEFINITIONS TO BE INSERTED HERE
200   REM
210   REM
5000  REM MAIN PROGRAM
5005  REM
5010  REM ENTER N AND ALL N DATA ITEMS (ARRAY X)
5020      PRINT "ENTER NUMBER OF DATA ITEMS";
5030      INPUT N
5040      PRINT "ENTER EACH DATA ITEM (FOLLOWED BY A RETURN)"
5050      FOR I = 1 TO N
5060          INPUT X(I)
5070      NEXT I
5080  REM
5090  REM COMPUTE THE RANGE, R
5100      LET R = FNL(N) - FNS(N)
5110      PRINT
5120      PRINT "THE RANGE IS "; R
5130  REM
5140  REM COMPUTE THE AVERAGE, A
5150      LET A = FNA(N)
5160      PRINT
5170      PRINT "THE AVERAGE IS "; A
5180  REM
5190  REM DETERMINE THE MEDIAN, M
5200      LET M = FNM(N)
5210      PRINT
5220      PRINT "THE MEDIAN IS "; M
5230  REM
5240      PRINT "CALCULATIONS COMPLETE"
5250  REM
5260      END
```

Fig. 8.7 Main program for Problem 8.1.

level one flow diagram for the statistics problem. It is easy to read as each major step stands out and is not obscured by the details required for implementation. We have skipped from line 190 to line 5000 in the main program to allow sufficient room for the insertion of the function definitions. To complete the data table for this program we should add the loop control variable I (as a program variable) and provide a list of the functions referenced at the bottom of the table.

Additional program variables

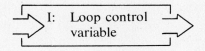

I: Loop control
      variable

Functions Referenced:
FNL—computes the largest of a collection of N data items in an array X.
FNS—computes the smallest of a collection of N data items in an array X.
FNA—computes the average of a collection of N data items in an array X.
FNM—computes the median of a collection of N data items in an array X.
(X is a global variable; N is an argument.)

Data tables and flow diagrams for each of the functions FNL, FNS, FNA, and FNM may now be designed independently of the main program except for the name of the global variable X and, of course, the line numbers for each function (to be inserted as indicated in the main program). The data tables, flow diagrams and BASIC statements for FNL, FNS and FNA are straightforward and are left as exercises. (See Exercise 8.8. The function FNL is shown in Fig. 8.3.)

We can complete the statistics problem by writing the function FNM, to find the median of a collection of N data items stored in the array X. In the process, we will once again illustrate many of the points made so far in this chapter, and provide some additional insights concerning the use of functions in BASIC.

Problem 8.2:   Write a function FNM to determine the median of a collection of N data items stored in an array X.

Discussion: Figure 8.8 shows the portion of the program system chart (Fig. 8.6) that is relevant to the median function, as well as a level one flow diagram for the function.

As is so often the case, the level one flow diagram simply reflects an ordering of the primary steps shown in the program system chart. The information involved in the solution of the problem at this level is shown on the program system chart and in the following data table.

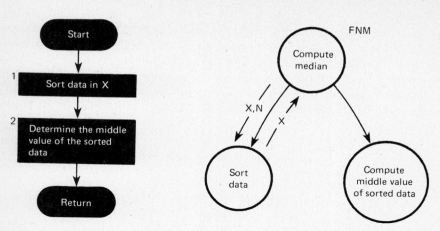

Fig. 8.8   Level one flow diagram and program system chart for the median problem (8.2).

Data Table for the Median Function (FNM)

Parameters

   N: The number of items in the array X

Global variables

   X: The array containing the data to be processed (input)

The next step in the solution of the problem is to decide how to implement steps 1 and 2 in the flow diagram. Since sorting a collection of data is a somewhat complicated task, we will implement the sort as a separate subroutine. (The sort does not return a value, so it cannot be implemented as a function.) Once the data has been sorted, finding the median is rather easy (see Fig. 8.9). This algorithm is based upon the definition of the median as the middle value in an ordered list of data.

We can now write the function FNM to find the median (see Fig. 8.10a). The sort subroutine shown in Fig. 8.10b is an implementation of the Bubble Sort algorithm (Problem 7.2) using the array X instead of M (see Fig. 7.22a, b).

Four new variables were used in the definition of the function. These should be added to the data table for FNM as follows:

Additional program variables for FNM

   P: Pointer (or index) to "middle" element of array X

   P$: Program flag—loop control variable for outer sort loop ⎫ As defined

   I: Loop control variable for inner sort loop   ⎬ for Prob-
                                                                                        ⎪ lem 7.2
   T: Temporary variable required for the exchange   ⎭

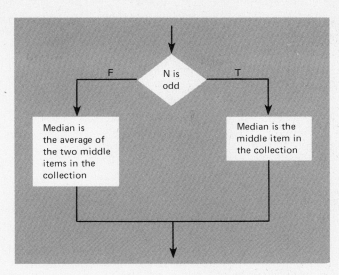

Fig. 8.9   Refinement of step 2 in Fig. 8.8—Determine middle value.

```
1110 REM FUNCTION TO COMPUTE THE MEDIAN OF N DATA ITEMS IN AN ARRAY X
1120 REM
1130     DEF FNM(N)
1140 REM
1150 REM PARAMETER DEFINITIONS -
1160 REM    N - NUMBER OF ITEMS IN X
1170 REM
1175 REM GLOBAL VARIABLES
1180 REM
1190 REM    IN:  X( ) - ARRAY OF DATA (UNSORTED)
1200 REM
1210 REM    OUT: X( ) - ORIGINAL ARRAY SORTED IN ASCENDING ORDER
1220 REM
1225 REM OTHER VARIABLES CHANGED - P, T, P$, I
1230 REM
1235 REM SORT DATA IN ASCENDING ORDER
1240     GOSUB 1400
1250 REM
1260 REM SET POINTER TO MIDDLE ELEMENT. CHECK IF N IS ODD OR EVEN
1270     LET P = N / 2 + 1
1280     IF INT(N/2)*2 < > N THEN 1285 ELSE 1315
                              [IF INT(N/2)*2 = N THEN 1315]
1285 REM THEN
1290        REM N IS ODD. USE MIDDLE ITEM
1300        LET FNM = X(P)
1310     GOTO 1340
1315 REM ELSE
1320        REM N IS EVEN. USE AVERAGE OF TWO MIDDLE ITEMS
1330        LET FNM = (X(P-1) + X(P)) / 2
1340 REM IFEND
1350 REM
1360 REM EXIT FROM FUNCTION
1370     GOTO 1680
```

Fig. 8.10a   Median function.

```
1400 REM BUBBLE SORT SUBROUTINE - SORT ARRAY X IN ASCENDING ORDER
1410 REM
1420 REM GLOBAL VARIABLES
1430 REM    IN:  X( ) - ORIGINAL DATA UNSORTED
1435 REM         N - NUMBER OF ITEMS IN X
1440 REM
1445 REM    OUT: X( ) - ORIGINAL ARRAY IN ASCENDING ORDER
1450 REM
1455 REM OTHER VARIABLES CHANGED - T, P$, I
1460 REM
1465 REM PASS THROUGH X COMPARING ADJACENT PAIRS OF DATA ITEMS
1470 REM EXCHANGE OUT-OF-ORDER PAIRS
1480 REM REPEAT PASS UNTIL NO MORE EXCHANGES TAKE PLACE
1490 REM
1500     LET P$ = "MORE"
1510 REM WHILE P$ = "MORE" MAKE ANOTHER PASS THROUGH X
1520     [DO] WHILE P$ = "MORE"                [IF P$ < > "MORE" THEN 1660]
1530         REM ASSUME NO MORE PASSES NEEDED AFTER THIS ONE
1540         LET P$ = "NOMORE"
1550         REM COMPARE ADJACENT PAIRS OF ELEMENTS,
1555         REM FROM FIRST PAIR TO LAST
1560         FOR I = 1 TO N-1
1570             IF X(I) > X(I-1) THEN 1575 ELSE 1630
                                              [IF X(I) <= X(I+1) THEN 1630]
1575 REM         THEN
1580                 REM -- EXCHANGE
1590                 LET T = X(I)
1600                 LET X(I) = X(I+1)
1610                 LET X(I+1) = T
1620                 LET P$ = "MORE"
1630 REM         IFEND
1640         NEXT I
1650     [LOOP] NEXT                          [GOTO 1510]
1660 REM
1670     RETURN
1680 REM
1690     FNEND
```

Fig. 8.10b Bubble Sort subroutine for median function.

The function FNM illustrates how subroutines may be defined internally within a function. Such subroutines may only be referenced from within the function, they return control to a statement inside the function definition. As usual, the subroutine must be entered only through the use of the GOSUB statement (line 1240); the GOTO statement (line 1370) is required to branch around the subroutine definition at the completion of execution of the function FNM. The FNEND statement (line 1690) comes after the subroutine, and not before, as the subroutine is part of the function definition.

FNM is an example of a function with a side effect. It computes not only a single value (the median of the N items in the array X) but also alters the array X by sorting the data in ascending order. Functions with side effects should normally be avoided; as a minimum, however, side effects should be clearly documented in the function definition.

There are additional side effects in that three of the variables listed as "other program variables" for FNM (P$, I, and T) are assigned new values during the execution of the sort subroutine. Any prior values assigned to these variables would be destroyed when the subroutine is executed. If these values are critical to the proper execution of some other portion of the program, these side effects could be extremely harmful. In choosing names of variables used "locally" within a function or subroutine, you should attempt to pick names that are not used elsewhere. If this is not possible, at least verify that these names do not contain valuable information prior to execution of the function or subroutine in which they are used.

In the next section, we will discuss another BASIC feature, the subprogram, which is useful in reducing the harmful interaction between various modules of a program and in eliminating undesirable side effects. If your BASIC system does not contain this feature, you may wish to skip this section.

Exercise 8.7:   In the program in Fig. 8.7, there is no reference to the computation of the sum or to the sorting of the data items (see the program system chart, Fig. 8.6). Why not?

Exercise 8.8:   Develop data tables and flow diagrams for the functions FNL, FNS and FNA. Write the functions FNA and FNS complete with documentation to complete the statistics problem.

Exercise 8.9:   In the program in Fig. 8.7, there is no validation check made on N to see if it is within the bounds of the array X. (N should be greater than 1 and less than or equal to 20.) Rewrite the main program using a subroutine to read and print N, validate N (print an error message if N is not valid), and read and print X. Your subroutine should be complete with documentation, such as that shown in the Bubble Sort subroutine (Fig. 8.10).

Exercise 8.10:   If we examine the program system chart for the statistics problem (Fig. 8.6) we can see that the sort subtask does not enter the picture until the third level, where sorting is required in finding the median of the data items. Yet the sort could have been quite helpful in the computation of the range. Since sorting is needed anyway, we might just as well have sorted the data in X before we computed the range. Once this has been done, the range could be computed by

$$\text{LET } R = X(N) - X(1)$$

and the functions FNL and FNS would no longer be needed. Rewrite the level one flow diagram and the program system chart if the sort is done immediately after the reading of the data.

8.4 SUBPROGRAMS*

8.4.1 Information Flow Between Independent Modules

While it is true that subroutines and functions can be useful in segmenting the programs that we write into modules, they are nevertheless limited in a number of ways.

The major shortcoming of the function and subroutine features of BASIC

---

*Optional if your BASIC system does not have this feature.

is that neither provides the degree of *module independence* that is so important in the implementation of larger program systems.

A reasonable degree of independence between modules can be achieved only through the use of programming language features that permit complete control of the *information flow interface* between these modules. The fundamental requirements of any such language features are:

1) that all information to be communicated between two modules can be passed through the use of arguments and parameters (in a manner similar to that of the user-defined functions),

2) that all other variables and arrays referenced in the module must be local to the module—i.e., distinct from data objects with the same name which appear outside the module.

Unfortunately, neither user-defined functions nor subroutines meet either of these two requirements. Subroutines do not have parameters; the user-defined functions allow only simple variables (and not arrays) to be used as parameters. User-defined functions also allow for the return from the function of only a single computed value. Furthermore, any variable used in a function or subroutine module and not listed as a parameter, is considered global to the module. This means that changes in the value of such a variable within the module are not confined to the module, but will propagate outside the module (side effects).

The global variable feature of a language makes it far more difficult to discern and control the information flow between modules. This is especially true in languages that require the use of global variables for transmitting certain types of data (such as arrays). Even if the side effects or changes in the global variables are carefully documented, these changes can still lead to unexpected and incorrect program behavior. The initial design of a program system containing global variable dependencies is more difficult, and the debugging and subsequent maintenance of the system are more complicated. Design considerations and changes and corrections that are relevant to one module may have an impact upon others. These problems are further aggravated in systems that are developed and maintained by teams of programmers over periods of years.

8.4.2 Independent Subprograms

A few versions of BASIC, e.g. Dartmouth BASIC and BASIC-PLUS-2 provide an additional language feature, called a *subprogram*, which satisfies the requirements of module independence listed earlier. Still other versions (including Dartmouth BASIC and BASIC-PLUS provide a *program chain* facility that is also useful, although in a more limited sense, in helping to produce independent program modules. Chaining will be discussed briefly in Chapter 11. In the remainder of this section, we will illustrate the use of the subprogram feature of Dartmouth BASIC and BASIC-PLUS-2 by rewriting the median function and the sort subroutine as independent subprograms. The new subprograms are shown in Fig. 8.11.

These subprograms are independent program modules; hence, they come after the END statement of the main program (line 5260 of Fig. 8.7). As illustrated in Fig. 8.11, the name of a subprogram appears in the subprogram header statement (lines 6130 and 6390) between the keyword SUB and the subprogram parameter list. The parentheses after the parameter X indicate that X is an array parameter. The SUBEND statement (lines 6340 and 6670) terminates a subprogram definition.

Some of the advantages and major features of subprograms are clearly demonstrated in Fig. 8.11. The sort and median subprograms are separated from each other (the sort module is not nested within the median module). One subprogram can call another (FNDMED calls SORT); all variables involved in the communication between subprograms are clealy indicated in one place, the subprogram call:

$$6230 \qquad \text{CALL SORT (X( ), N)} \quad \text{in FNDMED}$$

and

$$5200 \qquad \text{CALL FNDMED (X( ), N, M)} \quad \text{in the main program}$$

The call statement to subprogram FNDMED would replace the call to function FNM in the main program of Fig. 8.7 (line 5200).

```
6110 REM SUBPROGRAM TO COMPUTE THE MEDIAN OF N DATA ITEMS IN AN ARRAY
6120 REM
6130     SUB FNDMED (X( ), N, M)
6140 REM
6150 REM PARAMETER DEFINITIONS -
6155 REM
6160 REM IN:  X( ) - UNSORTED ARRAY OF DATA
6170 REM      N - NUMBER OF ITEMS IN X
6180 REM
6190 REM OUT: M - MEDIAN OF THE DATA
6200 REM      X( ) - ORIGINAL ARRAY IN ASCENDING ORDER
6210 REM
6220 REM SORT DATA IN ASCENDING ORDER
6230     CALL SORT (X( ), N)
6240 REM
6250 REM DETERMINE MIDDLE VALUE. CHECK IF N IS ODD OR EVEN
6260     LET P = N / 2 + 1
6270     IF INT(N/2)*2 < > N THEN 6280 ELSE 6300
6280 REM THEN
6285         REM N IS ODD. USE MIDDLE ITEM
6290         LET M = X(P)
6295     GOTO 6320
6300 REM ELSE
6305         REM N IS EVEN. USE AVERAGE OF TWO MIDDLE ITEMS
6310         LET M = (X(P-1) + X(P)) / 2
6320 REM IFEND
6330 REM
6340     SUBEND
```

Fig. 8.11a   Subprogram FNDMED.

```
6370 REM SUBPROGRAM TO SORT AN ARRAY IN ASCENDING ORDER
6380 REM
6390     SUB SORT (X( ), N)
6400 REM
6410 REM PARAMETER DEFINITIONS -
6420 REM
6430 REM IN:  X( ) - UNSORTED ARRAY OF DATA
6440 REM        N - NUMBER OF ITEMS IN X
6450 REM
6455 REM OUT: X ( ) - ORIGINAL ARRAY IN ASCENDING ORDER
6460 REM
6470 REM PASS THROUGH X COMPARING ADJACENT PAIRS OF DATA ITEMS
6480 REM EXCHANGE OUT-OF-ORDER PAIRS
6490 REM REPEAT UNTIL NO EXCHANGES TAKE PLACE
6500 REM
6510     LET P$ = "MORE"
6515 REM WHILE P$ = "MORE", MAKE ANOTHER PASS
6520     [DO] WHILE P$ = "MORE"
6530        REM ASSUME NO MORE PASSES NEEDED AFTER THIS ONE
6540        LET P$ = "NOMORE"
6550        REM COMPARE ADJACENT PAIRS OF ELEMENTS
6555        REM FROM FIRST PAIR TO LAST
6560        FOR I = 1 TO N-1
6570           IF X(I) > X(I+1) THEN 6580 ELSE 6630
6580 REM       THEN
6585              REM EXCHANGE
6590              LET T = X(I)
6600              LET X(I) = X(I+1)
6610              LET X(I+1) = T
6620              LET P$ = "MORE"
6630 REM       IFEND
6640        NEXT I
6650     [LOOP] NEXT
6660 REM
6670     SUBEND
```

Fig. 8.11b Subprogram SORT.

At each call, information is provided to a subprogram via the *input parameters;* all results are returned through the *output parameters*. Any number of values may be returned, such as the median, M (returned by FNDMED), and the sorted array X (returned by SORT). Some parameters, such as X, are used for both input and output; some, such as N, are used just for input; others, such as M in FNDMED are used solely for output purposes.

The argument names used in calling a subprogram are completely independent of the names used in the parameter list of the subprogram definition. Thus, subprograms can be called with different arguments in the same program or in different programs. Each argument must, however, agree in number and type (numeric variable, string variable or array), with the corresponding subprogram parameter.

When the subprogram call statement is executed, a correspondence is established between the actual arguments in the call statement and the parameters listed in the subroutine header statement. The correspondence is by position only and not by name; i.e., the first argument is substituted for the first parameter; the second argument for the second parameter, etc. This means that we could use FNDMED to determine the median value, M1, in an array A with 10 elements by using the call

```
CALL FNDMED (A( ), 10, M1)
```

Aside from the argument/parameter interface, subprogram modules are completely independent of one another. There can be no side effects, because there are no global variables. The variables P, P$, I, and T are all local to the subprograms in which they appear. Changes to these variables have no effect outside the subprograms. Hence, they can be used freely in more than one module without causing harmful interaction.

Thus, the various subprograms required for a program system can easily be written and used by different programmers. *Libraries* of subprograms can be created, thereby making the subprograms available to large numbers of users. The only information about a subprogram that a user needs to know is its name, a brief description of what it does, but not how it does it, and a complete description of the subprogram parameters.

All of these factors make the subprogram a far more powerful tool for programming than either the function or the subroutine. If the version of BASIC that you are using supports subprograms, you should consult your manual for the full details of how to use this feature. The displays that follow summarize the definition and call of subprograms in Dartmouth BASIC and BASIC-PLUS-2.

Subprogram Definition

Dartmouth BASIC and BASIC-PLUS-2 form:

      SUB name (parameter-list)

      _____

      _____ } subprogram description

      _____

      SUBEND

Interpretation: The subprogram name may be one to six characters in length. The parameter-list consists of the names of simple variables or arrays. All communication between the subprogram and the calling program (or calling subprogram) is through the parameter-list. The SUBEND statement terminates the subprogram definition and causes a return to the calling program.

Note: An array parameter is indicated by a pair of parentheses following the array name.

Subprogram Call Statement

Dartmouth BASIC and BASIC-PLUS-2 form:

CALL name (argument-list)

Interpretation: The name of the subprogram called or referenced follows the word CALL. Each argument may be a variable name, an array name or an array element. Expressions and constants may also be arguments. Each argument is associated with the parameter in the corresponding position in the parameter-list. Array names must be associated with array parameters; all other argument types (including array elements) must be associated with parameters that are simple variables.

 If the argument is an expression (not a variable, array or array element), the value of the expression is passed as input only to the subprogram; any changes in the associated parameter value are not returned to the calling program. If the argument is a variable, array or array element, any changes in the associated parameter value (or values for an array parameter) will be returned to the calling program. (The argument itself changes in value.)

Note: The use of an array as an argument is indicated by an empty pair of parentheses; the entire array is "passed" to the subprogram. A single array element is indicated by a subscript expression enclosed in parentheses; the subscript expression is evaluated when the call statement is executed to determine which array element is the argument.

Exercise 8.11: Rewrite the statistics problem function FNA (or FNL or FNS) as a subprogram with appropriate remarks. Also write the statements required to call your subprogram and print the result of its execution.

8.4.3 Dartmouth BASIC Subroutines Revisited*

 Dartmouth BASIC allows the use of the subprogram header, terminator and call statements when writing subroutines as well as subprograms. In Dartmouth BASIC, the statement

GOSUB line

may be replaced by the statement

CALL name

where the subroutine involved is indicated by name. The subroutine header

SUB name

may be used at the start of a subroutine definition and the terminator

SUBEND

may be used in place of the RETURN statement.

---

*This section may be omitted by nonusers of Dartmouth BASIC.

For example, in Fig. 8.10b the header statement

```
1390 SUB SORT
```

could be inserted in front of the subroutine and the statement

```
1670 SUBEND
```

could replace

```
1670 RETURN
```

Then, in Fig. 8.10a, the statement

```
1240 CALL SORT
```

could be used instead of

```
1240 GOSUB 1400
```

Despite the syntactic advantages offered by Dartmouth BASIC, remember that subroutines have no arguments and that all variables used in a subroutine are global. Consequently, side effects are still a problem. Also, subroutines are written as part of the program that calls them and are *local* or *internal* to that program. Thus, they must come before the main program END statement and must be separated from the rest of the program by an unconditional transfer, STOP or RETURN. Subprograms, on the other hand, are written external to the calling program (following the END or SUBEND of the previous module). They are separate, independent modules. All variables not included in the parameter list of a subprogram are local to that subprogram and have no meaning outside of the subprogram. Hence, there can be no side effects.

8.5 COMMON PROGRAMMING ERRORS

Some of the more common programming errors (and example diagnostics) associated with user-defined functions include forgetting the FNEND at the end of the definition (Unfinished Definition), attempting to nest function definitions (Nested Definition), referencing a function from within its own definition (Illegal Recursion), referencing an undefined function (Undefined Function), and using control statements for transferring in and out of a function definition (Undefined Line Number).

All of these errors should be detected by your BASIC system. Disagreement in argument list/parameter list correspondence should also be detected by the system. However, undesired function side effects will not be detected by the system; you will have to provide your own means of detecting or, better still, preventing such errors. Some suggestions for this are:

i) At least in the early debugging steps, the values of all multiple-line function arguments and input global variables should be printed upon function entry.

ii) Whenever possible, the values of argument and global input variables should be checked to see whether or not they fall within a meaningful range. For example, an argument or global variable used to indicate the number of items in an array must always be positive and should not exceed the largest legal subscript for the array. Meaningful diagnostics should be printed and appropriate action taken if the given range is violated.

iii)   Accurate, written descriptions of all arguments and global variables associated with a function should be maintained. These descriptions should be included as remarks in the function definition.

Steps similar to the above are also helpful in protecting against undesired side effects resulting from the execution of subroutines (of course there are no arguments in this case).

If you are working with subprograms, side effects will not be a problem. You should take special care, however, to ensure number and type agreement in your subprogram argument and parameter lists. The BASIC system that you are using should provide some assistance. Following steps i), ii) and iii) above for all subprogram input arguments should also prove helpful.

8.6 SUMMARY

Two additional features of BASIC, the *user-defined function* and the *subprogram* are discussed in this chapter. One-line, user-defined functions of zero or one argument are part of Minimal BASIC. Multiple-line functions and functions with more than one argument are permitted in many versions of BASIC. Subprograms are supported in only a few versions of BASIC, including Dartmouth BASIC and BASIC-PLUS-2. We described how to reference and define user-defined functions and subprograms, and showed how data are communicated among these modules using arguments and global variables.

To illustrate the use of user-defined functions and subroutines, we presented the solution to a simple statistics problem. We introduced the *program system chart* as a tool for describing the *functional relationships* and *information flow* among the different modules of a program system. The use of the program system chart is the same regardless of whether the modules used are subroutines, functions or subprograms.

The side effects caused by the use of *global variables* were described. Some suggestions were given for documenting the arguments and the global variables used in function and subroutine definitions.

Some of the shortcomings of functions and subroutines were discussed and the notion of *module independence* was introduced. Two requirements fundamental to the support of a reasonable level of module independence were described. These involved the exclusive use of argument/parameter lists for communication between modules and the definition of local variables within a module. The subprogram was introduced as one feature (though only available in a few BASIC versions) that met these requirements. The use of the subprogram was illustrated. The advantages of subprograms (over subroutines and functions) were summarized, and the importance of the subprogram as a programming tool was also briefly discussed.

Table 8.1 describes the Minimal BASIC one-line function. Table 8.2 de-

Statement	Effect
Function definition	
`DEF FNF(C) = (9/5)*C + 32`	Defines the function FNF. This function has a single parameter, C.
Function call	
`LET T = FNF(100)`	Calls the function FNF and substitutes the actual argument, 100, for C. The value returned, 212, is stored in T.

Table 8.1   Summary of Minimal BASIC statements

Statement	Effect
Multi-line function definition	
``` 100 DEF FND(X, Y) 110 REM 120 REM PARAMETER DEFINITIONS 130 REM IN: X, Y 140 REM 150 IF X > Y THEN 160 ELSE 190 160 REM THEN 170 LET FND = X - Y 180 GOTO 210 190 REM ELSE 200 LET FND = Y - X 210 REM IFEND 220 REM 230 FNEND ```	Defines the function FND with two parameters, X and Y. FND returns the positive number representing the difference between the parameter values.
Subprogram definition	
``` SUB ONES(X( ), N) 300 REM 310 REM PARAMETER DEFINITIONS 320 REM IN: N - SIZE OF X 330 REM 340 REM OUT: X( ) - ARRAY OF ONES 350 REM 360 REM LOCAL VARIABLES - I 370 REM 380 REM SET EACH ELEMENT OF X TO 1 390 FOR I = 1 TO N 400 LET X(I) = 1 410 NEXT I 420 REM 430 SUBEND ```	Defines the subprogram ONES with two parameters, array X and N. The FOR loop sets the first N elements of the array represented by X to 1.
Subprogram call	
`          CALL ONES (A( ), 10)`	Sets the first 10 elements of array A to 1.

Table 8.2   Summary of BASIC-PLUS/Dartmouth BASIC statements

scribes the more general form of function supported in BASIC-PLUS and Dartmouth BASIC, and the subprogram supported in BASIC-PLUS-2 and Dartmouth BASIC.

PROGRAMMING PROBLEMS

Unless otherwise noted, all problems listed can be solved using subroutines and functions and/or subprograms, depending upon the support provided by your BASIC system. Complete documentation, especially with respect to arguments/parameters and global variables (if any) should be included in all cases. Judicious use of global variables is suggested. If the subprogram feature is available, it should be used where needed to eliminate the use of global variables.

8.3   Given the lengths a, b, c of the sides of a triangle, write a function to compute the area, A, of the triangle; the formula for computing A is given by

$$A = \sqrt{s(s-a)(s-b)(s-c)}$$

where s is the semi-perimeter of the triangle:

$$s = \frac{a+b+c}{2}$$

Triangle

Write a program to read in values for a, b, and c, and call your function to compute A. Your program should print A, and a, b, and c.

8.4   Define a function FNQ that calculates the square root of a single argument without using SQR. *Hint:* One simple scheme for computing the square root, the Newton-Raphson method, requires that you start with an initial guess of the correct answer and then repeatedly refine this guess, obtaining more accurate ones. The formula for finding a more accurate guess from the old one is

$$\text{new guess} = 1/2(\text{old guess} + \frac{N}{\text{old guess}})$$

where N is the argument whose square root is required. When a new guess is found, it replaces the old guess in the formula, and "another new guess" is computed. This process continues until

$$| \text{new guess} - \text{old guess} | \leq \text{epsilon}$$

where epsilon is some suitably chosen small value (such as 0.0001). The brackets indicate that the absolute value of the difference between guesses is compared to epsilon.

Write a program to call FNQ and compare your result to the value computed by SQR. Test your program for the values 3, 9, 50, 99 and 100. Use N/2 as an initial value of old guess.

8.5   Two positive integers I and J are considered to be *relatively prime* if there exists no integer greater than 1 that divides them both. Write a function FNP that has two parameters, I and J, and returns a value of 1 if and only if I and J are relatively prime. Otherwise, FNP should return a value of 0.

8.6   The *greatest common divisor*, GCD, of two positive integers I and J is an integer N with the property that N divides both I and J (with 0 remainder), and N is the largest integer dividing both I and J. An algorithm for determining N was devised by the famous mathematician Euclid; a flow diagram description of that algorithm, suitable for direct translation into BASIC, is provided next. (In the diagram below, FNL and FNS are the BASIC largest value and smallest value functions (see Fig. 8.2), and FND is the mod function (see Exercise 8.6).

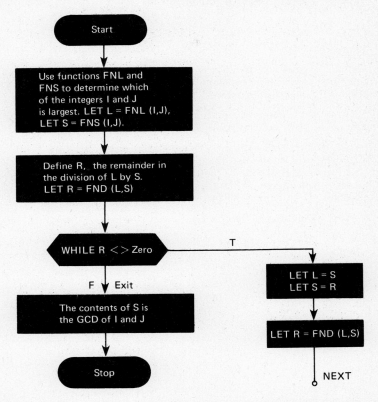

Write a main program to read in four positive integers N1, N2, N3, and N4 and find the GCD of all four numbers. [*Hint:* The GCD of the four integers is the largest integer N that divides all four of them.] Implement the above algorithm as an integer function and call it as many times as needed to solve the problem.

Note that GCD (N1, N2, N3, N4) = GCD[GCD(N1, N2), GCD(N3, N4)]. Print N1, N2, N3, and N4, and the resulting GCD.

8.7 The electric company charges its customers according to the following rate schedule:

8 cents a kilowatt-hour (kwh) for electricity used up to the first 300 kwh;
6 cents a kwh for the next 300 kwh (up to 600 kwh);
5 cents a kwh for the next 400 kwh (up to 1000 kwh);
3 cents a kwh for all electricity used over 1000 kwh.

Write a function to compute the total charge for each customer. Write a program to call this function using the following data:

Customer number	Kilowatt-hours used
123	725
205	115
464	600
596	327
601	915
613	1011
722	47

The calling program should print a three-column table listing the customer number, hours used and the charge for each customer. It should also compute and print the number of customers, total hours used and total charges.

8.8 Each week the employees of a local manufacturing company turn in time cards containing the following information:

i) an identification number (a five-digit integer),
ii) hourly pay rate (a real number),
iii) time worked Monday, Tuesday, Wednesday, Thursday and Friday (each a four-digit integer of the form HHMM, where HH is hours and MM is minutes).

For example, last week's time cards contained the following data:

Employee number	Hourly rate	Time worked (hours, minutes)				
		Monday	Tuesday	Wednesday	Thursday	Friday
16025	4.00	0800	0730	0800	0800	0420
19122	4.50	0615	0800	0800	0800	0800
21061	4.25	0805	0800	0735	0515	0735
45387	3.50	1015	1030	0800	0945	0800
50177	6.15	0800	0415	0800	0545	0600
61111	5.00	0930	0800	0800	1025	0905
88128	4.50	0800	0900	0800	0800	0700

Write a program system that will read the above data and compute for each employee the total hours worked (in hours and minutes), the total hours worked (to the nearest quarter-hour), and the gross salary. Your system should print the data shown above with the total hours (both figures) and gross pay for each employee. You should assume that overtime is paid at 1½ times the normal hourly rate, and that it is computed on a weekly basis (only on the total hours in excess of 40), rather than on a daily basis. Your program system should contain the following modules:

a) A function for computing the sum (in hours and minutes) of two four-digit integers of the form HHMM (*Example:* 0745 + 0335 = 1120);
b) A function for converting hours and minutes (represented as a four-digit integer) into hours, rounded to the nearest quarter hour (*Example:* 1120 = 11.25);
c) A function for computing gross salary given total hours and hourly rate;
d) A function for rounding gross salary accurate to two decimal places.
Test your program using the data above.

8.9 *Internal Sort/Merge.* Let A and B be two arrays of size 10, and C an array of size 20. Write a program system to read two lists of data, one of size N1 and the other of size N2 (N1, N2 ≤ 10) into A and B respectively, sort A and B in ascending order, and then merge A and B into C maintaining the ascending order. The merge process is illustrated below for N1 = 5, N2 = 3. The numbered lines between arrays A and B indicate the order of comparison of the pairs of elements in A and B. The smaller of each pair of numbers is always merged into array C; the larger is then compared with the next entry in the other array (either A or B).

A(1)	A(2)	A(3)	A(4)	A(5)	A(6)	A(7)	A(8)	A(9)	A(10)
-10.5	-1.8	3.5	6.3	7.2	?	?	?	?	?

1 2 3 4 5 6

B(1)	B(2)	B(3)	B(4)	B(5)		B(10
-2.5	3.1	5.7	?	?	. . .	?

C(1)	C(2)	C(3)	C(4)	C(5)	C(6)	C(7)	C(8)	C(9)		C(20)
-10.5	-2.5	-1.8	3.1	3.5	5.7	6.3	7.2	?	. . .	?

When one of the arrays A or B has been exhausted, do not forget to copy the remaining data from the other array into C.

8.10 An examination has been administered to a class of students, and the scores for each student have been provided as data along with the student's name. Write a program to do the following:
a) Determine and print the class average for the exam.
b) Find the median grade.
c) Scale each student's grade so that the class average will become 75. For example, if the actual class average is 63, add 12 to each student's grade.
d) Assign a letter grade to each student based on the scaled grade: 90-100 (A), 80-89 (B), 70-79 (C), 60-69 (D), 0-59 (F).
e) Print out each student's name in alphabetical order followed by the scaled grade and the letter grade.
f) Count the number of grades in each letter grade category.

8.11 Write a function that will compute the factorial, n!, of any small positive integer, n. [*Hint:* n! = n × (n−1) × (n−2) × . . . × 2 × 1]

8.12 The expression for computing C(n,r), the number of combinations of n items taken r at a time, is

$$C(n,r) = \frac{n!}{r!(n-r)!}$$

Assuming that we already have available a function for computing n! (see Problem 8.11), write a function for computing C(n,r). Write a program that will call this function for n = 4, r = 1; n = 5, r = 3; n = 7, r = 7; and n = 6, r = 2.

8.13 *For subprograms only.* Assume the existence of a main program containing a call to a subprogram SEARCH,

```
CALL SEARCH (B( ), N, K, F$, I)
```

Write the subprogram SEARCH to compare each of the N elements in the array B to the data item stored in K. If a match is found, SEARCH is to set F$ to "TRUE" and define I to be the index of the element in the array B in which the key, K, is located. If the key is not found, F$ should be set "FALSE" and I should not be defined by the subprogram.

8.14 A throw of dice may produce anywhere from a two (snake-eyes) to a twelve (box-cars). Write a program system to read the 36 two-digit integers representing all possible outcomes (1st digit 1-6, 2nd digit 1-6) into an array R of size 36, and produce the table shown below.

Roll value	Number of ways of getting this roll	Probability of getting this roll	Probability of a roll greater than or equal to this one
2	1	.028	1.000
3	2	.056	.972
.	.	.	.
.	.	.	.
.	.	.	.
11	2	.056	.084
12	1	.028	.028

For any roll value, X, the probability of getting that roll is

$$P(roll=X) = tally\ (X)/36$$

where tally(X) is the number of ways of getting X. Also, the probability of getting a roll greater than or equal to X is

Thus

$$P(roll \geq X) = P(roll=X) + P(roll=X+1) + \ldots P(roll=12)$$

and

$$P(roll=10) = tally(10)/36 = 3\ /36 = .083$$

$$P(roll \geq 10) = .083 + .056 + .028 = .167$$

Hints: Store the number of ways of getting a roll, and the probabilities of each roll X, and a roll greater than or equal to X, in three arrays N, P, and G, each of size 12 (do not use the first elements of these arrays).

Your main program should read the rolls into R, and call a function to compute N for each roll. Given the data in N, the probabilities of each roll can be determined by another function. All computations should be rounded to three decimal places.

Each roll is represented by a two-digit integer, r, in array R. The actual roll value, X, can be computed as

$$LET\ X = FND(r,10) + INT(r/10)$$

where FND is the mod function, described in Exercise 8.6. For example, if r is 36, then the actual value of the roll is

$$FND(36,10) + INT(36/10) = 6 + 3 = 9.$$

8.15 There are many ways of determining an approximate value for the number π. Here we describe one such technique.

Consider a quarter of a circle:

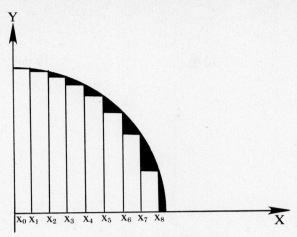

Fig. 8.12 Quarter circle.

The area of this quarter circle is $\frac{1}{4}\pi r^2$ which for $r = 2$ is π. Thus we can obtain an approximation to the value of π by approximating the area under the quarter circle.

To approximate the area under the quarter circle, we *partition* the interval $[0, 2]$ along the X-axis into n *subintervals* $[x_0 = 0, x_1], [x_1, x_2], [x_2, x_3] \ldots [x_i, x_{i+1}], \ldots [x_{n-1}, x_n = 2]$. In Fig. 8.12, the interval has been partitioned into 8 intervals:

$$[x_0, x_1] = [0, .25],$$
$$[x_1, x_2] = [.25, .50]$$
.
.
.
$$[x_7, x_8] = [1.75, 2.00]$$

We then compute the sum of the areas of the rectangles defined by these partitions. This sum yields the desired approximation. The larger the number of partitions, the better the approximation because there is less area lost (shaded areas). You should try your program for several different partition sizes.

The area underneath each rectangle can be computed as indicated in Fig. 8.13. The area of the ith rectangle is computed as

$$A_i = b_i \cdot h_i$$

The base of the rectangle has length $b_i = 2/n$, where n is the number of partitions of the interval $[0, 2]$ ($n = 8$ in the example in Fig. 8.13). The height, h_i, of the ith rectangle is computed as follows:

$$r^2 = x_i^2 + h_i^2$$

But $r = 2$; therefore:

$$h_i^2 = 2^2 - x_i^2, \quad h_i = \sqrt{4 - x_i^2}$$

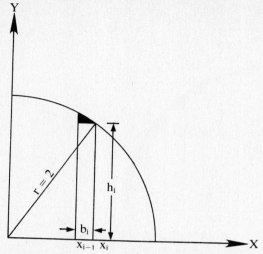

Fig. 8.13 Computing the area of the ith rectangle for Problem 8.15.

Also, $x_i = i \cdot b_i = i \cdot \dfrac{2}{n}$, so

$$h_i = 2\sqrt{1 - (i/n)^2}$$

Finally,

$$A_i = b_i \cdot h_i = \left(\frac{2}{n}\right) \cdot 2\sqrt{1 - (i/n)^2} = \frac{4}{n}\sqrt{1 - (i/n)^2}$$

The total area of all rectangles (for n partitions) is

$$T = \sum_{i=1}^{n} A_i = \frac{4}{n}\sum_{i=1}^{n} \sqrt{1 - (i/n)^2}$$

8.16 A mail order house with the physical facilities for stocking up to 20 items decides that it wants to maintain inventory control records on a small computer. For each stock item, the following data are to be stored on the computer:
1) the stock number (a five-digit integer);
2) a count of the number of items on hand;
3) the total year-to-date sales count (number of items sold);
4) the unit price;
5) the date (a four-digit integer of the form MMDD representing month and day) of the last order placed by the mail order house to the item manufacturer to restock an item.
6) the number of items ordered in 5.
Both items (5) and (6) will be zero if there is no outstanding order for an item.
   Design and implement a program system to keep track of the data listed in (1) through (6). You will need six arrays, each of size 20. Your system should contain subprograms (or subroutines and functions) to perform the following tasks:
   a) change the price of an item (given the item stock number and the new price);

b) add a new item to the inventory list (given the item number, the price, and the initial stock on hand);
c) enter information about the date and size of a new order for restocking an item;
d) reset the date and size of a new restock order to zero and update the amount on hand when a new order is received;
e) increase the total sales and decrease the count on hand each time a purchase order is received (if the order cannot be filled, print a message to that effect and reset the counts);
f) search for the array element that corresponds to a given stock number.

The following information should be stored initially in memory. This information should be printed at the start of execution of your program system.

Stock numbers	On-hand count	Price
02421	12	100.00
00801	24	32.49
63921	50	4.99
47447	100	6.99
47448	48	2.25
19012	42	18.18
86932	3	67.20

A set of typical transactions for this inventory system is given below.

Price Changes

Trans no.	Trans ID	Stock no.	New price
2	'PRIC'	19012	18.99
9	'PRIC'	89632	73.90

Add Items

Trans no.	Trans ID	Stock no.	Price	On-hand
4	'ADIT'	47447	14.27	36
5	'ADIT'	56676	.15	1500

New Orders

Trans no.	Trans ID	Stock no.	Date	Volume
3	'NUOR'	00801	1201	18
8	'NUOR'	47446	1116	15

Orders Received

Trans no.	Trans ID	Stock no.	Volume
6	'ORIN'	00801	18

Purchase Orders

Trans no.	Trans ID	Stock no.	Number wanted
11	'PRCH'	00801	30
1	'PRCH'	12345	1
7	'PRCH'	56676	150
10	'PRCH'	86932	4

Note: To obtain a reasonable test of your program, the data should be entered in order by *transaction number*.

Your main program should process the transactions, one at a time, as shown below.

Each subroutine (or subprogram) should print an appropriate informative message for each transaction, indicating whether or not the transaction was processed, and giving other pertinent information about inventory changes that resulted from the processing of the data.

After the last transaction is processed, all inventory data should be printed in tabular form.

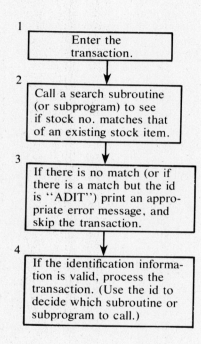

1 — Enter the transaction.

2 — Call a search subroutine (or subprogram) to see if stock no. matches that of an existing stock item.

3 — If there is no match (or if there is a match but the id is "ADIT") print an appropriate error message, and skip the transaction.

4 — If the identification information is valid, process the transaction. (Use the id to decide which subroutine or subprogram to call.)

CHARACTER STRING MANIPULATION

9

9.1 INTRODUCTION

Character strings were first introduced in Chapter 4, but we have made limited use of them so far. They have appeared primarily in print statements to annotate program output and as output column headings. We have also used string variables for storage of character strings and have written conditional statements involving character string comparison.

Many computer applications are concerned with the manipulation of character strings or textual data rather than numerical data. For example, computerized typesetters are used extensively in the publishing of books and newspapers; telephone directories and annual reports are updated on a regular basis using computer text editors; computers are used in the analysis of great works of literature.

Although there is little facility for manipulating character data in standard Minimal BASIC beyond what we have seen so far, many BASIC versions provide special functions and features for string manipulation. The features provided by these systems perform similar operations on character strings. However, the syntactical forms of these features vary significantly from system to system. In this chapter, we'll show both the Dartmouth BASIC and BASIC-PLUS forms of these features as they are representative of most BASIC implementations. A comparison chart, which illustrates the form of these features in other BASIC systems, is provided at the end of the chapter.

In the sections that follow, we will introduce some fundamental operations that can be performed on character-type data. We will describe how to reference a character *substring* and how to *concatenate* (or join) two strings. We will learn how to search for a substring in a larger string and to delete a substring or replace it with another. We will also discuss the use of the function LEN, which finds the length of its character string argument. Finally, we will see how to write expressions involving character-type data.

9.2 THE LENGTH OF A CHARACTER STRING

Recall from Chapter 4 that all string variable names consist of a letter followed by a "$". In addition to string variables, most versions of BASIC provide string arrays as well. These must be declared in DIM statements.

Example 9.1: The statement

```
DIM S$(80), A$(26)
```

allocates storage for two arrays of character strings: S$ is a one-dimensional array (list) that can store up to 80 character strings; A$ can store up to 26 strings. Most BASIC systems initialize string arrays and variables to the null string (or character string of length 0). The null string is written as "".

The concept of character string length is important to the discussion of character-type data. We will introduce this concept by defining what is meant by the length of a character string constant and a string variable. The definition of the length of other character entities will be given as they are introduced in later sections.

Length of Character String Constants and Variables

1. The length of a character string constant is equal to the number of characters in the constant excluding the quote marks used to delimit the constant.
2. The length of a string variable is equal to the number of characters stored in the variable. The length of a string variable may change when new information is stored in the variable.

The maximum allowable length for a character string constant or string variable is different for each BASIC system. Minimal BASIC specifies that strings of up to 18 characters in length must be accommodated. Many systems allow much larger size strings. (In BASIC-PLUS, string size is limited only by the amount of available memory.)

Many BASIC versions provide a function LEN that can be used to determine the length of its character-string argument. This function is described in the next display.

String Length Function LEN

Dartmouth BASIC and BASIC-PLUS form:

```
LEN (string)
```

Interpretation: The argument string may be a character string, string variable or string expression. The value returned is an integer denoting the number of characters in the argument string.

Example 9.2: The program segment below illustrates the use of the function LEN. The three numbers printed are the length of "BUTTER", "SILLY PUTTY", and "MARGARINE".

```
100 LET S$ = "BUTTER"
110 LET L1 = LEN(S$)
120 LET S$ = "SILLY PUTTY"
130 LET L2 = LEN(S$)
140 PRINT L1, L2, LEN("MARGARINE")
150 END

RUN
 6            11           9
```

9.3 SUBSTRINGS

9.3.1 Introduction

Character string manipulations frequently require references to segments of a larger character string called *substrings*. We can use special substring features to break a character string into sections or to extract part of a character string. For example, we might want to extract the day (25) from the string "JUNE 25, 1980".

There are two distinct approaches to extracting substrings: the first uses *substring notation* to reference the substring directly; the second uses special string functions which return the desired substring as value.

9.3.2 Substring Notation

Dartmouth BASIC uses substring notation as described below to reference a substring. The BASIC-PLUS substring functions are in Section 9.3.3.

Substring Notation

Dartmouth BASIC form:

$$\text{sname } (\text{exp}_1\colon \text{exp}_2)$$

Interpretation: The variable sname is a string variable or string array element and exp_1, exp_2 are numeric expressions. The expressions exp_1 and exp_2 are used to specify which substring of sname should be referenced. The value of exp_1 indicates the position in sname of the first character of the substring; the value of exp_2 indicates the position in sname of the last character of the substring.

Notes:
1. The reference sname ($\text{exp}_1\colon \text{exp}_2$) is called the *substring name*.
2. If the value of exp_1 or exp_2 is noninteger, that value is rounded to the nearest integer.
3. If the value of exp_1 is less than 1, then it is considered equal to 1.
4. If the value of exp_2 is greater than the length of sname, then exp_2 is considered equal to the length of sname.
5. If the value of exp_1 is greater than the value of exp_2, then the substring addressed is the null string preceding the character indicated by exp_1 and exp_2 is ignored.
6. If the value of exp_1 is greater than the length of sname, then the substring addressed is the null string immediately following the last character of sname.
7. Some versions of BASIC (Hewlett-Packard and Polymorphic BASIC) use a ",", instead of a ":" in the substring name; these systems don't support string arrays.

Example 9.3:   For the character assignment statement

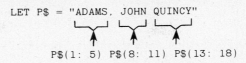

some substrings of P$ are indicated in brackets. From the notes in the preced-
ing display (on Substring Notation), we can infer the following:

Note 2:   P$(0.6*2: 0.6*8) is equivalent to P$(1.2: 4.8) or P$(1: 5).
Note 3:   P$(−3: 5) is equivalent to P$(1: 5).
Note 4:   P$(13: 20) is equivalent to P$(13: 18).
Note 5:   P$(9: 8) is the null string between the letter J and the letter O.
Note 6:   P$(23: 25) is the null string immediately following the letter Y.

Example 9.4:   The program segment below reads a social security number into
S$ and partitions it into the three substrings F$, M$, L$.

```
100 READ S$
110 DATA "042-30-0786"
120 LET F$ = S$(1: 3)
130 LET M$ = S$(5: 6)
140 LET L$ = S$(8: 11)
```

S$	F$	M$	L$
042-30-0786	042	30	0786

Before continuing with examples of substring notation, we shall introduce
the string functions used in BASIC-PLUS for extracting substrings. Section
9.3.4 will give additional examples for both methods.

9.3.3   String Functions for Extracting Substrings

In this section we will describe three BASIC-PLUS string extraction functions. These functions enable the programmer to extract substrings from either
the beginning (function LEFT$), middle (function MID$) or end (function
RIGHT$) of a string. The $ at the end of each function name indicates that the
function returns a string as its value. The name of any function that returns a
string value should end with a $.

Substring functions

BASIC-PLUS form:

LEFT$(sname, length)

Interpretation: The argument sname is a string constant, string variable
or string array element; length is a number or numeric expression. The

substring starting with the leftmost character in sname is extracted. The size of the substring is determined by the value of length.

RIGHT$(sname, length)

Interpretation: The substring ending with the rightmost character in sname is extracted. Its size is determined by length.

MID$(sname, first, length)

Interpretation: The argument first is a number or numeric expression. The substring extracted starts at position first in sname; its size is determined by the value of length. If length is omitted, the substring starting at first and ending with the last character of sname is extracted.

Notes:
1. Any noninteger-valued numeric expression for first or length will be truncated.
2. If the value of first in a reference to MID$ is 0, an error diagnostic may be printed.
3. If length exceeds the number of characters remaining in sname, the rest of the string will be extracted.
4. If the value of length is 0, an error diagnostic may be printed.

Each of the examples in section 9.3.1 is redone below using the substring functions. If exp_1 and exp_2 represent the position of the first and last characters, respectively, the length of the substring is equal to $exp_2 - exp_1 + 1$.

Example 9.3a: For the character assignment statement

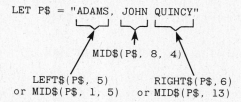

```
LET P$ = "ADAMS, JOHN QUINCY"
```

MID$(P$, 8, 4)

LEFT$(P$, 5)   RIGHT$(P$,6)
or MID$(P$, 1, 5)   or MID$(P$, 13)

some substrings of P$ are indicated in brackets.

Example 9.4a: The program segment below reads a social security number and partitions it into three substrings F$, M$, L$.

```
100 READ S$
110 DATA "042-30-0786"
120 LET F$ = LEFT$(S$, 3)
130 LET M$ = MID$(S$, 5, 2)
140 LET L$ = RIGHT$(S$, 4)
```

S$	F$	M$	L$
042-30-0786	042	30	0786

9.3.4   Additional Examples of Substring Extraction

Example 9.5:   In this example, we use a string array, G$, for storing substrings. Each substring is ten characters in length. The Dartmouth BASIC version is provided first, followed by the BASIC-PLUS version.

Dartmouth BASIC form:

```
100 DIM G$(4)
110 READ P$
120 DATA "JIMMY     CARTER    PEANUTS   GEORGIA"
130 FOR I = 1 TO 4
140    LET G$(I) = P$((10*I-9): 10*I)
150    PRINT G$(I) (1: 1);
160 NEXT I
170 END
```

BASIC-PLUS form:

```
100 DIM G$(4)
110 READ P$
120 DATA "JIMMY     CARTER    PEANUTS   GEORGIA"
130 FOR I = 1 TO 4
140    LET G$(I) = MID$(P$, 10*I-9, 10)
150    PRINT LEFT$(G$(I), 1);
160 NEXT I
170 END
```

The FOR loop shown in this example partitions the string stored in P$ into four substrings of ten characters each, which are stored in the string array G$ (line 140). This partitioning process is illustrated in Fig. 9.1. Line 150 causes the first character in each array element to be printed; the resulting program output would be the letters JCPG.

Substrings Referenced in FOR loop (line 140) for Each Value of I

I	Value of exp$_1$ 10*I-9	Value of exp$_2$ 10*I	G$(I)
1	1	10	"JIMMY "
2	11	20	"CARTER "
3	21	30	"PEANUTS "
4	31	40	"GEORGIA "

The Final Array G$

G$(1)	G$(2)	G$(3)	G$(4)
JIMMY□□□□□	CARTER□□□□	PEANUTS□□□	GEORGIA□□□

Fig. 9.1   Assignments of substrings to G$.

```
100 REM PRINT EACH WORD IN SENTENCE S$
105 REM
110     PRINT "ENTER SENTENCE"
115     INPUT S$
120 REM
125 REM FIRST WORD STARTS AT POSITION 1
130     LET B = 1
135     PRINT
140     PRINT "LIST OF WORDS"
150     FOR I = 1 TO LEN(S$)
160         REM SEARCH FOR NEXT BLANK
170         IF MID$(S$, I, 1) = " " THEN 180 ELSE 220
                                                        [IF S$(I: I) = " "]
180 REM     THEN
190             REM PRINT NEW WORD AND RESET B
200             PRINT MID$(S$, B, I-B)                  [PRINT S$(B: I-1)]
210             LET B = I + 1
220 REM     IFEND
230     NEXT I
240 REM
250 REM PRINT LAST WORD
260     PRINT MID$(S$, B)                               [PRINT S$(B: LEN(S$))]
265 REM
270     END

RUN

ENTER SENTENCE
?THE QUICK BROWN FOX JUMPED

LIST OF WORDS
THE
QUICK
BROWN
FOX
JUMPED
```

Fig. 9.2   Listing the words in a sentence.

Example 9.6:   The program in Fig. 9.2 prints each word in the sentence S$ on a separate line. It assumes that a single blank occurs between individual words.

The program variable B points to the start of the current word (B is initialized to 1). During each execution of the FOR loop, the next character in S$ is examined in line 170. If it is a blank, the substring consisting of all characters from the start of the current word up to the blank (character positions B through I−1) is printed (line 200) and B is reset to point to the first character following the blank (line 210). Line 260 prints the last word in the sentence.

Exercise 9.1:   Given the character variables S$, P$, and G$ (defined in Examples 9.3 through 9.5), list the characters that would be printed by the statements:

1)   PRINT LEFT$(S$, 3) [or PRINT S$(1:3)]

2)   PRINT MID$(P$, 6, 13) [or PRINT P$(6:18)]

3)   PRINT MID$(G$(1), 3, 7) [or PRINT G$(1)(3:9)]

Exercise 9.2:   Indicate how you could modify the program in Example 9.5 to convert a sentence to its "Pig Latin" form. In Pig Latin, the first letter of each word is moved to the end of the word and is followed by the letters AY. The Pig Latin form of THE QUICK BROWN FOX JUMPED would be HETAY UICKQAY ROWNBAY OXFAY UMPEDJAY. *Hint:* It is only necessary to change lines 200 and 260.

Program Form and Style

As in previous chapters, we have shown the BASIC-PLUS form of the program (Fig. 9.2) and used shading to highlight the Dartmouth BASIC decision structure. The equivalent Dartmouth BASIC string statements are shown on the right (lines 170, 200 and 260).

If you are not using either form shown, you should check the Table at the end of the chapter to see if the substring operations for your system are listed. If your compiler doesn't support the IF-THEN-ELSE decision structure or statement, you will have to replace line 170 in Fig. 9.2 with

```
170 IF MID$(S$, I, 1) < > " " THEN 220
```

9.4   CONCATENATION OF STRINGS

The only character string operator available in BASIC is the binary operator for *concatenation* (joining strings), written as an ampersand, &. (A + sign is used instead in BASIC-PLUS.)

The Concatenation Operator

Dartmouth BASIC form: *BASIC-PLUS form:*

     $string_1$ & $string_2$ $string_1$ + $string_2$

Interpretation: String₁ is concatenated with string₂. This means string₂ is joined to the right end of string₁. The length of the resulting string is equal to the sum of the lengths of string₁ and string₂.

Example 9.7:   In this example, the Dartmouth BASIC form of each statement is enclosed in square brackets.

a)   The assignment statement

```
LET A$ = "ABC" + "DE" [LET A$ = "ABC" & "DE"]
```

concatenates the strings ABC and DE together to form one string of length 5, "ABCDE", which is stored in A$.

b)   Given the string

```
"ADAMS, JOHN QUINCY"
```

stored in the string variable P$ (length 18), the statement

```
LET N$ = MID$(P$, 8, 5) + MID$(P$, 13, 1) + ". " + LEFT$(P$, 5)
[LET N$ = P$(8: 12) & P$(13: 13) & ". " & P$(1: 5)]
```

will result in the storage of the string.

"JOHN Q. ADAMS"

in the string variable N$.

c) Given the array G$ as defined in Example 9.5, the statement

```
LET R$ = LEFT$(G$(2), 6) + ", " + LEFT$(G$(1), 5)
[LET R$ = G$(2)(1: 6) & ", " & G$(1)(1: 5)]
```

will cause the string

"CARTER, JIMMY"

to be stored in the string variable R$.

Exercise 9.3: Given P$ and G$ as defined in Examples 9.3 and 9.5, evaluate the following:

1)   MID$(P$, 8, 4) + " " + LEFT$(G$(2), 5)
      [P$(8: 11) & " " & G$(2)(1: 5)]

2)   LEFT$(P$, 5) + MID$(P$, 7, 2) + ". " + MID$(P$, 13, 1) + "."
      [P$(1: 5) & P$(7: 8) & ". " & P$(13: 13) & "."]

9.5 STRING EXPRESSIONS AND COMPARISONS

String expressions may be used in string assignment statements, as operands of relational operators and as arguments in function calls. In this section we will describe the rules for the formation and use of string expressions.

9.5.1 String Assignment Statements

The string assignment statement assigns a value to a string or a substring, if substring notation is used. The rules of formation of the string assignment statement are summarized below.

String Assignment Statement

Dartmouth BASIC or BASIC-PLUS form:

LET svariable = sexpression

Interpretation: The variable svariable is a string variable (or substring reference written in substring notation) and sexpression is a string expression. A string expression consists of one or more character string constants, string variables, string array elements or substrings connected by the concatenation operator.

Notes: If svariable is a string variable, its new length will be equal to the length of sexpression. In Dartmouth BASIC, if svariable is a substring reference, the substring specified is replaced by the value of sexpression. The lengths of the specified substring and sexpression need not be the same; BASIC will adjust the position of the characters following the specified substring so that the replacement string fits perfectly.

We have used string assignment statements in earlier examples. The Dartmouth BASIC statements from Example 9.7

```
LET A$ = "ABC" & "DE"
LET N$ = P$(8: 12) & P$(13: 13) & ". " & P$(1: 5)
LET R$ = G$(2)(1: 6) & ", " & G$(1)(1: 5)
```

are all string assignment statements as are their BASIC-PLUS counterparts. The first of these assigns the value "ABCDE" to the string variable A$.

In the statement below, the substring A$(2: 4) is assigned a value:

```
LET A$(2: 4) = "LIV"
```

If A$ is the string "ABCDE", this statement would replace the substring in positions 2 through 4 ("BCD") with the string "LIV". The new value of A$ would be "ALIVE".

It is not necessary for the new substring and the old one to have the same length. For example:

```
LET A$(2: 4) = "GGRAVAT"
```

would redefine A$ (originally "ABCDE") as "AGGRAVATE".

Similarly, the statement:

```
LET A$(2: 4) = ""
```

would replace the substring in positions 2 through 4 of A$ by the null string, or delete it. The string A$ (originally "ABCDE") would be redefined as "AE." Finally, the statement

```
LET A$(3: 2) = "XY"
```

would replace the null string preceding position 3 in A$ (between the B and C in "ABCDE") by "XY". The effect would be to insert "XY" at position 3; the new value of A$ would be "ABXYCDE".

This capability of defining substrings is available only in those systems that use substring notation. In BASIC-PLUS it would be necessary to redefine the entire string A$. The BASIC-PLUS statement to replace the substring at positions 2 through 4 in A$ with new-string would have the form:

```
LET A$ = LEFT$(A$, 1) + new-string + MID$(A$, 5)
```

where LEFT$(A$, 1) is the original substring up to, but not including, position 2, and MID$(A$, 5) is the substring that formerly started at position 5 of A$ and continued to the end. Again, it would not be necessary for the length of new-string to be the same as the substring replaced.

Exercise 9.4: Write a program segment that reads the three character strings

```
"THE CHAIRMAN SAID"
"GENTLEMEN--WOULD EVERYONE"
"PLEASE TAKE HIS SEAT"
```

and modifies them to look like:

```
"THE CHAIRPERSON SAID"
"LADIES AND GENTLEMEN--"
"PLEASE BE SEATED"
```

9.5.2 String Comparison

We have already seen examples of string comparisons in earlier chapters: the relational operators were used to compare strings of letters for equality, or for order. The results of these comparisons were always determined by the alphabetical sequence of the operands involved. For example, if A$ and B$ contain letters only, then the relation B$ < A$ is true if the string in B$ would precede the string in A$ in the dictionary. In most BASIC versions, it is possible to compare arbitrary strings of characters containing not just letters, but also numbers and special characters such as $+, -, *, ?, /$, etc. In general the BASIC *collating sequence* is used to determine whether or not a string relation is true as described in the next display.

String Comparisons

Dartmouth BASIC and BASIC-PLUS form:

$$\text{string}_1 \text{ relop string}_2$$

Interpretation: String$_1$ and string$_2$ are string expressions that are evaluated; relop is a relational operator. The resulting strings are compared one character at a time, from left to right, until a pair of characters is reached that are different. The value of the string relation depends on the relative positions of these two (different) characters in the collating sequence (e.g., if relop is <, then the relation is true if the character from string$_1$ precedes the character from string$_2$ in the collating sequence).

BASIC collating sequence: □!"#$%&'()*+,-./01...9:;<=>?@AB...Z[\]↑
where □ is the symbol for a blank.   ⏟digits   ⏟letters

The null character, indicating the end of a string, precedes any character in the collating sequence.

Example 9.8: If the string variable W$ contains the string "PROGRAMS", then the relations below are true given the BASIC collating sequence. The first two "different" characters are indicated in parentheses following the relation.

```
W$ > "PROG"  (R follows null character)
LEFT$(W$, 4) [W$(1: 4)] = "PROG"
LEFT$(W$, 1) [W$(1: 1)] < "PR" (null character precedes R)
LEFT$(W$, 4) [W$(1: 4)] > = "PRANKS" (O follows A)
MID$(W$, 6, 3) [W$(6: 8)] < "A" + "PROG" ["A" & "PROG"] (M precedes P)
```

In the last relation, the substring to the left of < is the string "AMS"; the expression on the right evaluates to the string "APROG". M and P are the first "different" characters.

Example 9.9:   We mentioned that character strings can contain numbers and special symbols as well as letters. Sometimes character comparisons involving these other symbols lead to unexpected results as the dictionary relationship is no longer meaningful. The following relations are true for the BASIC collating sequence

```
"3" > "15"           (3 follows 1)
"1234" < "1236"      (4 precedes 5)
"1234 >= "12"        (3 follows null character)
"124" > "12398"      (4 follows 3)
"AB398" < "AC25"     (B precedes C)
"A*B+" <= "A+F$"     (* precedes +)
"ABC" > "□ABC"       (A follows □)
```

Exercise 9.5:   For each relation below, write all the relational operators that would yield a value of true. Substitute & for + in Dartmouth BASIC in parts a) and c).

a)   "A" + "35" relop "Z" + "12"
b)   "A*C" relop "A+Z"
c)   "A + 35" relop "A" + "35"
d)   "123" relop "12A4"
e)   "345" relop "32896"

9.5.3   Converting "Numeric" Character Strings to Numbers

There are many applications involving the manipulation of strings or substrings containing only the decimal digits 0, 1, 2, . . ., 9 with or without a sign or decimal point, e.g., "398" or "62.573". In Example 9.9, we have seen the rather surprising relation that "3" is greater than "15". We also know that expressions such as "3" * "15" are not permitted in BASIC since arithmetic operators can't be used with character string operands. Consequently, if we wish to perform arithmetic manipulations on these strings or to compare them numerically, we must first convert them from string data to numbers.

Many versions of BASIC provide a function VAL to convert numeric character strings into numbers. Often, a function, STR$, is also provided which is the *inverse* of VAL. This means that STR$ converts a number into a numeric string. The program below stores the numeric string "3.14" in A$ and the number 3.14 in M and N.

```
100 READ N
110 DATA 3.14
120 LET A$ = STR$(N)
130 LET M = VAL(A$)
140 PRINT "THE STRING "; A$; " IS THE NUMBER", M
150 END

RUN

THE STRING 3.14 IS THE NUMBER 3.14
```

The functions VAL and STR$ are described in the next displays.

The Function VAL

Dartmouth BASIC and BASIC-PLUS form:

```
VAL (numeric string)
```

Interpretation: If the argument is a numeric string of decimal digits (0 through 9) possibly including a sign or decimal point, then that number is returned as value; otherwise, the result is undefined and an error message will be printed.

The Function STR$

Dartmouth BASIC and BASIC-PLUS form:

```
STR$ (expression)
```

Interpretation: The argument expression may be a numeric expression, variable or constant. The argument is evaluated; its value is converted to a numeric string.

Example 9.10:   The string P$ contains a person's name (characters 1 through 10) followed by gross salary (characters 11 through 17) and number of dependents (characters 18 and 19).

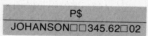

P$

JOHANSON□□345.62□02

The program in Fig. 9.3 computes taxable salary, T, by deducting 50 times the number of dependents from gross salary, G. Net salary, S, is 85 percent of the

Dartmouth BASIC form:

```
100 READ P$
110 DATA "JOHANSON  345.62 02"
120 LET G = VAL(P$(11: 17))
130 LET D = VAL(P$(18: 19))
140 LET T = G - 50 * D
150 LET S = .85 * T
160 PRINT P$(1: 10), "NET SALARY = $"; S
170 END
```

BASIC-PLUS form:

```
100 READ P$
110 DATA "JOHANSON  345.63 02"
120 LET G = VAL(MID$(P$, 11, 7))
130 LET D = VAL(MID$(P$, 18, 2))
140 LET T = G - 50 * D
150 LET S = .85 * T
160 PRINT LEFT$(P$, 10), "NET SALARY = $"; S
170 END
```

Fig. 9.3   Converting character strings to numbers.

taxable salary. The substrings representing gross salary and dependents are converted to numbers by use of the function VAL (lines 120 & 130).

9.6 SEARCHING FOR A SUBSTRING

In this section, we describe the BASIC function that searches a string (the *subject string*) for a substring (the *target string*). For example, if S$ is the subject string

we could use this function to determine whether or not the target string "AT" appeared anywhere in this string ("AT" is found in position 3). The string search function is described in the next display.

String Search Function

Dartmouth BASIC and BASIC-PLUS form:

```
POS (subject string, target string, start)
```

Interpretation: The subject string is examined from left to right, starting at position start, to determine the location of the next occurrence of the target string. If the target string is found, the value returned is the position in the subject string of the first character of the target string (value >= start); otherwise, the value returned is 0.

Note: If start is less than 1, it is considered to be 1 and the entire subject string is searched. If start is greater than the length of the subject string, the null string immediately following the subject string is searched. (In this case, the value returned should be 0 unless the target is also the null string.) If the target string is the null string, the value returned is always 1.

Some earlier versions of BASIC-PLUS use the function INSTR instead of POS. The arguments for INSTR are the same as for POS; however, their order is different:

```
INSTR (start, subject string, target string)
```

Example 9.11: The string search function POS is illustrated below.

Function Reference	Value
POS("SENTENCE", "E", 1)	2
POS("SENTENCE", "E", 3)	5
POS("SENTENCE", "E", 5)	5
POS("SENTENCE", "E", 6)	8
POS("SENTENCE", "E", 9)	0
POS("SENTENCE", "EN", −3)	2
POS("SENTENCE", "EN", 3)	5
POS("SENTENCE", "EN", 6)	0
POS("SENTENCE", "ACE", 1)	0
POS("SENTENCE", "NCE", 1)	6

```
100 REM REPLACE "AIN'T" BY "IS NOT"
105 REM
110     PRINT "ENTER SENTENCE"
120     INPUT S$
130     LET C = 0
135 REM
140 REM FIND FIRST OCCURRENCE OF AIN'T
150     LET M = POS (S$, "AIN'T", 1)
160 REM WHILE M < > 0, REPLACE AIN'T
165     [DO] WHILE M < > 0                    [IF M = 0 THEN 225]
170         REM REPLACE "AIN'T" BY "IS NOT"
180         LET S$ = LEFT$(S$,M-1)+"IS NOT"+MID$(S$,M+5)
                                              [LET S$(M:M+4) = "IS NOT"]
190         LET C = C + 1
200         REM SEARCH FOR NEXT OCCURRENCE
210         LET M = POS (S$, "AIN'T", M+6)
220     [LOOP] NEXT                           [GOTO 160]
225 REM
230     PRINT "NUMBER OF OCCURRENCES OF AIN'T = "; C
240     PRINT "NEW TEXT = "; S$
245 REM
250     END

RUN

ENTER SENTENCE
 ?HE AIN'T GOING IF JOE AIN'T
NUMBER OF OCCURRENCES OF AIN'T = 2
NEW TEXT = HE IS NOT GOING IF JOE IS NOT
```

Fig. 9.4   Replace "AIN'T by "IS NOT".

Example 9.12:   The program in Fig. 9.4 counts the number of occurrences, C, of the word "AIN'T" in the subject, S$, and replaces each occurrence with "IS NOT."

Line 150 searches for the first occurrence of "AIN'T" in S$ (starting position is 1). M is set to the location of the first occurrence and the WHILE loop is entered. Line 180 is used to replace the substring "AIN'T" (positions M through M+4 with "IS NOT". Line 210 is used to search for all occurrences of "AIN'T" after the initial one; the starting position for the next search of S$ is M+6 since the replacement string "IS NOT" now occupies positions M

Program Form and Style

The BASIC-PLUS form of the program is shown in Fig. 9.4. The WHILE loop is shaded; the statements on the right show the changes required if the WHILE loop is not available (lines 165 and 220); the Dartmouth BASIC form of line 180 is also shown on the right.

In Dartmouth BASIC, the substring of S$ originally at positions M through M+4 is redefined as "IS NOT". In BASIC-PLUS, the entire string S$ is redefined; the new S$ is the substring preceding "AIN'T" concatenated with "IS NOT" concatenated with the substring originally following "AIN'T".

through M+5. After all occurrences of AIN'T have been removed, the value
of M at line 210 will be zero, the loop repetition will fail, and the loop will be
exited.

Exercise 9.6:   Assume that we only have to count the number of occurrences of
"AIN'T". The loop below has been proposed as a substitute. Will it work? If not, fix
it.

```
165 [DO] WHILE M < > 0
170    LET C = C+1
180    LET M = POS(S$, "AIN'T", M)
190 [LOOP] NEXT
```

9.7 MANIPULATING INDIVIDUAL CHARACTERS IN A STRING*

Some versions of BASIC, including BASIC-PLUS, provide additional
functions that facilitate the manipulation of individual characters in a string.
The CHANGE function described next is used to store a numeric representation for each character of a string in consecutive array elements; each element of the array may then be manipulated. For example, the statements

```
100 DIM A(26)
110 READ A$
120 CHANGE A$ TO A
130 DATA "ABCDEFGHIJKLMNOPQRSTUVWXYZ"
```

could be used to store a numeric representation for each letter of the alphabet
in the numeric array A.

The numbers stored correspond to the *American Standard Code for In-*
formation Interchange (ASCII), part of which is shown in Table 9.1.

The array A defined by the CHANGE statement in line 120 is shown next.

Character	ASCII Equivalent	Character	ASCII Equivalent	Character	ASCII Equivalent
blank	32	A	65	O	79
+	43	B	66	P	80
−	45	C	67	Q	81
.	46	D	68	R	82
0	48	E	69	S	83
1	49	F	70	T	84
2	50	G	71	U	85
3	51	H	72	V	86
4	52	I	73	W	87
5	53	J	74	X	88
6	54	K	75	Y	89
7	55	L	76	Z	90
8	56	M	77		
9	57	N	78		

Table 9.1   ASCII Code

*This section is optional and may be omitted.

A(0)	A(1)	A(2)	A(3)		A(25)	A(26)
26	65	66	67	...	89	90

The number of characters in the string A$, or 26, is stored in element A(0). The CHANGE function may also be used to build the character string corresponding to a numeric array like A. The CHANGE function is described in the next display.

The CHANGE function

BASIC-PLUS form:

    CHANGE string TO numeric array

Interpretation: (From character string to numeric array.) The ASCII code for each character in string is stored in the corresponding element of numeric array. The array element with subscript zero is assigned the length of string as its value.

    CHANGE numeric array to string

Interpretation: (From numeric array to character string.) If each element of numeric array is a valid ASCII code for a character (normally a number less than or equal to 127), then each character in string will be determined by the corresponding code in numeric array. The length of string is determined by the array element with subscript zero.

There are two complementary functions in Dartmouth BASIC and BASIC-PLUS that manipulate the ASCII code: the function ASC converts a single character to its ASCII equivalent (e.g., the value of ASC("B") is 66), and the function CHR$ converts an ASCII number to its corresponding character (e.g., the value of CHR$(50) is the string "2"). These functions are described in the next display.

Functions ASC and CHR$

Dartmouth BASIC and BASIC-PLUS form:

    ASC(character)

Interpretation: The argument character is a string of length one. The value returned is the decimal number corresponding to the ASCII code for character.

    CHR$(numeric code)

Interpretation: The argument numeric code is a decimal number less than or equal to 127. The value returned is the character with numeric code as its ASCII equivalent.
Note: This function is named ORD in Dartmouth BASIC. In some systems quotation marks are not required around the character argument.

Example 9.13:　The program in Fig. 9.5 examines each character in a string, N$, to see if the string is a valid decimal number. A valid number may start with an optional + or − sign; it must contain only the digits 0 through 9 and possibly a decimal point. Imbedded blanks are ignored.

In Fig. 9.5, the CHANGE statement in line 150 stores the ASCII code for each character of N$ in the array N (N(0) represents the length of N$). The program variable D counts the number of decimal points so far (0 or 1) and S selects the first element in the array N to be processed by the FOR loop. If N(1) contains the ASCII code for + or −, the sign is printed (line 215), S is reset from 1 to 2 (line 220), and the FOR loop is entered. The multiple-alternative decision structure in the loop (lines 255-440) tests each element in the array N (following an optional + or −) to see if it represents a legal character. If the character is the first decimal point or a digit, it is printed (lines 290 and 350). If it is a blank, it is ignored and the next character is examined. If a character is illegal, an error message is printed (line 430). The data table is shown next; two sample runs of the program are provided in Fig. 9.5b.

Data Table for Example 9.13

Input variables	*Program variables*	*Output variables*
N$: Numeric string to be tested	S: First element of N to be tested as a digit	N(20):　Array of ASCII codes
	D: Count of decimal points (0 or 1)	
	I: Loop control variable	

Program Form and Style

The BASIC-PLUS form of the program is shown in Fig. 9.5. The Dartmouth BASIC SELECT structure is indicated by the shading.

The statements shown on the right must replace the corresponding IF-THEN-ELSE statements in any BASIC version that doesn't support this feature or the logical operators, AND and OR.

Exercise 9.7:　Improve the program in Fig. 9.5 so that it also accepts BASIC scientific notation.

Exercise 9.8:　Redo the program in Fig. 9.5, using only the string manipulation operations described in Sections 9.1 through 9.6.

```
100 REM TEST FOR VALID NUMBER
105 REM
110     DIM N(20)
120     PRINT "ENTER TEST STRING"
130     INPUT N$
135 REM
140 REM INITIALIZE PROGRAM VARIABLES
150     CHANGE N$ TO N
160     LET D = 0
170     LET S = 1
175 REM
180 REM SEE IF FIRST CHARACTER IS + OR -
190     IF N(1) = ASC("+") OR N(1) = ASC("-") THEN 200 ELSE 225
                                       [IF N(1) = ASC("+") THEN 200]
200 REM THEN                           [IF N(1) < > ASC("-") THEN 225]
210         REM + OR - SIGN; RESET S
215         PRINT CHR$(N(1));
220         LET S = 2
225 REM IFEND
230 REM
240 REM EXAMINE EACH CHARACTER STARTING AT POSITION S
250     FOR I = S TO N(0)
255 REM     SELECT
260 REM     CASE
265         IF N(I) = ASC(".") AND D = 0 THEN 270 ELSE 310
                                         [IF N(I) < > ASC(".") THEN 310]
270             REM FIRST DECIMAL POINT [IF D < > 0 THEN 310]
280             LET D = 1
290             PRINT ".";
300         GOTO 440
310 REM     CASE
330         IF N(I) >= ASC("0") AND N(I) <= ASC("9") THEN 340 ELSE 370
                                         [IF N(I) < ASC("0") THEN 370]
340             REM DECIMAL DIGIT        [IF N(I) > ASC("9") THEN 370]
350             PRINT CHR$(N(I));
360         GOTO 440
370 REM     CASE
380         IF N(I) = ASC(" ") THEN 400 ELSE 420
                                 [IF N(I) < > ASC(" ") THEN 420]
400             REM IGNORE IMBEDDED BLANK
410         GOTO 440
420 REM     DEFAULT
425             REM ILLEGAL CHARACTER; STOP
430             PRINT CHR$(N(I)); " THE LAST CHARACTER IS ILLEGAL"
435             GOTO 480
440 REM     SELECTEND
450     NEXT I
460 REM
470     PRINT " IS A VALID DECIMAL NUMBER"
480 REM
490     END
```

Fig. 9.5a Program to test for a valid number

```
RUN

ENTER TEST STRING
 ?"+ 34.  5  7"
+34.57 IS A VALID DECIMAL NUMBER

RUN

ENTER TEST STRING
 ?-  3  4.  A  69
-34.A THE LAST CHARACTER IS ILLEGAL
```

Fig. 9.5b Sample runs of program in Fig. 9.5a.

9.8 SAMPLE PROBLEMS

9.8.1 Generating Cryptograms

In the previous sections, we introduced the BASIC string manipulation operations and provided several examples of their use. We will now illustrate the application of these operations in the solution of three sample problems. The first problem is a program for generating cryptograms; the second problem involves a computer subroutine for processing a FOR loop header; the third problem is a text-editor program.

Problem 9.1:   A cryptogram is a coded message formed by substituting a code character for each letter of an original message. The substitution is performed uniformly throughout the original message, i.e., all A's might be replaced by B, all B's by P, etc. We will assume that all punctuation (including blanks between words) remains unchanged.

Discussion: The program must examine each character in a message, M\$, and add the appropriate substitution for that character to the cryptogram, S\$. This could be done by using the position of the original character in the alphabet string A\$ as an index to the string of code symbols, C\$ (e.g., the code symbol for the letter A should always be the first symbol in C\$; the code symbol for letter B should be the second symbol in C\$, etc.). The data table is shown below; the flow diagrams are drawn in Fig. 9.6 and the program is shown in Fig. 9.7.

Line 160 concatenates the punctuation symbols with the code C\$ to correspond with the punctuation symbols in A\$. Line 220 sets P to indicate the location in A\$ of the character in M\$ currently being coded. Line 260 builds the cryptogram by joining the code character in position P of C\$ to the right end of the solution so far, S\$. If P is zero, lines 300 and 305 print the first illegal character (not found in A\$) and an error message.

A sample run of the cryptogram generator is shown in Fig. 9.7 using a simple next letter code (substitute B for A, C for B, . . ., A for Z).

Data Table for Problem 9.1

Input variables	*Program variables*	*Output variables*
C$: Replacement code followed by punctuation marks	A$: String consisting of alphabet followed by punctuation marks	S$: Coded message (initially the null string)
M$: Original message	P: Position of original character in string A$, used as an index to C$	
	I: Loop control variable, indicates next character in M$ to encode	

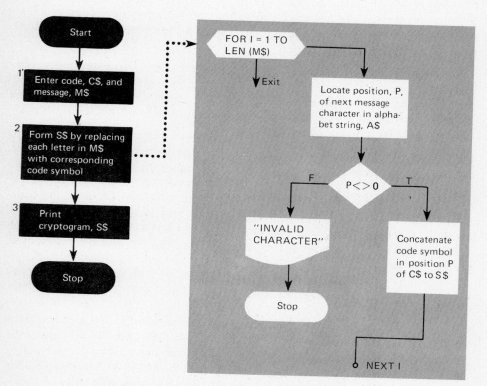

Fig. 9.6 Flow diagrams for cryptogram generator.

```
100 REM  PROGRAM TO GENERATE CRYPTOGRAMS
105 REM
110 REM  INITIALIZE ALPHABET STRING A$. SET SOLUTION S$ TO THE NULL STRING
115      LET A$ = "ABCDEFGHIJKLMNOPQRSTUVWXYZ,.?;:! "
120      LET S$ = ""
125 REM
130      PRINT "ENTER CODE SYMBOLS FOR EACH LETTER STARTING WITH A"
140      INPUT C$
150 REM  ADD PUNCTUATION SYMBOLS TO C$
160      LET C$ = C$ + ",.?;:! "              [LET C$ = C$ & ",.?;:! "]
165 REM
170      PRINT "ENTER ORIGINAL MESSAGE"
180      INPUT M$
185 REM
190 REM  SUBSTITUTE CODE SYMBOL FOR EACH LETTER
200      FOR I = 1 TO LEN(M$)
210         REM FIND CURRENT LETTER IN A$
220         LET P = POS(A$, MID$(M$, I, 1),1)   [LET P = POS(A$,M$(I:I), 1)]
230         IF P < > 0 THEN 240 ELSE 280      [IF P = 0 THEN 280]
240 REM     THEN
250            REM ADD CODE SYMBOL TO S$
260            LET S$ = S$ + MID$(C$, P, 1)   [LET S$ = S$ & C$(P:P)]
270         GOTO 320
280 REM     ELSE
290            REM ILLEGAL CHARACTER AT POSITION I IN M$; STOP
300            PRINT MID$(M$, I, 1);          [PRINT M$(I:I); ]
305            PRINT " IS AN ILLEGAL CHARACTER"
310         GOTO 360
320 REM     IFEND
330      NEXT I
340 REM
350      PRINT "CRYPTOGRAM:"
355      PRINT "   "; S$
360 REM
370      END

RUN

ENTER CODE SYMBOLS FOR EACH LETTER STARTING WITH A
?BCDEFGHIJKLMNOPQRSTUVWXYZA
ENTER ORIGINAL MESSAGE
?"JACK BE NIMBLE, JACK BE QUICK!"
CRYPTOGRAM:
   KBDL CF OJNCMF, KBDL CF RVJDL!
```

Fig. 9.7   Cryptogram generator.

Program Form and Style

In Fig. 9.7, we have shown the BASIC-PLUS form of the cryptogram program. The Dartmouth BASIC form of the decision structure is highlighted by shading, and the string manipulation statements are shown on the right.

The Minimal BASIC form of line 230 (the IF-THEN-ELSE statement) is also shown on the right.

9.8.2 Scanning a FOR Loop Header

One important function of a compiler is to scan each statement and extract all essential information contained in that statement. This process is illustrated next for a FOR loop header statement.

Problem 9.2: We can consider the FOR loop header statement as a character string of the form

```
FOR lcv = initval TO endval STEP stepval
```

For example,

```
"FOR I = F TO (L1 + 3) STEP 5"
```

One of the tasks of a compiler in translating this statement might be to separate the substrings representing the loop parameters initval, endval and stepval from the rest of the string and to save these substrings for future reference. We will write a program to perform this substring separation.

Discussion: The task of our program is to identify and copy each of the FOR loop parameters—initval, endval and stepval—into successive elements of the string array P$. In order to do this, our program must determine the start and end positions of the loop parameter strings. This, in turn, requires locating the equal sign and the words TO and STEP in the header string. We shall store the location of each of these target substrings in the array P. Once the positions of the equal sign and the words TO and STEP have been located, the substrings *delimited* by them can be copied into the array P$.

To make the program more general, we shall use a pair of arrays, T$(3) and T(3), for storage of the target strings *(delimiters)* and their lengths respectively. The target strings will be read into T$; the LEN function will be used to set T.

The data table for the main program follows; the level one flow diagram and program system chart are shown in Fig. 9.8. As indicated in the program system chart, the subroutine LOCATE will be used to find the substring delimiters ("=", "TO" and "STEP") and subroutine COPY will store the parameter substrings in P$. The main program is provided in Fig. 9.9.

Data Table for Scanning FOR Loop Header

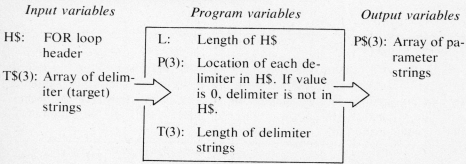

Input variables	*Program variables*	*Output variables*
H$: FOR loop header	L: Length of H$	P$(3): Array of parameter strings
T$(3): Array of delimiter (target) strings	P(3): Location of each delimiter in H$. If value is 0, delimiter is not in H$.	
	T(3): Length of delimiter strings	

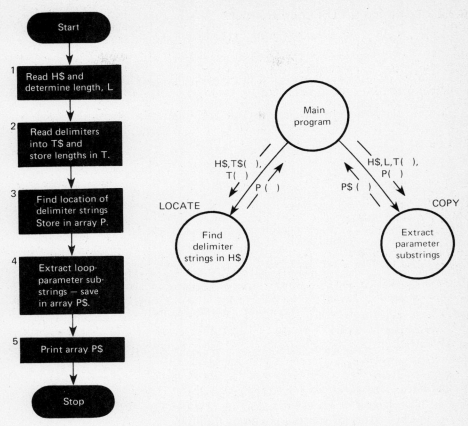

Fig. 9.8 Level one flow diagram and program system chart for FOR loop header
processor.

Subroutines Referenced

LOCATE: Finds the starting position in H$ of each delimiter.

> *Global variables*
> H$—header string (input)
> T$( )—array of delimiters (input)
> T( )—lengths of delimiters (input)
> P( )—array of starting positions in H$ of the delimiter strings
>   (output)

COPY: Copies each parameter substring into array P$. If "STEP" is missing,
the stepval substring is "1".

> *Global variables*
> H$, T$( ), T( )—(See above description for LOCATE)

```
100 REM PROCESS FOR LOOP HEADER
105 REM
110     DIM T$(3), T(3), P(3), P$(3)
115 REM
120 REM READ HEADER AND FIND LENGTH
130     READ H$
140     DATA "FOR I1 = K + 3 TO L2 STEP I + 2"
150     LET L = LEN(H$)
155 REM
160 REM READ TARGET STRINGS, T$, AND FIND LENGTHS, T
170     FOR I = 1 TO 3
180        READ T$(I)
190        LET T(I) = LEN(T$(I))
200     NEXT I
210     DATA "=", "TO", "STEP"
215 REM
220 REM LOCATE TARGET STRINGS
230     GOSUB 1000
235 REM
240 REM EXTRACT LOOP PARAMETER SUBSTRINGS
250     GOSUB 2000
260 REM
270 REM PRINT RESULTS
280     PRINT "FOR LOOP HEADER: "; H$
290     PRINT "INITIAL VALUE PARAMETER: "; P$(1)
300     PRINT "END VALUE PARAMETER: "; P$(2)
310     PRINT "STEP VALUE PARAMETER: "; P$(3)
320 REM
330     STOP
```

Fig. 9.9 Main program for FOR loop processor.

Additional global variables for COPY
    L—length of H$ (input)
    P( )—array of starting positions (input)
    P$( )—array of parameter substrings (output)

    The POS function can be used by LOCATE to search for the delimiters. We will introduce a program variable, B, which gives the starting position in H$ for each target search. The data table for LOCATE follows; the flow diagrams for LOCATE are shown in Fig. 9.10.

Data Table for LOCATE

Program variables

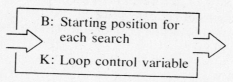

B: Starting position for each search

K: Loop control variable

    In Fig. 9.10, we see that the search for the first target string begins at position 1 of H$ (step 1.1). After each target search (step 1.3), B is reset so

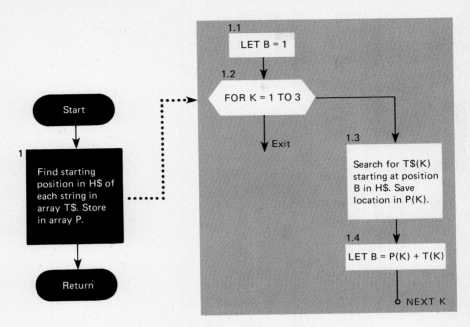

9.10   Flow diagrams for subroutine LOCATE.

Program Form and Style

The BASIC-PLUS form of the subroutine is shown in Fig. 9.12. The conditional transfer statements on the right should replace the corresponding IF-THEN-ELSE statements if your version of BASIC doesn't support this feature.

The Dartmouth BASIC form of the SELECT structure is shaded. The CASE statements and their conditions should be on the same line. The Dartmouth BASIC form of lines 2170 through 2280 is shown next.

```
2170 CASE P(3) = 0
2190    REM T$(3) IS MISSING; EXTRACT P$(1), P$(2), SET P$(3) TO "1"
2200    P$(1) = H$(P(1)+T(1): P(2)-1)
2210    P$(2) = H$(P(2)+T(2): L)
2220    P$(3) = "1"
2240 DEFAULT
2250    REM T$(3) IS PRESENT; EXTRACT P$(1), P$(2), AND P$(3)
2255    P$(1) = H$(P(1)+T(1): P(2)-1)
2260    P$(2) = H$(P(2)+T(2): P(3)-1)
2270    P$(3) = H$(P(3)+T(3): L)
2280 SELECTEND
```

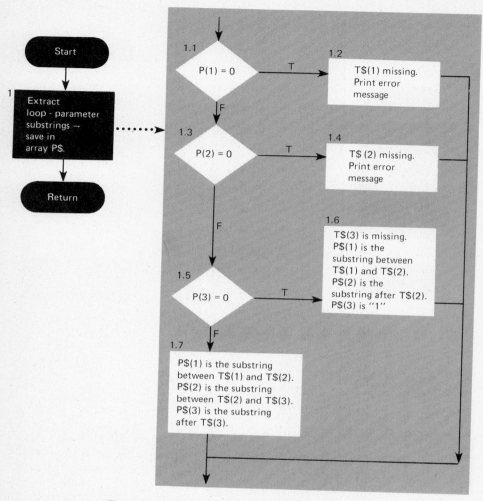

Fig. 9.11 Flow diagrams for the COPY subroutine.

that the next search begins with the first character following the target just located (step 1.4).

The flow diagrams for the COPY subroutine are drawn in Fig. 9.11. The level two flow diagram is a multiple-alternative decision structure. Steps 1.1 and 1.3 test to see whether either of the first two delimiters ("=", "TO") is missing; if so, an error message is printed. Step 1.5 tests to see whether the optional delimiter ("STEP") is missing; if so, step 1.6 extracts the initval and endval substrings and sets P$(1) to "1". Step 1.7 extracts the initval, endval and stepval parameter substrings when "STEP" is present.

```
1000 REM SUBROUTINE TO LOCATE TARGET STRINGS
1005 REM
1010 REM GLOBAL VARIABLES
1020 REM     IN:   H$, T$( ), T( )
1030 REM     OUT: P( )
1040 REM OTHER VARIABLES CHANGED: B, K
1050 REM
1060      LET B = 1
1070      FOR K = 1 TO 3
1080         LET P(K) = POS(H$, T$(K), B)
1090         LET B = P(K) + T(K)
1100      NEXT K
1110 REM
1120      RETURN
1130 REM
2000 REM SUBROUTINE TO COPY PARAMETER SUBSTRINGS
2005 REM
2010 REM GLOBAL VARIABLES
2020 REM     IN:   P( ), H$, T$( ), T( ), L
2030 REM     OUT: P$( ) – PARAMETER SUBSTRINGS
2040 REM
2050 REM COPY SUBSTRINGS INTO P$( )
2060 REM SELECT
2070 REM CASE
2080      IF P(1) = 0 THEN 2090 ELSE 2120        [IF P(1) <> 0 THEN 2120]
2090         REM T$(1) IS MISSING; RETURN
2100         PRINT T$(1); " IS MISSING"
2110      GOTO 2280
2120 REM CASE
2130      IF P(2) = 0 THEN 2140 ELSE 2170        [IF P(2) <> 0 THEN 2170]
2140         REM T$(2) IS MISSING; RETURN
2150         PRINT T$(2); " IS MISSING"
2160      GOTO 2280
2170 REM CASE
2180      IF P(3) = 0 THEN 2190 ELSE 2240        [IF P(3) <> 0 THEN 2240]
2190         REM T$(3) IS MISSING; EXTRACT P$(1), P$(2), SET P$(3) TO "1"
2200         LET P$(1) = MID$(H$, P(1)+T(1), P(2)-P(1)-T(1))
2210         LET P$(2) = MID$(H$, P(2)+T(2))
2220         LET P$(3) = "1"
2230      GOTO 2280
2240 REM DEFAULT
2250         REM T$(3) IS PRESENT; EXTRACT P$(1), P$(2) AND P$(3)
2255         LET P$(1) = MID$(H$, P(1)+T(1), P(2)-P(1)-T(1))
2260         LET P$(2) = MID$(H$, P(2)+T(2), P(3)-P(2)-T(2))
2270         LET P$(3) = MID$(H$, P(3)+T(3))
2280 REM SELECTEND
2290 REM
2300      RETURN
2310      END

RUN

FOR LOOP HEADER: FOR I1 = K + 3 TO L2 STEP I + 2
INITIAL VALUE PARAMETER: K + 3
END VALUE PARAMETER: L2
STEP VALUE PARAMETER: I + 2
```

Fig. 9.12 Subroutines LOCATE and COPY and a sample run.

Subroutines LOCATE and COPY are shown in Fig. 9.12 along with a sample run of the program. These subroutines should be implemented as subprograms if that feature is supported on your system. Refer to the Program Form and Style box on page 313 for additional discussion.

Exercise 9.9:   Modify the main program and subroutines so that the section that prints final results (lines 260-310) is skipped if T$(1) or T$(2) is missing.

Exercise 9.10:   What changes would be required to enable this program to process a one line IF-THEN-ELSE statement and extract the relation, the THEN statement and the ELSE statement as shown below.

```
IF    X > Y    THEN    LET X = X-1    ELSE    LET Y = Y-1
```
relation   THEN statement   ELSE statement

9.8.3   Text Editing Problem

In this section, we will write a subroutine for a text editor that can be used to replace any string with another. We have already written a specific program that replaces all occurrences of the string "AIN'T" with "IS NOT" (Example 9.12).

Problem 9.3:   There are many applications for which it is useful to have a computerized text editing program. For example, if you are preparing a laboratory report, it would be convenient to edit or modify sections of the report (improve sentence and paragraph structure, change words, correct spelling mistakes, etc.) at a computer terminal and then have a fresh, clean copy of the text typed at the terminal without erasures or mistakes.

Discussion: A Text Editor System is a relatively sophisticated system of subroutines that can be used to instruct the computer to perform virtually any kind of text alteration. At the heart of such a system is a subroutine that replaces one substring in the text with another substring. As an example, consider the following sentence prepared by an overzealous member of the Addison-Wesley advertising group.

"THE BOOK BY FRIEDMEN AND KOFFMAN
IN FRACTURED PROGRAMING IS GRREAT?"

To correct this sentence we would want to specify the following edit operations:

1)   Replace "MEN" with "MAN"
2)   Replace "IN" with "ON"
3)   Replace "FRA" with "STRU"
4)   Replace "AM" with "AMM"
5)   Replace "RR" with "R"
6)   Replace "?" with "!"

The result is now at least grammatically correct.

> "THE BOOK BY FRIEDMAN AND KOFFMAN
> ON STRUCTURED PROGRAMMING IS GREAT!"

We will write the replacement program module as the subroutine RE-
PLACE. The data table is shown below.

Data Table for REPLACE

Input global variables	*Program variables*	*Output global variables*
T$: Text to be edited		T$: Edited text
M: Maximum possible length of text		
O$: Old string (to be replaced)		
N$: New string (to be inserted)		

M is an input global variable that is defined to be equal to the maximum
length of the text string.

The initial task to be performed by REPLACE is to locate the first occurrence of the string to be replaced, O$, in T$ (only the first occurrence will
be replaced). This can be accomplished using the string search function POS.

The additional data table entries required for REPLACE are shown next.
The flow diagrams are drawn in Fig. 9.13.

Additional Data Table Entries for REPLACE

Program variables

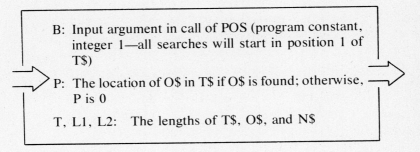

B: Input argument in call of POS (program constant, integer 1—all searches will start in position 1 of T$)

P: The location of O$ in T$ if O$ is found; otherwise, P is 0

T, L1, L2: The lengths of T$, O$, and N$

As indicated in the refinement of step 2.2, if L2 is larger than L1, it is
possible that the length of the revised text, R, would exceed the maximum text
size, M. In this case, an error message should be printed and the replacement

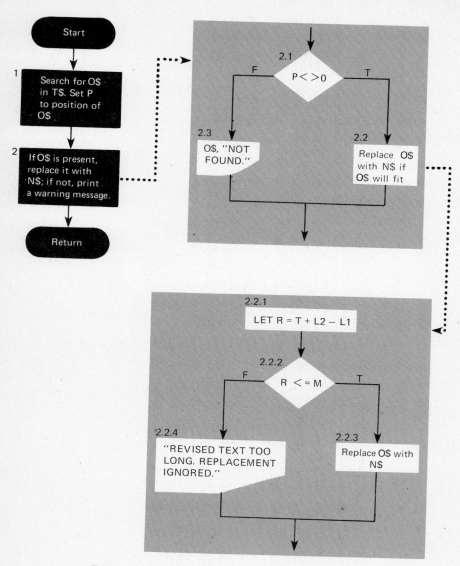

Fig. 9.13   Flow diagrams for subroutine REPLACE.

```
1000 REM SUBROUTINE TO REPLACE O$ IN T$ WITH N$
1005 REM
1010      GLOBAL VARIABLES
1015 REM IN:  T$ — TEXT TO BE EDITED
1020 REM      M  — MAXIMUM TEXT LENGTH
1025 REM      O$ — SUBSTRING TO BE REPLACED
1030 REM      N$ — REPLACEMENT SUBSTRING
1035 REM OUT: T$
1040 REM OTHER VARIABLES CHANGED — B, P, R, T, L1, L2
1045 REM
1050 REM SET STRING LENGTHS
1060      LET T = LEN(T$)
1070      LET L1 = LEN(O$)
1080      LET L2 = LEN(N$)
1085 REM
1090 REM SEE IF O$ IN T$ AND SET P TO START OF O$.
1100      LET B = 1
1110      LET P = POS(T$, O$, B)
1120      IF P < > 0 THEN 1130 ELSE 1240          [IF P = 0 THEN 1240]
1130 REM THEN
1140         REM O$ FOUND IN T$. CHECK REVISED LENGTH R.
1150         LET R = T + L2 — L1
1160         IF R <= M THEN 1170 ELSE 1210        [IF R > M THEN 1210]
1170 REM     THEN
1180            REM LENGTH O.K.; REPLACE O$ WITH N$
1190            LET T$ = LEFT$(T$, P—1) + N$ + MID$(T$, P+L1)
1200            GOTO 1230
1210 REM     ELSE
1220            PRINT "REVISED TEXT TOO LONG. REPLACEMENT IGNORED"
1230 REM     IFEND
1235 REM GOTO 1260
1240 REM ELSE
1250         PRINT O$; "NOT FOUND. REPLACEMENT IGNORED."
1260 REM IFEND
1270 REM
1280      RETURN
```

Fig. 9.14 REPLACE subroutine.

operation ignored. The new data table entry follows. The subroutine is given in Fig. 9.14.

Additional Data Table Entries for REPLACE

Program variables

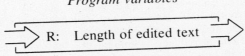

R: Length of edited text

Line 1190 replaces the substring O$ in T$ with N$. The characters replaced were in positions P through P+L1−1 (L1 is the length of O$). The position of the substring that followed O$ will be automatically adjusted to follow N$.

There is a potential problem with the BASIC-PLUS version of the program. If the text, T$, starts with the substring O$, P would be set to 1 in line 1110 and the value of P−1 in line 1190 would be zero. This would cause an error diagnostic to be printed. An IF-THEN-ELSE decision structure should be used to test for P equal to 1 before redefining T$.

Program Form and Style

The BASIC-PLUS version of the subroutine is shown in Fig. 9.14, the Dartmouth BASIC form of the nested decision structure is indicated by shading. The only other change required in Dartmouth BASIC would be the substitution of the line below for line 1190.

```
1190 LET T$(P: P+L1-1) = N$
```

This statement replaces the substring O$ in T$ (positions P through P+L1−1 of T$) with N$.

The statements on the right of Fig. 9.14 should be used in those systems that don't support the IF-THEN-ELSE statement.

Exercise 9.11:   Write the IF-THEN-ELSE decision structure described above to prevent the error at line 1190 when P is equal to one.

Exercise 9.12:   Write a main program that could be used with the subroutine REPLACE. The main program should read and print the text to be edited and also read a set of edit commands of the form

```
R, MEN, MAN
```

or

```
RA, MEN, MAN
```

The first command means replace the first occurrence of the string "MEN" with the string "MAN"; the second command means replace all occurrences of the string "MEN" with the string "MAN". After each editing command has been processed, the edited text should be printed.

Exercise 9.13:   The REPLACE subroutine shown in Fig. 9.14 always begins its search for O$ at position one of T$. In many instances, it is useful to be able to provide REPLACE with an additional piece of information—namely, the position in T$ where the search is to begin. Such flexibility can be provided in REPLACE simply by changing B from a local variable to a global input variable. In this way, we provide REPLACE with a starting point that is closer to the substring to be replaced and reduce the amount of searching done by POS.

We may also be able to reduce the amount of *contextual information* required in order to have the correct replacement done. For example, if B is set to 18 before REPLACE is called, then it would only be necessary to replace "E" by "A" (instead of "MEN" by "MAN") to change the spelling of FRIEDMEN to FRIEDMAN. (See the example at the start of section 9.8.3.) The additional contextual information "M" and "N" was needed to prevent the earlier occurrences of "E" from being replaced by "A."

For each of the editing operations listed below, write two sets of values for the global variables O$ and N$. Write the first set assuming B is a local variable and the second set with B as an input global variable (also include the value of global variable B).

a)   Replace "FRA" with "STRU"
b)   Replace the "I" in "IN" with an "O"
c)   Replace "BOOK" by "TEXT"
d)   Insert an extra "M" into "PROGRAMING"
e)   Delete an "R" from "GRREAT"

Exercise 9.14:   From Exercise 9.13, parts (d) and (e), it is clear that REPLACE can be used to perform both insertions into and deletions from T$ simply by providing enough contextual information in the global variables representing the new and old strings. Nevertheless, we might wish to write subroutines DELETE and INSERT to handle all deletions and insertions.

a)   Using the REPLACE subroutine as a guide, write a subroutine DELETE to delete the first occurrence of a string O$ from T$. The search for O$ in T$ will start at B.
b)   We can write a subroutine INSERT to insert a character string N$ into T$. In addition to N$ this subroutine will need a third input global variable, B, which in this case marks the exact position in T$ in which the insertion is to be performed. For example, if N$ were "ELLIOT" and B were 26, the subroutine would insert the string "ELLIOT" in front of "KOFFMAN" in the original version of T$. Again using REPLACE as a guide, write the subroutine INSERT. If you have the subprogram feature, write all three of these as subprograms instead. All the global variables should be parameters.

9.9   COMMON PROGRAMMING ERRORS

Now that we know how to manipulate different types of data, we must be especially careful not to misuse these data types in expressions. Character strings can be operands of the concatenation operator (& or +) and relational operators only. Remember that string variables and character string constants can be manipulated only with other string variables and constants.

The string manipulation functions introduced in this chapter require string expressions as well as numeric expressions as arguments. Make sure that your arguments are in the proper order and that string arguments are not used in place of numeric arguments (or vice versa), as attempts to use these functions with incorrect argument types will cause compiler errors. In user-defined functions, if the parameter is a string variable, indicated by a $ in its name, then the matching argument must be a string expression.

In using substrings, care must be taken to ensure that the numeric expressions indicating the start and end positions of a substring (or the start and length of a substring) are correct. If they are not correct, the wrong substring will be referenced. The compiler normally will not detect incorrect values for these numeric expressions; consequently, it is advisable to double check them yourself and print their values if you are in doubt.

Feature	Dartmouth BASIC 7	Digital Equipment BASIC-PLUS	Sperry Univac UBASIC	Honeywell 60/6000	CDC Basic 3
1. string length	LEN(string)	LEN(string)	LEN(string)	LEN(string)	LEN(string)
2. substring extraction	string(start:end)	LEFT$(string, length) RIGHT$(string, length) MID$(string, start, length)	CPY$(string, start, length) (like MID$)	SST(string, start, length) (like MID$)	SUBSTR(string, start, length) (Like MID$)
3. concatenation operator	&	+	+	&	+
4. substring search	POS(subject, target, start)	POS(subject, target, start) INSTR(start, subject, target)	SEP(subject, target, start) (like POS)	not available	not available
5. functions for converting from strings to numbers, and single characters to ASCII code	CHANGE string TO array CHANGE array TO string VAL(string) STR$(number) ORD(character) (like ASC) CHR$(code)	CHANGE string TO array CHANGE array TO string VAL(string) STR$(number) ASC(character) CHR$(code)	VAL(string)	CHANGE string TO array CHANGE array TO string VAL(numeric-string) STR$(number) ASC(character)	VAL(numeric-string) STR$(number) CHR$(code)
6. string arrays	string arrays are permitted	string arrays are permitted	string arrays are permitted	string arrays with twenty characters/ element	string arrays are permitted

Feature	Digital Equipment RT/11 BASIC	Burroughs B6000/B7000	Hewlett Packard 2000E/2000C	Dartmouth BASIC (edition 6)	TRS/80-level II and Commodore BASIC
1. string length	LEN(string)	LEN(string)	LEN(string)	LEN(string)	LEN(string)
2. substring extraction	SEG$(string, start, end)	LEFT(string, length) RIGHT(string, length)	string(start, end) (like Dartmouth)	SEG$(string, start, end)	LEFT$(string, length) RIGHT$(string, length) RIGHT$(string,

			BASIC substring notation)	
(returns the substring in positions start through end of string)	(like LEFT$ and RIGHT$) EXT$(string, start, end) (returns the substring in positions start through end of string)	...BASIC substring notation)	(returns the substring in positions start through end of string)	length) MID$(string, start, length)
3. concatenation operator &	+	not available	&	+
4. substring search POS(subject, target, start)	SCN(subject, target, occurrence, start) (like POS except the occurrence number desired must be specified; POS always finds the first occurrence)	not available	POS(subject, target, start)	not available
5. functions for converting from strings to numbers, and single characters to ASCII code VAL(numeric-string) STR$(number) ASC(character) CHR$(code)	VAL(string) STR$(number) ASC(character)	not available	CHANGE string TO array CHANGE array TO string VAL(string) STR$(number) ASC(character) CHR$(code)	VAL(string) STR$(number) CHR$(code) ASC(character)
6. string arrays string arrays are permitted	string arrays are permitted	string arrays are not permitted. The DIM statement declares the maximum length of a string variable, not an array	string arrays are permitted	string arrays are permitted

Table 9.2 Comparison of BASIC string manipulation statements

9.10   SUMMARY

In this chapter, we reviewed earlier work with character strings and introduced several new functions (LEN, POS, MID$, LEFT$, RIGHT$, VAL, etc.) and a new operator for concatenation (& or +). We also discussed substring notation for referencing substrings and the use of string functions for extracting substrings. Table 9.2 provides a description of the form of these features in several BASIC systems.

Many examples of these new features for manipulating character strings were presented. We have applied these features to generate cryptograms, to solve a problem that might arise in compiler design (processing a FOR loop header), and in the design of a text editor replacement subroutine.

These kinds of problems are called non-numerical problems and they are among the most challenging in computer science. This is because the computer is a numerical device and, consequently, is well suited for use as a tool for manipulating numerical data. However, many of the concepts that interest us most are not quantitative or numerical; hence, we are often unable to apply the computer effectively in helping to solve these problems. The techniques presented in this chapter should give you a better idea of how to use the computer to solve non-numerical problems.

PROGRAMMING PROBLEMS

9.4   LET F$ contain the string "DINGBAT" and L$ the string "WOMBAT". Write a program to read in a set of words and determine whether or not the words fall between the words in F$ and L$. Print the words in F$ and L$ and print each word read in (except the last) along with the identifiers "BETWEEN" or "NOT BETWEEN", whichever applies. Use the following data:

```
              HELP
              ME
              STIFLE
              THE
              DINGBAT
              AND
              THE
              WOMBATS
              BEFORE
              IT
              IS
              TOO
              LATE
```

9.5   Assume a set of sentences is to be processed. Each sentence consists of a sequence of words, separated by one or more blank spaces. Write a program that will read these sentences and count the number of words with one letter, two letters, etc., up to ten letters.

9.6   Write a program that will scan a sentence and replace all multiple occurrences of a blank with a single occurrence of a blank.

9.7 Write a program to read in a collection of character strings of arbitrary length. For each string read, your program should do the following:

  i) print the length of the string;

  ii) count the number of occurrences of four letter words in each string;

  iii) replace each four letter word with a string of four asterisks and print the new string.

9.8 Write a program that removes all of the blanks from a character string and "compacts" all non-blank characters in the string. You should only have to scan the input string once from left to right.

9.9 Use the subroutine REPLACE (Problem 9.3) and subroutines DELETE and INSERT (Exercise 9.14), and write a simple Text Editor System to perform the following tasks:

  a) Delete the first occurrence of a character string from T$;
  b) Replace the first occurrence of a character string with another string;
  c) Insert a character string at a specified position of T$.

The program system chart (PSC) for the Text Editor is as follows:

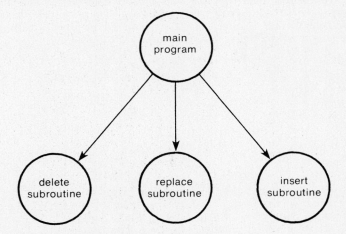

Test your system with the following input data:

```
"THE ORGANIZATION OF A PROGRAM IS A VERY MISERABLE EXPERIENCE. EVERY
PROGRAMMER HAS HIS OWN INEFFICIENT WAY OF GOING ABOUT THE DEVELOPMENT
PROCESS. PROGRAMMING IS STILL A WASTE OF TIME, BUT EVEN TEACHERS
WASTE TIME."

"REPLACE", "MISERABLE", "PERSONAL"
"DELETE", "THIS IS NONSENSE"
"INSERT", "DESIGN AND", 5
"REPLACE", "A WASTE OF TIME," , "AN ART."
"DELETE", "INEFFICIENT"
"DELETE", "BUT EVEN TEACHERS WASTE TIME."
"PRINT"
"QUIT"
```

For this problem, T$ should be a character string of maximum length 300. The main program should begin by reading the character string into T$.

Next, the main program should enter a loop in which text edit directives, REPLACE, INSERT, DELETE, PRINT and QUIT are processed. The main program should read a directive, then read the data associated with that directive, and call the appropriate subroutine to perform the indicated edit. If QUIT is read, the program should terminate.

9.10 Write an arithmetic expression translator that compiles fully-parenthesized arithmetic expressions involving the operators *, /, +, and −. For example, given the input string

(i) "((A+(B*C))−(D/E))"

the compiler would print out:

```
Z = (B*C)
Y = (A+Z)
X = (D/E)
W = (Y−X)
```

Assume only the letters A through F can be used as variable names. *Hint:* Find the first right parenthesis. Remove it and the four characters preceding it and replace them with the next unused letter at the end of the alphabet. Print out the assignment statement used. For example, the following is a summary of the sequence of steps required to process expression (i). The arrow points to the first right parenthesis at each step.

expression status	*print*
((A+(B*C))−(D/E)) ↑	Z = (B*C)
((A+Z)−(D/E)) ↑	Y = (A+Z)
(Y−(D/E)) ↑	X = (D/E)
(Y−X) ↑	W = (Y−X)

9.11 Write a program to read in a string of up to 10 characters representing a number in the form of a Roman numeral. Print the Roman numeral form and then convert to Arabic form (a BASIC integer). The character values for Roman numerals are

M	1000
D	500
C	100
L	50
X	10
V	5
I	1

Test your program on the following input.

LXXXVII	87
CCXIX	219
MCCCLIV	1354
MMDCLXXIII	2673
MDCDLXXVI	?

Positions	Data description
1–6	Employee number (an integer)
7–19	Employee last name
20–27	Employee first name
28–32	Number of hours worked (to the nearest ½ hour) for this employee
33–37	Hourly pay rate for this employee
38	Contains a C if employee works in the City Office and an S if he works in the Suburban Office
39	Contains an M if the employee is a union member
40–41	Number of dependents
42–46	Number of overtime hours worked (if any) (also to the nearest ½ hour)

Table 9.3 Employee record string for Problem 9.12

9.12 Write a data table, flow diagram and program that will process the employee records described in Table 9.3 (each record is represented as a character string) and perform the following tasks:

a) For each employee compute the gross pay:
Gross pay = Hours worked * Hourly pay +
Overtime hours worked * Hourly pay * 1.5
b) For each employee compute the net pay as follows:
Net pay = Gross pay − Deductions

Deductions are computed as follows:

Federal Tax = (gross pay − 13 * no. of dependents) * .14

FICA = gross pay * .052

City Tax = $\begin{cases} \$0.00 \text{ if employee works in the suburbs} \\ 4\% \text{ of gross pay if employee works in city} \end{cases}$

Union Dues = $\begin{cases} 0.00 \text{ if employee not a union member} \\ 6.75\% \text{ of gross pay otherwise} \end{cases}$

For each employee, print one or more lines of output containing:

1. Employee number
2. First and last name
3. Number of hours worked
4. Hourly pay rate
5. Overtime hours
6. Gross pay
7. Federal tax
8. FICA
9. City wage tax (if any)
10. Union dues (if any)
11. Net pay

Also compute and print:

1. Number of employees processed
2. Total gross pay
3. Total federal tax withheld

4. Total hours worked
5. Total overtime hours worked

9.13 Shown below is the layout of a string that the registrar uses as input for a program to print the end-of-the-semester final grade report for each student.

Positions	Data description
1–6	Student number
7–19	Last name
20–27	First name
28	Middle initial
29	Academic year:
	1 = Fr, 2 = So, 3 = Jr, 4 = Sr
30–32	First course—Department ID (3 letters)
33–35	First course—Number (3 digits)
36	First course—Grade A, B, C, D, or F
37	First course—Number of credits: 0–7
40–42	
43–45	
46	Second course: data as described above
47	
50–52	
53–55	
56	Third course data
57	
60–62	
63–65	
66	Fourth course data
67	
70–72	
73–75	
76	Fifth course data
77	

Write a data table, flow diagram and program to print the following grade report sheet for each student.

```
Line  1                    MAD RIVER COLLEGE
Line  2                    YELLOW GULCH, OHIO
Line  3
Line  4              GRADE REPORT, SPRING SEMESTER
Line  5
Line  6  (student number)          (year)        (student name)
         ------------------        ------        --------------
Line  7
Line  8                    GRADE SUMMARY
Line  9        COURSE
Line 10      DEPT   NMBR              CREDITS       GRADE
Line 11  1.  ----   ----               _             _
Line 12  2.  ----   ----               _             _
Line 13  3.  ----   ----               _             _
Line 14  4.  ----   ----               _             _
Line 15  5.  ----   ----               _             _
Line 16
Line 17  SEMESTER GRADE POINT AVERAGE = _.__
```

Compute the grade point average as follows:

   i)   Use 4 points for an A, 3 for a B, 2 for a C, 1 for a D, and 0 for an F
  ii)   Compute the product of points times credits for each course
 iii)   Add together the products computed in (ii)
 iv)   Add together the total number of course credits
  v)   Divide (iii) by (iv) and print the result.

Your program should work for students taking anywhere from one to five courses. You will have to determine the number of courses taken by a student from the input data.

9.14 Do the hangman problem (Problem 6.17) using character strings instead of string arrays to hold the word to be guessed and the solution so far.

TWO-DIMENSIONAL ARRAYS AND MATRICES

10

10.1 INTRODUCTION

In previous chapters, we have written programs that manipulate both numerical and string data. In addition, we have used one data structure, the array, for identifying and referencing a collection of data items of the same type. The array enables us to save a list of related data items in memory. All of these data items are referred to by the same name, and the array subscript is used to distinguish among the individual array elements.

In this chapter, the use of the array will be extended to facilitate the organization of related data items into tables of two dimensions. For example, we will see how a two-dimensional array with three rows and three columns can be used to represent a tic-tac-toe board. This array has nine elements, each of which can be referenced by specifying the *row subscript* (1, 2 or 3) and *column subscript* (1, 2 or 3), as shown in Fig. 10.1. The two-dimensional array is available in Minimal BASIC.

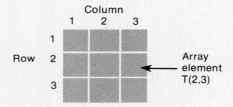

Fig. 10.1 Representation of a tic-tac-toe board as a two-dimensional array.

10.2 DECLARATION OF TWO-DIMENSIONAL ARRAYS

The general form of an array declaration can be expanded to handle arrays of two dimensions, as shown in the next display.

Two-Dimensional Array Declaration

Minimal BASIC form:

```
DIM name (row–range, column–range)
```

Interpretation: Row-range and column-range are integer constants representing the permissible range of values for the row subscript (number of rows) and column subscript (number of columns) respectively.

    1, 2, . . ., row-range   row subscript

    1, 2, . . ., column-range   column subscript

Note: Many compilers start the row and column subscripts at 0 instead of 1.

Example 10.1:

$$DIM \ T(3,3), \ R(7,5)$$

The array T is a two-dimensional array consisting of nine elements where each subscript may take on the values 1, 2, or 3 (16 elements if the subscript 0 is allowed). In the array R, the first subscript may take on values from 1 to 7; the second, from 1 to 5. There are a total of 7×5 or 35 elements in the array R (8×6 or 48 elements if the subscript value 0 is allowed).

10.3   MANIPULATION OF TWO-DIMENSIONAL ARRAYS

10.3.1   Manipulation of Individual Array Elements

Since the computer can manipulate only individual memory cells, we must be able to identify the individual elements of a two-dimensional array. This is accomplished by using a subscripted reference to the array, as shown next.

Subscripted Array Reference (Two-dimensional Arrays)

Minimal BASIC form:

$$\text{array name } (s_1, s_2)$$

Interpretation: s_1 and s_2 are subscript expressions. The forms permitted are the same as those discussed in Section 6.3 for one-dimensional arrays.

In the case of two-dimensional arrays, the first subscript of an array reference is considered the row subscript and the second subscript the column subscript. Consequently, the subscripted array reference

$$T(2,3)$$

selects the element in row 2, column 3 of the array T shown in Fig. 10.1. This row/column convention is derived from the area of mathematics called *matrix algebra*. A *matrix* M is a two-dimensional arrangement of numbers. Each element in M is referred to by the symbol M_{ij}, where i is the number of its row and j is the number of its column.

Example 10.2:   Consider the array T drawn below.

This array contains three zero elements (T(1,2), T(2,1), T(2,3)); three elements with value 1 (T(1,1), T(3,1) T(3,2)); and three elements with value 2 (T(1,3), T(2,2), T(3,3)).

Example 10.3:   A university offers 50 courses at each of five campuses. We can conveniently store the enrollments of these courses in an array declared by

DIM E(50,5)

This array consists of 250 elements; E(I,J) represents the number of students in course I at campus J.

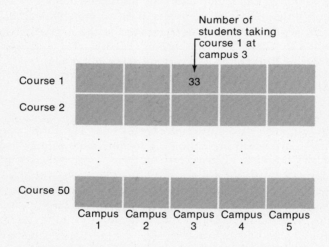

Fig. 10.2   Two-dimensional array of class enrollments, E.

The program segment below could be used to find the total number of students enrolled in course 3 at all campuses.

```
100      LET C = 3
110      LET S = 0
120 REM ADD UP ALL STUDENTS IN COURSE C
130      FOR I = 1 TO 5
140         LET S = S + E(C,I)
150      NEXT I
160      PRINT "NUMBER OF STUDENTS IN COURSE "; C; "="; S
```

We might also be interested in determining the total number of students enrolled in all classes at all campuses. To accomplish this, a pair of nested FOR loops is required.

```
210    LET S = 0
220 REM ACCUMULATE SUM OF ALL ELEMENTS OF E IN S
225 REM PROCESS ONE ROW AT A TIME
230    FOR I = 1 TO 50
240       REM ADD IN THE ELEMENTS OF ROW I
250       FOR J = 1 TO 5
260          LET S = S + E(I,J)
270       NEXT J
280    NEXT I
290    PRINT "TOTAL NUMBER OF STUDENTS = "; S
```

This program segment accumulates the sum of all elements of array E in S. It starts with the five elements of row 1 (E(1,1), . . ., E(1,5)), followed by the five elements of row 2 (E(2,1), . . ., E(2,5)) until it finally adds in the five elements of row 50 (E(50,1), . . ., E(50,5)).

Exercise 10.1:

a) For the array E in Fig. 10.2, write a program segment to count the number of students in all classes at campus 3. Students will be counted once for each course in which they are enrolled.
b) For the array T in Example 10.2, write a program segment which will count the total number of 1's.

10.3.2 Relationship between Loop Control Variables and Array Subscripts

Sequential referencing of array elements is frequently required when working with two-dimensional arrays. This process often requires the use of nested loops, since more than one subscript must be incremented in order to process all or a portion of the array elements. It is very easy to become confused in this situation and interchange subscripts, or nest the loops improperly. If you are in doubt as to whether or not your loops and subscripts are properly synchronized, you should include extra print statements to display the subscript and array element values.

Example 10.3 and Exercise 10.1(b) provide some examples of writing nested loops to process two-dimensional arrays. The following problem, which processes the array T (see Example 10.2), provides further illustration.

Problem 10.1:   Write a subroutine that will be used after each move is made in a computerized tic-tac-toe game to see if the game is over. When the game is over, the subroutine should indicate the winning player or the fact that the game ended in a draw.

Discussion: Each move made by the computer is represented by a 1; the opponent's moves are indicated by the number 2; an empty cell is indicated by a 0. To see whether a player has won, the subroutine must check each row, column and diagonal on the board to determine if all three squares are occupied by the same player. A draw occurs when all squares are occupied but neither player has won. The flow diagrams for this problem are shown in Fig. 10.3. The data table follows.

Data Table for Tic-Tac-Toe Problem

Input global variables	*Output global variables*
T(3,3): An array that shows the current state of the tic-tac-toe board after each move	F\$: Program flag used to indicate whether the game is over (F\$ will be defined as "OVER" if the game is over; otherwise it will be "NOTOVER")
	W: An indicator used to define the winner of the game (1, 2, or 0 for draw) when the game is over

Other program variables

> R: Row subscript for array T; used as loop control variable
>
> C: Column subscript for array T; used as loop control variable

(If you have the subprogram feature, all information should be communicated via the argument/parameter interface. Hence, the "global variables" would become subprogram parameters; the "other program variables" would be local to the subprogram.)

The refinements of steps 2.2 and 3.2 (Fig. 10.3) all involve the same operation—a comparison of the contents of three elements of the array T to see whether they are identical. (In step 4, there are two diagonals to be checked.) To perform this operation, we will use a function FNS that will return a value of 1 if three array elements are the same (and not zero), and will return 0 otherwise. The input arguments for FNS will be the three elements of T that are to be compared; therefore, step 4 will require two calls to function FNS (one for each diagonal). With this lowest-level detail now handled, we can write the subroutine for Problem 10.1 (see Fig. 10.4). Additional data table entries are shown below and continue on page 339.

Additional Data Table Entries for Problem 10.1

Other program variables

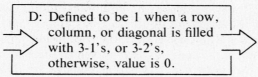

> D: Defined to be 1 when a row, column, or diagonal is filled with 3-1's, or 3-2's, otherwise, value is 0.

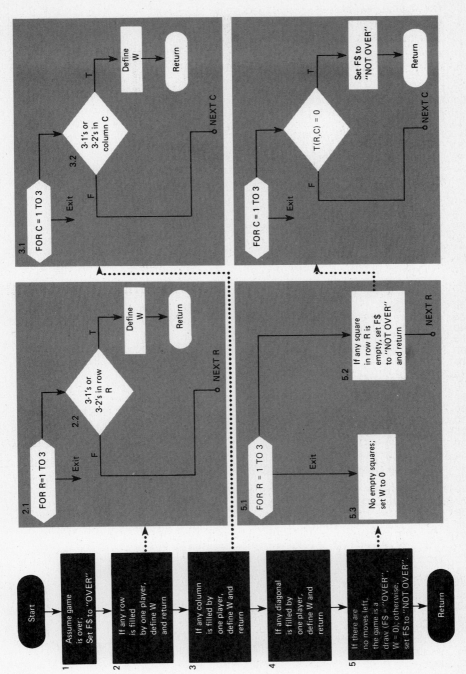

Fig. 10.3 Flow diagrams for tic-tac-toe.

```
1000 REM SUBROUTINE TO CHECK IF TIC-TAC-TOE GAME
1010 REM IS OVER AND DETERMINE WINNER (IF ANY)
1020 REM
1030 REM GLOBAL VARIABLES
1040 REM    IN:  T(,) - REPRESENTS THE CURRENT STATE OF THE GAME BOARD
1050 REM
1060 REM    OUT: F$ - INDICATES WHETHER GAME IS OVER
1070 REM         W  - INDICATES WINNER (1 OR 2) OR DRAW (0)
1080 REM    OTHER VARIABLES CHANGED - R, C, D
1085 REM    FUNCTION CALLED - FNS
1090 REM
1100 REM ASSUME GAME IS OVER
1110 REM LET F$ = "OVER"
1115 REM
1120 REM CHECK ROWS FOR A WINNER
1130     FOR R = 1 TO 3
1140         LET D = FNS(T(R,1),T(R,2),T(R,3))
1145         IF D = 1 THEN 1150 ELSE 1180      [IF D < > 1 THEN 1180]
1150 REM     THEN
1155             REM WIN IN ROW R. SET W AND RETURN
1160             LET W = T(R,1)
1170             GOTO 1490
1180 REM     IFEND
1190     NEXT R
1195 REM
1200 REM NO WINNER BY ROWS - CHECK COLUMNS
1210     FOR C = 1 TO 3
1220         LET D = FNS(T(1,C),T(2,C),T(3,C))
1225         IF D = 1 THEN 1230 ELSE 1260      [IF D < > 1 THEN 1260]
1230 REM     THEN
1235             REM WIN IN COLUMN C. SET W AND RETURN
1240             LET W = T(1,C)
1250             GOTO 1490
1260 REM     IFEND
1270     NEXT C
1275 REM
1280 REM NO WINNER BY ROWS OR COLUMNS - CHECK DIAGONALS
1290     LET D = FNS(T(1,1),T(2,2),T(3,3)) + FNS(T(1,3),T(2,2),T(3,1))
1300     IF D = 1 THEN 1310 ELSE 1340          [IF D < > 1 THEN 1340]
1310 REM THEN
1315         REM WIN IN DIAGONAL. SET W AND RETURN
1320         LET W = T(2,2)
1330         GOTO 1490
1340 REM IFEND
1350 REM
1360 REM NO WINNER. SEE IF GAME IS A DRAW
1370 REM CHECK EACH ROW FOR AN EMPTY CELL (0)
1380     FOR R = 1 TO 3
1390         FOR C = 1 TO 3
1400             IF T(R,C) = 0 THEN 1410 ELSE 1440
                                              [IF T(R,C) < > 0 THEN 1440]
1410 REM         THEN
1415                 REM EMPTY CELL -T(R,C)- GAME NOT OVER, RETURN
1420                 LET F$ = "NOTOVER"
1430                 GOTO 1490
1440 REM         IFEND
1450         NEXT C
1460     NEXT R
1470 REM NO EMPTY SPACES, GAME IS A DRAW
1480     LET W = 0
1490 REM
1500     RETURN
```

Fig. 10.4 Subroutine for Problem 10.1.

Functions Referenced

FNS: Tests a row, column or diagonal; returns a value of 1 if all three elements are the same (1 or 2); otherwise, returns a value of 0.

Argument	*Definition*
1,2,3	The arguments are the elements of a row, column or diagonal of T. The order in which these elements are specified is immaterial.

The function FNS is called in lines 1140, 1220, and 1290 of Fig. 10.4. The
actual arguments listed in each call are all elements of the array T. Each
argument is implemented as a subscripted variable consisting of the array name
(T) followed by a pair of subscripts. If the header statement in the definition
of function FNS had the form:

```
DEF FNS(C1, C2, C3)
```

a different set of array elements would be associated with the parameters C1,
C2, C3 each time FNS was called.

Exercise 10.2:   Write the function FNS.
Note: Make sure FNS properly handles the situation in which all three items being
compared are 0; the value returned should be 1 only if all three items are 1 or all three
are 2.

10.4   MATRIX OPERATORS

10.4.1   Introduction

As we have seen, the manipulation of two-dimensional arrays or matrices
often requires a pair of nested loops. In order to make it easier to program
some of the most common matrix manipulations, many extended versions of
BASIC provide some special matrix operators. These include operators for
reading and printing matrices, matrix initialization, matrix addition, subtraction
and multiplication.

The matrix operators in the new Dartmouth BASIC (edition 7) are quite
different from those available in BASIC-PLUS and the other extended versions
of BASIC. We will describe the BASIC-PLUS operators since they are more
generally available.

We will explain all these operations assuming that the lower bound for
subscript values is one. If your compiler normally uses a lower bound of zero,
it may be necessary to insert the *option statement*

```
OPTION BASE 1
```

before any array declarations in your program. This statement should reset the
lower bound from zero to one.

10.4.2   Matrix Operators

The matrix READ and PRINT operators are described in the next display.

Matrix Read and Print

BASIC-PLUS form:

```
MAT READ list of matrices
MAT PRINT list of matrices
```

Interpretation: The list of matrices is a list of matrix names. For a MAT READ, the data are stored in each matrix on a row-by-row basis: the first set of values is stored in row 1 of the first matrix, the next set in row 2 of the first matrix, etc. For a MAT PRINT, the values of each matrix will be printed in row order. All rows for the first matrix will be printed first, then the second matrix, etc.

Notes: It is permissible to specify the dimensions of the matrix in the READ statement, e.g., MAT READ B(2,3). However, we recommend using a DIM statement for this purpose and simply listing the matrix name (without dimensions) in the READ statement.
     Some versions of BASIC allow only one matrix name to be listed in each MAT PRINT statement.

Example 10.4:   The following program enters data into matrices A and B and prints their contents.

```
110      DIM A(4,4), B(3,2)
120      MAT READ A, B
130      MAT PRINT A, B
140      DATA 10, 20, 30, 40, 20, 30, 40, 50
150      DATA 30, 40, 50, 60, 40, 50, 60, 70
160      DATA 1, 2, 3, 4, 5, 6
170      END

RUN
```

10	20	30	40
20	30	40	50
30	40	50	60
40	50	60	70

Matrix A

1	2
3	4
5	6

Matrix B

BASIC also provides special instructions for initializing matrices to all zeros, or all ones, or the identity matrix. These are described next.

Matrix Initialization Statements

BASIC-PLUS form:

```
MAT name = ZER
MAT name = CON
MAT name = IDN
```

Interpretation: Name indicates the matrix to be initialized. ZER causes this matrix to be initialized to all zeros; CON to all ones; and IDN to the identity matrix.

Note: Only square matrices (same number of rows as columns) may be initialized to the identity matrix. The identity matrix contains ones along its major diagonal (upper left corner to lower right corner) and zeros everywhere else.

Example 10.5:   The next program segment illustrates the effect of the matrix initialization statements.

```
110        DIM A(2,2), B(2,4), C(3,3)
120        MAT A = ZER
130        MAT B = CON
140        MAT C = IDN
150        MAT PRINT A, B, C
160        END

RUN
```

Matrix A	0	0		
	0	0		

Matrix B	1	1	1	1
	1	1	1	1

Matrix C	1	0	0
	0	1	0
	0	0	1

10.4.3   Matrix Arithmetic Operations

BASIC provides some more operators to simplify the programming of matrix arithmetic. Statements using these operators all begin with the word MAT; they are listed in Table 10.1.

Statement	Effect
MAT C = A	Copy matrix A into matrix C
MAT C = A + B	Add matrix A to matrix B—store the sum in matrix C
MAT C = A − B	Subtract matrix B from matrix A— store the difference in matrix C
MAT C = A * B	Multiply matrix A by matrix B—store the product in matrix C
MAT C = (e) * A	Multiply each element of matrix A by e (an arithmetic expression) and store the result (scalar product) in matrix C
MAT C = INV(A)	Store the inverse of matrix A in matrix C
MAT C = TRN(A)	Store the transpose of matrix A in matrix C

Table 10.1   Matrix Arithmetic Operators

For the operations of copy, addition, subtraction, and scalar multiplication, each element of the result matrix, C, is determined by the values of the corresponding elements of the operand matrix (or matrices) as shown below:

Copy: $C(i,j) = A(i,j)$
Addition: $C(i,j) = A(i,j) + B(i,j)$
Subtraction: $C(i,j) = A(i,j) - B(i,j)$
Scalar Multiplication: $C(i,j) = (e) * A(i,j)$

If there are two operand matrices, they must have the same dimensions; the result matrix, C, will always have the same dimensions as the operand matrix (or matrices).

The matrix multiplication operation, however, is somewhat more complicated. The product of two matrices (A * B) is defined only when matrix A has the same number of columns as matrix B has rows. If A is a matrix with M rows and N columns (M × N matrix) and B is a matrix with N rows and P columns (N × P matrix), the result matrix will have M rows and P columns (M × P matrix).

Each element, C(i,j), of the result matrix is determined by forming the *dot-product* of row i of matrix A with column j of matrix B. The formula for the dot-product is shown below where N is the number of columns of matrix A and the number of rows of matrix B:

$$C(i,j) = A(i,1) \times B(1,j) + A(i,2) \times B(2,j) + \ldots + A(i,N) \times B(N,j)$$

or

$$C(i,j) = \sum_{k=1}^{N} A(i,k) \times B(k,j)$$

In the example below, a matrix with 2 rows and 3 columns (2×3 matrix) is multiplied by a matrix with 3 rows and 2 columns (3×2 matrix); the result is a matrix with 2 rows and 2 columns (2×2 matrix).

$$
\begin{vmatrix} 6 & 8 & 7 \\ 3 & 4 & 5 \end{vmatrix}
*
\begin{vmatrix} 1 & 2 \\ 2 & 1 \\ -1 & 0 \end{vmatrix}
=
\begin{vmatrix} 15 & 20 \\ 6 & 10 \end{vmatrix}
$$

A(2×3)   B(3×2)   C(2×2)

Element	Dot-Product of Row (in A) ×	Column (in B)	Computation
C(1,1)	1	1	$6 \times 1 + 8 \times 2 + 7 \times (-1) = 15$
C(1,2)	1	2	$6 \times 2 + 8 \times 1 + 7 \times 0 = 20$
C(2,1)	2	1	$3 \times 1 + 4 \times 2 + 5 \times (-1) = 6$
C(2,2)	2	2	$3 \times 2 + 4 \times 1 + 5 \times 0 = 10$

As shown above, C(1,1) is computed by first multiplying corresponding elements of row 1 of A (6, 8, 7) and column 1 of B (1, 2, −1), and then adding these three products together.

In the next example, a 2×3 matrix is multiplied by a 3×1 matrix. The result is a 2×1 matrix (2 rows, 1 column). A matrix with a single column is called a *column vector*. A column vector with N rows is the same as a one-dimensional array with N elements.

$$
\begin{vmatrix} 6 & 8 & 7 \\ 3 & 4 & 5 \end{vmatrix}
*
\begin{vmatrix} 2 \\ 1 \\ 0 \end{vmatrix}
=
\begin{vmatrix} 20 \\ 10 \end{vmatrix}
$$

A(2×3)   B(3×1)   C(2×1)

Element	Dot-Product of Row (in A) ×	Column (in B)	Computation
C(1,1)	1	1	$6 \times 2 + 8 \times 1 + 7 \times 0 = 20$
C(2,1)	2	1	$3 \times 2 + 4 \times 1 + 5 \times 0 = 10$

Problem 10.2: A businessman owns three stores; each store carries the same five items of merchandise. He has kept a record of the number of items sold at each store for the four quarters of the current year, and now needs to compute the annual gross sales for each store and the total gross for all three stores.

Discussion: The sales record for each quarter should be entered into a 3×5 matrix, Q, and accumulated in a second 3×5 matrix, A. Q(i,j) will contain the quantity of item j sold at store i during a quarter. The final contents of matrix A represent the annual sales figures for all items in all stores. This matrix must be multiplied by the price of each item (stored in a column vector P) in order to determine the dollar volume for each store (stored in a column vector V). The elements of the column vector V must then be summed to find the total gross volume, G, for the business. The data table is shown below; The flow diagrams are drawn in Fig. 10.5 and the program is listed in Fig. 10.6.

Data Table for Problem 10.2

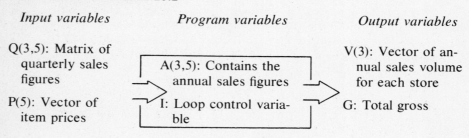

Input variables	*Program variables*	*Output variables*
Q(3,5): Matrix of quarterly sales figures	A(3,5): Contains the annual sales figures	V(3): Vector of annual sales volume for each store
P(5): Vector of item prices	I: Loop control variable	G: Total gross

In the program of Fig. 10.6, each of the first four data statements contains 15 numbers representing the sales figures for one quarter. The first five numbers in each data statement are stored in the first row of matrix Q; they represent the sales for Store 1 for that quarter. The last number in each of these data statements would be read into Q(3,5) and accumulated in A(3,5); the resulting sum represents the quantity of item five sold at store 3 over the entire year. The last data statement provides the prices for all items (stored in P).

For the data provided, the initial contents of matrix Q and the column vector P are shown below:

	Items						
	1	2	3	4	5		
Store 1	18	20	30	40	55	15.5	Price of item 1
Store 2	60	90	80	55	23	37.83	Price of item 2
Store 3	40	37	62	15	10	42.55	Price of item 3
						95.63	Price of item 4
		Q(3 × 5)				110.87	Price of item 5

$$P(5 \times 1)$$

Exercise 10.3a: Indicate what changes would be necessary to the program and data of Fig. 10.6 if we wished to compute and display the annual dollar volume by item instead of store. [*Hint:* Multiplying a row vector by a rectangular matrix yields a row vector.]

Exercise 10.3b: Indicate what changes would be necessary to the program and data of Fig. 10.6 if the price of each item changed quarterly and we desired to compute the gross volume for each store on a quarterly basis as well as an annual basis.

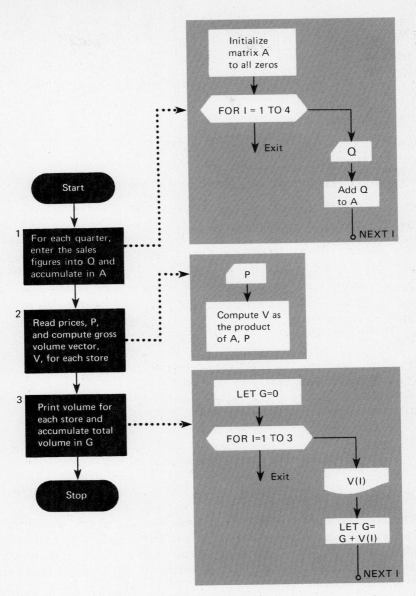

Fig. 10.5 Flow diagrams for Problem 10.2.

```
100 REM   DETERMINE GROSS SALES VOLUME
105 REM
110       DIM Q(3,5), A(3,5), P(5), V(3)
120 REM   ACCUMULATE ANNUAL SALES FIGURES IN MATRIX A
130       MAT A = ZER
140       FOR I = 1 TO 4
150          MAT READ Q
160          MAT A = A + Q
170       NEXT I
180       DATA 18, 20, 30, 40, 55, 60, 90, 80, 55, 23, 40, 37, 62, 15, 10
190       DATA 25, 33, 40, 60, 77, 30, 100, 60, 45, 15, 38, 45, 90, 20, 8
200       DATA 37, 20, 55, 65, 70, 50, 80, 40, 33, 20, 60, 70, 60, 55, 18
210       DATA 25, 28, 42, 53, 60, 75, 85, 93, 90, 80, 60, 73, 82, 91, 25
215 REM
220 REM   ENTER PRICES AND COMPUTE VOLUME, V, FOR EACH STORE
230       MAT READ P
240       DATA 15.50, 37.83, 42.55, 95.63, 110.87
250       MAT V = A * P
260 REM
270 REM   COMPUTE TOTAL GROSS VOLUME, G, AND
280 REM   DISPLAY ANNUAL VOLUME FOR EACH STORE
290       LET G = 0
300       FOR I = 1 TO 3
310          PRINT "GROSS VOLUME AT STORE "; I; " = $"; V(I)
320          LET G = G + V(I)
330       NEXT I
340 REM
350       PRINT "TOTAL GROSS = $"; G
360 REM
370       END

RUN

GROSS VOLUME AT STORE 1 = $ 62449.5
GROSS VOLUME AT STORE 2 = $ 65003.8
GROSS VOLUME AT STORE 3 = $ 48162.5
TOTAL GROSS = $ 175616.
```

Fig. 10.6 Computation of gross volume.

10.4.4 Matrix Transpose and Inverse*

The last two operations listed in Table 10.1 are matrix transpose and inverse. The *transpose of a matrix* is a new matrix with rows and columns interchanged. Hence, if matrix A has M rows and N columns, its transpose will have N rows and M columns. Row i of matrix A will be identical to column i of its transpose as shown below.

$$
\begin{vmatrix} 6 & 8 & 7 \\ 3 & 4 & 5 \end{vmatrix}
\qquad
\begin{vmatrix} 6 & 3 \\ 8 & 4 \\ 7 & 5 \end{vmatrix}
$$

Matrix A (2 × 3)   Matrix B (3 × 2)

---

*This section is optional.

The *inverse of a matrix* is defined to be that matrix which, when multiplied by the original matrix, yields the identity matrix. The inverse of matrix A is represented in mathematical formulas as A^{-1}; hence, A^{-1} times A equals I (the identity matrix). This property of matrices is used in solving systems of simultaneous equations as illustrated in the next example. (*Note:* Not all matrices have inverses.)

Example 10.6: In many scientific and engineering problems, it is necessary to find a set of values that satisfy several constraints expressed in the form of a set of *linear equations*. In the example at the top of page 348, a set of linear equations is solved for values of x_1, x_2, and x_3.

```
100 REM PROGRAM TO SOLVE A SET OF SIMULTANEOUS
110 REM EQUATIONS IN 3 UNKNOWNS
120 REM
130     DIM A(3,3), X(3), B(3), V(3,3)
150 REM
160     MAT READ A
170     DATA 3, 2, 1
180     DATA 1, 3, -7
190     DATA -2, 1, 5
210     PRINT "COEFFICIENT MATRIX"
220     MAT PRINT A
230 REM
240     MAT READ B
250     DATA 7, -8, 11
260     PRINT "VECTOR OF CONSTANTS"
270     MAT PRINT B
280 REM
290 REM INVERT MATRIX A
300     MAT V = INV(A)
310 REM
320 REM SOLVE FOR UNKNOWNS X
330     MAT X = V * B
340     PRINT "SOLUTION VECTOR--X"
350     MAT PRINT X
360 REM
370     END

RUN

COEFFICIENT MATRIX
 3              2              1
 1              3             -7
-2              1              5

VECTOR OF CONSTANTS
 7
-8
 11

SOLUTION VECTOR--X
 .428571
 1.85714
 2.
```

Fig. 10.7 Solving simultaneous equations.

$$3x_1 + 2x_2 + x_3 = 7$$
$$x_1 + 3x_2 - 7x_3 = -8$$
$$-2x_1 + x_2 + 5x_3 = 11$$

This set of equations can be represented by the matrix equation

$$1) \quad AX = B$$

where A is the coefficient matrix, X is the solution vector of unknowns and B is the constant vector.

$$A = \begin{vmatrix} 3 & 2 & 1 \\ 1 & 3 & -7 \\ -2 & 1 & 5 \end{vmatrix} \quad X = \begin{vmatrix} x_1 \\ x_2 \\ x_3 \end{vmatrix} \quad B = \begin{vmatrix} 7 \\ -8 \\ 11 \end{vmatrix}$$

Multiplying both sides of matrix equation 1) by A^{-1} (inverse of A), we get

$$A^{-1}AX = A^{-1}B$$
or
$$IX = A^{-1}B$$

where I is the identity matrix. Since any matrix (or vector) multiplied by I is that matrix, IX equals X; hence, the product of A^{-1} and B is a vector that represents the values of x_1, x_2 and x_3, which satisfy the original set of equations. The program for computing X is listed in Fig. 10.7.

Exercise 10.4:   Modify the program and data in Fig. 10.7 to solve the pair of equations:

$$3x_1 + 2x_2 = 14$$
$$x_1 - x_2 = 2$$

10.5 ADDITIONAL APPLICATION OF TWO-DIMENSIONAL ARRAYS

To further illustrate the use of two-dimensional arrays or matrices, we will present a solved problem in which this data structure plays a central role.

Problem 10.3:   The little red high school building in Sunflower, Indiana, has three floors, each with five classrooms of various sizes. Each semester the high school runs 15 classes that must be scheduled for the rooms in the building. We will write a program which, given the capacity of each room in the building and the size of each class, will attempt to find a satisfactory room assignment that will accommodate all 15 classes in the building. For those classes that can't be satisfactorily placed, the program will print a "ROOM NOT AVAILABLE" message.

Discussion: As part of the data table definition, we must decide how the table of room capacities is to be represented in the memory of the computer. Since the building may be pictured as a two-dimensional structure with three floors (vertical dimension) and five rooms (horizontal dimension), a two-dimensional array should be a convenient structure for representing the capacities of each room in the building. We will read the room capacities into a 3×5 array C.

By using a two-dimensional array, we will be able to determine the number of the room assigned to each class directly from the indices of the array element that represents that room. For example, if a class is placed in a room with capacity given by C(2,4), we know that the number of this room is 204. In general, C(F,N) represents the capacity of the room whose number is the value of the expression:

$$F * 100 + N$$

Data Table for Problem 10.3

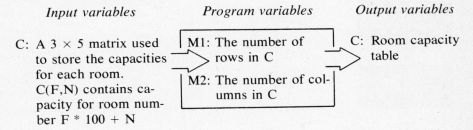

Input variables	Program variables	Output variables
C: A 3×5 matrix used to store the capacities for each room. C(F,N) contains capacity for room number F * 100 + N	M1: The number of rows in C M2: The number of columns in C	C: Room capacity table

The level one flow diagram for this problem is shown in Fig. 10.8 along with the program system chart. We will handle steps 1 and 3 through the use of a subroutine PRINTC which, given as input, the room capacity table and its dimensions will print the table in a readable form. Step 2 will be performed by a subroutine, PROCESS, which will read and process room requests and print the room assigned, if any. The subroutines referenced by the main program are described next; the main program is shown in Fig. 10.9.

Subroutines Referenced by Main Program

PRINTC: Used to print the contents of the two-dimensional array C

Global variables
C(,)—array to be printed (input)
M1, M2—dimensions of C (input)

PROCESS: Reads and processes each room request consisting of a class ID and a class size. Determines the room number to be assigned (if one is available) and prints the room number.

Global variables
C(,)—room capacity table (input and output)
M1, M2—dimensions of C (input)

For each room request, subroutine PROCESS will read a pair of data items representing the course identification number and class size. Subroutine

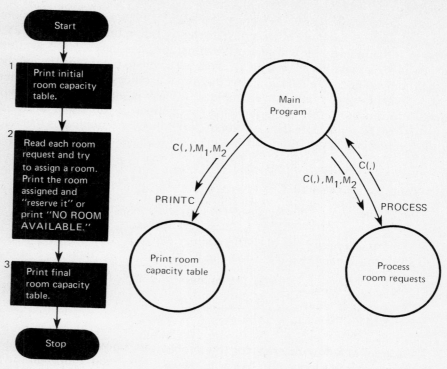

Fig. 10.8 Level one flow diagram and program system chart for room scheduling problem (10.3).

PROCESS should find a room that is large enough to hold each class if one is available. (The ideal situation would be to find a room whose capacity exactly matches the class size.) For each class, PROCESS will print, in tabular form, the class ID (ID$) and size (S) and the number (R) and capacity of the room assigned to the class. The flow diagrams for PROCESS are shown in Fig. 10.10 along with a third level addition to the program system chart. The data table for PROCESS follows.

Data Table for PROCESS

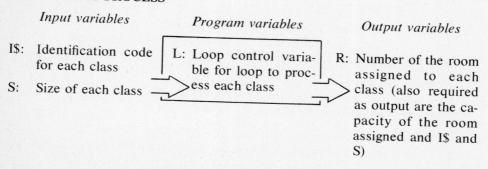

Input variables	Program variables	Output variables
I$: Identification code for each class	L: Loop control variable for loop to process each class	R: Number of the room assigned to each class (also required as output are the capacity of the room assigned and I$ and S)
S: Size of each class		

```
100 REM ROOM SCHEDULING PROGRAM
110     DIM C(3,5)
115 REM
120 REM ENTER ROOM CAPACITIES TABLE
130     READ M1, M2
140     DATA 3, 5
150     MAT READ C
160     DATA 30, 30, 15, 30, 40
170     DATA 25, 30, 25, 10, 110
180     DATA 62, 30, 40, 40, 30
190 REM
200 REM PRINT CAPACITY TABLE — CALL PRINTC
210     GOSUB 1000
215     PRINT
220 REM
230 REM SET UP HEADING FOR ROOM ASSIGNMENT TABLE
240     PRINT "ROOM ASSIGNMENT TABLE"
250     PRINT "CLASS ID", "SIZE", "ROOM",
260     PRINT "CAPACITY"
270 REM
280 REM PROCESS EACH ROOM REQUEST — CALL PROCESS
290     GOSUB 2000
300 REM
310 REM PRINT FINAL CAPACITY TABLE — CALL PRINTC
315     PRINT
320     GOSUB 1000
330 REM
340     STOP
```

Fig. 10.9   Main program for room scheduling problem (10.3).

As shown in Fig. 10.10, a third level subroutine, ASSIGN, will be called by PROCESS to perform step 1.3. This subroutine will search the room capacity table, C, to find a room of size, S, or greater. It will return the subscripts F and N of an assigned room, if one is found, and indicate success or failure by setting a program flag, A$, to "FOUND" or "NOTFOUND". The additional data table entries for PROCESS are shown next along with a description of subroutine ASSIGN.

Additional Data Table Entries for PROCESS

Program variables

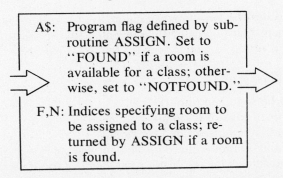

A$: Program flag defined by subroutine ASSIGN. Set to "FOUND" if a room is available for a class; otherwise, set to "NOTFOUND."

F,N: Indices specifying room to be assigned to a class; returned by ASSIGN if a room is found.

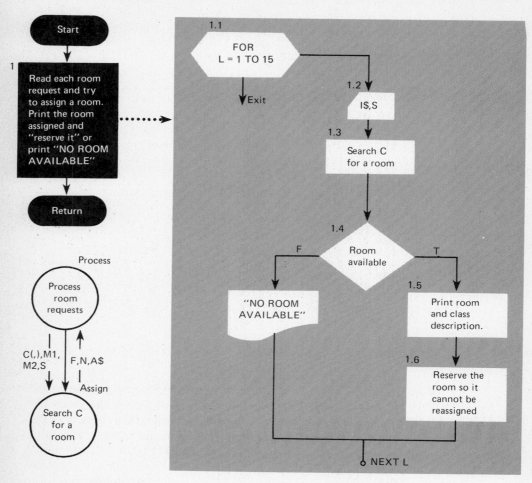

Fig. 10.10   Flow diagram and program system chart for PROCESS.

Subroutines Referenced by PROCESS

ASSIGN: Searches the two-dimensional array, C, to find the indices, F and
N, of an element that is greater than or equal to a specified value, S. If no
such element is found, a flag, A$, is set to "NOTFOUND".

Global variables

C—array to be searched (input)
M1, M2—dimensions of C (input)
S—value that is being searched for (input)
F, N—row and column indices of element selected (output)
A$—flag: indicates whether or not a satisfactory room was found (output)

```
2000 REM SUBROUTINE TO PROCESS EACH ROOM REQUEST
2010 REM
2020 REM GLOBAL VARIABLES
2030 REM      IN:  C(,) - ROOM CAPACITY TABLE
2040 REM           M1, M2 - DIMENSION OF C
2050 REM
2060 REM      OUT: C(,) - CAPACITY TABLE WITH INDICATION OF ASSIGNMENT
2070 REM OTHER VARIABLES CHANGED - L, I$, S, A$, R, F, N
2080 REM
2090 REM READ AND PROCESS EACH ROOM REQUEST
2100      FOR L = 1 TO 15
2110          READ I$, S
2120          REM SEARCH FOR A ROOM; CALL ASSIGN TO SET A$, F, AND N;
2130          GOSUB 3000
2140          IF A$ = "FOUND" THEN 2145 ELSE 2195
                                     [IF A$ < > "FOUND" THEN 2195]
2145 REM      THEN
2150              REM COMPUTE NUMBER OF ROOM ASSIGNED AND RESERVE IT
2160              LET R = F * 100 + N
2170              PRINT I$, S, R, C(F,N)
2180              LET C(F,N) = -C(F,N)
2190          GOTO 2220
2195 REM      ELSE
2200              REM NO ROOM ASSIGNED
2210              PRINT "NO ROOM AVAILABLE FOR CLASS "; I$
2220 REM      IFEND
2230      NEXT L
2240 REM
2250      DATA CIS1, 37, CIS2, 55, CIS3, 100, CIS10, 26
2260      DATA CIS11, 26, CIS25, 39, CIS30, 30, CIS31, 56
2270      DATA CIS101, 20, CIS120, 15, CIS203, 22, CIS301, 10
2280      DATA CIS302, 5, CIS324, 28, CIS330, 25
2290 REM
2300      RETURN
```

Fig. 10.11   PROCESS subroutine for Problem 10.3.

There are probably many ways to resolve the problem indicated in step 1.6 of the flow diagram for PROCESS (Fig. 10.10). Once a room is assigned, we must ensure that it can't be reassigned to another class. We will provide this protection simply by negating the capacities of each room assigned to a class when the assignment is made. Exactly why this works will become clearer when subroutine ASSIGN is written. We can now write the subroutine PROCESS (see Fig. 10.11).

The only step left in the design process is the specification of subroutine ASSIGN. The algorithm that we will use to find a room for a class size S may be summarized as follows:

> Search C and find the smallest room that is greater than or equal to S and is still not assigned.

This is called the *best fit* algorithm because the unassigned room with the least excess capacity is chosen for each class. The ideal situation is to find a room

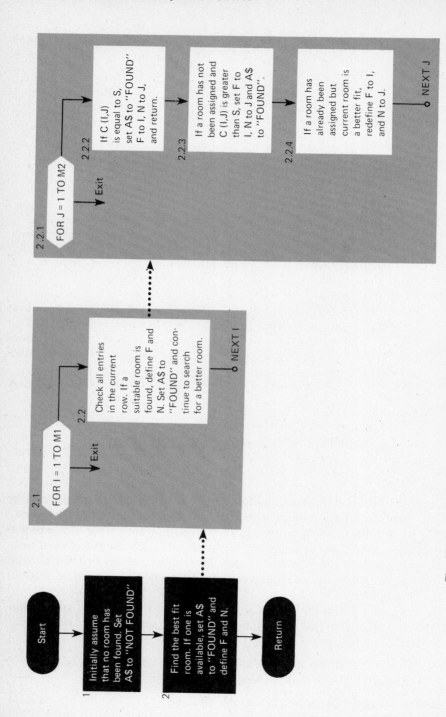

Fig. 10.12   Flow diagrams of ASSIGN subroutine for room scheduling problem (10.3).

that fits exactly. This algorithm assigns as many classes to suitable rooms as is physically possible without later juggling room assignments. The implementation of this search requires two nested loops with loop control variables I and J. The flow diagrams for ASSIGN are drawn in Fig. 10.12.

Program variables for ASSIGN

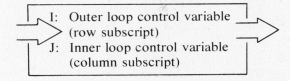

I: Outer loop control variable (row subscript)

J: Inner loop control variable (column subscript)

As shown in Fig. 10.12, subroutine ASSIGN uses the following criteria to locate the room with smallest capacity that is larger than S.
1. If a room is found with a capacity equal to S, this room is chosen as the best-fit room, and the search is complete (step 2.2.2).
2. When the first room with capacity larger than S is found, it is chosen (perhaps temporarily) to be the best-fit room (step 2.2.3). If, subsequently, a room of sufficient capacity is located that is smaller than the current best-fit room, the new room becomes the best-fit room (step 2.2.4). We will implement these steps using a multiple-alternative decision structure.

The implementation of subroutine ASSIGN is shown in Fig. 10.13. A sample run of the complete program is shown in Fig. 10.14.

Program Form and Style

In Fig. 10.13, we have used the BASIC-PLUS form of the SELECT structure without a DEFAULT alternative. As before, the Dartmouth BASIC form of the SELECT structure is indicated by shading. If the logical AND operator is not available on your BASIC system, lines 3230 and 3290 should each be replaced by the corresponding pair of conditional transfer statements shown in brackets to the right of the program. If the IF-THEN-ELSE statement is not available, line 3170 should also be changed as shown in brackets.

If the subprogram feature is available, PROCESS, ASSIGN and PRINTC should be implemented as subprograms.

Exercise 10.5: Complete the program system for Problem 10.3 by writing the subroutine PRINTC. Your subroutine output should be similar to the tables in Fig. 10.14.

Exercise 10.6: Modify the main program so that the final contents of the array C can be used to determine the number of empty seats in each classroom. Make sure that it is not possible to assign a large room to 2 small classes after your modification.

```
3000 REM SUBROUTINE TO ASSIGN A ROOM
3010 REM
3020 REM GLOBAL VARIABLES
3030 REM     IN:  C(,), M1, M2 - ROOM CAPACITY TABLE AND DIMENSIONS
3040 REM          S - SIZE OF CLASS
3050 REM
3060 REM     OUT: F, N - INDICES OF ASSIGNED ROOM
3070 REM          A$ - PROGRAM FLAG
3080 REM OTHER VARIABLES CHANGED - I, J
3090 REM
3100 REM ASSUME NO ROOM AVAILABLE
3120     LET A$ = "NOTFOUND"
3125 REM
3130 REM OUTER LOOP - CHECK EACH FLOOR
3140     FOR I = 1 TO M1
3150         REM INNER LOOP - CHECK EACH ROOM ON FLOOR
3155         FOR J = 1 TO M2
3160 REM         SELECT
3165 REM         CASE
3170             IF C(I,J) = S THEN 3180 ELSE 3225
                                    [IF C(I,J) < > S THEN 3225]
3180                 REM SIZE MATCH. MAKE BEST FIT ASSIGNMENT AND RETURN
3190                 LET A$ = "FOUND"
3200                 LET F = I
3210                 LET N = J
3220                 GOTO 3370
3225 REM         CASE
3230             IF C(I,J) > S AND A$ = "NOTFOUND" THEN 3240 ELSE 3285
                                    [IF C(I,J) <= S THEN 3285]
3240                 REM - FIRST AVAILABLE ROOM FOUND
                                    [IF A$ < > "NOTFOUND" THEN 3285]
3250                 LET A$ = "FOUND"
3260                 LET F = I
3270                 LET N = J
3280             GOTO 3330
3285 REM         CASE
3290             IF C(I,J) > S AND C(I,J) < C(F,N) THEN 3300 ELSE 3330
                                    [IF C(I,J) <= S THEN 3330]
3300                 REM SUBSEQUENT AVAILABLE ROOM, BETER FIT
                                    [IF C(I,J) >= C(F,N) THEN 3330]
3310                 LET F = I
3320                 LET N = J
3330 REM         SELECTEND
3340         NEXT J
3350     NEXT I
3360 REM ALL FLOORS SEARCHED
3370 REM
3380     RETURN
3385 REM
3390     END
```

Fig. 10.13 ASSIGN subroutine for Problem 10.3.

```
                                    ROOM NUMBER
     FLOOR                   01     02     03     04     05
       1                     30     30     15     30     40
       2                     25     30     25     10    110
       3                     62     30     40     40     30
                                       CAPACITIES

     ROOM ASSIGNMENT TABLE
     CLASS ID          SIZE            ROOM            CAPACITY
     CIS1               37             105                40
     CIS2               55             301                62
     CIS3              100             205               110
     CIS10              26             101                30
     CIS11              26             102                30
     CIS25              39             303                40
     CIS30              30             104                30
     NO ROOM AVAILABLE FOR CLASS CIS31
     CIS101             20             201                25
     CIS120             15             103                15
     CIS203             22             203                25
     CIS301             10             204                10
     CIS302              5             202                30
     CIS324             28             302                30
     CIS330             25             305                30

                                    ROOM NUMBER
     FLOOR                   01     02     03     04     05
       1                    -30    -30    -15    -30    -40
       2                    -25    -30    -25    -10   -110
       3                    -62    -30    -40     40    -30
                                       CAPACITIES
```

Fig. 10.14 Sample run of room scheduling problem, (10.3).

Exercise 10.7: The algorithm used in subroutine ASSIGN is called a *best-fit* algorithm, because the room having the capacity that was closest to class size was assigned to each class. Another algorithm that might have been used is called a *first-fit* algorithm. In this algorithm, the first room having a capacity greater than or equal to the class size is assigned to the class (no further searching for a room is carried out). Modify the flow diagram (Fig. 10.12) and program (Fig. 10.13) to reflect the first-fit algorithm. (You will see that this algorithm is simpler than best-fit.) Apply both algorithms using the room capacities shown earlier and the following 15 class sizes: 38, 41, 6, 26, 28, 21, 25, 97, 12, 36, 28, 27, 29, 30, 18. Exactly what is wrong with the first-fit algorithm?

10.6 COMMON PROGRAMMING ERRORS

The errors encountered using two-dimensional arrays are similar to those encountered in processing one-dimensional arrays. The most frequent errors are likely to be subscript range errors. These errors may be more common now because two subscripts are involved in an array reference, introducing added complexity and confusion.

Some compilers will check each subscript to see whether it is within range and some will not. Consequently, it is important to verify for yourself that all subscripts are correct by printing any suspect subscript values.

Other kinds of errors arise because of the complex nesting of FOR loops when they are used to manipulate two-dimensional arrays. Care must be taken to ensure that the subscript order is consistent with the nesting structure of the loops. Inconsistent usage will not result in an error diagnostic but will likely produce incorrect program results.

If your system has subprograms, an additional source of error involves the use of arrays as subprogram arguments. If the range of a subscript is passed through the argument list, care must be taken to ensure that the value passed is correct. Otherwise, the address computation performed within the subprogram will cause the wrong array elements to be manipulated and out-of-range errors may occur.

10.7 SUMMARY

In this chapter, we have introduced a more general form of the array. This form is useful in representing data that are most naturally thought of in terms of tables or other two-dimensional structures. The two-dimensional array is convenient for representing rectangular tables of information such as matrices, game-board patterns and business-related tables.

We have seen examples of the manipulation of individual array elements

Statement	Effect
Matrix declaration	
`DIM A(4,2), B(3,3)`	Declares A to be a matrix with four rows and two columns; B has three rows and three columns.
Matrix manipulation	
`LET B(1,2) = 3`	Assigns a value of three to the element in row one, column two of B.

`LET S = 0`
`FOR I = 1 TO 4`
`  FOR J = 1 TO 2`
`    LET S = S + A(I,J)`
`  NEXT J`
`NEXT I`
`PRINT "SUM ="; S`
	Accumulates and prints the sum of all values stored in matrix A.

Table 10.2 Summary of Minimal BASIC statements

Statement	*Effect*
Matrix declaration	
DIM A(4,2), B(3,3)	Declares A to be a matrix with four rows and two columns; B has three rows and three columns.
Matrix read	
MAT READ A, B	Reads first eight data items into matrix A and next nine data items into matrix B.
Matrix print	
MAT PRINT A	Prints the eight elements of matrix A in four rows and two columns.
Matrix initialization	
MAT A = ZER	Initializes A to all zeros.
MAT A = CON	Initializes A to all ones.
MAT B = IDN	Initializes B to the identity matrix.
Matrix arithmetic	
MAT C = A	Copy matrix A into matrix C
MAT C = A + B	Add matrix A to matrix B—store the sum in matrix C
MAT C = A − B	Subtract matrix B from matrix A—store the difference in matrix C
MAT C = A * B	Multiply matrix A by matrix B—store the product in matrix C
MAT C = (e) * A	Multiply each element of matrix A by e (e is an arithmetic expression) and store the result (scalar product) in matrix C
MAT C = INV(A)	Store the inverse of matrix A in matrix C
MAT C = TRN(A)	Store the transpose of matrix A in matrix C

Table 10.3   Summary of BASIC-PLUS statements

through the use of nests of FOR loops. The correspondence between the loop control variables and the array subscripts determines the order in which the array elements are processed.

Special matrix operators for reading, printing and initializing two-dimensional arrays were also described in this chapter; the matrix arithmetic operators were introduced and their use was illustrated. Table 10.2 shows the matrix operations permitted in Minimal BASIC; Table 10.3 summarizes the operations available in most extended versions of BASIC.

PROGRAMMING PROBLEMS

10.4 Write a program that reads in a tic-tac-toe board and determines the best move for player X. Use the following strategy. Consider all squares that are empty and evaluate potential moves into them. If the move fills the third square in a row, column, or diagonal that already has two X's, add 50 to the score; if it fills the third square in a row, column or diagonal with two O's, add 25 to the score; for each row, column or diagonal containing this move that will have 2 X's and one blank, add 10 to the score; add 8 for each row, column or diagonal through this move that will have one O, one X, and one blank; add four for each row, column or diagonal that will have one X and the rest blanks. Select the move that scores the highest.

The possible moves for the board below are numbered. Their scores are shown to the right of the board. Move five is selected.

1	O	X
2	X	3
O	4	5

1—10 + 8 = 18
2—10 + 8 = 18
3—10 + 10 = 20
4—8
5—10 + 10 + 8 = 28

10.5 Each card of a poker deck will be represented by a pair of integers: the first integer represents the suit (1 through 4); the second integer represents the value of the card. For example, 4, 10 would be the 10 of spades, 3, 11 the jack of hearts, 2, 12 the queen of diamonds, 1, 13 the king of clubs, 4, 14 the ace of spades. Read five cards in and represent them in a 4 × 14 array. A mark should be placed in the five array elements with row and column indices corresponding to the cards entered. Evaluate the poker hand. Provide subroutines to determine whether the hand is a flush (all one suit), a straight (five consecutive cards of different suits), a straight flush (five consecutive cards of one suit), 4 of a kind, a full house (3 of one kind, 2 of another), 3 of a kind, 2 pair, or 1 pair.

10.6 Represent the cards of a bridge check by a pair of integers, as described in Problem 10.5. Read the thirteen cards of a bridge hand into a 4 × 14 array. Compute the number of points in the hand. Score four for each ace, three for a king, two for a queen, one for a jack. Also, add three points for any suit not represented, two for any suit with only one card which is not a face card (jack or higher), one for any suit with only two cards, neither of which is a face card.

10.7 If, in the room scheduling problem (10.3), we removed the restriction of a single building and wished to write the program to accommodate an entire campus of buildings, each with a different number of floors and rooms on each floor, the choice of a two-dimensional array for storing room capacities may prove inconvenient. Instead, it might be easier to use two *parallel arrays* to store the identification of each room (building and number) and its size. In fact, we may wish to represent the building ID and room number in separate arrays. Write a program, with appropriate subroutines (or subprograms), to solve the room scheduling problem using the 15 class sizes given in Exercise 10.7, and the campus room table shown below.

Room ID

Building	Number	Room size
HUMA	1003	30
MATH	11	25
MUSI	2	62
LANG	701	30
MATH	12	30
ART	2	30
EDUC	61	15
HUMA	1005	25
ART	1	40
ENG	101	30
MATH	3	10
EDUC	63	40
LANG	702	40
MUSI	5	110
HUMA	1002	30

10.8 Write a set of subroutines (or subprograms) to manipulate a pair of matrices. You should provide subroutines for addition, subtraction, and multiplication. Each subroutine should validate its input arguments (i.e., check all matrix dimensions) before performing the required data manipulation. Do not use the special matrix arithmetic operators.

10.9 The results from the mayor's race have been reported by each precinct as follows:

Precinct	Candidate A	Candidate B	Candidate C	Candidate D
1	192	48	206	37
2	147	90	312	21
3	186	12	121	38
4	114	21	408	39
5	267	13	382	29

Write a program to do the following:
A. Print out the table with appropriate headings for the rows and columns.
B. Compute and print the total number of votes received by each candidate and the percent of the total votes cast.
C. If any one candidate received over 50% of the votes, the program should print a message declaring that candidate the winner.
D. If no candidate received 50% of the votes, the program should print a message declaring a run-off between the two candidates receiving the highest number of votes; the two candidates should be identified by their letter names.
E. Run the program once with above data and once with candidate C receiving only 108 votes in precinct 4.

10.10 The game of Life, invented by John H. Conway, is supposed to model the genetic laws for birth, survival and death. (See *Scientific American*, October, 1970, p. 120.) We will play it on a board consisting of 25 squares in the horizontal and vertical directions. Each square can be empty or contain an X indicating the presence of an organism. Each square (except the border squares) has eight neighbors. The small square shown in the segment of the board drawn below connects the neighbors of the organism in row three, column three.

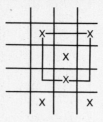

Generation 1

The next generation of organisms is determined according to the following criteria:
1. *Birth:* An organism will be born in each empty location that has exactly three neighbors.
2. *Death:* An organism with four or more organisms as neighbors will die from overcrowding. An organism with fewer than two neighbors will die from loneliness.
3. *Survival:* An organism with two or three neighbors will survive to the next generation.

Generations 2 and 3 for the sample follow:

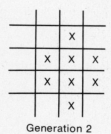

Generation 2

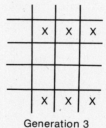

Generation 3

Read in an initial configuration of organisms. Print the original game array, calculate the next generation of organisms in a new array, copy the new array into the original game array and repeat the cycle for as many generations as you wish. Provide a program system chart. [*Hint:* Assume that the borders of the game array are infertile regions where organisms can neither survive nor be born; you will not have to process the border squares.]

FORMATTED OUTPUT AND FILES

11

11.1   INTRODUCTION

In this chapter, we describe two additional features of input and output in BASIC: formatted output and files. Although these features are not part of standard Minimal BASIC, they are supported on a number of versions of BASIC. Unfortunately, each version has its own unique syntax for formatted output and files features. We will describe the BASIC-PLUS and Dartmouth BASIC forms of these features. In addition, we have provided a table at the end of the chapter that outlines the differences among files features supported on several BASIC systems. You should consult your BASIC manual for the exact forms of both the formatted output and files features that are available on your computer.

11.2   FORMATTED OUTPUT: PRINT USING AND IMAGE FEATURES

11.2.1   Introduction

Until now we have been restricted to using commas, semicolons and the TAB function for arranging program results on a page. Using these features, it was relatively easy to program the output steps required in our programs. It was possible to print columns of results and to exercise some control over the spacing of program output. However, we could not instruct the computer to print results in the precise form that we desired. For example, we could not line up the decimal point in a column of numbers, or specify the number of decimal digits to be printed. We also had only limited control over the horizontal spacing between items printed on the same line. With the PRINT USING and image features we can achieve complete control over the form of any output line. We also get automatic rounding when printing numeric values.

11.2.2   Formatting Output with PRINT USING

In this section, we will illustrate how the PRINT USING statement controls the appearance or *format* of our program output.

Example 11.1:   This example shows the printing of numeric values with the PRINT USING and image features.

```
100 READ X, Y, N
110 DATA 13.86, 210.582, 7
120 PRINT USING "X = ##.###   Y = ###.#   N = ##", X, Y, N
130 END

RUN

X = 13.860   Y = 210.6   N =  7
```

In the example, the *PRINT USING statement* (line 120) causes the values of X, Y and N to be printed. The *image* part of the statement (enclosed in quotes) is a description of the format of the output line. The image contains three *fields* (##.###, ###.# and ##) that determine the position and form of the output items. Normally, there are as many fields as there are variables in the output list following the image. The image is printed exactly as shown, with each output value inserted in its field. The decimal point is always aligned with the decimal point in the corresponding field; decimal values are rounded and the number of digits printed after the decimal point is the same as in the corresponding field (3 for X, 1 for Y).

Integer values are printed in fields without decimal points. If the integer value doesn't fill the entire field, it is printed right-justified (aligned with the rightmost # symbol) and blanks are printed in the extra field positions.

It is also possible to use a string variable to represent the image portion of a PRINT USING statement. In this case, the image must be stored in the string variable before the PRINT USING statement is executed. For example, the statements

```
115 LET A$ = "X = ##.###   Y = ###.#   N = ##"
120 PRINT USING S$, F$, F$, F$
```

would have the same effect as line 120 in the program above.

Example 11.2: In BASIC-PLUS, an output field for a string is indicated in an image by using a single quote followed by a series of capital L's, C's or R's. The placement of the string in the output field is determined by the letter used: L for *left-justified* (starting at the single quote), R for right-justified (ending at the last R), and C for centered. Blanks are printed in any "extra" field positions.

```
100 LET F$ = "SAM"
110 LET S$ = " 'LLLL 'RRRR 'CCCC"
120 PRINT USING S$, F$, F$, F$
130 END

RUN

    SAM      SAM  SAM
```

In Dartmouth BASIC, the symbols < and > are used to indicate the placement of a string value. The Dartmouth BASIC form of line 110 would be

```
110 LET S$ = " <#### >#### #####"
```

The string value is printed left-justified if the field starts with a <, right-justified if the field starts with a > and centered if it starts with a #.

These and other points are summarized in the following display and table.

PRINT USING Statement

BASIC-PLUS and Dartmouth BASIC form:

         PRINT USING image-string, output-list

Interpretation: The image-string indicates the image to be used to determine the format of the output; it may be a string constant or variable. The output-list specifies the values to be printed and their order.

Note: It is permissable for the output-list to be empty. In this case, the comma following image-string should be omitted.

Summary of Image Features

1. (For fields without a decimal point)
   a. Numeric values are printed right-justified in the field. If the value does not fill the entire field, blanks are assigned to the leftmost #'s.
   b. In Dartmouth BASIC, string values are printed centered in the field unless the first character of the field is a > or <. If the symbol < is used, string values are printed left-justified. If the symbol > is used, string values are printed right-justified. In BASIC-PLUS, string output fields are indicated by a single quote followed by a string of L's (for left justification) R's (for right-justification) or C's (for centered output).
2. (For fields with a decimal point) The decimal point in a numeric value is aligned with the decimal point in its corresponding field. A numeric value is rounded to as many significant digits as there are # symbols following the decimal point. Blanks are assigned to any extra # symbols to the left of the decimal point, and zeros are assigned to any extra # symbols to the right of the decimal point, e.g., 35.3 prints as □35.300 in the field specified by ###.###. (The symbol □ represents a space.)
3. In Dartmouth BASIC, if the field width specified is too small to hold a numeric value, a string of *'s (one for each field symbol) may be printed instead. If the field width is too small to hold a string value, excess characters are lost. In BASIC-PLUS if a numeric field is too small to hold the value to be printed, the entire value is printed anyhow, but it is preceded by a percent sign (%). In this case, the field specification is ignored. If an L, R or C string field is too small to hold the string value to be printed, BASIC-PLUS left-justifies the string and doesn't print the excess characters. In both Dartmouth BASIC and BASIC-PLUS, fields must be large enough to accommodate the MINUS sign for negative values.
4. If there are no fields in the line image, then the line image represents a column heading or output message and will be printed exactly as it appears.

In some versions of BASIC, the image is provided in a separate *image statement*. In this case, the line number of the associated image statement is specified instead of the image in the PRINT USING statement. Each image statement begins with a colon; the quote marks aren't used. Image statements may be placed anywhere in a program since they aren't executable statements.

Example 11.3:

```
170      PRINT USING 180, F$, I, X
180      :#######  AGE = ###   WEIGHT = ###.#
```

The PRINT USING statement specifies that line 180, which contains three output fields, is the image statement that determines the placement and form of the three variable values that are to be printed (F$, I, X). The output that would be produced for a sample set of values is shown next.

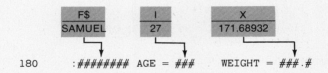

```
180      :#######  AGE = ###   WEIGHT = ###.#
```

Output line

```
SAMUEL   AGE =  27    WEIGHT = 171.7
```

The character string "SAMUEL" is printed centered in the first field while the integer 27 is printed right-justified in the second field. The real number 171.68932 is rounded to the nearest tenth because the image allows for only one position to the right of the decimal, and its decimal point is aligned with the decimal point in the third field.

Example 11.4: The following BASIC-PLUS program segment reads and prints a table of savings account transactions.

```
100      LET H$ = "ID NUMBER       NAME          TRANSACTION"
105      LET F$ = "########       'LLLLLLLL    #######.##"
110      PRINT USING H$
115 REM
120      READ N
130      FOR L = 1 TO N
140         READ I, P$, T
145         PRINT USING F$, I, P$, T
150      NEXT L
160      PRINT "END OF TRANSACTION LIST"
170 REM
180      DATA 2
190      DATA 12345, KLEIN, 555.75
200      DATA 54321, JACKSON, -6200.00
205 REM
210      END

RUN
```

```
ID NUMBER        NAME           TRANSACTION
   12345         KLEIN             555.75
   54321         JACKSON         -6200.00
END OF TRANSACTION LIST
```

The program segment may also be run in Dartmouth BASIC if line 105 is changed to read

```
105     LET F$ = "########        <########    ######.##"
```

11.2.3 Matching Fields and PRINT USING List Items

If the number of fields in an image exceeds the number of items in the PRINT USING output-list, the portion of the image beginning with the first extra field is ignored. If an insufficient number of fields is provided, then the image is reused as often as needed until the list of items is exhausted.

Example 11.5:   For the statements

```
110 LET F$ = "X = ###.#,   Y = ###.##"
120 PRINT USING F$, 3.5, 16.82, 199.185
```

the output would be:

```
X =    3.5,  Y =   16.82
X = 199.2,  Y =
```

Here the image statement is used twice; the second time the field following "Y = " is not needed.

Exercise 11.1:   Write the output line printed by the statements

```
150 LET F$ = " 'LLLLL  ###.# SECONDS"
                    [for Dartmouth BASIC use " <####   ###.# SECONDS"]
160 PRINT USING F$, L$, X
```

a) for L$ = "FABIAN" and X = 62.5
b) for L$ = "THE DOCTOR" and X = 125.27
c) for L$ = "HOSS" and X = 1026.2
d) for L$ = "ACE" and X = − 41

Exercise 11.2:   Consider the variable definitions shown below.

S1	S2	S3	L$	F$	H	R	P
219	40	0677	DOG	HOT	40	4.50	180.0

Write the PRINT USING statements required to produce the following output:

```
Line 1       SOCIAL SECURITY NUMBER 219-40-0677
Line 2
Line 3       DOG,    HOT
Line 4
Line 5       HOURS   RATE    PAY
Line 6       40.00   4.50   180.00
```

Exercise 11.3:
a) Let W be an array of size seven containing values falling in the range $-130°$F to $50°$F. Let T be a variable with values in the range $-50°$F to $+50°$F. Write the PRINT USING statement to print the contents of T and W in one row:

      T   W(1)   W(2)   W(3)   W(4)   W(5)   W(6)   W(7)

The value of T should be separated from W(1) by eight blanks and the values of the elements of W should be separated from one another by three blanks. The values of W should be printed as whole numbers without a decimal point.
b) Suppose you wished to put your PRINT USING statement from part (a) in a loop in which T ranges from $-50°$ to $+50°$ in increments of five, and the contents of W are recomputed for each of these 21 values of T. Would any changes be required in either your PRINT USING statements or your images. Describe the result of the execution of such a loop.
c) Write the PRINT USING statements to print the following:

```
WIND CHILL FACTOR TABLE (DEGREES F)
TEMPERATURE              WIND VELOCITY(MILES PER HOUR)
READING (DEG F)     0    10    20    30    40    50    60
```

11.2.4 Exponential Fields

It is often desirable to specify images for the printing of numeric data in exponential or scientific notation (see Section 4.2.4 for a discussion of BASIC scientific notation). In BASIC-PLUS, this can be done by placing four ↑ symbols at the end of a group of #'s.

Example 11.6: Let X contain .0000625, and Y contain 85260000.0. The BASIC-PLUS statements

```
120 LET F$ = " X = #.###↑↑↑↑    Y = ###.#↑↑↑↑"
130 PRINT USING F$, X, Y
```

would print the line

```
X = 6.250E-05    Y = 852.6E+05
```

Dartmouth BASIC requires five ↑ symbols in the exponential field. Some systems use an exclamation point (!) or a circumflex (∧) for the exponential field instead of an arrow.

Scientific notation can be convenient when numeric values of small magnitude (such as .0000625) or large magnitude (such as 85260000.0) are to be printed. They can also be extremely useful in printing values whose magnitude cannot be easily determined. In such cases, rather than risk specifying a field that is too small, it is better to specify an exponential field.

Exercise 11.4: Write the statements needed to produce the output described below.
a) Let X be a real array of 20 elements each containing positive values ranging from 0 to 99999.99. Print the contents of X, accurate to two decimal places, four elements per line.
b) Do the same as for part (a), but print the contents of the variable N (containing an

integer ranging in value from one to 20) on one line, and then print the contents of the first N elements of the array X, four per line.

c) Let Q be a 1000-element array of real numbers whose range of values is not easily determined but is known to be very large. Print the contents of Q, six per line, each with six significant digits.

d) Let R and T be 120-element arrays. R contains the numbers of the rooms in a nine-story building (these range from 101 through 961). T contains the temperature of these rooms on a given day, accurate to one decimal place. Print two parallel columns of output, one containing room numbers and the other containing temperatures.

Exercise 11.5: Consider the variable definitions shown below.

I	A	B	C
36	610.7	39930.0	−.000926

Write the image required to produce the following line of output.

```
3.6E+01    6.107E+03    3.99300E+04    −9.260E−04
```

11.3 FILES

11.3.1 Introduction to Files

All of the examples and problems that we have examined so far share the limitation that the input data must be typed in with the program (in DATA statements) or interactively as the program executes. In problems involving large amounts of data, this approach is not very practical. Furthermore, it prevents the sharing of the same data among several programs. It would be very desirable if data generated by one program could be manipulated by other programs.

There is also little sense of "permanency" for the data that we have used in our programs. Data items appearing in DATA statements may be saved with the program, but these data can't be used by other programs. Data items entered as the program executes are processed immediately and can't normally be reused. What is needed is a means for storing or saving data items so that they may easily be used and reused by a number of programs.

Storing a collection of data in the computer can be accomplished through the use of files. A *file* is a linear arrangement of data that is given a unique name (the *file name*). Files are usually stored on *permanent storage devices* such as a disk, drum or a tape (see Fig. 11.1). Once saved, the file can be referenced by name and used by any number of programs.

The statements and rules for working with files vary considerably from one BASIC system to another. In this section, we shall study a subset of the files features provided by BASIC-PLUS and Dartmouth BASIC. At the end of the chapter (in the summary section, 11.8) we provide a table listing the files features in several other versions of BASIC. If you are not using BASIC-PLUS

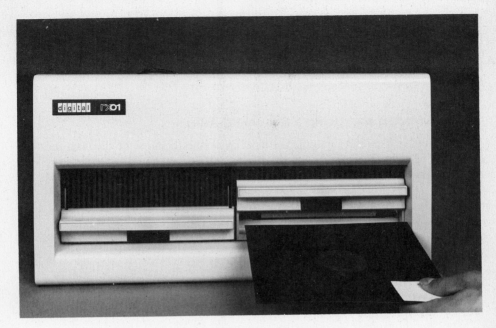

Fig. 11.1   A disk. (Photo courtesy Digital Equipment Corp.)

or Dartmouth BASIC, you should refer to this table and to your BASIC system manual to note the differences between your version of BASIC and the version described in the text.

11.3.2   Types of Files

BASIC-PLUS and Dartmouth BASIC support two types of files: *sequential* files and *random access* files. Sequential files look as if they had been entered directly at the terminal; hence, they are sometimes called *terminal files*. They are stored in a form that allows them to be listed simply by using the system command LIST. Programs, in fact, are saved on disk as sequential files.

Sequential files must be processed serially (in order) beginning with the first item. Thus, to obtain the seventh item in a sequential file, we must first read items one through six; there is no way to start reading such a file in the middle. In addition, we cannot change an item in a sequential file without rewriting the entire file.

On the other hand, items in a random access file can be referenced in any desired order. They can also be rewritten or updated on an individual basis without rewriting the entire file. Random access files are analogous to arrays in that any item in these files can be referenced as easily as the first item.

Unfortunately, not all BASIC systems support random access files. Among those that do, there are widely differing implementations. For these reasons, we will include the details of the use of sequential files in this chapter and only summarize a few of the concepts fundamental to the use of random access files.

11.3.3   Creating and Using a Sequential File

Sequential files may be created directly at the terminal or through the use of a program. Before entering data in a new file, it is necessary to define the name of the file to be created. Sequential file creation generally proceeds as follows:

1. Enter the system command NEW (followed by pressing the RETURN key, of course).
2. The computer requests the name of the file by typing NEW PROGRAM NAME—.
3. Respond by typing the name that you wish to call the file, such as INVEN. On most systems a file name must start with a letter; some systems restrict the length of the name to a maximum of six characters.
4. The computer responds by typing READY.
5. If you have a program to create your file, go to step 6. If you are going to create your file without a program, you next enter the data for the file, line-by-line, following each line number.
6. Type SAVE (and press RETURN) to save the file. If you plan to create the file using a program, typing SAVE will store a file that is initially empty.

This sequence of steps is illustrated in the following example. The directives issued by the system are underlined. The commands used may differ on your system, but the creation process should be quite similar.

Example 11.7:   The short interactive session (below) creates a file named INVEN directly at the terminal. Each line of data is preceded by a BASIC line number (lines 10-50); a comma separates the line number from the data.

```
NEW

NEW PROGRAM NAME-INVEN
READY

10, 1, TY COBB, NO PLACE LIKE HOME, 5.95, 6
20, 2, PETE ROSE, GREATEST HITS, 6.34, 3
30, 3, JIM RICE, I BOMBED NEW YORK, 4.99, 1
40, 4, HOYT WILHELM, KNUCKLING UNDER, 3.44, 8
50, 5, BILLY MARTIN, USA TRAVEL GUIDE, 2.50, 500

SAVE
```

The created file consists of information about five books, including the stock number, author, title, cost, and count-on-hand of each. Typing the system command SAVE will store this information on disk in the form shown below. Note that the line numbers (10, 20, etc.) are also saved.

file INVEN

10	1	TY COBB	NO PLACE LIKE HOME	5.95	6	20	2	...

Having saved this file, we can now write a program to read and print the information it contains, and count the number of books on hand (see Fig. 11.2).

Before we can reference a file in a program we must inform the computer of the name of the file to be used. This is done through the use of an OPEN

```
110 REM READ AND PRINT BOOK STORE INVENTORY
120 REM
130      OPEN "INVEN" AS FILE 1                          [OPEN #1: "INVEN"]
140      PRINT "BOOK STORE INVENTORY    01-04-80"
145      PRINT
150      LET H$ = "STOCK NO     AUTHOR         TITLE       PRICE    INV"
155      LET F$ = " ####    'LLLLLLLLLLL  'LLLLLLLLLLLLLLLLLL  ##.##   ###"
160      PRINT USING H$
165 REM
170 REM LOOP TO READ AND PRINT EACH DATA ITEM AND
175 REM ACCUMULATE TOTAL, T
180      LET T = 0
190      FOR I = 1 TO 5
195          INPUT #1, L, S, A$, T$, P, C            [INPUT #1: L, S,..., C]
200          PRINT USING F$, S, A$, T$, P, C
205          LET T = T + C
210      NEXT I
215 REM
220      PRINT "TOTAL NUMBER OF BOOKS = "; T
250      CLOSE #1
260 REM
270      END

RUN

BOOK STORE INVENTORY    01-04-80
```

STOCK NO	AUTHOR	TITLE	PRICE	INV
1	TY COBB	NO PLACE LIKE HOME	5.95	6
2	PETE ROSE	GREATEST HITS	6.34	3
3	JIM RICE	I BOMBED NEW YORK	4.99	1
4	HOYT WILHELM	KNUCKLING UNDER	3.44	8
5	BILLY MARTIN	USA TRAVEL GUIDE	2.50	500

TOTAL NUMBER OF BOOKS = 518

Fig. 11.2 Reading and printing a sequential file.

statement (line 130). The OPEN statement associates file number 1 with the file "INVEN". The BASIC-PLUS form is shown on the left of Fig. 11.2; the Dartmouth BASIC form is in brackets on the right.

The FOR loop in Fig. 11.2 is executed five times. Each time the next six data items are read from file #1 ("INVEN") by the INPUT #1 statement at line 195. The last five of these data items (all except the line number, L) are printed at the terminal (line 200) using image F$ (line 155).

The CLOSE statement (line 250) is used to terminate input or output for a file. Normally, all files that have been opened must be closed prior to the end of program execution. All of the new file-related statements are described in the following displays.

The OPEN Statement

BASIC-PLUS form: *Dartmouth BASIC form:*

```
OPEN file name AS FILE fileno        OPEN #fileno: file name
```

Interpretation: The file name may be a character string constant, variable or expression. The file number (fileno) must be a numeric constant, variable or numeric expression having a positive integer value. The OPEN statement associates the indicated file name with the value of fileno.

Notes: BASIC-PLUS places an upper limit of 12 on the value of fileno. In Dartmouth BASIC, the upper limit is 4095, although only 16 files can be active at one time.

The CLOSE Statement

BASIC-PLUS and Dartmouth BASIC form:

```
                    CLOSE file list
```

Interpretation: The file list is a list of one or more file numbers, separated by commas. Each file number may be an integer constant, variable or expression and must be preceded by a # sign.

Notes: Older versions of Dartmouth BASIC don't have a CLOSE statement. On some systems, files are automatically closed when a program terminates execution. You should check your BASIC system manual to see whether or not your system has a CLOSE statement and, if so, when it must be used.

The INPUT # Statement (for reading from sequential files)

BASIC-PLUS form: *Dartmouth BASIC form:*

```
    INPUT #fileno, input list              INPUT #fileno: input list
```

Interpretation: Fileno is a numeric expression that indicates which sequential file is to be read. The value of fileno must be equal to one of the file numbers designated in a previous OPEN statement. The input list is a list of the variables and array elements that are to receive the data.

Example 11.8:   Given the file association indicated below:

BASIC-PLUS   *Dartmouth BASIC*

```
        OPEN "APRIL" AS FILE 2          [OPEN #2: "APRIL"]
        OPEN "MAY" AS FILE 3            [OPEN #3: "MAY"]
```

a)   The statement

```
            INPUT #2, X, Y, Z$          [INPUT #2: X, Y, Z$]
```

will read two numbers (into X, Y) and one character string (into Z$) from the sequential file APRIL.

b)   The statements

```
        LET I = 2                       LET I = 2
        INPUT #2*I−1, A, B, S$          [INPUT #2*I−1: A, B, S$]
```

will read two numbers (into A, B) and one character string (into S$) from the sequential file MAY.

In the program in Fig. 11.2, an extra variable (L) appears in the INPUT# statement at line 195. L is used solely for reading the line numbers entered during file creation. It appears nowhere else in the program. Some systems

```
110 REM CREATE THE FILE INVEN UNDER PROGRAM CONTROL
120 REM
130     OPEN "INVEN" AS FILE 1                      [OPEN #1: "INVEN"]
140     PRINT "ENTER − STOCK NO, AUTHOR, PRICE, INVENTORY −−";
145     PRINT "IN THAT ORDER"
150 REM
160 REM LOOP FOR DATA ENTRY
170     FOR I = 1 TO 5
180         INPUT S, A$, T$, P, C
190         PRINT #1, S, A$, T$, P, C          [PRINT #1: S, A$, T$, P, C]
200     NEXT I
210 REM
220     PRINT "END OF FILE CREATION"
230     CLOSE #1
240 REM
250     END
```

Fig. 11.3 Sequential file creation using a program.

permit files without line numbers to be created at the terminal. If you use this feature, then you do not need an extra variable for reading line numbers.

Files without line numbers may also be created under program control. Fig. 11.3 illustrates the use of a program to create the file INVEN. Five items of data should be entered at the teletype after each "?" printed by the computer (INPUT statement at line 180). The PRINT # statement (line 190) writes the values just entered (S, A$, T$, P, C) on the file INVEN. The BASIC-PLUS form is shown on the left of Fig. 11.3; the Dartmouth BASIC changes are on the right. The PRINT # statement is described in the next display.

The PRINT # Statement (for writing on sequential files)

BASIC-PLUS form: *Dartmouth BASIC form:*

```
PRINT #fileno, output list        PRINT #fileno: output list
```

Interpretation: The fileno designation is the same as in the INPUT # statement. The output list specifies the values that are to be copied into the file.

Regardless of the way in which a sequential file is created, it may be listed using the system LIST command. The name of the file must be specified, using the system command OLD, before it can be deleted.

Exercise 11.6:   Write a program that reads a name and a list of three exam scores for each student in a class, and copies this information onto a sequential file called GRADES. Test your program on the following data:

```
IVORY, 47, 82, 93
CLARK, 86, 42, 77
MENACE, 99, 88, 92
BEAR, 53, 69, 62
BUMSTEAD, 88, 74, 81
```

List the file GRADES using the LIST command after your program has executed.

11.3.4   End of File Test for Sequential Files

When we have finished creating a sequential file (with or without program control), the system places a mark on the file following the last data value. This mark, called an *end-of-file mark (EOF)*, is used to indicate that there is no more data on the file.

Often when reading from a file we don't know how much information is stored on the file. We would like to be able to instruct our program to continue reading from the file "as long as more data is available." We can, in fact, do this by checking for the EOF before each read of the file. To illustrate this, the loop portion of the program shown in Fig. 11.2 is rewritten below in Dartmouth BASIC. The difference between the new loop and the old one is that loop repetition is now controlled through the condition MORE #1 rather than through the use of the loop control variable I.

```
185 REM WHILE MORE DATA CONTINUE TO READ
190     DO WHILE MORE #1
195         INPUT #1: L, S, A$, T$, P, C
200         PRINT USING F$, S, A$, T$, P, C
205         LET T = T + C
210     LOOP
```

END #1 and MORE #1 are conditions that evaluate to true or false. END #1 is true if the EOF has been reached (last data item has been read) on file #1; MORE #1 is true as long as the EOF has not been reached (more data to be read).

The End of File Test (for sequential files)

Dartmouth BASIC form:

```
                    END #fileno
                    MORE #fileno
```

Interpretation: The condition END #fileno will evaluate to true only when the EOF marker has been reached on the designated file. In all other cases, END #fileno evaluates to false. The condition MORE #fileno will evaluate to true as long as the EOF marker has not yet been reached on the designated file.

In BASIC-PLUS, two new statements (IFEND # and IFMORE #) are provided to test for the end of a sequential file. The BASIC-PLUS form of the loop is shown below. The IFEND # and IFMORE # statements are described in the next display.

```
185 REM WHILE MORE DATA CONTINUE TO READ
190     IFEND #1 THEN 215
195         INPUT #1, L, S, A$, T$, P, C
200         PRINT USING F$, S, A$, T$, P, C
205         LET T = T + C
210     GOTO 185
215 REM
```

End of File Test (for sequential files)

BASIC-PLUS form:

```
IFEND # expression THEN line number
IFMORE # expression THEN line number
```

Interpretation: For the IFEND statement, control is transferred to the designated line number when the EOF marker is reached. For the IFMORE statement, control is transferred to the designated line number as long as the EOF marker has not yet been reached.

Example 11.9: In Exercise 11.6, you were asked to create under program control a file (GRADES) containing four data items for each student in a class: the student's name, followed by three exam scores. In this example we will read the file GRADES, compute and print the average score for each student, and save the student's average along with the other four data items in a new file, AVERAG (See Fig. 11.4). The file AVERAG could be processed later by a program that computes the standard deviation or a program that assigns a letter grade.

Program Form and Style

In Fig. 11.4, we have shown the Dartmouth BASIC form of the program as its loop structure more clearly indicates what is happening. The changes required to implement the loop in BASIC-PLUS, or BASIC systems without the WHILE loop, are shown in brackets to the right. In addition to the changes shown, the ":" in lines 200 and 250 should be replaced by a "," in BASIC-PLUS. and the words IF and END in line 190 should be written together as IFEND.

Exercise 11.7: Take the GRADES file from Example 11.9, and write a program that will read the exam data on the GRADES file, and write this data to a new file (NEWGRA), along with the score from a fourth exam. For each student on the GRADES file, your program should print the student's name, request from the user the fourth exam score for this student, and then write the new exam data on the file NEWGRA.

11.3.5   Resetting a Sequential File

In some cases, the same file may be processed more than once by a program. To accomplish this, the file must be *rewound* (reset to the beginning) using the RESTORE statement in BASIC-PLUS (RESET in Dartmouth BASIC). The first data item on the file would be the next item read.

```
100 REM READ NAME AND TEST SCORES FROM FILE GRADES
110 REM COMPUTE AND PRINT EACH STUDENT'S AVERAGE SCORE
120 REM COPY NAME, SCORES, AND AVERAGES INTO FILE AVERAG
130 REM
140     OPEN FILE #1: "GRADES"              [OPEN "GRADES" AS FILE 1]
150     OPEN FILE #2: "AVERAG"              [OPEN "AVERAG" AS FILE 2]
160 REM
170     PRINT "NAME", "AVERAGE"
180 REM WHILE MORE DATA ON FILE GRADES, COMPUTE AVERAGE
190     DO WHILE MORE #1                    [IFEND #1 THEN 270]
195         REM READ NAME AND SCORES
200         INPUT #1: N$, S1, S2, S3
210         REM COMPUTE AND PRINT AVERAGE
220         LET A = (S1 + S2 + S3)/ 3
230         PRINT N$, A
240         REM COPY DATA INTO FILE AVERAG
250         PRINT #2: N$, S1, S2, S3, A
260     LOOP                                [GOTO 180]
270 REM
280     CLOSE #1, #2
290 REM
300     END
```

Fig. 11.4 Adding information to a sequential file.

Setting a File to the Beginning (for sequential files)

BASIC-PLUS form: *Dartmouth BASIC form:*

    RESTORE #fileno   RESET #fileno

Interpretation: The fileno designation is the same as in the OPEN statement. This statement resets the indicated file to the beginning.

The RESTORE (RESET) statement is useful in programs in which the data on a file must be read more than once or in programs in which a file is first written and then read.

11.4 APPLICATION OF SEQUENTIAL FILES

11.4.1 The File Merge Problem

A common problem when working with files is to update one file (master file) by merging in information from a second file (update file). This process is illustrated in the following problem.

Problem 11.1: The Junk Mail Company has recently received a new mailing list (file UPDATE) that it wishes to merge with its master file (file OLDMST). Each of these files is in alphabetical order by name. The company wishes to produce a new master file (NEWMST) that is also in alphabetical order. Each client name and address on either mailing list is represented by four consecutive character strings as shown below:

"CLAUS, SANTA"
"1 STAR LANE"
"NORTH POLE"
"ALASKA, 99999"

There is a sentinel name and address at the end of each of the files UPDATE and OLDMST. The sentinel is the same for both files; one copy should be written at the end of the NEWMST file. The sentinel entry consists of four

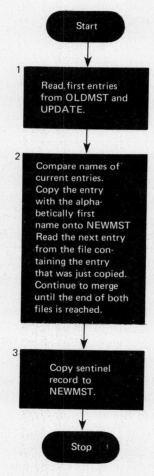

Fig. 11.5 Level one flow diagram for Problem 11.1.

character strings, each containing 3 Z's. We assume that there are no names that appear on both files.

Discussion: In addition to the two input files (OLDMST and UPDATE) we will need an output file (NEWMST) that will contain the merged data from OLDMST and UPDATE. NEWMST will then serve as the new master file of mailing labels. The files information is summarized in the data table shown below.

Data Table for Merge Problem

Input files	*Output files*
OLDMST: The original mailing list in alphabetical order by name (file #1)	NEWMST: The final mailing list, formed by merging OLDMST and UPDATE (file #3)
UPDATE: The additions to be made to OLDMST, also in alphabetical order by name (file #2)	

The level one flow diagram is shown in Fig. 11.5. As indicated here, the program reads one name and address entry at a time from each input file. These two entries are compared and the one that comes first alphabetically is copied to the output file (NEWMST). Another entry is then read from the file containing the entry just copied and the comparison process is repeated. When the end of one of the input files (OLDMST or UPDATE) is reached, the program should copy the remaining information from the other input file to NEWMST followed by the sentinel record.

To simplify the implementation of the algorithm, we will use two string arrays, O$ and U$, to hold the current client data from OLDMST and UPDATE, respectively. The layout of these arrays is shown below.

	1	2	3	4
O$ (from OLDMST)	$name_1$	$street_1$	$city_1$	$state_1$ & zip_1
U$ (from UPDATE)	$name_2$	$street_2$	$city_2$	$state_2$ & zip_2

The additional data table entries are shown below. The refinement of step 2 is shown in Fig. 11.6.

Additional Data Table Entries for Problem 11.1

Input variables   *Program variables*

O$(4): String array to
  hold current client
  data from OLDMST

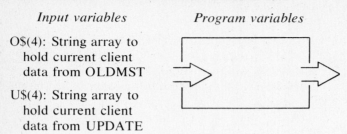

U$(4): String array to
  hold current client
  data from UPDATE

It is important to verify that all the remaining data on a file will be merged into NEWMST when the end-of-file mark on the other file has been reached. Just before reaching the end-of-file mark on UPDATE (or OLDMST), the sentinel record will be read into U$ (or O$). Since the sentinel name ("ZZZ") alphabetically follows any other client name, the remaining client data on the unfinished file will be copied to NEWMST as desired. When loop repetition terminates, both O$ and U$ will contain the sentinel record.

The main program is shown in Fig. 11.7a; the subroutine (MERGE) is used to implement step 2 (see Fig. 11.7b). The MAT INPUT # and MAT PRINT # statements are analogous to the MAT READ and MAT PRINT statements described in Chapter 10. They transfer an entire array of data be-

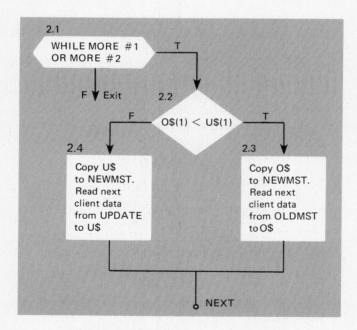

Fig. 11.6 Refinement of step 2 from Fig. 11.5.

```
100 REM PROGRAM TO MERGE OLD MASTER AND UPDATE FILES
110 REM TO BUILD A NEW MASTER FILE
120 REM
130     DIM O$(4), U$(4)
140     OPEN #1: "OLDMST"                        [OPEN "OLDMST" AS #1]
150     OPEN #2: "UPDATE"                        [OPEN "UPDATE" AS #2]
160     OPEN #3: "NEWMST"                        [OPEN "NEWMST" AS #3]
170 REM
180 REM READ FIRST CLIENT NAMES AND ADDRESSES INTO O$ AND U$
190     MAT INPUT #1: O$
200     MAT INPUT #2: U$
210 REM
220 REM MERGE OLDMST AND UPDATE TO NEWMST
230     GOSUB 1000
240 REM
250 REM COPY SENTINEL RECORD TO NEWMST
260     MAT PRINT #3: O$
270 REM
280     PRINT "MERGE COMPLETE"
290     CLOSE #1, #2, #3
300 REM
310     STOP
```

Fig. 11.7a　Main program for file merge problem (11.1).

```
1000 REM SUBROUTINE TO MERGE TWO FILES
1010 REM
1020 REM GLOBAL DATA
1030 REM    IN:  FILE 1, FILE 2, O$( ), U$( )
1040 REM    OUT: FILE 3, O$( ), U$( )
1050 REM
1060 REM WHILE MORE DATA ON EITHER FILE, CONTINUE MERGE
1070     DO WHILE MORE #1 OR MORE #2           [IF MORE #1 THEN 1090]
1080 REM                                       [IF END #2 THEN 1200]
1090        REM COPY ALPHABETICALLY SMALLER RECORD
1100        IF O$(1) < U$(1) THEN 1110 ELSE 1150
                                               [IF O$(1)>=U$(1) THEN 1150]
1110 REM    THEN
1120            MAT PRINT #3: O$
1130            MAT INPUT #1: O$
1140        GOTO 1180
1150 REM    ELSE
1160            MAT PRINT #3: U$
1170            MAT INPUT #2: U$
1180 REM    IFEND
1190     LOOP                                  [GOTO 1060]
1200 REM MERGE COMPLETE
1210 REM
1220     RETURN
1225 REM
1230     END
```

Fig. 11.7b　Merge subroutine for file merge problem (11.1).

tween memory and a data file. These operations will be described in the next section. If they are not available on your system, you should use a FOR loop for data input and output.

Program Form and Style

As in Fig. 11.4, we have departed a bit from the normal procedure in Fig. 11.7a and shown the Dartmouth BASIC program form with BASIC-PLUS changes in brackets. The major difference between the two versions in Fig. 11.7a is in the form of the OPEN statement; the ":" must also be changed to "," in the INPUT # and PRINT # statements for BASIC-PLUS.

In Fig. 11.7b, the merge loop is implemented as a WHILE loop in Dartmouth BASIC. In BASIC-PLUS, the INEND and IFMORE statements must be used as shown to determine whether either file has additional data. The GOTO 1060 statement causes a transfer back to the loop repetition test after each loop execution. These statements would be needed, as well, in any version of BASIC that doesn't support the WHILE loop.

The IF-THEN-ELSE decision structure inside the loop is implemented using the BASIC-PLUS form with the Dartmouth BASIC form shaded as in earlier programs. The statement in brackets to the right of line 1100 should replace the IF-THEN-ELSE statement if it is not supported on your system.

Exercise 11.8:   Modify the program for Problem 11.1 to handle the situation in which the UPDATE file may contain some of the same names as the OLDMST file. In this case only one address should appear on the NEWMST file; the address in file UPDATE should be used as it is more recent. Also, print a count of the number of file entries in each of the three files.

Exercise 11.9:   Let FILEA and FILEB be two files containing the name (a character string) and identification number of the students in two different programming classes. Assume that these files are arranged in ascending order by student number and that no student is in both classes. Write a program to read the information on FILEA and FILEB, and merge them onto a third file (FILEC) retaining the ascending order.

11.4.2   Matrix Input and Output on Files

The input and output of matrices on files is handled in a manner that is completely analogous to the input and output of matrices at the terminal (see Chapter 10). The forms of the file input and output statements for matrices are identical to those described earlier in this chapter except that they are preceded by the word MAT. When a file is specified in a matrix input or output statement, as many data items as there are elements in the specified arrays are read or written.

Example 11.10:   Assume the matrices A and B are declared in the dimension statement

```
DIM A(4,2), B(3,3)
```

a)   `MAT INPUT #1, A`
reads a list of eight values stored on the sequential file (designated by #1) into the matrix A.

b)   `MAT PRINT #3, A, B`
writes eight values from the matrix A followed by nine values from B onto the file designated by #3.

11.5   RANDOM ACCESS FILES

A random access file has the advantage that any part of it may be read or written without disturbing the rest of the file. Random access files are, therefore, very similar to arrays in that all items in a random file may be accessed with equal ease. Random files may be created and listed only under program control, not directly from the terminal. The commands for reading and writing random files are similar to those for sequential files. However, the end-of-file test and file reset operations for random files have a somewhat different interpretation than their counterparts for sequential files.

Not all BASIC systems support random access files and those that do differ considerably in the actual implementation. For this reason, we will illustrate the use of random files in an example, avoiding the details of any particular implementation. You should consult your BASIC manual for the statements required to process random files in your system.

Example 11.11:   We will consider a random inventory file (named INVENR) that is similar to the file INVEN (see Example 11.7) but without the string information. The data for each inventory item is shown in Table 11.1.

Entry Number	Description	
0	stock number S--1	
1	wholesale cost W	
2	retail price R	item 1
3	count-on-hand C	
4	year-to-date sales Y	
5	stock number S--2	
6	wholesale cost W	
7	retail price R	item 2
8	count-on-hand C	
9	year-to-date sales Y	
.	.	
.	.	
.	.	

Table 11.1   The Random Inventory File—INVENR

As is the case with all random files, the inventory file consists of a list of *entries*. Each entry in the file has a unique *file entry number*; the first file entry number is zero. In this example there are five entries for each of the items in the inventory. The group of five entries for each item is called the *record of information* (or, simply, the *record*) pertaining to that item.

Suppose we wish to write a program to update the inventory file to reflect the past day's sales. It is unlikely that all inventory records will be affected by a single day's sales or that the sales records will be arranged in any particular order. Furthermore, only certain entries for each record will normally need to be altered (for example, the count-on-hand or year-to-date sales entries).

This is precisely the sort of problem in which it is advantageous to use random files for data storage: in any given execution of the update program, only some of the entries on certain records are processed, and the records involved are not processed in any prespecified order. In a sequential file, an item in the middle of the file can't be accessed without first reading through all of the entries that precede the item. Furthermore, in a sequential file, you can't alter any single entry without recopying the entire file.

On a random file, all we need do to access or change a particular item of a record is to position the file to that item. If we imagine a *pointer to the file*, then to access a particular entry on the file, we must first set the pointer to the desired entry number. The entry number can be computed using a formula and the pointer can be set by using the reset operation for random files.

If each record has N entries, the assignment statement

$$\text{LET E } = \text{ (S}-1\text{) } * \text{ N}$$

could be used to compute the first file entry number corresponding to a particular stock number S as illustrated below for S = 2 and N = 5.

record for item 2

. . .	stock number (S)	wholesale cost (W)	retail price (R)	count-on-hand (C)	YTD sales (Y)	. . .

(entry numbers) 5 6 7 8 9
                 ↑
                 E

The value assigned to E (5 in this case) corresponds to the first entry in the record for item 2. To access the ith entry in this record ($0 \le i \le N - 1$), we can specify a reset to file position E + i, and then execute a read (or a write) for the file. For example, to directly access the count-on-hand for item 2, we can execute the statement below:

$$\text{RESET \#1: E } + \text{ 3}$$

which will set the file pointer for file one to entry number 8 as required. After entry 8 is accessed, the file pointer automatically advances to entry 9. Hence, the statements

```
RESET #1: E + 3
INPUT #1: Cl, Yl
```

would read the count-on-hand and year-to-date sales for item 2 into C1 and Y1 respectively; the file pointer would advance to entry 10.

In addition to defining the entry number of a file item to be accessed as just shown, we may also define the entry number of a file item based upon the current location of the file pointer. This may be done through the use of a special function with one argument (named LOC in many BASIC systems) which returns the current position of the pointer to its argument file. For example, the reset operation

```
RESET #1: LOC(1) - 2
```

will reposition the pointer for file #1 two positions to the left of its current position.

The statement sequence

```
RESET #1: E + 3
INPUT #1: Cl, Yl
RESET #1: LOC(1) - 2
PRINT #1: Cl - A, Yl + A
```

would update the count-on-hand and year-to-date sales entries (C1 and Y1 respectively) by the amount sold, A.

The use of the reset operation for a random access file has an effect that is analogous to the specification of a subscript for an array. The value of the expression in the reset operation accesses a particular file entry in the same way that the value of the subscript selects a specific element in an array.

11.6 CHAINING

Many BASIC versions provide an additional feature, the *CHAIN statement*, which enables a long program to be divided into more manageable segments. This feature allows each segment to be designed relatively independently. Once the segments are completed, they can be executed serially (one after the other) without programmer intervention to complete the desired programming task.

The CHAIN Statement

Dartmouth BASIC and BASIC-PLUS form:

```
CHAIN next program
```

Interpretation: The CHAIN statement terminates the execution of the program in which it occurs, and initiates the execution of the program specified by next program. On most BASIC systems, next program is a string expression designating the name of the file containing the program to be executed.

When chaining is used, there is complete independence between the names of variables and arrays used in the current program and those used in the new program. No information is transferred from one module of a chain to another except through files. Hence, it is impossible for variables altered in one program to have any effect upon the values of variables in the other program, even if these variables have the same name. The CHAIN feature is, therefore, an important aid in the construction, debugging and maintenance of large-scale systems. If the subprogram feature (see Chapter 8) is not available, then chaining is the only means of segmenting a large-scale system into a set of compact, independent modules.

When the CHAIN statement is executed, the new program segment is placed in memory and program execution continues. Any files used in common by several programs should be opened in each program.

Example 11.12:   The two programs shown in Fig. 11.8 are chained together via the statement

```
280 CHAIN "PRNTCK"
```

where PRNTCK is the name of the file containing the second program. The first program reads file PAYROL (#1) containing payroll data for all employees (name—N$, hours—H and rate—R). It then computes each employee's pay, P, and writes it on file CHECKS (#5) along with the employee's name. The second program (contained on file PRNTCK) reads file CHECKS and prints it at the terminal. The first entry on each file is the number of employees processed.

It is important to remember that there is no transfer of data between these two programs except as provided through file 5. Even the names N, N$ and P used in the second program have no connection to the names N, N$ and P in the first program; the names used in the second program are completely independent of those used in the first one. We could have just as easily used the names X, Y$ and Z in place of N, N$ and P in the second program without affecting the results.

11.7   COMMON PROGRAMMING ERRORS

11.7.1   Print Using and Image Errors

The most common error in the construction of images is the failure to provide a field specification of sufficient size to accommodate the value printed. Recall (see Sec. 11.2.2) that the use of images of insufficient size for character strings will prevent the excess characters from being printed. If an image for a numeric value is not large enough to accommodate the integral part of the value, the field that is printed may be filled with asterisks. If there is any possibility that a value might be negative, enough space should be left in the field to guarantee that the minus sign will be accommodated.

```
110 REM PAYROLL PROBLEM
115 REM
120 REM READ NAME, HOURS, RATE FOR EACH EMPLOYEE. COMPUTE PAY.
125 REM WRITE NAME AND PAY TO FILE "CHECKS" FOR LATER PROCESSING.
130 REM
135     OPEN "PAYROL" AS FILE 1
140     OPEN "CHECKS" AS FILE 5
145 REM
150 REM READ AND PRINT NUMBER OF EMPLOYEES
160     INPUT #1, N
170     PRINT "NUMBER OF EMPLOYEES IS ", N
180     PRINT #5, N
185 REM
190 REM LOOP TO PROCESS EACH EMPLOYEE PAYROLL DATA
200     FOR I = 1 TO N
210        INPUT #1, N$, H, R
220        LET P = H * R
230        PRINT #5, N$, P
240     NEXT I
250     CLOSE #1, #5
260 REM
270 REM PRINT PAYCHECKS
280     CHAIN "PRNTCK"
285 REM
290     END

100 REM PRINT CONTENTS OF CHECK FILE
115 REM
120     OPEN "CHECKS" AS FILE 5
130 REM
140 REM READ THE COUNT OF EMPLOYEES ON FILE CHECKS
150     INPUT #5, N
170     PRINT "NAME", "AMOUNT PAID"
180     FOR I = 1 TO N
190        INPUT #5, N$, P
200        PRINT N$, P
210     NEXT I
215 REM
220     CLOSE #5
225 REM
230     END
```

Fig. 11.8 Example of CHAIN statement.

Image statements are reused as often as necessary if the output list statement contains more items than there are field specifications in the image. If this reuse is not carefully planned, it can easily result in a size mismatch between output list items and the field specification.

11.7.2 Errors in File Usage

There are a number of errors that can result from the improper definition or use of files. We list some of the more common errors along with a representative error message. Your version of BASIC should provide similar diagnostic messages.

Feature	Dartmouth BASIC	Digital Equipment BASIC-PLUS and RT/11	Sperry Univac UBASIC	Honeywell 60/600
1. Types of files supported	Sequential Random	Sequential Random	Sequential Random	Sequential
2. Opening a sequential file	OPEN #fileno: name	OPEN AS FILE fileno name	OPEN name AS FILE fileno	FILES statement with names separated by semicolons
3. File naming conventions	From 1-8 chars. (incl. letters, digits, + or −). Must start with a letter	No name length limits; any legal string is allowed	From 1-12 chars. (incl. letters, digits, dashes or $)	No name length limits (any legal string allowed)
4. Sequential file read	INPUT #fileno: list	INPUT #fileno, list	INPUT FROM fileno: list	INPUT #fileno, list
5. Sequential file write	PRINT #fileno: list	PRINT #fileno, list	WRITE ON fileno: list PRINT ON fileno: list	PRINT #fileno, list
6. Sequential file EOF test	conditions: END #fileno MORE #fileno	IFEND #fileno THEN ln IFMORE #fileno THEN ln	ON END FILE fileno GOTO ln (transfers control to ln if EOF reached)	conditions: END #file MORE #file
7. Sequential file rewind	RESET #fileno	RESTORE #fileno	RESTORE-for input via READ/DATA statements only	RESTORE #fileno (places file in read mode)
8. Maximum value for file designator	4095 (up to 16 may be open at one time)	System dependent (file designator 0 not allowed)	9	8

Feature	CDC Basic 3	DECSYSTEM 10 Conversational BASIC	Burroughs B6000/B7000	Hewlett Packard 2000E/2000C
1. Types of files supported	Sequential	Sequential Random	Sequential Random Numeric Random String	Sequential Random
2. Opening a sequential file	FILE statement of form FILE #fileno = name	FILES statement with names separated by semicolon	FILES statement with names separated by semicolons	FILES statement with names separated by commas
3. File naming conventions	1 to 7 alphanumeric characters beginning with a letter	Any combination of letters and digits up to and including 6 characters in length	1 to 6 alphanumeric characters beginning with a letter	1 to 6 alphanumeric characters beginning with a letter
4. Sequential file read	INPUT #fileno, list READ #fileno, list	INPUT #fileno, list READ #fileno, list	INPUT #fileno, list	READ #fileno; list
5. Sequential file write	PRINT #fileno, list WRITE #fileno, list	PRINT #fileno, list WRITE #fileno, list	PRINT #fileno, list	PRINT #fileno; list
6. Sequential file EOF test	conditions: END #file MORE #file	IFEND #fileno THEN ln	conditions: END #fileno MORE #fileno	conditions: END #fileno
7. Sequential file rewind	RESTORE #fileno	RESTORE #fileno (places file in read mode)	RESTORE #fileno	RESET #fileno
8. Maximum value for file designator	$2^{18} - 1$	9 (range from 1 to 9)	16	4

Table 11.2 Summary of files features

Error	Message
1. Failure to provide a numeric-valued expression as a file designator (following a # sign—for example, in INPUT # or PRINT # statements)	FILE NUMBER REQUIRED
2. Use of an expression as a file designator that is less than zero or larger than the number of files permitted on your system	ILLEGAL FILE NUMBER
3. Failure to OPEN a file in a program; attempt to use a file designator in a statement that precedes the OPEN statement	NO FILE FOR FILE NUMBER
4. Use of a string that is not a legal file name in an OPEN statement	ILLEGAL FILE NAME
5. Attempt to read beyond the end of a file	READING PAST END OF FILE

You may encounter numerous other error messages in working with files and in using the chain statement. Since many of these errors are highly dependent upon your computer system and the version of BASIC that you are using, you should consult your BASIC manual to interpret these messages.

11.8 SUMMARY

In this chapter we have described two features of input and output that are supported in a number of BASIC systems. Both the formatted output and files features are described in a form that is similar to that used in most BASIC systems. However, it is highly likely that your implementation doesn't conform exactly to that described in the text. It is a good idea to consult the manual for your BASIC system before attempting to use any of these features. As a summary and reference aid, we have provided a list of the files statements supported in several popular versions of BASIC (see Table 11.2).

PROGRAMMING PROBLEMS

11.2 Assume that the table below reflects the current market value of six well-known stocks:

LEAVEM COLD ELEC CO., 13.66
WE FLEECEM GAS CO., 19.27
US THIEVES SUGAR CO., 8.01
TAINTED COFFEE INC., 6.45
DRYWELL OIL OF MAINE, 27.42
HOT PRODUCTS INC., 2.82

Write an interactive program to read the above table from a sequential file and write a sequential file containing three entries for each stock: company name, number of shares and market value per share. Allow the user to enter the number of shares of each of the stocks at the terminal.

11.3 Write a program that reads the file created in Problem 11.2 and prints the following table:

CORPORATION NAME	STOCK VALUE PER SHARE	NO. OF SHARES	TOTAL VALUE
XX . . . X	XXX.XX	XXXX	XXXXXXX.XX
.	.	.	.
.	.	.	.
.	.	.	
(allow for a max of 25 characters)			
XX . . . X	XXX.XX	XXXX	XXXXXXX.XX
TOTALS		XXXXX	XXXXXXXX.XX

Use PRINT USING and image features to obtain the table.

11.4 A local music school has the following payroll data on a sequential file called PAYROL.

Employee Name	Year-to-Date Earnings	YTD Federal Tax	YTD Social Security
BEETHOVEN	9132.83	913.28	657.56
MOZART	7781.35	778.14	560.26
ROSSINI	1847.51	184.75	133.02
GERSHWIN	7951.38	759.14	572.50
PACHELBEL	5699.16	569.92	410.34
BALIN	6222.81	622.28	448.04
CLIBURN	4995.88	499.59	359.70

The weekly payroll figures are:

Name	Hours	Rate
BEETHOVEN	40	8.50
MOZART	44	6.45
ROSSINI	36	4.75
GERSHWIN	35.5	8.50
PACHELBEL	50	6.00
BALIN	16.5	20.00
CLIBURN	0	2.90

Write an interactive program to read and update the payroll file. Federal tax is computed as a straight 10 percent of earnings. The Social Security tax is computed as 7.2 percent of earnings up to a maximum tax of $750 a year. List the updated sequential file after the program is run.

11.5 Revise the program in Problem 11.4 to read the updated payroll file and print a table containing employee name, earnings, Federal tax, Social Security tax, and net pay. Use PRINT USING and image features.

11.6 a) Write a program with PRINT USING and image features to print n copies of the questionnaire in Fig. 11.9, where n is read interactively from the terminal.

b) Write a program that will read in the responses to the questionnaire for all students in your class and tabulate the results as follows: Compute and print the total number of responses and a breakdown according to class and according to age: less than 18; 18-22; over 22. Compute and print the number of Yes and No answers to each of questions 4-10 for all students.

Label all output appropriately, and use PRINT USING and image features for all output.

POLITICS AS USUAL—A PREFERENCE POLL

1. Name: _____, _____ ____
             Last   First   M.I.

2. Academic year: ____ ____
   (Fr, So, Jr, Sr, Use "O" for other)

3. Age ____ ____

For items 4. through 10., answer yes (Y) or no (N).

4. Have you ever voted in a presidential election?   _____

5. Do you think that most politicians are honest?   _____

6. Do you think that most politicians are responsive to the needs of their constituents?   _____

7. Do you think that the Federal government has taken sufficient steps to prevent another Watergate?   _____

8. Have you ever taken a Political Science course?   _____

9. Are you very interested in national politics?   _____

10. Have you ever paid any Federal income taxes?   _____

Fig. 11.9 Questionnaire for Problem 11.6.

11.7 Consider the inventory file shown in Table 11.1. In Example 11.11, we assumed that the entries on this file were in sequence according to stock number, ordered from 1, 2, and so on. Write a program to read from the terminal the stock entries for a dozen or so inventory items and build a sequential file containing these items. (You are not to make any assumptions concerning the ordering of the stock numbers of these items).

11.8 Write a program to read the sequential file created in Problem 11.7, sort the file in ascending order according to stock number and write the results on a new file. You may assume that the entire sequential file will fit in memory at once (Use arrays large enough to accommodate the sequential file entries that you made in Problem 11.7).

11.9 Chain together the programs for Problems 11.7 and 11.8. Then chain a third program to read the resulting sequential file and print it at the terminal with the appropriate PRINT USING and image features.

11.10 Create a sequential file SALMEN containing the salaries of 10 men, and a second sequential file SALWOM containing the salaries of 10 women. For each employee on these files, there is an employee number (four digits), an employee name (a string) and an employee salary. Each file is arranged in ascending order by employee number. Write a program that will read each of these files and merge the contents onto a third file, SALARY, retaining the ascending order of employee numbers. For each employee written to the file SALARY, write an "M" (for male) or an "F" (for female) following the employee number.

11.11 Write a program to read and print the file SALARY and compute the average salary for all employees. Chain together this program and the program from Problem 11.10. Use the PRINT USING statement with appropriately designed images.

11.12 Do Problem 9.12 with the PRINT USING statement.

11.13 Do Problem 9.13 with the PRINT USING statement.

GLOSSARY OF
BASiC STATEMENTS and STRUCTURES

REFERENCE TABLES

INDEX OF
PROGRAMS

STANDARD, MINIMAL BASIC FEATURES (Supported by all BASIC systems)

Statement or Structure	Purpose	Examples	Section Introduced
LET	Assignment: compute and assign a new value	LET A = B + 3 LET N$ = "HARRY"	1.3.3 (See also 4.2)
READ	Read data from list specified in DATA statement	READ X, Y(3,I), N$	1.3.5
DATA	Designate a list of data to be read by READ statement	DATA 3.5, -16, 'JOE'	1.3.5
PRINT	Display values	PRINT "X=", X	1.3.6
END	Last statement in a program	END	1.3.7
INPUT	Read data interactively	INPUT, X, L$	1.5.3
REM	For remarks or comments	REM COMPUTE SUM	2.2.3
FOR–NEXT	Counter-controlled loop	FOR I=1 TO 10 STEP 1	2.4.2 (See also 3.3)
GOTO	Transfer of control	GOTO 250	3.2.2
IF–THEN	Conditional transfer	IF X > 1000 THEN 420	3.2.2
STOP	Stop program execution	STOP	5.4.3
GOSUB	Transfer to a subroutine	GOSUB 1000	5.4.3
RETURN	Return to statement following GOSUB	RETURN	5.4.3

DIM	Declaring array sizes	DIM A(12), B(3,5)	6.2
ON–GOTO	Multiple alternative branch	ON A GOTO 180,220,260	7.5.1
DEF	Single line function definition	DEF FNR(X) = X ↑ 2	8.2
Double Alternative Decision Structure	For writing decisions having two alternatives	IF X < Y THEN 200 REM THEN ||| GOTO 300 200 REM ELSE ||| 300 REM IFEND	3.2.4
Single Alternative Decision Structure	For writing decisions having one alternative	IF X < 0 THEN 280 REM THEN ||| 280 REM IFEND	3.2.5
While Loop	For writing conditional loops	120 REM WHILE Y < 100 IF X >= 100 THEN 270 ||| GOTO 120 270 REM	5.2.3

STANDARD MINIMAL BASIC FEATURES (Supported by all BASIC systems) (Continued)

Statement or Structure	Purpose	Examples	Section Introduced
Multiple Alternative Decision Structure	For writing decisions having more than two alternatives	``` REM SELECT REM CASE IF X >= 60 THEN 220 ———— ———— GOTO 420 220 REM CASE IF X >= 80 THEN 320 ———— ———— GOTO 420 320 REM DEFAULT ———— ———— ———— 420 REM SELECTEND ```	7.3.3

BASIC-PLUS FEATURES

Statement or Structure	Purpose	Example	Section Introduced
IF-THEN-ELSE Statement	Single statement for specifying decisions having two alternatives. Alternatives can be statement numbers or single statements	IF X < 0 THEN 360 ELSE 390 IF X < 0 THEN LET X = −Y ELSE LET X = Y	3.2.1
Double Alternative Decision Structure	For writing decisions having two alternatives	210 REM IF X > Y THEN 210 ELSE 290 THEN ——— GOTO 370 290 REM ELSE ——— 370 REM IFEND	3.2.3
Single Alternative Decision Structure	For writing decisions having one alternative	210 REM IF X > 0 THEN 210 ELSE 250 THEN ——— 250 REM IFEND	3.2.5
While Loop (BASIC-PLUS 2)	For writing conditional loops	WHILE X < 100 ——— NEXT	5.2.2
While Loop	For writing conditional loops	FOR Z9 = 0 WHILE X < 100 ——— NEXT Z9	5.2.4

BASIC PLUS FEATURES (Continued)

Statement or Structure	Purpose	Examples	Section Introduced

Multiple Alternative Decision Structure	For writing decisions having more than two alternatives	REM SELECT
		REM CASE
		    140 IF X < 60 THEN 140 ELSE 220
		    ||
		    ||
		    GOTO 420
		— 220 REM CASE
		    240 IF X < 80 THEN 240 ELSE 320
		    ||
		    ||
		    GOTO 420
		320 REM DEFAULT
		    ||
		    ||
		420 REM SELECTEND
			7.3.3

ON-GOSUB	Multi-way subroutine call switch	ON I GOSUB 100,200,300	7.5.2

Multi-line Function Definition	Definition of multi-argument and multi-line functions	DEF FNM(X,Y)
		  ||
		  ||
		FNEND
			8.2

Subprogram Definition	Definition of independent program module	SUB ONES (X( ),N)
		  ||
		  ||
		SUBEND
			8.4.2

Subprogram Call	Call independent modules	CALL ONES(A( ),10)	8.4.2
MAT READ MAT PRINT	Read a matrix Display a matrix	MAT READ X,Y MAT PRINT W	10.4.2 10.4.2

MAT initialization	To initialize a matrix to all zeros (ZER), all ones (CON), or the identity matrix (IDN)	MAT C = ZER MAT C = CON MAT C = IDN	10.4.2
MAT Arithmetic	For performing matrix arithmetic (multiply, subtract, add)	MAT C = A * B MAT C = A – B MAT C = A + B	10.4.3
MAT Inverse	Compute the inverse of a matrix	MAT C = INV(A)	10.4.4
MAT Transpose	Compute the transpose of a matrix	MAT C = TRN(A)	10.4.4
MAT Copy	To copy one matrix to another	MAT C = A	10.4.3
MAT Scalar Multiply	To multiply a matrix by a scalar expression	MAT C = (2*K) * A	10.4.3
PRINT USING	Print with formatting	PRINT USING A$, X	11.2.2
Files OPEN	Open a sequential file	OPEN MASTER AS FILE #1	11.3.3
Files CLOSE	Close a sequential file	CLOSE #1	11.3.3
Files INPUT	Read from a sequential file	INPUT #1, X, Y	11.3.3
Files PRINT	Write on a sequential file	PRINT #1, X, Y	11.3.3
End-of-File Test	Check for EOF on a sequential file	IFEND #1 THEN 610 IFMORE #1 THEN 610	11.3.4
Files Reset	RESET a file back to beginning	RESTORE #1	11.3.5
MAT Files INPUT	Read a matrix from a sequential file	MAT INPUT #1, A	11.4.2
MAT Files PRINT	Write a matrix to a sequential file	MAT PRINT #1, A	11.4.2
CHAIN	Terminate execution of current program; initiate execution of next program.	CHAIN NEXT	11.6

DARTMOUTH BASIC FEATURES

Statement or Structure	Purpose	Example	Section Introduced
IF-THEN-ELSE Statement	Single statement for specifying decisions having two alternatives. Alternatives can be statement numbers or single statements	IF X < 0 THEN 360 ELSE 390 IF X < Y THEN LET X = Y ELSE LET X = Y	3.2.1
Double Alternative Decision Structure	Structure for writing decisions having two alternatives	IF X < Y THEN ——— ——— ELSE ——— ——— IFEND	3.2.1
Single Alternative Decision Structure	Structure for writing decisions having one alternative	IF X < Y THEN ——— ——— IFEND	3.2.5
While Loop	For writing conditional loops	DO WHILE X < 100 ——— ——— LOOP	5.2.2
Multiple Alternative (SELECT) Decision Structure	For writing decisions having more than two alternatives	SELECT CASE X < 60 ———	7.3.3

		CASE X < 80	
		──────	
		DEFAULT	
		──────	
		SELECTEND	
ON-GOSUB	Multi-way subroutine call switch	ON I GOSUB 100,200,300	7.5.2
Multi-line function definition	Definition of multi-argument and multi-line functions	DEF FNM(X,Y) ────── ────── FNEND	8.2
Subprogram Definition	Definition of independent program module	SUB ONES(X( ),N) ────── ────── SUBEND	8.4.2 8.4.3
Subprogram Call	Call independent modules	CALL ONES(A( ),10)	8.4.2 8.4.3
PRINT USING	Print with formatting	PRINT USING A$, X	11.2.2
Files OPEN	Open a sequential file	OPEN #1: MASTER	11.3.3
Files CLOSE	Close a sequential file	CLOSE #1	11.3.3
Files INPUT	Read from a sequential file	INPUT #1: X, Y	11.3.3
Files PRINT	Writing on a sequential file	PRINT #: X, Y	11.3.3
End-of-File Test	Check for EOF on a sequential file	IF END #1 THEN IF MORE #1 THEN	11.3.4

DARTMOUTH BASIC FEATURES (Continued)

Statement or Structure	Purpose	Examples	Section Introduced
Files Reset	Reset a file back to beginning	RESET #1	
MAT Files INPUT	Read a matrix from a sequential file	MAT INPUT #1 : A	11.4.2
MAT Files PRINT	Write a matrix to a sequential file	MAT PRINT #1 : A	11.4.2
CHAIN	Terminate execution of current program; initiate execution of next program	CHAIN NEXT	11.6

REFERENCE TABLES

Table	Description	Section	Page
1.1	BASIC Arithmetic Operators	1.3.3	13
1.2	Summary of BASIC Statements	1.6	28
2.2	BASIC Relational Operators	2.3.1	40
3.1	BASIC Relational Operators and Complements	3.2.4	69
3.2	Summary of Minimal BASIC Statements	3.7	94
3.3	Summary of BASIC-PLUS Statements	3.7	95
3.4	Summary of Dartmouth BASIC Statements	3.7	95
4.1	Rules of Evaluation of Arithmetic Expressions	4.2.2	101
4.2	Eleven BASIC Mathematical Functions	4.5	112
4.3	Summary of Minimal BASIC Statements	4.9	125
5.1	Summary of Minimal BASIC Statements	5.7	162
5.2	Summary of BASIC-PLUS WHILE Loop	5.7	162
5.3	Summary of Dartmouth BASIC WHILE Loop	5.7	162
6.3	Summary of BASIC Statements	6.8	200
7.2	Summary of Minimal BASIC Statements	7.9	240
7.3	Summary of Dartmouth BASIC Statements	7.9	241
7.4	Summary of BASIC-PLUS Statements	7.9	242
8.1	Summary of Minimal BASIC Statements	8.6	277
8.2	Summary of BASIC-PLUS/Dartmouth BASIC Statements	8.6	277
9.1	ASCII Code	9.7	303
9.2	Comparison of BASIC String Manipulation Statement (String functions included)	9.10	322
10.1	Matrix Arithmetic Operators	10.4.3	342
10.2	Summary of Minimal BASIC Statements	10.7	358
10.3	Summary of BASIC-PLUS Statements (for matrix manipulation)	10.7	359
11.1	The Random Inventory File—INVENR	11.5	385
11.2	Summary of Files Features	11.8	390

INDEX OF PROGRAMS

ANSWERS TO
SELECTED EXERCISES

Chapter 1

1.1   −27.2, MINE, 0.05

1.2   legal: A, M, G2, N1

1.3   The DATA statement can be moved anywhere. Line 140 can be moved down. Lines 110 and 120 can be transposed.

1.4   35   3.8
               133   108

1.5   40   16.25   650   117   533

1.6
```
100 PRINT "   I   I"
110 PRINT " X I   I"
120 PRINT "---I---I---"
130 PRINT "   I O I X"
140 PRINT "---I---I---"
150 PRINT "   I O I"
160 PRINT "   I   I"
```

1.7   Changes to Fig. 1.13
```
120 PRINT "ENTER HOURS AND RATE SEPARATED BY A COMMA"
130 INPUT H, R
```

Changes to Fig. 1.15

```
100 PRINT "ENTER DISTANCE AND SPEED SEPARATED BY A COMMA"
110 INPUT D, S
170 PRINT "ENTER MILAGE RATE IN MPG ";
175 PRINT "AND COST IN DOLLARS"
180 INPUT M, C
```

Chapter 2

2.1

Input variables	*Program variables*	*Output variables*
N1: First number		S: Sum of N1,
N2: Second number	S1: Sum of N1, N2	N2, N3, N4
N3: Third number	S2: Sum of N3, N4	A: Average
N4: Fourth number		

```
100 REM COMPUTE SUM AND AVERAGE OF FOUR NUMBERS
110 REM
120 REM ENTER DATA
130     PRINT "ENTER FOUR NUMBERS TO BE SUMMED";
140     INPUT N1, N2, N3, N4
150 REM
160 REM COMPUTE SUM AND AVERAGE
170     LET S1 = N1 + N2
180     LET S2 = N3 + N4
190     LET S = S1 + S2
195     LET A = S / 4
200 REM
210     PRINT "SUM = "; S, "AVERAGE = "; A
220 REM
230     END
```

2.2   a)   b)

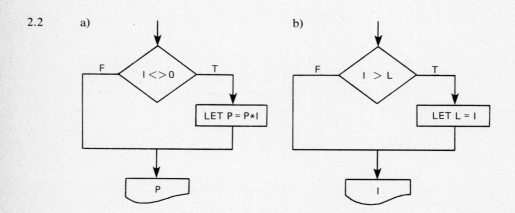

c)

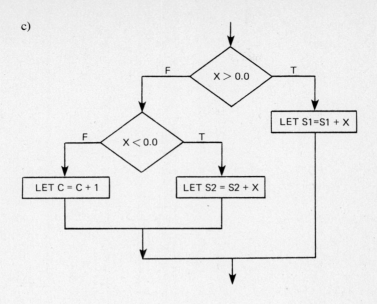

2.3   115.625 if H = 37.5, R = 3.75
        80 if H = 20, R = 4

2.6

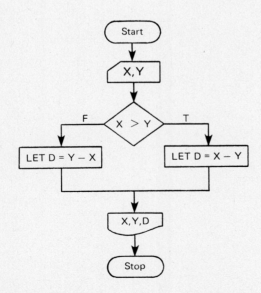

2.7   a)   b)

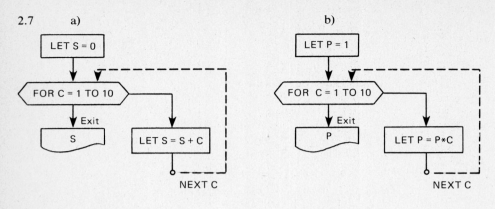

2.11   a)

```
100  REM FIND SUM OF 1-10
110  REM
120      LET S = 0
130      FOR C = 1 TO 10
140         LET S = S + C
150      NEXT C
160  REM
170      PRINT "SUM OF 1-10 ="; S
180  REM
190      END
```

b)

```
100  REM FIND PRODUCT OF 1-10
110  REM
120      LET P = 1
130      FOR C = 1 TO 10
140         LET P = P * C
150      NEXT C
160  REM
170      PRINT "PRODUCT OF 1-10 ="; P
180  REM
190      END
```

Chapter 3

3.1
```
100 REM MODIFIED PAYROLL PROGRAM
110 REM
120 REM INITIALIZE M, T, AND ENTER INPUT DATA
130     LET M = 100
140     LET T = 25
150     PRINT "ENTER HOURS WORKED AND RATE";
160     INPUT H, R
170 REM
```

```
180 REM COMPUTE GROSS, G, AND NET, N
190     LET G = H * R
200     IF G > M THEN 210 ELSE 250          [IF G <= M THEN 250]
210 REM THEN
220         REM DEDUCT TAX, T
230         LET N = G - T
240     GOTO 280
250 REM ELSE
260         REM G TOO SMALL, NO TAX
270         LET N = G
280 REM IFEND
290 REM
300     PRINT "GROSS = "; G, "NET = "; N
310 REM
320     END
```

3.2
```
100 REM LARGEST OF THREE NUMBERS
110 REM
120     PRINT "ENTER 3 NUMBERS IN ANY ORDER";
130     INPUT N1, N2, N3
140 REM
150 REM FIND LARGEST
160     IF N1 > N2 THEN 170 ELSE 200          [IF N1 <= N2 THEN 200]
170 REM THEN
180         LET L = N1
190     GOTO 220
200 REM ELSE
210         LET L = N2
220 REM IFEND
230     IF N3 > L THEN 240 ELSE 260          [IF N3 <= L THEN 260]
240 REM THEN
250         LET L = N3
260 REM IFEND
270 REM
280     PRINT "LARGEST ="; L
290 REM
300     END
```

Lines 160–260 may be rewritten using the IF-THEN-ELSE statement.

```
160 IF N1 > N2 THEN LET L = N1 ELSE LET L = N2
230 IF N3 > L THEN LET L = N3
```

3.3   Data Table for Exercise 3.3

Input variables	Program variables	Output variables
M: Boundary value	I: Loop control variable	S1, C1: Sum and count of items greater than M
N: Total count of data items		
X: Current data item		S2, C2: Sum and count of items less than or equal to M

Flow diagram

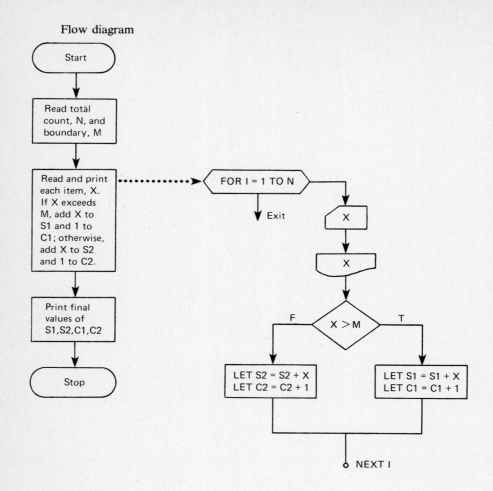

Program

```
100 REM FORM SUM AND COUNT OF ITEMS GREATER THAN M
110 REM AND ITEMS LESS THAN OR EQUAL TO M
120 REM
130 REM ENTER COUNT AND BOUNDARY M
140     READ N, M
150     DATA 20, 50
160 REM
170 REM PROCESS EACH ITEM X
180     PRINT "LIST OF "; N; "DATA ITEMS"
190     FOR I = 1 TO N
200        READ X
210        PRINT X
220        IF X > M THEN 230 ELSE 270        [IF X <= M THEN 270]
230 REM     THEN
240            LET C1= C1 + 1
250            LET S1 = S1 + X
```

```
260        GOTO 300
270 REM    ELSE
280            LET C2 = C2 + 1
290            LET S2 = S2 + X
300 REM    IFEND
310     NEXT I
320 REM
330 REM PRINT FINAL RESULTS
340     PRINT "THERE WERE"; C1; "ITEMS GREATER THAN"; M
350     PRINT "THEIR SUM WAS"; S1
360     PRINT
370     PRINT "THERE WERE"; C2; "ITEMS NOT GREATER THAN"; M
380     PRINT "THEIR SUM WAS"; S2
390 REM
400     END
```

3.4   a)   b)

c)

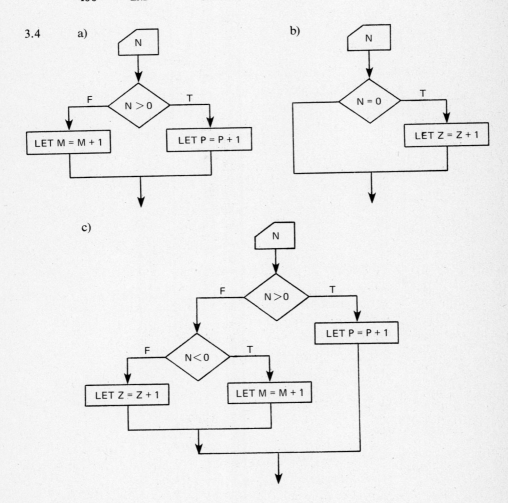

3.5   Both sequences will store 7.2 in X and Y. Correct sequence b) would be:

```
LET T = Y
LET Y = X
LET X = T
```

3.7   Implementation of:

```
                     FOR Y = 1 TO P STEP S
180 REM INITIALIZE LOOP CONTROL VARIABLE Y
190     LET Y = 1
200 REM IF Y <= P REPEAT LOOP BODY
210     IF Y <= P THEN 220 ELSE 260          [IF Y > P THEN 260]
220 REM LOOP BODY
            ----
            ----
            ----
240     LET Y = Y + S
250     GOTO 200
260 REM LOOPEND
```

3.8

```
140 REM COMPUTE SUM OF ODDS AND PRODUCT OF EVENS
150     LET N = 10
160     LET S = 0
170     LET P = 1
180     FOR T = 1 TO N STEP 2
190         LET E = T + 1
200         LET S = S + T
210         LET P = P * E
220     NEXT T
230 REM
240     PRINT "SUM OF ODDS LESS THAN ";
250     PRINT "OR EQUAL TO "; N; "="; S
260     PRINT "PRODUCT OF EVENS LESS THAN ";
270     PRINT "OR EQUAL TO "; N; "="; P
280 REM
290     END
```

3.9

```
100 REM FAHRENHEIT TO CELSIUS CONVERSION
110 REM
120     PRINT "ENTER INITIAL FAHRENHEIT TEMPERATURE,"
130     PRINT "HIGHEST TEMPERATURE, AND STEP VALUE"
140     INPUT I, H, S
150 REM
160     PRINT "FAHRENHEIT", "CELSIUS"
170     FOR F = I TO H STEP S
180         LET C1 = F - 32
190         LET C2 = 5 * C1
200         LET C = C2 / 9
210         PRINT F, C
220     NEXT F
230 REM
240     END
```

3.10

```
100 REM SQUARE ROOT TABLE
110 REM
120     PRINT "NUMBER", "SQUARE ROOT"
```

```
130     FOR I = 1 TO 50
140       LET R = I ↑ 0.5
150       PRINT I, R
160     NEXT I
170 REM
180     END
```

3.11

Step	I1	I2	R	U	C	N	A	S
1	75					6		
2		75		0				
3		55	20		1			
3		5	50		2			
3			100	100	3			
3		2	3		4			
3			15	115	5			
3			12	127	6			
4								73
5							125	

Chapter 4

4.1

a) $\dfrac{w + x}{y + z}$

b) $g \cdot h - f \cdot w$

c) $a^{(b^2)}$

d) $(b^2 - 4 \cdot a \cdot c)^{.5}$

e) $(x \cdot x - y \cdot y)^{.5}$

f) $x^2 + r/365^N$

g) $p2 - \dfrac{p1}{t2} - t1$

4.2

a) $^5/_7$

b) $2\frac{1}{2}$

c) 17

d) $3\frac{1}{3}$

e) $\frac{1}{4}$ (2^{-2})

f) 3

4.3

a) LET C = (A ↑ 2 + B ↑ 2) ↑ .5
b) LET Y = 3 * X ↑ 4 + 2 * X ↑ 2 − 4
c) LET W = 3 * K ↑ 4 * (7 * K + 4) − K ↑ 3
d) LET X = A ↑ 2 * (B ↑ 2 − C ↑ 2)/(B * C)
e) LET D = (A ↑ 2 + B ↑ 2 + C ↑ 2) ↑ .5
f) LET Z = 3.14159 * R ↑ 2
g) LET R = 6.27 * 10 ↑ (−45) * S
h) LET P = C0 + C1 * X − C2 * X ↑ 2 + C3 * X ↑ 3 − C4 * X ↑ 4
i) LET B = A ↑ (−5)

4.4
```
100 REM AVERAGE AND STANDARD DEVIATION
105     PRINT "ENTER THE NUMBER OF DATA ITEMS"
110     INPUT N
120     LET S1 = 0
130     LET S2 = 0
140     FOR I = 1 TO N
150         PRINT "ENTER NEXT NUMBER"
160         INPUT X
170         LET S1 = S1 + X
180         LET S2 = S2 + X ↑ 2
190     NEXT I
200     LET M = S1/N
210     LET S = (S2/N - M ↑ 2) ↑ 0.5
220     PRINT "AVERAGE = "; M, "STANDARD DEVIATION = "; S
230     END
```

4.5 a) Reads three data items, the string 033-30-0785, and the numbers 40 and 5.63 into the memory cells S$, H, and R respectively. Then prints the string to the right of the label "SOCIAL SECURITY NUMBER."

b) The data item 033-30-0785 is not enclosed in quotes, and is therefore illegal.

c) Reads and prints three string data items, FLOW, ROSE, and THORN. When the fourth data item, DONE, is read, loop repetition terminates.

d) The statements

```
LET S = X$
LET T = S + X$
```

are illegal: string data may not be assigned to a numeric variable, and may not be used in arithmetic expressions.

4.6

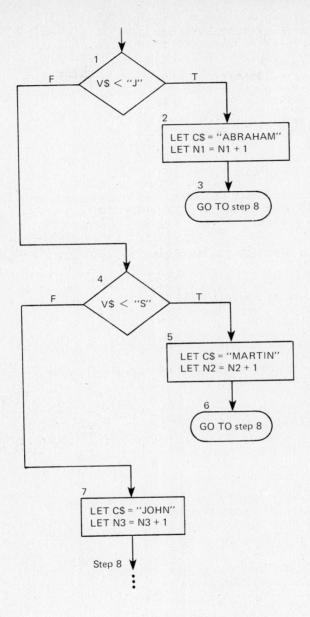

4.7
```
110 REM ANOTHER EXAMPLE OF SIN AND COS
120     LET R = 3.14159265 / 180
130     PRINT "NUMBER OF RADIANS IN ONE DEGREE "; R
140     PRINT "     X", "          Y", " SIN(Y)", "COS(Y)"
150     PRINT "(IN DEGREES)", "(RADIANS/DEGREE)"
160     FOR X = 0 TO 180 STEP 15
170         LET Y = X * R
180         PRINT X, Y, SIN(Y),
190         PRINT COS(Y)
200     NEXT X
210     END
```

4.8
```
100 REM QUADRATIC EQUATION ROOTS
110 REM
120     PRINT "ENTER A, B, AND C--THE COEFFICIENTS OF"
130     PRINT "THE EQUATION AX↑2 + BX + C"
140     INPUT A, B, C
150 REM
160     LET D = B↑2 - 4*A*C
170     IF D >= 0 THEN 180 ELSE 240        [IF D < 0 THEN 240]
180 REM THEN
190         LET D1 = SQR(D)
200         LET R1 = (-B+D1)/(2*A)
210         LET R2 = (-B-D1)/(2*A)
220         PRINT "ROOTS ARE "; R1; "AND "; R2
230     GOTO 260
240 REM ELSE
250         PRINT "EQUATION HAS NO REAL ROOTS"
260 REM IFEND
270 REM
280     END
```

4.9
```
100 LET N = 10
110 PRINT "NATURAL LOGARITHM TABLE"
120 PRINT "X", "LOG(X)", "EXP(X)"
130 FOR I = 1 TO N
140     PRINT I, LOG(I), EXP(I)
150 NEXT I
160 END
```

4.11
```
100 REM COMPUTING VELOCITY OF A BODY DROPPED FROM REST
110 REM AT TEN SECOND INTERVALS
120 REM
125     LET G = 9.81
130     LET S = 600
135 REM
140 REM DETERMINE WHEN PICKLE HITS GROUND
145     LET T1 = INT(SQR(2*S/G))
150 REM
160 REM COMPUTE VELOCITY
170         PRINT "TIME", "VELOCITY"
180         FOR T = 0 TO T1 STEP 10
190             LET V = G * T
200             PRINT T, V
210         NEXT T
220 REM
230     END
```

4.12   (Program changes only)

```
380 REM  COMPUTE TRAVEL TIME(T) AND HEIGHT(H) OF ARROW
390          LET T = D/(V*COS(R))
400          LET H = V*T*SIN(R)-(G*T↑2)/2
410 REM
420 REM  CHECK TO SEE IF ARROW HEIGHT AT BASE OF TOWER
430 REM  IS BETWEEN 100 AND 110 FEET.
440 REM  IF NOT, ADJUST VELOCITY AND RECOMPUTE
450 REM
460      IF H < 100 THEN 470 ELSE 510    [IF H >= 100 THEN 510]
470 REM  THEN
480          REM ARROW TOO LOW
490          LET V = V + 10
500          GOTO 380
510 REM  ELSE
520          IF H > 110 THEN 530 ELSE 570  [IF H <= 110 THEN 570]
530 REM      THEN
540              REM ARROW TOO HIGH
550              LET V = V - 8
560              GOTO 380
570 REM      ELSE
580              PRINT "ARROW THROUGH WINDOW"
590              PRINT "FINAL VELOCITY = "; V
600 REM      IFEND
610 REM  IFEND
```

4.13   `LET X = I - INT(I/J) * J`

4.14
```
100 LET Y = INT(100 * X + 0.5)
110 LET X = INT(Y)/100
```

4.15   Change the line

```
        FOR D = 2 TO N - 1
to      FOR D = 2 TO INT(SQR(N))
```


Chapter 5

5.1   a) 5, 3, 1, −1, −3, −5

   b) I, HIM, HER, IT, YOU

   c) 3, 5, 7

5.2   *Using the WHILE Structure*   *Without the WHILE Structure*
```
100     READ C$
110 REM
115     [DO] WHILE C$ < > "."           [IF C$ = "." THEN 180]
120         IF C$ < "I" THEN 130 ELSE 150
                                        [IF C$ >= "I" THEN 150]
130 REM     THEN
140             PRINT C$
150 REM     IFEND
160         READ C$
170     [LOOP] NEXT                     [GOTO 110]
180 REM
```

5.3   *Using the WHILE Structure*   *Without the WHILE Structure*

```
100     LET P = 0
110     LET R = 0
120 REM
130     [DO] WHILE R < 100000        [IF R >= 100000 THEN 190]
140         READ V
150         LET R = V * 2↑P
160         PRINT "P="; P; "V="; V; "R="; R
170         LET P = P + 1
180     [LOOP] NEXT                  [GOTO 120]
190 REM
```

5.4   *Using the WHILE Structure*   *Without the WHILE Structure*

```
100     LET P1 = 1
105     LET N = 0
110 REM
120     [DO] WHILE P1 < 10000        [IF P1 >= 10000 THEN 170]
130         LET P = P1
140         LET N = N + 1
150         LET P1 = P1*N
160     [LOOP] NEXT                  [GOTO 110]
170 REM
180     PRINT "LARGEST PRODUCT ="; P
190     END
```

5.5   L would be set equal to the sentinel value, and this value would be printed as the largest item.

5.6   Modifications:
        Add to the data table the output variable K
            K: Contains the count of the number of scores processed at any time during program execution
        In the flow diagram, insert step 2.05 at top of loop

2.05
| LET K = 0 |

Also, insert step 2.45:

2.45
| Increment the counter K by 1 |

Change step 3 in the flow diagram to read

3
| Print L and K |

The program must be altered as indicated in the flow diagram changes

5.7   Any set of data containing values that are all less than 0 will do.

5.8   Modifications:
        Add to the data table the output variables M and R:
            M: Contains the value of the smallest of all scores processed at any point during program execution
            R: Contains the range of scores processed

In the flow diagram:
    change step 1 to read

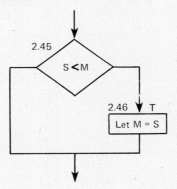

    add step 1.3

Insert steps 2.45 and 2.46

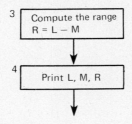

replace step 3 with steps 3 and 4

3   Compute the range
    R = L − M

4   Print L, M, R

5.10   The loop at lines 240 to 470 should be renumbered as lines 1240 to 1470.
    Change the following lines:

```
230   GOSUB 1240
610   STOP
```

and add the lines

```
1480  RETURN
1490  END
```

5.13
```
1010 REM SUBROUTINE TO COMPUTE ACTUAL ANSWER (A)
1020 REM COMPARE (A) TO STUDENT RESPONSE (R)
1030 REM INDICATE IF RESPONSE IS CORRECT AND IF NOT
1040 REM GIVE STUDENT THREE TRIES
```

```
1050      LET A = M1 * M2
1060      FOR I = 1 TO 3
1070         IF A = R THEN 1080 ELSE 1110
                                  [IF A < > R THEN 1110]
1080 REM     THEN
1090            PRINT "CORRECT"
1100            GOTO 1260
1110 REM     ELSE
1120            REM--WRONG ANSWER. INDICATE IF TOO
1130            REM  LARGE OR SMALL AND GIVE TWO
1140            REM  MORE CHANCES
1150            IF A < R THEN 1160 ELSE 1190
                                  [IF A >= R THEN 1190]
1160 REM        THEN
1170              PRINT "ANSWER TOO LARGE. TRY AGAIN."
1180              GOTO 1210
1190 REM        ELSE
1200              PRINT "ANSWER TOO SMALL. TRY AGAIN"
1210 REM        IFEND
1220            INPUT R
1230 REM     IFEND
1240      NEXT I
1250      PRINT "ANSWER STILL WRONG "; M1; "* "; M2; " = "; A
1260 REM
1270      RETURN
```

Chapter 6

6.1   X(I) is X(4), X(2*I) is X(8), X(5*I−6) is an illegal reference to X(14), X(I+ 3) is X(7).

6.2   legal references are a, c, d (X(6), X(10), X(6)).

6.3   a) 12   b) 8.2   c) true; false   d) 1

	G(1)	G(2)	G(3)	G(4)	G(5)	G(6)	G(7)	G(8)	G(9)	G(10)
e)	2	4	6	8	10	4	8	12	16	20
f left)	12	18	22	−9.3	8.2	1.3	−.7	388.8	9	10
f right)	0	−11.2	12	−6.1	400	8.2	1.3	−.7	388.8	9
g)	0	−11.2	−11.2	−11.2	−11.2	−11.2	−11.2	−11.2	−11.2	−11.2

6.4   a)   b)

```
100 DIM A$(26)                    100 DIM S(10)
110 FOR I = 1 TO 26               110 FOR I = 1 TO 10
120    READ A$(I)                 120    LET S(I) = I
130 NEXT I                        130 NEXT I
140 DATA A,B,C,D,E,F,G,H,I
150 DATA J,K,L,M,N,O,P,Q,R
160 DATA S,T,U,V,W,X,Y,Z
```

      c)   d)

```
100 DIM T(10)                     100 DIM U(10)
110 FOR I = 10 TO 1 STEP −1       110 FOR I = 1 TO 10
120    T(I) = I                   120    LET U(I) = I ↑ 3
130 NEXT I                        130 NEXT I
```

6.5 and 6.6

```
100 DIM P(10)
110 PRINT "N", "PRIME(N)"
120 FOR N = 1 TO 10
130    READ P(N)
140    PRINT N, P(N)
150 NEXT N
160 DATA 2, 3, 5, 7, 11, 13, 17, 19, 23, 29
```

6.7   Replace lines 250-300 with:

```
250        GOSUB 1000
260  REM
270        STOP
1000 REM
1010 REM SUBROUTINE TO COMPUTE AND PRINT F(3) THROUGH F(15)
1020       FOR N = 3 TO 15
1030          LET F(N) = F(N-2) + F(N-1)
1040          PRINT N; TAB(24); F(N)
1050       NEXT N
1060 REM
1070       RETURN
1080       END
```

6.8

F(1)	F(2)	F(3)	F(4)	F(5)	F(6)	F(7)	F(8)		F(15)
1	1	3	5	7	9	11	13	⋯	27

6.9

```
100 REM FACTORIAL PROGRAM
110      DIM F(7)
120 REM
130 REM INITIALIZE F(1) AND SUM, S
140      LET F(1) = 1
150      LET S = 1
160      PRINT "N" , "N FACTORIAL"
170      PRINT 1, F(1)
180 REM
190 REM FIND F(2) THROUGH F(7)
200      FOR N = 2 TO 7
210         LET F(N) = F(N-1) * N
220         LET S = S + F(N)
230         PRINT N, F(N)
240      NEXT N
250 REM
260      PRINT "SUM OF FACTORIAL 1 THROUGH 7 = "; S
270 REM
280      END
```

6.10   Only the lines that would be changed are listed

```
140  DIM N$(100), S(100), G$(100), N(3)
3135 PRINT "A", N(1)
3140 PRINT "B", N(2)
3150 PRINT "C", N(3)
5040 FOR I5 = 1 TO 3
5050    LET N(I5) = 0
5060 NEXT I5
5130 LET N(1) = N(1) + 1
5190 LET N(2) = N(2) + 1
5230 LET N(3) = N(3) + 1
```

6.11   Add line 175 and the subroutine below:

```
170        INPUT C
175        GOSUB 1000
                .
                .
                .
1000 REM SUBROUTINE TO VALIDATE CLASS SIZE, C
1010       IF C < 0 THEN 1020 ELSE 1070    [IF C >= 0 THEN 1070]
1020 REM THEN
1030           PRINT "NEGATIVE CLASS SIZE NOT PERMITTED"
1040           PRINT "ENTER CLASS SIZE AGAIN ";
1050           INPUT C
1060           GOTO 1010
1070 REM ELSE
1080           IF C > 100 THEN 1090 ELSE 1160
                                    [IF C <= 100 THEN 1160]
1090 REM    THEN
1100             PRINT "MAXIMUM CLASS SIZE IS 100"
1110             PRINT "BREAK YOUR CLASS INTO SMALLER ";
1120             PRINT "GROUPS OF 100 OR LESS."
1130             PRINT "ENTER FIRST GROUP SIZE ";
1140             INPUT C
1150             GOTO 1010
1160 REM    IFEND
1170 REM IFEND
1180 REM
1190       RETURN
```

The statements GOTO 1010 (lines 1060 and 1150) transfer control back to the structure header in order to validate the new value of C that has been entered. These backward GOTO's should normally be avoided.

Insert the call statements below and the subroutine at line 4000.

```
255 REM COMPUTE STANDARD DEVIATION
260        GOSUB 4000
```

6.13
```
4000 REM COMPUTE STANDARD DEVIATION OF ARRAY S; THE
4010 REM AVERAGE, A, HAS ALREADY BEEN COMPUTED.
4020 REM
4030 REM COMPUTE SUM OF SQUARES
4040       LET T1 = 0
4050       FOR I = 1 TO C
4060           LET T1 = T1 + S(I) ↑ 2
4070       NEXT I
4080       LET T2 = (T1/C) − (A ↑ 2)
4090 REM
4100 REM COMPUTE STANDARD DEVIATION D
4110       LET D = SQR(T2)
4120       PRINT "STANDARD DEVIATION ="; S
4130 REM
4140       RETURN
```

6.16   The statement

```
          LET B(I4) = B(I4) + T
```

should be replaced by the structure

```
IF -T > B(I4)
THEN
    PRINT "OVERDRAFT-WITHDRAWAL NOT PERMITTED"
ELSE
    LET B(I4) = B(I4) + T
IFEND
```

6.17   Two arrays, D(20) and W(20), should be allocated for storing the count of deposits and withdrawals for each account. Both arrays should be initially set to all zeros. If T > 0, then D(I4) should be increased by one when T is added to B(I4); otherwise, W(I4) should be increased by one. The total number of deposits (or withdrawals) can be found by adding up all the elements of array D (or W).

6.18
```
1000 REM SUBROUTINE TO FIND TAX BRACKET - B
1010 REM
1020     IF S <= T(10) THEN 1030 ELSE 1110
                                          [IF S > T(10) THEN 1110]
1030 REM THEN
1040         LET I = 1
1045 REM     SEARCH THROUGH TABLE T
1050         [DO] WHILE T(I) <= S            [IF T(I) > S THEN 1080]
1060             LET I = I + 1
1070         [LOOP] NEXT                  [GOTO 1045]
1080         REM BRACKET IS I-SET B AND RETURN
1090         LET B = I
1100         GOTO 1140
1110 REM ELSE
1120         PRINT "SALARY"; S; "EXCEEDS TABLE VALUES"
1130 REM IFEND
1140 REM
1150     RETURN
```

6.21   *Array search solution.*
```
1000 REM SUBROUTINE TO DETERMINE GRADE FOR SCORE, S, BY SEARCH
1010 REM
1020 REM INITIALIZE G AND G$
1030     DIM G(5), G$(5)
1040     FOR I = 1 TO 5
1050         READ G(I), G$(I)
1060     NEXT I
1070     DATA 60, "F", 70, "D", 80, "C", 90, "B", 101, "A"
1080 REM
1090 REM COMPARE GRADE BOUNDARIES IN G TO S
1100     FOR I = 1 TO 5
1110         IF G(I) > S THEN 1120 ELSE 1160      [IF G(I) <= S
                                                      THEN 1160]
1120         THEN
1130             REM ASSIGN GRADE AND RETURN
1140             PRINT "SCORE -"; S, "GRADE -"; G$(I)
1150             GOTO 1180
1160 REM     IFEND
1170     NEXT I
1180 REM
1190     RETURN
```

Direct computation solution

```
1000 REM SUBROUTINE TO DETERMINE GRADE FOR SCORE, S, BY DIRECT
1005 REM COMPUTATION
1010     DIM G$(5)
1020     FOR I = 1 TO 5
1030         READ G$(I)
1040     NEXT I
1050     DATA F, D, C, B, A
1060     IF S < 50 THEN 1070 ELSE 1100    [IF S >= 50 THEN 1100]
1070 REM THEN
1080         LET I = 1
1090         GOTO 1190
1100     IFEND
1110     IF S = 100 THEN 1120 ELSE 1150 [IF S < > 100 THEN 1150]
1120 REM THEN
1130         LET I = 5
1140         GOTO 1190
1150 REM IFEND
1160 REM GRADE BETWEEN 50 and 99
1170     LET I = INT(S/10) − 4
1180 REM
1190 REM ASSIGN GRADE
1200     PRINT "SCORE −"; S, "GRADE −"; G$(I)
1210 REM
1220     RETURN
```

Chapter 7

7.1 The FOR loop terminator precedes the IF structure terminator. One possible correction is:

```
200     FOR I = 1 TO N
            ———
            ———
            ———
300     IF X + Y = Z
310     THEN
320         ———
            ———
            ———
400         IFEND
410     ———
        ———
        ———
500     NEXT I
```

7.2
```
100     FOR I = 1 TO 20
110         IF X(I) < 0 THEN 120 ELSE 150 [IF X(I) >= 0 THEN 150]
120 REM     THEN
130             PRINT, I, "IS THE INDEX OF FIRST NEGATIVE ITEM"
140             GOTO 190
150 REM     IFEND
160     NEXT I
170 REM
180 REM PRINT "ALL ITEMS ARE NON−NEGATIVE"
190 REM
```

7.3
```
100 REM PRINT NAME, N$, IF SEX, S$, IS "FEMALE"
110 REM AND AGE, A, IS BETWEEN 25 AND 35
120 REM
130     IF S$ = "FEMALE" AND A>=25 AND A<=35 THEN 140 ELSE 160
140 REM THEN
150         PRINT N$, "IS A FEMALE BETWEEN 25 AND 35"
160 REM IFEND
```

Minimal BASIC changes:
```
130     IF S$ < > "FEMALE" THEN 160
133     IF A < 25 THEN 160
136     IF A > 35 THEN 160
```

7.4 a)
```
100     FOR I = 1 TO 100
110         IF X(I) < 50 OR X(I) > 100 THEN 120 ELSE 140
120 REM     THEN
130             PRINT "X(" ; I; ") IS OUT OF RANGE"
140 REM     IFEND
150     NEXT I
```

Minimal BASIC changes:
```
110     IF X(I) < 50 THEN 120
115     IF X(I) <= 100 THEN 140
```

b)
```
100     FOR I = 1 TO 50
110         IF X(I) >= 50 AND X(I) <= 100 THEN 120 ELSE 140
120 REM     THEN
130             PRINT "50 >= X(" ; I; ") <= 100"
140 REM     IFEND
150     NEXT I
```

Minimal BASIC changes:
```
110     IF X(I) < 50 THEN 140
115     IF X(I) > 100 THEN 140
```

7.5
```
100 REM SELECT
110 REM CASE
120     IF P >= 3.5 THEN 130 ELSE 150
130         PRINT "DEAN'S LIST"
140     GOTO 250
150 REM CASE
160     IF P > 1.0 AND P <= 1.99 THEN 170 ELSE 190
170         PRINT "PROBATION WARNING"
180     GOTO 250
190 REM CASE
200     IF P <= 1.0 THEN 210 ELSE 230
210         PRINT "YOU ARE ON PROBATION NEXT SEMESTER"
220     GOTO 250
230 REM DEFAULT
240         PRINT "NO SPECIAL STATUS"
250 REM SELECTEND
```

Minimal BASIC changes:
```
120     IF P < 3.5 THEN 150
160     IF P <= 1.0 THEN 190
165     IF P > 1.99 THEN 190
200     IF P > 1.0 THEN 230
```

7.7   *Changes to Fig. 7.15a, b*

```
140      DIM P(30), S(10)
4190     LET S(F) = P(I) + P(I+1) + P(I+2)
4200     LET I = I + 3
```

7.8   The conditions that determine which alternative will be executed can't be specified by a single expression.

7.9
```
100      LET E = INT(X/5) + 1
110      IF E < 1 OR E > 5 THEN LET E = 5
120      ON E GOTO 130, 200, 300, 400, 500
130 REM  0 <= X < 5 - TASK 1
         ___
         ___
         ___
190      GOTO 520
200 REM  5 <= X < 10 - TASK 2
         ___
         ___
         ___
290      GOTO 520
300 REM  10 <= X < 15 - TASK 3
         ___
         ___
         ___
390      GOTO 520
400 REM  15 <= X < 20 - TASK 4
         ___
         ___
         ___
490      GOTO 520
500 REM  X < 0 OR X > 19 - TASK 5
510      PRINT "X OUT OF RANGE 0-19"
520 REM  ENDON-GOTO
```

7.10
```
OUTER       1
INNER J     1    1
INNER J     1    3
INNER K     1    2
INNER K     1    4
OUTER       2
INNER J     2    1
INNER J     2    3
INNER K     2    2
INNER K     2    4
```

7.11   Set up a counter, K, to keep track of the number of passes. Initialize K to 0 just before step 2.2 (see Fig. 7.22b), and increment K by 1 just before step 2.3. Step 2.3.2 should read

$$FOR \ I = 1 \ TO \ N - K$$

7.12   In the subroutine to pass through M, change the test

$$IF \ M(I) > M(I+1) \ ...$$

to read

$$IF \ M(I) < M(I+1) \ ...$$

7.13   In the main program, insert the statements

```
233 REM DETERMINE THE MEDIAN
236     GOSUB 5010
```

Then write the subroutine to determine the median:

```
5010 REM SUBROUTINE TO COMPUTE AND PRINT MEDIAN (H)
5020 REM
5025    LET N1 = INT(N/2)*2
5030    IF N = N1 THEN 5040 ELSE 5070    [IF N < > N1 THEN 5070]
5040 REM THEN
5050       REM N IS EVEN
5060       LET H = (M(N/2) + M(N/2 + 1))/2
5065    GOTO 5100
5070 REM ELSE
5080       REM N IS ODD
5090       LET H = M(N/2 + 1)
5100 REM IFEND
5110    PRINT "THE MEDIAN IS "; H
5120 REM
5130    RETURN
```

7.14

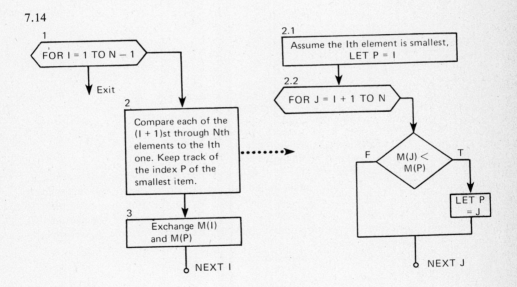

Chapter 8

8.1   LET L4 = FNM(FNM(FNM(A,B), C), D)
      or LET L4 = FNM(FNM(A,B), FNM(C,D))

8.2   a)

```
110    DEF FNA(X)
120 REM
130    IF X < 0 THEN 140 ELSE 160
140 REM THEN
```

```
150        LET FNA = X
155      GOTO 180
160 REM ELSE
170        LET FNA = -X
180 REM IFEND
185 REM
190      FNEND
```

b)
```
210      DEF SGN(X)
220 REM
230 REM SELECT
240 REM CASE
250      IF X > 0 THEN 260 ELSE 280        [IF X <= 0 THEN 280]
260        LET FNS = 1
270    · GOTO 340
280 REM CASE
290      IF X < 0 THEN 300 ELSE 320        [IF X >= 0 THEN 320]
300        LET FNS = -1
310      GOTO 340
320 REM DEFAULT
330        LET FNS = 0
340 REM SELECTEND
350 REM
360      FNEND
```

8.3 a) i) B is a global array

```
        DEF FNC(K, N)
    REM
    REM PARAMETER DEFINITIONS
    REM    K - KEY BEING SEARCH FOR IN THE ARRAY B
           N - NUMBER OF ITEMS IN B
    REM GLOBAL VARIABLES
    REM    IN: B( ) - ARRAY TO BE SEARCHED
```

   ii) L is assigned a value of 8.

   iii) L is assigned a value of 8.

   iv) The external variable K is assigned the value 5 by the first statement. When the function is called, the parameters K and N are assigned the values 1 and 12 respectively. When the function execution is completed, L is assigned a value of 6, the values of the parameters K and N become irrelevant; the external variable K retains its original value of 5.

   v) L is assigned a value of 5.

b)
```
FOR I = 1 TO M
   LET B(I) = X(I)
NEXT I
LET L = FNC(V, M)
```

c)
```
FOR I = 1 TO K
   LET B(I) = Y(I)
NEXT I
LET L = FNC(V, K)
```

d)
```
110      DEF FNP(K, F, L)
120      LET C = 0
```

```
130     FOR I = F TO L
140         IF B(I) = K THEN 150 ELSE 170          [IF B(I) < > K
                                                       THEN 170]
150 REM     THEN
160             LET C = C + 1
170 REM     IFEND
180         NEXT I
190     LET FNP = C
200 REM
210     FNEND
```

8.4   DEF FNR(X,N) = SGN(X)*(INT(ABS(X)*10↑N + 0.5)/10↑N)

8.5   Insert the function definition for FNR following line 110. Change the output lists for lines 180 and 190 as follows:

SIN (X*P/180) becomes FNR (SIN(X*P/180), 3)
COS (X*P/180) becomes FNR (COS(X*P/180), 3)

8.6   a) DEF FND(I,J) = I – INT(I/J) * J

Rewrite of line 270
```
              IF FND(I,J) = 0 THEN 275 ELSE 310
```
b) DEF FNF(X) = SGN(X)*(ABS(X)–INT(ABS(X)))

c) DEF FNI(X) = SGN(X)*(INT(ABS(X)))

d) DEF FNC(X) = INT(X) + 1

8.7   The sort is carried out as part of the step to find the median.
The sum is computed as part of the step to compute the average.

8.9   In the main program (Fig. 8.6), replace lines 5020 through 5070 with the single line
                    GOSUB 1010

At line 1010 we would write the subroutine:

```
1010 REM SUBROUTINE TO READ, PRINT AND VALIDATE N
1020 REM ALSO READ AND PRINT DATA
1030 REM
1040 REM GLOBAL VARIABLES
1050 REM     IN:  (NONE)
1060 REM     OUT: N    – NUMBER OF ITEMS TO BE READ INTO X
1070              X( ) – ARRAY TO RECEIVE INPUT DATA
1080 REM
1090 REM OTHER VARIABLES CHANGED: I
1100 REM
1110 REM READ AND CHECK N
1120     PRINT "ENTER NUMBER OF ITEMS ";
1130     INPUT N
1140     IF N < 2 OR N > 20 THEN 1150 ELSE 1190
1150 REM THEN
1160         PRINT N, "IS OUTSIDE RANGE OF 2 TO 20."
1170         PRINT "EXECUTION TERMINATED"
1180         STOP
1190 REM IFEND
1195 REM
```

```
1200 REM READ AND PRINT ARRAY X
1210    PRINT "ENTER EACH DATA ITEM FOLLOWED BY A RETURN"
1230    FOR I = 1 TO N
1240        INPUT X(I)
1250    NEXT I
1260 REM
1270    RETURN
```

Minimal BASIC changes

```
1140    IF N < 2 THEN 1150
1145    IF N <= 20 THEN 1190
```

Chapter 9

9.1   "042", ",□JOHN□QUINCY", "MMY□□□□"

9.2   *BASIC-PLUS changes*

```
200 PRINT MID$(S$, B+1, I-B-1) ; MID$(S$, B, 1) ; "AY"
260 PRINT MID$(S$, B+1) ; MID$(S$, B, 1) ; "AY"
```

Dartmouth BASIC changes

```
200 PRINT S$(B+1:I-1) ; S$(B:B) ; "AY"
260 PRINT S$(B+1:LEN(S$)) ; S$(B:B) ; "AY"
```

9.3   "JOHN□CARTE", "ADAMS□J.Q."

9.4   *BASIC-PLUS form*

```
100 READ Q$, R$, S$
110 DATA "THE CHAIRMAN SAID"
120 DATA "GENTLEMEN--WOULD EVERYONE"
130 DATA "PLEASE TAKE HIS SEAT"
140 LET Q$ = LEFT$(Q$, 9) + "PERSON" + RIGHT$(Q$, 5)
150 LET R$ = "LADIES AND " + LEFT$(R$, 11)
160 LET S$ = LEFT$(S$, 7) + "BE" + RIGHT$(S$, 4)
170 LET S$ = S$ + "ED"
180 END
```

Dartmouth BASIC form

```
140 LET Q$(10:12) = "PERSON"
150 LET R$ = "LADIES AND" & R$(1:11)
160 LET S$(8:11) = "BE"
170 LET S$ = S$ & "ED"
```

9.5   a-d)   <, <=, < >
       e)   >, >=, < >

9.6   Replace line 180 with

```
180 LET M = POS(S$, "AIN'T", M+5)
```

9.7 Add a counter, E, to keep track of the number of occurrences of the letter E (0 or 1). Initialize E to 0 and insert the following alternative in the SELECT structure:

```
CASE N(I) = ASC("E") AND E = 0
   LET E = 1
   PRINT "E";
```

9.8 The FOR loop header should become:

```
250 FOR I = S TO LEN(N$)
```

The references to N(1) should become LEFT$(N$, 1) [N$(1:1)]; all references to N(I) should become MID$(N$, I, 1) [N$(I:I)]. Each reference to ASC should be replaced by its argument (e.g., ASC (''0'') becomes ''0'').

9.9 A flag should be set if either T$(1) or T$(2) is missing. This flag could be tested in the main program before printing the final results.

9.10 Change the data statement in the main program

```
DATA "IF", "THEN", "ELSE"
```

9.11
```
IF P = 1
THEN
   LET T$ = N$ + MID$(T$, P+L1)
ELSE
   LET T$ = LEFT$(T$, P-1) + N$ + MID$(T$, P+L1)
IFEND
```

9.12 Asssume a command "QUIT" terminates text editing.

```
100 REM TEXT EDITOR MAIN PROGRAM
110 REM
120     PRINT "INITIAL VERSION OF TEXT"
130     PRINT T$
140 REM
150     PRINT "ENTER COMMAND"
160     INPUT C$, O$, N$
170 REM
180 REM WHILE C$ < > "QUIT" PROCESS COMMAND
190     [DO] WHILE C$ < > "QUIT"
200         REM TEST FOR "R" OR "RA"
210         IF C$ = "R" THEN 220 ELSE 250
220 REM     THEN
230             GOSUB 1000
240             PRINT T$
245         GOTO 310
250 REM     ELSE
255 REM         C$ = "RA"
260             LET P = 1
265 REM         WHILE P < > 0 REPLACE O$ WITH N$
270             [DO] WHILE P < > 0
280                 GOSUB 1000
290                 PRINT T$
300             [LOOP] NEXT
310 REM     IFEND
```

```
320         PRINT "ENTER COMMAND"
330      [NEXT] LOOP
340 REM
350         PRINT "FINAL VERSION OF TEXT"
360         PRINT T$
370 REM
380      STOP
```

The Minimal BASIC changes are:

```
190 IF C$ = "QUIT" THEN 340
210 IF C$ < > "R" THEN 250
270 IF P = 0 THEN 310
300 GOTO 260
330 GOTO 180
```

9.13

	O$	N$	O$	N$	B
a)	FRA	STRU	FRA	STRU	1
b)	IN	ON	I	O	33
c)	BOOK	TEXT	BOOK	TEXT	1
d)	AM	AMM	M	MM	45
e)	RR	R	RR	R	60
f)	?	!	?	!	60

Chapter 10

10.1 a)
```
300      LET C = 3
310      LET S = 0
320 REM
330 REM COUNT NUMBER OF STUDENTS AT CAMPUS C
340      FOR I = 1 TO 50
350         LET S = S + E(I, C)
360      NEXT I
370 REM
380      PRINT "NUMBER OF STUDENTS AT CAMPUS"; C; "="; S
```

b)
```
200      LET C = 0
210      FOR I = 1 TO 3
220         FOR J = 1 TO 3
230            IF T(I, J) = 1 THEN 240 ELSE 260
                        [IF T(I, J) < > 1 THEN 260]
240 REM         THEN
250                LET C = C + 1
260 REM         IFEND
270         NEXT J
280      NEXT I
```

10.2
```
100      DEF FNS(X, Y, Z)
110 REM
120 REM FUNCTION TO CHECK IF X = Y = Z < > 0
130 REM
140      IF X = Y AND Y = Z AND Z < > 0 THEN 150 ELSE 170
150         LET FNS = 1
160      GOTO 190
170      ELSE
180         LET FNS = 0
```

```
190      IFEND
195 REM
200      FNEND
```

Minimal BASIC changes:

```
140      IF X < > Y THEN 170
143      IF Y < > Z THEN 170
146      IF Z = 0 THEN 170
```

10.3 a) If P were a row vector of prices, the computation

$$\text{MAT V} = \text{P} * \text{A}$$

would yield a row vector, V, of annual volume by item. The declarations
for P and V should be changed to:

$$\text{DIM P}(1, 5), \text{V}(1, 5)$$

b) The computations

$$\text{MAT V} = \text{P} * \text{Q}$$
$$\text{MAT T} = \text{T} + \text{V}$$

should be performed after each set of quarterly sales figures are entered.
The array T will be used to accumulate the total volume by store. The
declaration and initialization of T should be:

$$\text{DIM T}(3)$$
$$\text{MAT T} = \text{ZER}$$

10.4   The changes are listed below:

```
120 DIM A(2, 2), X(2), B(2), V(2, 2)
140 DATA 2
170 DATA 3, 2
180 DATA 1, −1
190
250 DATA 14, 2
```

10.5
```
1000 REM SUBROUTINE TO PRINT ROOM CAPACITY TABLE
1010 REM
1020 REM GLOBAL VARIABLES
1030 REM    IN: C(,) − ROOM CAPACITY TABLE
1040 REM OTHER VARIABLES CHANGED − I1, J1
1050 REM
1060 REM PRINT TABLE HEADING
1070      PRINT TAB(25); "ROOM NUMBER"
1080      PRINT "FLOOR "," 01   ";" 02   ";
1090      PRINT " 03   ";" 04   ";" 05    "
1100 REM
1110 REM FOR I1= 1 TO 3
1120        REM PRINT FLOOR NUMBER AND FLOOR CAPACITIES
1130        PRINT I1,
1140        FOR J1 = 1 TO 5
1150          PRINT C(I1, J1);" ";
1160        NEXT J1
1170        PRINT
1180      NEXT I1
1190 REM
1200      RETURN
```

Chapter 11

11.1   For BASIC-PLUS, the line   For Dartmouth BASIC, the line
       images are: images are:

   a) `FABIAN    62.5 SECONDS`   `FABIAN    62.5 SECONDS`
   b) `THE DO   125.3 SECONDS`   `THE DO   125.3 SECONDS`
   c) `HOSS     %1026.5 SECONDS`   `HOSS     ***.* SECONDS`
       (The % indicates insufficient   (insufficient space for X)
       space for X)
   d) `ACE      -41.0 SECONDS`   `ACE      -41.0 SECONDS`

11.2   ```
       PRINT USING "SOCIAL SECURITY NUMBER###-##-####", S1, S2, S3
       PRINT USING "'LL,   'LL", L$, F$ (BASIC-PLUS)
       [PRINT USING "<##,   <##", L$, F$] (Dartmouth BASIC)
       PRINT USING "HOURS   RATE   PAY"
       PRINT USING "##.##   #.##   ###.##", H, R, P
       ```

11.3 a) `LET F$ = "###         ####   ####   ####   ####   ####   ####   ####"`

       `PRINT USING F$, T, W(1), W(2), W(3), W(4), W(5), W(6), W(7)`

   b) No changes. Twenty-one lines of the form prescribed by F$ would be
      printed.

   c) ```
      PRINT USING "WIND CHILL FACTOR TABLE (DEGREES F)"
      PRINT
      PRINT USING "TEMPERATURE        WIND VELOCITY (MILES PER HOUR)"
      PRINT
      PRINT USING "READING (DEG F)   0    10    20    30    40    50    60"
      ```

11.4 b) ```
      PRINT USING "THE VALUE OF N IS ##", N
      LET F$ = " #####.##"
      FOR I = 1 TO N STEP 4
         PRINT USING F$, X(I), X(I+1), X(I+2), X(I+3)
      NEXT I
      ```

   c) ```
      LET F$ = " #.#####↑↑↑↑"
      FOR I = 1 TO 1000 STEP 6
         PRINT USING F$, X(I), X(I+1), X(I+2), X(I+3), X(I+4), X(I+5)
      NEXT I
      ```

      for Dartmouth BASIC:

      `LET F$ = " #.#####↑↑↑↑"`

   d) ```
      PRINT USING "ROOM NUMBER   TEMPERATURE"
      FOR I = 1 TO 120
         PRINT USING "   ###   ##.#", R(I), T(I)
      NEXT I
      ```

11.5   `"#.#↑↑↑↑   #.###↑↑↑↑   #.#####↑↑↑↑   ##.###↑↑↑↑"`

11.6   *BASIC-PLUS form*

       ```
       110 REM PROGRAM TO CREATE SEQUENTIAL FILE GRADES
       120 REM
       130   OPEN "GRADES" AS FILE 1
       ```
       ```

```
140       PRINT "EXAM GRADES FOR CIS 123"
150       PRINT
160       LET H$ = "    NAME     EXAM 1   EXAM 2   EXAM 3"
165       LET F$ = " 'LLLLLLLLL     ###      ###      ###"
170 REM
180 REM READ AND PRINT CLASS SIZE
190       READ N
200       PRINT "NUMBER OF STUDENTS IN THE CLASS IS "; N
205 REM
210 REM LOOP TO READ AND PRINT EACH DATA ITEM AND WRITE TO FILE
220       PRINT
230       PRINT USING H$
240       FOR I = 1 TO N
250          READ N$, E1, E2, E3
260          PRINT USING F$, N$, E1, E2, E3
270          PRINT #1, N$, E1, E2, E3
280       NEXT I
290 REM
300       CLOSE #1
310 REM
320       END
```

For the Dartmouth BASIC version, make the following changes

```
130       OPEN #1: "GRADES"
165       LET F$ = "<######### ### ### ###"
270         PRINT #1: N$,       E1,  E2,  E3
```

11.7   Program follows the same pattern as the program for Example 11.9
       (see Fig. 11.4). Instead of computing the average, your program should
       read the fourth exam score, S4, from the terminal and write N$, S1,
       S2, S3, S4 to the file NEWGRA.

11.8   Replace lines 1100-1180 as shown below:

```
1100 REM SELECT
1105 REM CASE
1110      IF O$(1) = U$(1) THEN 1115 ELSE 1135
1115         MAT PRINT #3: U$
1120         MAT INPUT #1: O$
1125         MAT INPUT #2: U$
1130      GOTO 1175
1135 REM CASE
1140      IF O$(1) < U$(1) THEN 1145 ELSE 1160
1145         MAT PRINT #3: O$
1150         MAT INPUT #1: O$
1155      GOTO 1175
1160 REM DEFAULT
1165         MAT PRINT #3: U$
1170         MAT INPUT #2: U$
1175 REM SELECTEND
```

INDEX

ABOUT THE AUTHORS

Elliot B. Koffman is a Professor of Computer and Information Sciences at Temple University, Philadelphia. He has also been an Associate Professor in the Electrical Engineering and Computer Science Department at the University of Connecticut. Dr. Koffman received his Bachelor's and Master's degrees from the Massachusetts Institute of Technology and earned his Ph.D. from Case Institute of Technology in 1967.

Frank L. Friedman is an Associate Professor of Computer and Information Sciences at Temple University. Formerly, he was an instructor in mathematics at Goucher College, Towson, Maryland. Dr. Friedman did his undergraduate work at Antioch College and received Master's degrees from Johns Hopkins University and Purdue University. He was awarded the Ph.D. in Computer Sciences from Purdue University in 1974.